COMPETITION, STRATEGY AND MANAGEMENT IN CHINA

Competition, Strategy and Management in China

Fang Lee Cooke

The University of Manchester, UK

First published 2008 by
PALGRAVE MACMILLAN
Houndmills, Basingstoke, Hampshire RG21 6XS and
175 Fifth Avenue, New York, N.Y. 10010
Companies and representatives throughout the world

PALGRAVE MACMILLAN is the global academic imprint of the Palgrave
Macmillan division of St. Martin's Press, LLC and of Palgrave Macmillan Ltd.
Macmillan® is a registered trademark in the United States, United Kingdom
and other countries. Palgrave is a registered trademark in the European
Union and other countries.

ISBN-13: 978–0–230–51694–6 paperback
ISBN-10: 0–230–51694–7 paperback

This book is printed on paper suitable for recycling and made from fully
managed and sustained forest sources. Logging, pulping and manufacturing
processes are expected to conform to the environmental regulations of the
country of origin.

A catalogue record for this book is available from the British Library.

A catalog record for this book is available from the Library of Congress.

10   9   8   7   6   5   4   3   2   1
17 16 15 14 13 12 11 10 09 08

Printed and bound in China

Contents

List of Tables   *vi*
List of Figures   *viii*
Abbreviations   *ix*
Acknowledgements   *x*

1   Introduction   1

PART I   Macro Business Environment and Firms' Strategy

2   Business Environment in China   21
3   Competition Strategy of Leading Chinese (Private) Firms   67

PART II   Analysis of Selected Industries

4   Automotive Industry   117
5   Pharmaceutical Industry   136
6   Information Technology Industry   154
7   Retail and Exhibition Industry   176

PART III   FDI Into and Out of China: Motives, Barriers and Management Implications

8   Acquisitions of Chinese State-Owned Enterprises by Foreign
    MNCs: Driving Forces, Barriers and Implications for HRM   207
9   Chinese MNCs Abroad: Internationalization Strategies and
    Implications for HRM   229
10 Conclusions   261

Notes   *281*
References   *284*
Index   *303*

List of Tables

1.1   Structure of China's economy   3
1.2   Output of major industrial products   4
2.1   Composition of gross domestic product   25
2.2   Number of employed persons at the year-end by sector   27
2.3   Employment statistics by ownership in urban and rural areas in China   30
2.4   Source of funds for investment and newly increased fixed assets in urban area by sector in 2004   32
2.5   Foreign direct investment by sector in 2004   37
2.6   Ratio of R&D investment to GDP of selected countries   41
2.7   Government expenditure for science and research   42
2.8   National science and technology financing indictors (1999–2004)   43
2.9   Structure of source of funding for scientific and technological activities in China   43
2.10   Gross expenditure of R&D by source of funds, flow of funding and sector of performance in 2004   44
2.11   National R&D personnel indicators (1999–2004)   46
2.12   Number of patents applied for and granted by the State Intellectual Property Office (SIPO) of the People's Republic of China (2003–4)   51
2.13   Domestic service invention patent applications filed and patents granted by SIPO by sector (2001–4)   52
2.14   National imports and exports of high-tech products (1999–2004)   53
2.15   National imports and exports of high-tech products by field (2004)   54
2.16   Educational attainment composition of employment (total and by selected sectors)   55
2.17   Number of staff and workers and number of scientific and technical personnel in urban units by sector at the year-end   56
2.18   Most needed skills in enterprises in China   59
2.19   Number of technical colleges, students, teachers and staff (1985–2005)   62
3.1   Industrial enterprises of state-owned and non-state-owned above designated size   68
4.1   Possession of civil vehicles and private vehicles in China (1985–2004)   120
4.2   Vehicle production by types in China (2002–4)   121

4.3   World motor vehicle production by country 2003–4, OICA
       correspondents survey   122
4.4   Country share in percentage of automotive sales (units)   122
4.5   Annual average wage of staff and workers by sector (2003–5)   133
5.1   Expenditure on public health   138
5.2   New drugs approved in China   145
6.1   The structure of the Chinese computer industry   156
6.2   Comparison of the Chinese IT market in 2001 and 2002   156
7.1   Total retail value of commodities in China in selected years   177
7.2   The added value of the wholesale and retail industry and the
       goods transportation industry as percentage of the tertiary
       sector of selected countries in the year 2000   178
7.3   The added value of the wholesale and retail industry and the
       goods transportation industry as percentage of the GDP of
       selected countries in the year 2000   179
7.4   General information of retail chain store enterprises of above
       designated size by status of ownership   181
7.5   Employment in the wholesale and retail industry and the
       goods transportation industry as percentage of the total
       employment of selected countries in the year 2000   189
8.1   Utilization of foreign capital between 1979–2005
       (end-of-year figures)   208
8.2   Examples of utilization of foreign capital and foreign
       investment (end-of-year figures)   210
8.3   Information on enterprises of selected ownership forms in
       China (end of 2003 figures)   222
9.1   Chinese FDI overview in selected years   230
9.2   Cross-border merger and acquisition overview, 1995–2003   231
9.3   Reasons for and patterns of Chinese firms investing overseas   235
9.4   Investment strategy of Chinese MNCs and choice of host
       countries   241
9.5   A comparison of the key characteristics of the HRM
       environment encountered by Chinese MNCs in developed
       and developing countries   251
10.1   Competitive pressure and strategic response of selected
       industries in China   265
10.2   Competition strategy and implications for Chinese firms   270
10.3   Key resources and constraints of foreign firms versus Chinese
       firms   273

List of Figures

1.1   An analytical framework of business environment and firms'
      strategy   6
2.1   Chinese innovation policy institutions   39
2.2   Chinese innovation policy   40
2.3   Gross expenditure on R&D in selected countries by sector of
      performance   44
2.4   R&D expenditures in selected countries by type of activity 45
2.5   R&D personnel in selected countries   45
7.1   Number of employees in the retail industry (end-of-year
      figures)   190
7.2   Number of employees employed in retail enterprises of other
      ownership forms   191
7.3   Number of employees employed in retail enterprises by
      ownership forms   192
7.4   Annual average wage of employees in retail enterprises of
      different ownership forms   193
7.5   A diagram of the compositional structure of the exhibition
      industry   199
7.6   Industrial chain of the exhibition industry   200
9.1   Transfer of HR practices between Chinese MNC home
      country and host countries   257
9.2   Transfer of HR practices between Chinese MNC home
      country and host countries in knowledge-intensive businesses 258

Abbreviations

CNNIC	China Internet Network Information Centre
COE	Collectively owned enterprise
CSR	Corporate social responsibility
FDI	Foreign direct investment
GDP	Gross domestic product
GMP	Good manufacturing practice
HR	Human resource
HRM	Human resource management
IT	Information technology
M&A	Merger and acquisition
MII	Ministry of Information Industry
MNC	Multinational corporation
MOST	Ministry of Science and Technology
OTC	Over-the-counter
R&D	Research and development
SFDA	State Food and Drug Administration
S&T	Science and technology
SOE	State-owned enterprise
WTO	World Trade Organization

Acknowledgements

My hunger to learn more about China seems to be growing by the day, but it is the unfailing support of my family that has enabled me to complete this book and hopefully many more to come. My family's tolerance of my obsession in writing during our holiday periods was however somewhat stretched when the draft plan of another book popped out of the suitcase when they helped me to unpack upon my return from my most recent trip to China. This means another two years absence from much of the family activities. Young and optimistic, our son turned to his speechless father, 'Well, at least we can do what we like for another two years!'

My parents, as always, are far more prepared to put up with my absence for the sake of my study. Even during my visits to China, I spend much more time conducting interviews and visiting libraries and bookshops than spending time with them. I must mention my sister here too to relieve her deep sense of injustice as a result of not being mentioned in my first book. After accompanying me on many of my interview trips, to try out new delicacies and sample latest fashions, such sentiment is entirely justified.

I would also like to thank the production team of Palgrave Macmillan, particularly Ursula Gavin and Lee Ann Tutton, for their continuing support that has made the publication of this book happen.

Finally, I would like to acknowledge the publishers of the following publishers for allowing me to reuse the materials for this book: part of Chapter 3 comes from Cooke, F. L., 50, 1 (2008), 'Competition and strategy of Chinese firms: an analysis of top performing Chinese private enterprises', *Competitiveness Review*, 18:1/2.

Chapter 8 is a revised version of Cooke, F. L. (2006), 'Acquisitions of Chinese state-owned enterprises by MNCs: driving forces, barriers and implications for HRM', *British Journal of Management*, 17:1, S105–S121, Blackwell Publishing.

Table 1.1 came from The World Bank, 2005a, 'China at a glance', http://devdata.worldbank.org/AAG/chn_aag.pdf.

Figures 2.1 and 2.2 came from C. Huang, C. Amorim, M. Spinoglio, B. Gouveia and A. Medina, 'Organization, Programme and Structure: An Analysis of the Chinese Innovation Policy Framework', *R&D Management*, 34, 4(2004): 367–87, Blackwell Publishing.

Fang Lee Cooke
28 January 2007, Manchester

CHAPTER 1

Introduction

Introduction

With around 20 per cent of the world's population and a sustained high rate of economic growth in the last two decades, China has risen as a nation with great market potential and a high level of production activities (see Box 1.1, Tables 1.1 and 1.2). As one of the world's largest foreign direct investment (FDI) recipient countries, China is now renowned for its position as 'the world's workshop', offering low-cost competitive advantage, abundant labour supply and the ability to expand production capacity rapidly. Some '25 per cent of the world's washing machines are produced in China, 30 per cent of the world's television sets, 40 per cent of the world's microwaves, 50 per cent of the world's cameras, 70 per cent of the world's photocopiers, and 90 per cent of the world's toys' (Brown, 2005, p. 2).

Meanwhile, China's primarily manufacturing-based economy makes it the world's largest user of cement, steel, copper, iron ore and tin. It has been responsible for one-third of the recent growth in demand for oil (Brown, 2005). It has been estimated that 'China is consuming 40 per cent of the world's coal and 30 per cent of its steel' (*The World Agenda*, 2005, p. 9). China uses 103 cubic meters of water to produce 10,000 yuan worth of output whereas the United States and Japan use only 8 and 6 cubic meters, respectively (Hofman, 2005). According to the World Bank, 20 of the 30 most polluted cities in the world are in China, largely due to high coal use and motorization (The World Bank, 2006). Low efficiency in production activities and difficulties in enforcing environmental protection laws are also contributing factors (Hofman, 2005). It is evident that China's rapid economic growth has been achieved at a high price – exhausting its natural resources and creating a legacy of ecological and environmental problems. The impact of these will be long-lasting. The Chinese economy is also in danger of being trapped in the low-cost and low-value-added end of the spectrum whose competitive advantage is increasingly being eroded by the rising comparative advantage of other developing countries whose wage levels and labour standards are even lower.

What is the economic structure of China? How has China's business environment evolved in the last two decades? What is the nature of its market competition? What are the major sources of competitive advantages of local firms and multinational corporations (MNCs)? Competition on quality as well as cost, innovation, customer service, and strategic alliance to maximize corporate resources are now the main strategies adopted by leading international firms in the context of a globalized economy and competition. What strategies

BOX 1.1

China Quick Facts

Poverty

- More than 400 million people were lifted above the $1 dollar a day poverty level in the last 20 years. Between 1981 and 2001 poverty fell by 422 million.
- China is still home to 18 per cent of the world's poor.
- About 150 million people in China live on less than $1 a day.
- China's income inequality has risen from 28 per cent in 1981 to 41 per cent today (according to the Gini index).
- Poverty reduction efforts, first initiated in 1980, have reduced the number of poor in the rural western province of Gansu by 18.5 million as of 2000 (more than 60 per cent of the population).

Growth

- Real GDP grew stronger than expected – 9.5 per cent in the first half of 2005.
- GDP growth is projected to be 9 per cent in 2005 and about 8 per cent in 2006.
- As Asia's fastest-growing economy over the past 20 years, China saw a sixfold increase in GDP from 1984 through 2004.
- In 1985, average income in China was $280; in 2005 the average income was $1,290.

China and the global economy

- China made up 12 per cent of the world economy on purchasing power parity basis in 2004 (second to the United States).
- China contributed one-third of global economic growth in 2004.
- In 2004, China accounted for half of global growth in metal demand, and one-third global growth in oil demand.
- China's economy has a high energy intensity. The country uses 20–100 per cent more energy than OECD countries for many industrial processes. Automobile standards lag behind European standards by ten years. And China has 20 of the world's 30 most polluted cities, largely due to high coal use and motorization.
- Foreign exchange reserves exceed $700 billion (second to Japan), and are growing at about $200 billion a year.
- About 40 per cent of China's exports go to the United States.

Source: adapted from the World Bank (2006), *http://web.worldbank.org/WBSITE/EXTERNAL/ COUNTRIES/EASTASIAPACIFICEXT/CHINAEXTN*.

Table 1.1 Structure of China's economy

	1984	1994	2003	2004
Percentage of GDP				
Agriculture	32.0	20.2	14.6	15.2
Industry	43.3	47.8	52.2	52.9
Manufacturing	35.5	34.4	36.7	37.3
Services	24.7	31.9	33.2	31.9
Household final consumption expenditure	51.2	44.5	44.9	43.1
General government final consumption expenditure	14.2	12.8	12.6	12.0
Imports of goods and services	11.4	23.4	31.7	36.7
	1984–94	*1994–04*	*2003*	*2004*
Average annual growth				
Agriculture	4.0	3.3	2.5	6.3
Industry	12.3	10.0	12.7	11.1
Manufacturing	11.7	10.1	14.9	13.2
Services	9.8	8.2	7.3	8.3
Household final consumption expenditure	8.1	7.9	6.1	7.9
General government final consumption expenditure	9.4	8.6	4.8	6.8
Gross capital formation	9.1	9.5	18.9	13.0
Imports of goods and services	9.9	15.5	24.8	22.5

2004 data are preliminary estimates (original note).
Source: The World Bank (2005a), 'China at a glance', http://devdata.worldbank.org/AAG/chn_aag.pdf.

are the Chinese firms adopting to improve their competitiveness? How does the loose governance on intellectual property rights (IPR) affect market competition in China and the level of innovation at firm level? Does the emergence of elite local firms as strong competitors against foreign firms threaten to erode the latter's initial competitive advantage in China? What may be the patterns of competition and collaboration between Chinese-owned and foreign firms? What may be the potential effects on and implications for a number of Chinese industries? As the Chinese economy grows and competition intensifies, some indigenous firms are spreading their wings overseas to seek new markets and develop global brands. But short of international exposure and experience, do they have the necessary resources to realize their global dreams? What is the role of the Chinese government in shaping competition and performance at industrial level and in the Chinese firms' international expansion aspirations?

Table 1.2 Output of major industrial products

Year	Household refrigerator (10,000 units)	Air-conditioners (10,000 units)	Household washing machines (10,000 units)	Colour TV sets (10,000 units)	Coal (100 million tons)	Crude oil (10,000 tons)	Natural gas (100 million cu.m)
1978	2.80	0.02	0.04	0.38	6.18	10,405.00	137.30
1980	4.90	1.32	24.53	3.21	6.20	10,595.00	142.70
1985	144.81	12.35	887.20	435.28	8.72	12,490.00	129.30
1989	670.79	37.47	825.40	940.02	10.54	13,764.00	150.50
1990	463.06	24.07	662.68	1,033.04	10.80	13,831.00	152.98
1991	469.94	63.03	687.17	1,205.06	10.70	14,099.00	160.73
1992	485.76	158.03	707.93	1,333.08	11.16	14,210.00	157.88
1993	596.66	364.41	895.85	1,435.76	11.50	14,524.00	167.65
1994	768.12	393.42	1,094.24	1,689.15	12.40	14,608.00	175.59
1995	918.54	682.56	948.41	2,057.74	13.61	15,004.95	179.47
1996	979.65	786.21	1,074.72	2,537.60	13.97	15,733.39	201.14
1997	1,044.43	974.01	1,254.48	2,711.33	13.73	16,074.14	227.03
1998	1,060.00	1,156.87	1,207.31	3,479.00	12.50	16,100.00	232.79
1999	1,210.00	1,337.64	1,342.17	4,262.00	12.80	16,000.00	251.98
2000	1,279.00	1,826.67	1,442.98	3,936.00	12.99	16,300.00	272.00
2001	1,351.26	2,333.64	1,341.61	4,093.70	13.81	16,395.87	303.29
2002	1,598.87	3,135.11	1,595.76	5,155.00	14.55	16,700.00	326.61
2003	2,242.56	4,820.86	1,964.46	6,541.40	17.22	16,959.98	350.15
2004	3,007.59	6,390.33	2,533.41	7,431.83	19.92	17,587.33	414.60
2005	2,987.06	6,764.57	3,035.52	8,283.22	22.05	18,135.29	509.44

Source: adapted from *China Statistical Yearbook* (2006, pp. 561–4).

These are the issues to be addressed in this textbook – *Competition, Strategy and Management in China*. Aimed as a text for international business and management studies and Chinese studies, this book outlines major sources of competition, changes and business strategies in a selection of Chinese industries. Existing works on business and management in China have accentuated the important role of the state in shaping organizational practices and competition strategy. This book takes a broader approach that combines the role of the state and the market to explore the development of Chinese businesses and business environment. These developments include, for example, the growing strength of the private sector, the entry of MNCs into China and the global competition that Chinese industries are increasingly facing. Whilst the role of the government remains important, organizational leaders are taking more responsibility in the choice of organizational strategies as a result of the loosening state grip and China's opening up towards the market economy. The growing freedom of enterprises in managing their own businesses, the maturing of these firms as the market economy is gradually taking shape and the growing competence and confidence of Chinese managers as enterprise decision makers all enable firms to contemplate their business strategy more proactively. In other words, firms are becoming more autonomous and strategic in shaping their strategy, although the speed of organizational learning and the business approach

Table 1.2 (Continued)

Electricity (100 million kwh)		Rolled steel (10,000 tons)	Cement (10,000 tons)	Motor vehicles (10,000 units)		Micro-computers (10,000 units)	Integrated circuit (10,000 units)	Mobile phones (10,000 units)
Total	Hydropower			Total	Cars			
2,566.00	446.00	2,208.00	6,524.00	14.91	–	–	3,041	–
3,006.00	582.00	2,716.11	7,986.00	22.23	0.54	–	1,684	–
4,107.00	924.00	3,693.00	14,595.00	43.72	0.90	–	6,385	–
5,848.00	1,183.00	4,859.00	21,029.00	58.35	3.58	7.54	13,156	–
6,212.00	1,267.00	5,153.00	20,971.00	51.40	3.50	8.21	10,838	–
6,775.00	1,247.00	5,638.00	25,261.00	71.42	6.87	16.25	17,049	–
7,539.00	1,307.00	6,697.00	30,822.00	106.67	16.17	12.62	16,099	–
8,395.00	1,518.00	7,716.00	36,788.00	129.85	22.29	14.66	20,101	–
9,281.00	1,674.00	8,428.00	42,118.00	136.69	26.87	24.57	48,462	–
10,070.30	1,905.77	8,979.80	47,560.59	145.27	33.70	83.57	551,686	–
10,813.10	1,879.66	9,338.02	49,118.90	147.52	38.29	138.83	388,987	–
11,355.53	1,959.83	9,978.93	51,173.80	158.25	48.60	206.55	255,455	–
11,670.00	1,988.90	10,738.80	53,600.00	163.00	50.71	291.40	262,577	–
12,393.00	1,965.80	12,109.78	57,300.00	183.20	57.10	405.00	415,000	–
13,556.00	2,224.14	13,146.00	59,700.00	207.00	60.70	672.00	588,000	5,248
14,808.02	2,774.32	16,067.61	66,103.99	234.17	70.36	877.65	636,288	8,032
16,540.00	2,879.74	19,251.59	72,500.00	325.10	109.20	1,463.51	963,101	12,146
19,105.75	2,836.81	24,108.01	86,208.11	444.39	207.08	3,216.70	1,483,101	18,231
22,033.09	3,535.44	31,975.72	96,681.99	509.11	227.63	5,974.90	2,355,100	23,752
25,002.60	3,970.17	37,771.14	106,884.79	570.49	277.01	8,084.89	2,699,729	30,354

adopted differ significantly across firms. It is in this context that issues related to competition, strategy and human resource management (HRM) in China at both industry and enterprise level are discussed in this book. This state-and-market and institution-and-management approach is in line with that adopted by Lazonick (2004) in his analysis of organizational learning and innovation and by White and Liu (2001). White and Liu (2001, p. 121) argue that formal institutional influence (e.g. state planning) on managerial choice has been diminishing during China's economic transition period 'as decision-making autonomy has been devolved to organizations'. This is in spite of the fact that the process towards marketization and privatization that characterize emerging economies are still heavily regulated (Hoskisson *et al.*, 2000).

Analytical framework

The business environment under which businesses operate is shaped by a broad range of institutional and cultural factors played out at international, national and industrial and organizational level, although the macro environment is in turn influenced by corporate strategies adopted by firms (see Figure 1.1). At the international level, a country's business environment is influenced by policies, regulations and other forms of pressure and incentive from international

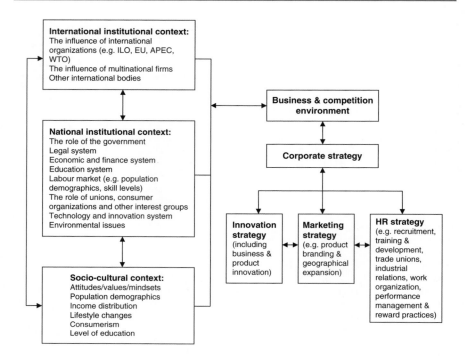

Figure 1.1 An analytical framework of business environment and firms' strategy

Sources: adapted and expanded from Clark and Mallory (1996, p. 27); Johnson and Scholes (2002, p. 102).

organizations. It is also influenced by the way multinational firms operate, both globally and in the host country. For example, an increasing number of Chinese firms and industries are now subject to a rising level of competitive pressure as a result of China's accession to the World Trade Organization (WTO) in 2001 and the subsequent gradual removal of barriers to MNCs operating in China. At the national level, the role of the government, the legal system, the economic and finance system, the technological innovation system, the education and training system, and the stock of human capital in the labour market are all important institutional factors that determine the business environment. The role of the government includes: 'the extent to which markets are administratively regulated, the degree of centralization in government economic policy, and the extent of government ownership in business' (Child, 2001, p. 696). The technology and innovation environment includes: government spending on research and development (R&D), government and industry focus on technological effort, new discoveries and developments, speed of technology transfer and rates of obsolescence (Johnson and Scholes, 2002). The education and training system is important as it determines the pool of human capital of the country, including knowledge, skills and managerial competence essential to its competitiveness. It is also a determinant of the workforce's earning power and the nation's living standard and consumption power. At the industry level, many of the factors identified at the international and national level manifest themselves but exhibit characteristics that are specific to particular industries.

Porter (1990) argues that national environment plays an important role in the competitive success of firms. He identifies four sets of factors that are important in shaping the business environment that may 'promote or impede the creation of competitive advantage' for a particular industry in a nation:

1. *'Factor conditions.* The nation's position in factors of production, such as skilled labour or infrastructure, necessary to compete in a given industry.

2. *Demand conditions.* The nature of home demand for the industry's products or service.

3. *Related and supporting industries.* The presence or absence in the nation of supplier industries and related industries that are internationally competitive.

4. *Firm strategy, structure, and rivalry.* The conditions in the nation governing how companies are created, organized, and managed, and the nature of domestic rivalry' (Porter, 1990, p. 71).

In addition to these four determinants of national competitive advantage, Porter identifies the role of the government as being vital in influencing the four determinants. Here, the government's role is only partial and can be positive and negative 'in the process of creating competitive advantage' (Porter, 1990, p. 128). In critiquing Porter's model of national competitive advantage, Dunning (1993) highlighted the significant impact of globalization of production and market and added the role of foreign MNCs in shaping the host country's competitive advantage. Given the high level of FDI into China, this is highly relevant and important in the discussion of competitive pressures for businesses and patterns of industrial development in China. Further, Li and Zhou (2005, p. 3) identified six major institutional environmental factors that firms in China must scan, monitor and design strategies to deal with. These include:

- Continued transition to a market economy;
- Opening up to world stages;
- Continued development of laws and regulations governing economic activities;
- Paramount role that various levels of governments play in economic activities;
- Geographical diversity and development stage disparity; and
- Rapidly developing emerging product markets.

The above framework and factors identified serve as a guide in the analysis of the business environment, competitive pressure and business strategy of the Chinese industries and firms throughout this book. The rapid changes in China's institutional and social environment provide a timely opportunity to explore how the nature of competition may have evolved and how firms' competitive advantages are changing.

Thematic focus

This book focuses on three main themes, as its title suggests: competition, strategy and management, with more attention to human resources. Competition is increasingly a central issue in China's business and economic growth, largely as a result of China's shift from the state planned economy towards the market economy. Whilst competitive pressure has intensified across all industries, the pressure is perhaps more strongly felt by firms and industries that were previously most sheltered by the state. In the industry-specific chapters (Chapters 4–7), sources of competitive pressure are analysed. These pressures are often a consequence of deficiencies of institutional infrastructure as well as organizational competence.

There are various definitions of the term 'strategy' and different perspectives of corporate strategy.[1] This book adopts the 'strategic choice' perspective in the understanding of strategy of firms (Boxall and Purcell, 2003; Child, 1972). In this perspective, a firm's strategy is seen 'as a set of strategic choices' that includes critical choices about ends as well as means, 'outward' as well as 'inward' elements (Boxall and Purcell, 2003, p. 34). As Boxall and Purcell (2003, p. 29) argue:

> There are strategic dimensions of all the key disciplines that constitute the business. Making a business successful is about giving due attention to the critical aspects of all the essential parts of the system, ensuring they are genuinely supporting the firm's mission and one another.

Johnson and Scholes (2002, p. 16) pointed out that strategic management include three important aspects: '*understanding the strategic position* of an organization, *strategic choice* for the future and *turning strategy into action*' (original emphases). Johnson and Scholes (2002, p. 16) define strategic position as the impact of external environment, internal resources and competences, and the expectations and influence of stakeholders on strategy. They further define that strategic choice involves 'understanding the underlying bases for future strategy [. . .] and the options for developing strategy in terms of both the directions in which strategy might move and the methods of development' (Johnson and Scholes, 2002, p. 19). It follows that 'strategy in action is concerned with ensuring that strategies are working in practice' (Johnson and Scholes, 2002, p. 21).

In analysing sources and forms of competitive pressure in selected industries (Chapters 4–7) in China and the motives of Chinese firms' internationalization strategy (Chapter 9), this book explores the strategic positions of foreign firms (see Chapter 8) as well as Chinese-owned firms. It also summarizes strategic responses taken by firms and strategic implications at firm and industrial level. In addition, business strategies adopted by leading Chinese (private) firms are analysed (Chapter 3). Key elements of business strategy analysed in this book include: business expansion strategy (e.g. diversification, internationalization, mergers and acquisitions), R&D and innovation, product and production strategy, marketing and corporate branding strategy and HRM. Particular focus is given to innovation, marketing and HRM (see Figure 1.1), as these strategic elements are seen as crucial in enhancing an organization's competitiveness.

Although human resource (HR) strategy forms part of the corporate strategy, this thematic element needs to feature more prominently because different industries face different types of competitive pressure and respond differently even to the same type of pressure (Purcell, 2001; Schuler *et al.*, 2001). Different industries are also positioned differently in the labour market, in part due to differences in their skill requirements, the competitiveness of a particular industry and firms within the industry, the bargaining power of the workforce, wage levels, career patterns and other elements of the employment package. Therefore the HR implications at firm and industry level tend to differ (Purcell, 2001; Schuler *et al.*, 2001). What is common across firms and industries in China, however, as we shall see in the chapters that follow, is the worsening problem of skill shortages that is becoming a bottleneck for economic growth and the fact that HRM is not yet a top priority of the majority of Chinese firms. This makes HRM a particularly important topic for discussion in a book on competition and strategy of Chinese firms as well as MNCs in China.

In discussing the HRM implications, this book focuses mainly on the level of human capital at national and industrial level as one of the factor conditions for competitiveness (Porter, 1990), instead of providing a detailed analysis of HR policies and practices at firm level. In particular, it looks at the role of national factors such as government policy, education and training systems and culture in shaping the quality of the labour force and ultimately patterns of HRM at industry and national level. But more broadly, HRM in China is shaped within a specific institutional context which exhibits a number of characteristics that are often generic among developing countries.[2] Some of these characteristics are outlined below and elaborated on in Chapter 9:

- Relatively tight government regulations of how companies should operate – prone to corruption to bypass regulations and restriction in HRM (e.g. recruitment and wage determination);
- A major recipient of FDI – economic and sectoral structure may be over influenced by and dependent upon MNCs;
- Economic growth largely based on manufacturing in mass production mode – FDI more concentrated in the manufacturing industry;
- High-tech industry and service industry remain relatively underdeveloped – but the former may receive more government support for growth, hence more resources to develop human capital and easier to attract talent;

■ Limited pool of management and technical skills, especially at senior level – leading to war for talent and widening wage gaps;

■ Technological capacity less advanced than developed countries, with lower level of R&D and innovation – leading to more low-paid and low-skilled jobs;

■ Relatively low living standards in general – wage payment may be the main concern of workers instead of non-financial rewards;

■ Limited social welfare provision – may force people to remain employed and accept low wages;

■ Incomplete provision and slack enforcement of employment regulations, and low level of awareness of employment regulations – may lead to higher level of job insecurity and labour disputes, and lower level of health and safety protection for workers;

■ High level of management prerogative due to societal cultural norm and unemployment pressure – lack of employees voice and bargaining power;

■ Lack of effective mechanism of collective representation (e.g. trade unions) to protect labour rights and advance labour interests; and

■ Less sophisticated HR techniques, more traditional personnel management specific to the particular country and industries;

■ Perspectives on ethics different from that of developed countries – for example, nepotism and corruption may be more common practices in recruitment selections, promotion and redundancy.

In short, the three key themes on competition, strategy and HRM run through the book at different level of analysis. For example, Chapters 2 and 3 provide an overview of the role of the government, sources of competitive pressures, product and production strategy, internationalization strategy, R&D and innovation, HRM, organizational culture and value and corporate branding strategy. The same themes will then be discussed again in Chapters 4–9 where specific industries and FDI activities are discussed.

Key features of this book

This book has the following four features:

Level of analysis This book analyses issues related to competition, strategy and HRM at international, national, industrial and firm level, although the primary focus is at national and industry level. At the international and national level, it contemplates the competitive pressures from foreign firms, the motives for Chinese firms investing overseas and the role of the governments, the business and economic context of China and so on. At the industry and firm level, more detailed discussions are given to analyse the dynamics of competition, characteristics of strategies and patterns of organizational practices of specific industries. It is at the industry level that industry-specific characteristics are most evident which provide both opportunities for and constraints to the industry's performance and growth. As Johnson and Scholes (2002) pointed out, the impact of general forces in the environment is more clearly felt by firms in the immediate environment in which they operate. As far as possible, examples of firms are provided to illustrate the points.

Coverage of industries and ownership This book covers a number of industries which include both the traditional industries and the relatively new industries. While five key industries are selected for detailed discussion in the four chapters that deal with specific industries (see below for more detail), the remaining chapters draw on examples from other industries for analysis to ensure the widest possible coverage of industries. The intention of selecting several key industries as case studies is to provide a more detailed analysis of pressures encountered by each specific industry and the responding strategies adopted by firms in the industry. These case study chapters are meant to be informative for illustrative purposes rather than authoritative and comprehensive accounts of what has been happening in the selected industries. The selection of industries for discussion is a semi-pragmatic decision based on the data available, the need to provide representative industries to cover both traditional and new industries in the manufacturing and service sector, the level of changes that have occurred in the industry and the significance of the industry to the economy. As a result, five industries are selected as case study industries. They are: the automotive, pharmaceutical, IT, retail and exhibition industries.

The automotive industry and pharmaceutical industry are chosen because both are old manufacturing industries. They were primarily state-owned but have been through major changes as a result of the state's effort to improve the efficiency of state-owned enterprises (SOEs) and the industry as a whole. They are subject to intensive competition from abroad, as they were amongst the sectors that first opened up to foreign-invested joint ventures (JVs) in the early 1980s. This is particularly the case for the automotive industry. China has the world's third largest automotive market and is the fourth largest automotive producer in the world. However, foreign brands made in China occupy over 90 per cent of the domestic market, with JVs as a mainstay (*China Economic Net*, 18 May 2005). The information technology (IT) industry is chosen due to its significance to China's national competitiveness in recent and coming years. Chinese-owned IT firms are emerging as strong competitors in the global arena, flag-shipped by Lenovo. The retail industry and exhibition industry represent two industries in the service sector. The former is an old one that has faced severe competitive pressure from foreign household name retail giants. The latter is a relatively new industry that is diverse and fragmented but plays a vital role in bridging China and the rest of the world through exhibitions. Despite not yet being one of the key industries in China, it is a growing industry that is unregulated in terms of both government regulations and market norms. In general, both industries have received relatively little intervention from the Chinese government in their restructuring (for the retail industry) and development (for the exhibition industry). Like many other Chinese industries, these five sample industries have been experiencing a high level of growth. Whilst the automotive industry is listed as a pillar industry in the future economic development of China, the IT industry is regarded as a strategic industry and a future pillar industry by the Chinese government. Both of them are significant to China's economy.

In addition, the book covers a range of ownership forms, including SOEs, foreign-owned and Chinese-owned MNCs, JVs and Chinese private enterprises. It must be noted that the Chinese public sector and small businesses are not a focus of discussion in this book mainly because the former is not yet in a competitive environment and the latter usually operate in a rather different environment that requires a different approach to analysis. A spread of ownership is helpful in illustrating the competitive positions and hence strategic responses taken by firms. This is because firms in different ownership forms are exposed to different business environments with resultant heterogeneous institutional advantages and disadvantages (Boisot and Child, 1996; Shenkar and Von Glinow, 1994; Tan, 2002). Tan (2002) argues that ownership type has a significant impact on the environment-strategy configuration which in turn has important performance implications for the firm. Similarly, Peng *et al.* (2004, p. 1105) argue that 'different ownership types lead to different managerial outlook and mentality due to a number of macro and micro foundations giving rise to various managerial cognitions'. For example, it has been noted that managers in the Chinese SOEs are more concerned with their political careers as the majority of them are appointed by the Party and are less entrepreneurial (Child, 1994; Tan, 2001; Tsang, 2001). By contrast, the emerging private entrepreneurs are far more adventurous, have stronger motivation to innovate and are more entrepreneurial in maximizing their performance with their limited resources (Tan, 2001).

Due to the rapid development and the growing size and diversity of China's economic profile, a level of over-generalization and simplification is unavoidable. Where possible, I avoid citing business strategies of the most high-profile cases, for example, Microsoft in China, for two reasons. One is that information on these case studies is more readily accessible to readers from a variety of sources. Another reason is that these are elite cases that may not be widely representative of what is happening in China.

Inter-disciplinary approach This book adopts an inter-disciplinary approach. It covers a number of thematic topics, albeit in various levels of depth, that span across a number of sub-disciplines within business and management studies. These include, for example, corporate strategies, technological innovation, marketing and product branding, HRM and international business studies. It needs to be pointed out here that the primary objective of this textbook is to provide information on a relatively wide range of issues encountered by business organizations in the Chinese context. It is not aimed to be an in-depth academic analysis of chosen topics or a text that deals with theoretical advancement in conceptualizing business and management issues in China. Many issues are only touched upon superficially, in part due to space constraints, and require readers to carry out much more study if they wish to gain a deeper understanding of the subject. Where possible, references of scholarly works on specific topics are provided. There are some important omissions in this book for the same reason. Some important topics have not been selected to feature as a chapter, particularly if there is already a good range of literature available on the subject. For example, foreign MNCs or international JVs in China have not been featured as a chapter, even though it is a crucial aspect of China's economic development and an important subject in international business. However, it is featured in various chapters as an integral part of the discussion of the topics in those chapters concerned. Readers interested in the subject can find out more from other readings, for example, Child and Faulkner (1998) and Luo (2002).

Two-way approach Although not intended to be an international and comparative study of foreign and Chinese firms in their home and host country environment, this book takes a two-way approach. It not only looks at the impact of inward FDI on Chinese industries, but also contemplates the growth of Chinese outward FDI that is fuelled by a number of factors, including resource and market seeking. It is important to adopt this two-way approach in order to identify how the interactions between foreign businesses and Chinese businesses may form a dual force that helps shape the global patterns of economy. This is in spite of the fact that the substantial global impact of Chinese outward FDI has yet to be felt. Whilst the business opportunities China offers have long been spotted and increasingly captured by foreign firms, the potential emergence of Chinese firms as global competitors is beginning to be recognized by global business leaders. According to a survey conducted by the Economist Intelligence Unit (EIU) of *The Economist* on CEOs on corporate priorities for 2005,

> China is cited by 35% of executives as the country offering the greatest opportunities for business expansion. Those opportunities will only increase as the economy opens up further: 43% of executives believe WTO-related liberalizations, which should further reduce China's protective tariffs across a range of industries, will be an important development for business. However, executives know that any turbulence in China's economy could have major repercussions for the global business environment. Some Western executives also believe it is only a matter of time before Chinese companies come to compete 'in their own backyard'.
>
> (The Economist Intelligence Unit, 2005, pp. 2–3)

As we shall see in Chapters 8 and 9, international JVs, often through acquisitions, is a main mode of international expansion of both Chinese firms abroad and foreign firms in China. As Tan (2001) observed, differential environmental opportunities tend to motivate firms to form strategic alliances that cross or blur organizational and national boundaries. Globalization has significantly reduced the ability of nation states to regulate and control economic activities (Ohmae, 1990, cited in Edwards and Rees, 2006) and 'a country's competitive position is not primarily determined by "national" firms but rather by "global" ones' (Reich, 1991, cited in Edwards and Rees, 2006, p. 59).

Sources of data

This book draws on a wide range of literature and statistical information from secondary sources in both the English and Chinese languages. These include: statistics from national and international institutions, business press, academic journals and books, published consultancy reports, empirical studies conducted by myself and obtained from secondary sources and company information from websites. As far as possible, information from authoritative sources is used and statistics on China is provided in the international context for comparison. However, statistics on China is not always accurate and discrepancies tend to exist in statistics obtained from different sources. As Lau *et al.* (1999, p. 32) observed, '[R]eliable and complete statistics on Chinese businesses both at macro and firm level is often not available' and it is very difficult to build 'a full picture of the Chinese economy and firm characteristics'. While statistics from China are gradually becoming more comprehensive, there is still a long way to go in improving its accuracy and level of details.

It needs to be noted that statistics referred to in this book are related to mainland China and does not include those of Hong Kong and Macau as Special Administration Regions unless otherwise specified. In fact, most of the discussion of industries and firms' practices relates to mainland China and does not include Hong Kong and Macau, in part because their institutional environments are significantly different from that of mainland China due to historical sovereignty reasons. However, investment from Hong Kong and Macau in mainland China is included in the discussion as part of the inward FDI and MNCs.

Where possible, the discussion of each topic concerned draws on various sources of information to provide a balanced and comprehensive view. However, this is not always achieved and sometimes one or two sources are heavily relied upon. For example, in Chapter 6, I am heavily indebted to Rui and Tao's (2004) work in providing the summary of the development of the IT industry. Constrained by the varying degree of availability of data accessible to me, some chapters are more informative than others. This is particularly the case for the retail and exhibition industry.

Finally, due to the lead time for the information to become available and the lead time for the publishing of this book, even the latest statistics included in the book at the time of its writing may be two years out of date by the time it reaches the market. For example, a main source of statistical information for this book – the China Statistical Yearbook – is published in September/October each year which contains statistics of the previous year. Similarly, the competitive position and strategy of companies reported in this book as examples may have changed by the time the book is published.

Structure of the book

The structure of this book is both by themes and by industries, consisting of a total of ten chapters. The book is divided into three focal parts, in addition to the Introduction and Conclusions chapters. Chapter 1 is this introductory chapter that outlines China's economy profile and the analytical framework adopted in this book. It also summarizes the thematic focuses, key features, sources of data, as well as the structural organization of the book. The first part that follows contains two substantial chapters which deal with the macro institutional environment (Chapter 2) and business strategy at firm level (Chapter 3). More specifically, Chapter 2 maps out the development of the Chinese institutional environment as a macro context for business and management. It focuses on the role of the Chinese government in shaping economic policy and growth, China's industrialization and the development of industries, technology and innovation environment and the stock of its human capital. This chapter contains key statistics and diagrams related to these thematic topics to provide an overview. An overview of these key national institutions is important in order to understand how they constitute distinctive contexts for businesses and impact upon the policies and operations of firms (Child, 2001).

Chapter 3 analyses key elements of leading Chinese firms' strategy, with a particular focus on private firms. While foreign multinational firms and SOEs have been the focus of a large number of studies, Chinese-owned private businesses have attracted relatively less attention. This is in spite of the fact that this sector has been witnessing significant changes and is playing an increasingly important role in China's economic development (Garnaut and Huang, 2001; Parris, 1999; Saich, 2001). The chapter draws on a range of studies but primarily from 30 of the Top 50 Chinese Private Enterprises of 2004 reported in Liu and Xu (2004). A close examination of the business strategy and reported key success factors of well-performing enterprises in China reveals that business diversification and internationalization, product innovation and quality enhancement, product and corporate branding, good HRM policy, improvement of corporate governance and entrepreneurship of enterprise leaders appear to be these Chinese firms' key elements of strategy that are associated with their success.

The second part of this book consists of four chapters (Chapters 4–7) that provide an analysis of the competitive pressure and operating environment of each of the five case study industries and firms' responding strategies with these industries. The five broad industries selected are representative of the spectrum, as explained earlier. The automotive industry and pharmaceutical industry form Chapters 4 and 5, respectively. These two chapters are put together because they are both in the manufacturing sector and share broadly more similar features than they do, for example, with the retail sector. Chapter 6 covers the IT industry. It is a new industry in China that is developing rapidly, privileged with special support from the state and benefiting from booming consumer demands. Chapter 7 covers two industries in the service sector – the retail and exhibitions industries – in part due to the limited availability of data. As far as possible, these four chapters follow a similar structure to cover similar issues in each industry. These include: the history of the industry, product market characteristics, major competitive pressures encountered by each industry as a whole and by firms of specific ownership forms within the industry, the role of the Chinese government, strategies adopted by firms in the industries and HR implications. Variations in the chapter structures do exist, however, as the business nature of each industry and the pressures they face may differ. The review of these issues in these five industries shows that they share a number of common problems, especially the Chinese firms. These include: small firm size and lack of economies of scale, lack of industrial clusters or supporting industries, low level of technology and innovation, lack of human resources for the development of the industry and lack of domestic brand-name products, with foreign firms often taking the lead positions and premium product markets. By comparison, the IT industry fares better and suffers from these problems to a considerably lesser extent. In addition, while Sino-foreign JVs were a key feature during the early period of China's market economy, these may be replaced by real and intensifying competition in the market where foreign and indigenous firms compete head on for their market share through refined business strategies.

The third part of this book consists of two chapters (Chapters 8 and 9) that explore FDI activities in China by foreign MNCs and outward FDI by Chinese firms. Both chapters cover similar thematic issues to look at the two-way flow of investment and the associated strategies of both FDI into China and Chinese outward investment. The intention is to offer some comparison and also to fill the gap in existing literature of FDI that focuses primarily on FDI into China but much less so on Chinese outward investment. These two chapters offer further examples of competitive pressures and strategies of firms. In particular, Chapter 8 explores the driving forces for, barriers to, as well as trends and patterns of acquisitions of Chinese SOEs by foreign investors. It questions the level of alignment of objectives between the Chinese side and the foreign partner during the acquisition of Chinese SOEs. Issues related to Chinese managerial skills and behaviour in acquisition negotiations are discussed, so is the policy making, administrative and practical role of local governments. The chapter argues that FDI's acquisitions of Chinese firms create unique management issues, particularly in the area of HRM.

Chapter 9 provides an overview of the growth of Chinese outward FDI and analyses the driving forces for this relatively new development. The chapter identifies a number of investment strategies adopted by the Chinese firms as well as a range of barriers they may encounter in their overseas' investment drive. The chapter contains an extensive section on the implications for HRM for Chinese MNCs. A major reason for this extensive discussion is that while a number of studies on Chinese outward FDI now exist in Western academic literature (e.g. Cai, 1999; Wu and Chen, 2001; Young et al., 1998; Zhang and Van Ben Bulcke, 1996), they have not sufficiently explored the relationships between the FDI motives, investment strategies and implications of these for HRM. In particular, Chinese MNCs' investment motive and strategy has a direct effect on the mode of entry (e.g. through acquisitions) and location (host country). The implications for managing human resources in host countries may differ significantly due to differences in national business systems and employment environments. Given the additional challenges in and the importance of managing human resources in the successful operation of MNCs, a detailed analysis is necessary to identify the likely problems that may be encountered by Chinese MNCs in developed countries where they are seen as the downstream firms, as opposed to the HR challenges they may face in developing countries where their competitive advantages may be more apparent and employment practices more similar. A number of propositions are put forward in this chapter which require further testing through large-scale empirical studies.

Chapter 10 is the concluding chapter that summarizes the main themes from the previous chapters. It reflects on the characteristics, trends and prospects of issues related to business environment, the role of the Chinese government, and the competitive positions of foreign-invested and Chinese-owned firms in China. Whilst key challenges facing Chinese firms are highlighted as they face intensifying competition both at home and abroad, the potential disadvantages of foreign MNCs in China are also acknowledged. The chapter concludes by drawing the readers' attention to a number of research implications.

To conclude, writing this textbook has provided me an opportunity to learn about subjects of which I had little prior knowledge and has helped me to understand the Chinese business environment better. Nevertheless, important knowledge gaps exist and unspotted errors remain. What is more, writing a textbook alone that covers a wide range of subject matters is a challenging undertaking in both the time and expertise required to complete the task satisfactorily. Trying to keep up with the rapid changes in China and the bourgeoning research publications that document these changes proves to be an impossible race. And I encourage students and researchers to read more widely on the topics discussed here and many others that have not been dealt with.

Recommended readings

R. Grant, *Contemporary Strategy Analysis* (6th edition) (Malden, MA: Blackwell Publishing, 2008).

G. Johnson and K. Scholes, *Exploring Corporate Strategy: Text and Cases* (6th edition) (Harlow: Pearson Education Ltd, 2002).

M. Porter, *The Competitive Advantage of Nations* (Basingstoke: Palgrave Macmillan, 1990).

R. Whittington, *What Is Strategy and Does It Matter?* (London: Routledge, 1993).

PART I

Macro Business Environment and Firms' Strategy

CHAPTER 2

Business Environment in China

Introduction

In Chapter 1, we have identified a number of macro (e.g. national level) and micro (firm level) factors which play a role in shaping the competitiveness of a nation, its industries and firms (see Figure 1.1). In this chapter, we will examine some of the macro factors as part of the business environment under which firms operate in China. In particular, we focus on the following: the role of the Chinese government, industrialization and the development of industries, the technology and innovation environment, and the level of human capital in China. Many of the factors that are not covered here will be discussed in later chapters where they are better explained as part of the analysis of particular industries or strategies at firm level. Some of the themes discussed here, for example, the role of the Chinese government, innovation and human resources, will be revisited throughout the book where it is appropriate.

This chapter consists of four main sections. The first section examines the role of the Chinese government as a legislator and an economic manager and how this role is sometimes compromised by its role as an employer. As is the case in many developing countries with centralized government control, the role of the Chinese government is pervasive in shaping the business environment through a wide range of legislative, policy and administrative interventions. The second section outlines the sectoral shift of China's economic structure in recent decades from an agricultural and heavy industry driven economy to an urban industrial oriented economy that is increasingly dominated by lighter manufacturing and service industries. The third section then investigates the technology and innovation environment in China. This includes: the innovation policy framework and institutions of China, the overall investment into R&D, types of R&D programmes sponsored by the government and the output of science and technology (S&T). The final main section analyses how human capital, a key factor in determining a nation's competitiveness, is becoming a bottleneck in China's economic development due to the worsening skill shortages experienced by many sectors. This chapter makes extensive use of statistical tables and charts. They provide a broad overview of background information based on which the ensuing thematic and industry-specific chapters are discussed.

The role of the Chinese government

As a socialist country with a legacy of state planned economy that runs deeply in the country's political and economic system, the role of the Chinese government, or more broadly the state, as an employer, a legislator and an economic manager remains dominant. This is in spite of the fact that state sector employment has been making up a reducing proportion of the total employment over the last two decades. For example, in 1980, 76 per cent of the urban workforce was employed in the state sector. This had been reduced to 24 per cent by 2005 (see Table 2.3), mainly through downsizing, plant closure and privatization (Cooke, 2005a; Morris *et al.*, 2001; also see Chapter 8). There was also a significant reduction in the number of state-owned or state-holding industrial enterprises of above designated size (see Table 3.1), also see the next section for further discussion). In the meantime, the government has been promulgating a wide range of regulations and industry-specific policies to regulate the disorderly behaviour endemic across many industries as a result of the opening up of the economy, as well as to facilitate the growth of new and key industries.

Following the footsteps of the Japanese and Korean governments who had adopted their industrial policy[1] in the 1950s–1960s and the 1960s–1970s, respectively during the important periods of their economic development, the Chinese government promulgated an industrial policy for the first time in 1987 (Eun and Lee, 2002). The introduction of an industrial policy by the Chinese government was said to be triggered by the bottlenecks created by the previous decade's decentralization strategy in its economic development (Eun and Lee, 2002). In 1994, the State Council promulgated 'The Outline of State Industrial Policy in the 1990s'. The 'Outline' announced an 'industrial organization policy' that was aimed to 'promote "rational competition", reap economies of scale, and exploit coordinative specialization' (Eun and Lee, 2002, p. 8). Based on the 'Outline', industry-specific policies were then drafted for a number of industries, including the automotive, telecommunication, transportation, construction, and electronics industries (Eun and Lee, 2002).

The Chinese government adopts an interventionist and protectionist approach in designing its industrial policies to foster competitive advantages of particular industries. These policies have the following missions (Eun and Lee, 2002; Linden, 2004; Perkins, 2001; Steinfeld, 2004):

■ Setting standards through the introduction of regulatory framework that forces firms in a specific industry to upgrade their operating standard (e.g. the good manufacturing practice (GMP) and good sales practices (GSP) of the pharmaceutical industry);

■ Establishing pillar industries (e.g. the automotive industry) and strategic industries (e.g. the IT industry) through:

- Launching new industries (e.g. the IT industry) to make them internationally competitive (see Chapter 6 for further discussion);
- Restrictive and conditional entry of foreign firms (usually through JVs and technology transfer) to protect the market of national firms;

- Reorganizing the industrial structure – support the growth of large firms through directive policy and allow the growth of smaller firms through freedom to operate and financial support incentives (e.g. the 'grasping the large and release the small' policy on SOEs);
- Providing time for the loss-making SOEs to return to profit-making or to go into liquidation without being politically disruptive.

■ Providing export subsidies and preferential loans to incentivize export-driven production that is in line with China's export-oriented economic growth policy;
■ R&D investment and government sponsorship of S&T programmes (see below and Box 6.1 for further discussion and examples); and
■ Promoting educational and training programmes to combat skill shortages.

Interventions by the Chinese government have attracted wide criticism widely as an obstacle for economic development and undue interference to market forces. This is especially true when the government has a vested interest as a large employer. For example, the government's protection of the auto industry has reduced the pressure for auto firms to increase their efficiency and competitiveness (see Chapter 4). However, a level of state intervention is always needed in the development of any given economy as a remedy of market failure and to ensure the alignment between the interests of enterprises and that of the overall economy (Nolan, 2004). For example, the introduction of new tax regulations and decrees to tighten the product and production quality standards (if effectively enforced) in the rice wine making industry will increase the cost of production and force shoddy rice wine producers to close down en masse, therefore raising the operational and competition standard of the industry. This is in spite of the fact that higher production cost will affect the profit margin and stock market performance of good manufacturers in the industry. Another purpose of the government's intervention is to safeguard the development of industries that are of national strategic importance (e.g. fuel, telecommunication, IT). The IT industry is a case in point. Here, the government's support in the growth of the IT industry has helped the industry to take off in a very short period of time and the globalization of the industry (see Chapters 6 and 9). It is 'an important example of how strong government policy combined with entrepreneurial local companies can lead to development and upgrading of industrial capabilities' (Kraemer and Dedrick, 2001, p. 3).

In short, the Chinese government plays an important role, whether it is appropriate and desirable or not, in the industrial activities through various means. This role will be further explored throughout the book, though not always in a separate section, in the discussion of various themes and industries (also see Chapter 10 for the barriers to implement industrial policy). The decision of whether the government's role is discussed in a self-contained section or as an integral part of the discussion of industries and business activities is a pragmatic one. This is because on the one hand, the role of the government permeates in all aspects of enterprises' activities, for example, from the pricing of drugs to an merger and acquisition (M&A) decision. On the other hand, the level of government intervention may differ in degree across different industries and business activities.

Industrialization and the development of industries

Over the past five decades, China's industrial sector has developed much more rapidly than its agricultural (farming, forestry, animal husbandry and fishery) sector. In 1952, the total output value of the former comprised only 43.1 per cent of the combined agricultural–industrial output value, this rose to 72.8 per cent in 1980 (Li *et al.*, 1998). It continued to rise in the next two and a half decades and in 2004, it made up 86 per cent (*China Statistical Yearbook*, 2006). Since the late 1970s, we have been witnessing a steady decline in the proportion of the national gross domestic product (GDP) from the primary (agricultural) industry (see Table 2.1, also see Tables 1.1 and 1.2). By contrast, the secondary and tertiary (service) industries have been experiencing a small but again steady increase in its proportion of the national GDP.

More specifically, certain industries such as construction, transport, storage, post and telecommunication services, wholesale, retail trade and catering services, finance and insurance, real estate and social services have experienced a higher growth rate, measured by employment growth, than other industries in the last twenty-five years (see Table 2.2).

The significant shift from the agricultural to industrial sector and from the heavy industry to the light manufacturing and service industries in the Chinese economic structure in recent decades has been accompanied by a relatively moderate shift from the rural to urban employment. For example, in 1952, those employed in the agricultural sector constituted 83.5 per cent of the total workforce in the country. The percentage was reduced to 68.7 per cent in 1980. In 2005, workers employed in this sector still made up 44.8 per cent of the total workforce (*China Statistical Yearbook*, 2006, also see Table 2.2). China faces continuous pressure to create employment opportunities not only for urban workers but more so to absorb the vast surplus rural labour force. According to the national statistics, there were some 50 million rural migrant workers working in urban areas by 1995, representing a quarter of those working in the urban area (Chen *et al.*, 2001). By 2003, there were over 98 million rural migrant workers working away from their hometown (*Workers' Daily*, 12 October 2004). They work on construction sites, in foreign-owned factories, JV plants, private enterprises, township and village enterprises (TVEs) or community services where sub-standard employment terms and conditions may be the norm and the level of state intervention has been deliberately weak (Cooke, 2005a). Rural migrant workers now make up over 46 per cent of the workforce in the secondary and tertiary industrial sectors. In the catering and construction industries, rural labour consists of 70 per cent and 80 per cent

Table 2.1 Composition of gross domestic product

Year	Gross domestic product	Primary industry	Secondary industry			Tertiary (service) industry		
			Sub-total	Industry*	Construction	Sub-total	Transport, post and telecom services	Wholesale, retail trade and catering services
1978	100.0	28.1	48.2	44.4	3.8	23.7	4.8	7.3
1979	100.0	31.2	47.4	43.8	3.6	21.4	4.6	5.5
1980	100.0	30.1	48.5	44.2	4.3	21.4	4.5	4.7
1981	100.0	31.8	46.4	42.1	4.3	21.8	4.3	5.3
1982	100.0	33.3	45.0	40.8	4.2	21.7	4.5	3.8
1983	100.0	33.0	44.6	40.0	4.6	22.4	4.5	3.9
1984	100.0	32.0	43.3	38.9	4.4	24.7	4.6	5.8
1985	100.0	28.4	43.1	38.5	4.6	28.5	4.5	9.8
1986	100.0	27.1	44.0	38.9	5.1	28.9	4.7	9.2
1987	100.0	26.8	43.9	38.3	5.6	29.3	4.6	9.7
1988	100.0	25.7	44.1	38.7	5.4	30.2	4.4	10.8
1989	100.0	25.0	43.0	38.3	4.7	32.0	4.6	10.0
1990	100.0	27.1	41.6	37.0	4.6	31.3	4.2	7.7
1991	100.0	24.5	42.1	37.4	4.7	33.4	6.5	9.7
1992	100.0	21.8	43.9	38.6	5.3	34.3	6.3	10.3
1993	100.0	19.9	47.4	40.8	6.6	32.7	6.1	8.9

Table 2.1 (Continued)

Year	Gross domestic product	Primary industry	Secondary industry			Tertiary (service) industry		
			Sub-total	Industry*	Construction	Sub-total	Transport, post and telecom services	Wholesale, retail trade and catering services
1994	100.0	20.2	47.9	41.4	6.5	31.9	5.7	8.7
1995	100.0	20.5	48.8	42.3	6.5	30.7	5.2	8.4
1996	100.0	20.4	49.5	42.8	6.7	30.1	5.1	8.2
1997	100.0	19.1	50.0	43.5	6.5	30.9	5.1	8.3
1998	100.0	18.6	49.3	42.6	6.7	32.1	5.3	8.4
1999	100.0	17.6	49.4	42.8	6.6	33.0	5.4	8.4
2000	100.0	16.4	50.2	43.6	6.6	33.4	6.0	8.2
2001	100.0	15.8	50.1	43.5	6.6	34.1	6.1	8.1
2002	100.0	15.3	50.4	43.7	6.7	34.3	6.1	8.1
2003	100.0	14.4	52.2	45.2	7.0	33.4	5.7	7.9
2004	100.0	15.2	52.9	45.9	7.0	31.9	5.6	7.4

Data in this table are calculated at current prices (Figures in %)

*Industry refers to the material production sector which is engaged in extraction of natural resources and processing and reprocessing of minerals and agricultural products, including (1) extraction of natural resources, such as mining, salt production (but not including hunting and fishing); (2) processing and reprocessing of farm and sideline produces, such as rice husking, flour milling, wine making, oil processing, silk reeling, spinning and weaving and leather making; (3) manufacture of industrial products, such as steel making, iron smelting, chemicals manufacturing, petroleum processing, machine building, timber processing, water and gas production and electricity generation and supply; (4) repairing of industrial products such as the repairing of machinery and means of transport (including cars) (original note from *China Statistical Yearbook*, 2005, p. 524).

Source: adapted from *China Statistical Yearbook* (2005, p. 52).

Table 2.2 Number of employed persons at the year-end by sector*

Industry	1978	1985	1990	1995	1998	2000	2002
Farming, forestry, animal husbandry and fishery	283,180	311,300	341,170	330,180	332,320	333,550	324,870
Mining and quarrying	6,520	7,950	8,820	9,320	7,210	5,970	5,580
Manufacturing	53,320	74,120	86,240	98,030	83,190	80,430	83,070
Electricity, gas and water production and supply	1,070	1,420	1,920	2,580	2,830	2,840	2,900
Construction	8,540	20,350	24,240	33,220	33,270	35,520	38,930
Geological prospecting and water conservancy	1,780	1,970	1,970	1,350	1,160	1,100	980
Transport, storage, post and telecommunication services	7,500	12,790	15,660	19,420	20,000	20,290	20,840
Wholesale, retail trade and catering services	11,400	23,060	28,390	42,920	46,450	46,860	49,690
Finance and insurance	760	1,380	2,180	2,760	3,140	3,270	3,400
Real estate	310	360	440	800	940	1,000	1,180
Social services	1,790	4,010	5,940	7,030	8,680	9,210	10,940

Table 2.2 (Continued)

Industry	1978	1985	1990	1995	1998	2000	2002
Health care, sports and social welfare	3,630	4,670	5,360	4,440	4,780	4,880	4,930
Education, culture and art, radio, film and Television	10,930	12,730	14,570	14,760	15,730	15,650	15,650
Scientific research and Polytechnic service	920	1,440	1,730	1,820	1,780	1,740	1,630
Governmental organizations, party agencies and social organizations	4,670	7,990	10,790	10,420	10,970	11,040	10,750
Others	5,210	13,190	17,980	44,840	51,180	56,430	62,450
Total	401,520	498,730	647,490	680,650	706,370	760,850	737,400

Figures in 1000 persons

* Employed persons refer to the persons aged 16 and over who are engaged in social working and receive remuneration payment or earn business income. This indicator reflects the actual utilization of total labour force during a certain period of time and is often used for the research on China's economic situation and national power (original note from *China Statistical Yearbook*, 2005, p. 181).

Source: adapted from *China Statistical Yearbook* (2005, p. 125).

of the workforce, respectively (*Workers' Daily*, 9 November 2004). Whilst millions of rural migrant workers continue to enter employment in urban areas and have played a pivotal role in the urban economic development, this labour force is largely unskilled and lowly educated. This imposes a strong constraint on China's capability to upgrade its economic structure by developing high value-added products and employing highly skilled workers working in knowledge-intensive industries (see further discussion later on human capital).

The continuous growth of the light manufacturing and service industries in the last twenty-five years took place in parallel with the contraction of the state-owned and collectively owned sector and the growth of the domestic privately owned and foreign-invested sector, as well as that of other ownership forms, again, measured by employment growth (see Table 2.3). For example, in 1978, the state provided over 78 per cent of the urban employment. In 2005, it provided less than 24 per cent of the urban employment (see Table 2.3). It is also interesting to note that the proportion of rural employed persons had shrunk from being over 76 per cent of the national total employment in 1978 to about 64 per cent in 2005. This is in part a result of the continuous industrialization and development of the urban economy that has largely been sustained by domestic private and foreign funds. Even in the rural employed persons category, an increasing proportion of people are engaged in industrial production and commercial activities in township and villages enterprises, private enterprises and self-employed businesses.

Indeed, private and foreign funds have been a major source of investment for the growth of the Chinese industries (see Tables 2.4 and 2.5). The proportion of state investment funds for the majority of the industries is now very small. This is with the exception of a few industries such as the utilities, telecommunications, education, health and other public services, where the state continues to be a major employer. Even in these industries, the proportion of state investment funds has diminished. Ever since China's adoption of its open door policy in the late 1970s, the manufacturing industry has been the major beneficiary of foreign investment funds (see Tables 2.4 and 2.5, also see Tables 7.1 and 7.2). In recent years, real estate, leasing and business services, scientific research and technical services, and culture, sports and entertainment industries have also begun to benefit from an increasing level of FDI (see Table 2.5). We will provide a more in-depth analysis of the development of some of the industries and of issues related to FDI in later chapters in this book.

Developing the service sector is an important and necessary step forward for China. China is a relatively resource-scarce country with many of the important natural resources falling below the world average. With the economic growth in the last three decades relying heavily on the manufacturing industry, China is facing a worsening resource shortage problem as well as environmental and ecological problems. In 2003, three shortages (known as '*san huang*') emerged in China: shortages of coal, electricity and fuel. These shortages are likely to persist for a number of years and production capacity has been constrained

Table 2.3 Employment statistics by ownership in urban and rural areas in China*

Ownership	1978	1980	1985	1990	1995	1998	2000	2002	2005
Total	401.52	423.61	498.73	647.49	680.65	706.37	720.85	737.40	758.25
Number of urban employed persons	95.14	105.25	128.08	166.16	190.93	206.78	231.51	247.80	273.31
State-owned units	74.51	80.19	89.90	103.46	112.61	90.58	81.02	71.63	64.88
Collectively owned units	20.48	24.25	33.24	35.49	31.47	19.63	14.99	11.22	8.10
Co-operative units	–	–	–	–	–	1.36	1.55	1.61	1.88
Joint ownership units	–	–	0.38	0.96	0.53	0.48	0.42	0.45	0.45
Limited liability corporations	–	–	–	–	–	4.84	6.87	10.83	17.50
Share-holding corporations ltd	–	–	–	–	3.17	4.10	4.57	5.38	6.99
Private enterprises	–	–	–	0.57	4.85	9.73	12.68	19.99	34.58
Units with funds from Hong Kong, Macao and Taiwan	–	–	–	0.04	2.72	2.94	3.10	3.67	5.57
Foreign funded units	–	–	0.06	0.62	2.41	2.93	3.32	3.91	6.88
Self-employed individuals	0.15	0.81	4.50	6.14	15.60	22.59	21.36	22.69	27.78

Number of rural employed persons	306.38	318.36	370.65	472.93	488.54	492.79	489.34	489.60	484.94
Township and village enterprises	28.27	30.00	69.79	92.65	128.62	125.37	128.20	132.88	142.72
Private enterprises	–	–	–	1.13	4.71	7.37	11.39	14.11	23.66
Self-employed individuals	–	–	–	14.91	30.54	38.55	29.34	24.74	21.23

Figures in million persons

* Since 1990, data on economically active population, the total employed persons and the sub-total of employed persons in urban and rural areas have been adjusted in accordance with the data obtained from the 5th National Population Census. As a result, the sum of the data by region, by ownership or by sector is not equal to the total (original note from *China Statistical Yearbook*, 2003, p. 123).

Source: adapted from *China Statistical Yearbook* (2003, pp. 126–7) and (2006, p. 125).

Table 2.4 Source of funds for investment and newly increased fixed assets in urban area by sector in 2004

Item	Total funds in 2004	State budgetary appropriations	Domestic loans	Foreign investment	Self-raising fund	Others	Investment sum	Newly increased fixed assets	Rate of projects completed and put into operation (%)
National total	63,116.2	2,855.7	12,842.9	2,706.6	32,826.4	11,884.6	59,028.2	34,755.9	58.9
Farming, forestry, animal husbandry and fishery	644.4	127.7	49.4	20.2	333.6	113.6	645.1	459.0	71.1
Mining	2,173.9	31.4	317.1	27.7	1,627.1	170.6	2,126.3	1,398.0	65.7
Manufacturing	15,039.1	91.5	2,192.0	1,841.0	10,178.8	735.8	14,657.2	9,024.1	61.6
Manufacture of medicines	606.3	2.8	92.0	34.5	450.7	26.3	594.5	390.6	65.7
Manufacture of transport equipment	1,068.4	11.9	116.0	104.0	787.3	49.2	1,033.2	573.7	55.5

Manufacture of communication equipment, computers and other electronic equipment	1,103.8	2.8	203.9	453.7	423.9	19.2	1,021.2	680.8	66.7
Electricity, gas and water production and supply	5,643.6	253.2	2,372.6	224.5	2,411.1	382.3	5,525.1	3,110.2	56.3
Construction	530.6	42.6	46.6	4.2	359.0	78.2	526.3	365.6	69.5
Transport, storage, post and telecommunication services	6,759.3	830.5	2,369.6	180.0	2,959.0	420.3	7,091.5	4,257.8	60.0
Information transmission, computer service and software	1,644.9	16.1	118.1	11.0	1,468.6	31.1	1,638.0	1,153.3	70.4

Table 2.4 (Continued)

Item	Total funds in 2004	State budgetary appropriations	Domestic loans	Foreign investment fund	Self-raising investment fund	Others	Investment sum	Newly increased of fixed assets	Rate of projects completed and put into operation (%)
Telecom and other information transmission services	1,593.5	13.4	104.2	9.4	1,438.2	28.4	1,589.9	1,134.4	71.3
Computer services	14.3	0.9	3.1	1.0	9.0	0.4	11.7	5.1	43.0
Software	37.0	1.9	10.8	0.7	21.4	2.3	36.4	13.9	38.1
Wholesale and retail trade	1,158.3	6.2	101.6	26.6	874.8	149.2	1,117.2	717.5	64.2
Wholesale trade	454.8	4.6	34.6	6.1	354.8	54.8	447.4	268.0	59.9
Retail trade	703.5	1.6	66.9	20.5	520.0	94.5	669.8	449.4	67.1
Hotels and restaurants	453.3	7.5	57.1	30.6	322.8	35.4	438.1	267.6	61.1
Finance and insurance	94.4	2.8	1.5	–	75.7	14.5	97.6	111.4	114.2

Real estate	1,389.6	32.0	112.8	14.2	1,085.8	144.8	14,547.0	7,893.3	54.3
Leasing and business services	17,531.0	18.3	3,224.8	233.0	5,450.2	8604.7	361.7	160.6	44.4
Scientific research, technical services and geological prospecting	318.8	56.5	17.3	10.1	198.2	36.6	311.8	200.4	64.3
Management of water conservancy, environment and public facilities	4,764.4	607.5	1,207.8	42.0	2,504.4	402.8	4,890.8	2,408.9	49.3
Services to households and other services	109.6	1.3	6.6	2.2	80.3	19.2	107.6	74.4	69.2

Table 2.4 (Continued)

Item	Total funds in 2004	State budgetary appropriations	Domestic loans	Foreign investment	Self-raising fund	Others	Investment sum	Newly increased fixed assets	Rate of projects completed and put into operation (%)
Education	1,755.9	157.3	389.2	9.4	1,056.6	143.0	1,803.0	1,209.5	67.1
Health, social securities and social welfare	450.4	51.9	56.7	7.1	303.3	31.6	446.9	308.5	69.0
Culture, sports and entertainment	530.3	58.6	57.6	11.2	357.8	45.1	531.2	243.3	45.8
Public management and social organizations	2,123.8	462.9	144.3	11.6	1,179.2	325.8	2,165.6	1,392.5	64.3
International organizations	0.3	–	–	0.1	0.1	0.1	0.3	0.2	56.2

Figures in 100 million yuan
Source: adapted from *China Statistical Yearbook* (2005, pp. 212–5).

Table 2.5 Foreign direct investment by sector in 2004

Sector	No. of projects (units)	Contracted value (million US$)	Actually used value (million US$)
Total	43,664	153,478.95	60,629.98
Farming, forestry, animal husbandry and fishery	1,130	3,270.96	1,114.34
Mining	279	1,155.81	538.00
Manufacturing	30,386	109,735.76	43,017.24
Electricity, gas and water production and supply	455	3,960.49	1,136.24
Construction	411	1,768.89	771.58
Transport, storage, post and telecommunication services	638	2,372.90	1,272.85
Information transmission, computer service and software	1,622	2,021.37	906.09
Wholesale and retail trade	1,700	2,500.53	739.59
Hotels and restaurants	1,174	2,168.87	840.94
Finance and insurance	43	575.41	252.48
Real estate	1,767	13,488.02	5,950.15
Leasing and business services	2,661	6,742.48	2,824.23
Scientific research, technical services and geological prospecting	629	1,006.41	293.84
Management of water conservancy, environment and public facilities	164	822.09	229.11
Services to households and other services	251	542.51	157.95
Education	59	172.74	38.41
Health care, social securities and social welfare	21	147.20	87.38
Culture, sports and entertainment	272	1,012.81	447.76
Public management and social organization	2	13.70	1.80

Source: adapted from *China Statistical Yearbook* (2005, p. 648).

due to power cuts in many areas. In 2004, China's GDP made up only 4 per cent of the world's GDP. However, it consumed 38 per cent of the world's coal, 27.4 per cent of steel, 21.4 per cent of aluminium and 45.8 per cent of cement (Shu, 2005; also see Chapter 1). The Chinese manufacturing firm receives only 10 per cent of the sales revenue to produce the product while the foreign firm takes 90 per cent of it. For example, the first set of DVD that China exported was sold for US$32, of which China needed to pay US$18 as a patent fee to the foreign firm, to produce the product cost US$13, and so the Chinese manufacturer was left with US$1 on each set of DVD sold. Similar is true for the production of other products, such as MP3s and computer mice (*Workers' Daily*, 9 August 2005). This model of manufacturing economy – 'Made in China' with 'one-dollar profit' – is clearly not sustainable with regard to the country's economic growth and environmental and ecological protection.

The conversion of farming land into industrial sites also causes social and political problems as farmers who have lost their land have not always been able to gain employment, in part due to their low level of education and skills. Whilst land-loss compensation provides them with a moderate level of financial support in the initial years, their livelihood is difficult to sustain without the support of a proper state welfare system. There are therefore all sorts of reasons and pressures for the Chinese economy to shift from a manufacturing economy towards a service-oriented economy. In many ways, such a shift is not a radical departure from its economic trajectory, but an evolutionary journey which many developed countries have already been through.

Technology and innovation environment

There is now a wide consensus that knowledge, technology and innovation are the key drivers for sustained economic growth and national competitiveness (e.g. Leonard-Barton, 1995; Nonaka and Takeuchi, 1995; OECD, 1992; Porter, 1990; Teece *et al.*, 1997; Utterback, 1994). In this section, we will first look at the innovation policy framework and institutions of China, the overall investment into R&D activities and where they come from. We will then introduce a number of national R&D programmes that are sponsored and participated in by the Chinese government. Finally, we will investigate the output of S&T.

Innovation policy framework and institutions

China has a complex structure of innovation policy institutions, which is headed by the State Steering Committee of S&T and Education of the State Council and the Ministry of Science and Technology (MOST) (see Figure 2.1). These institutions are responsible for the design, implementation and monitoring of China's innovation policies, S&T programmes and other R&D initiatives at the national level (Huang *et al.*, 2004).[2]

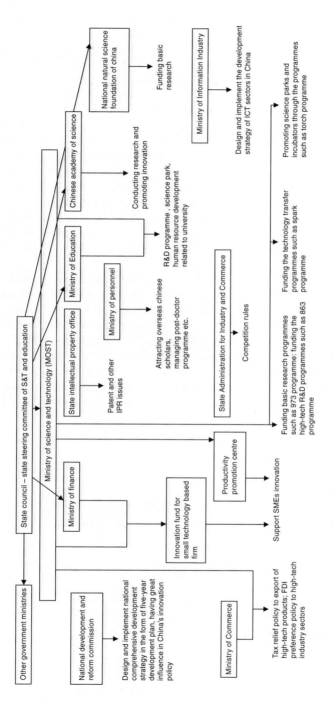

Figure 2.1 Chinese innovation policy institutions

Sources: Huang *et al.* (2004, p. 368).

Influenced by the state planned economy regime, the innovation system of China is a centralized one that is substantiated by three categories of R&D institutions (Huang *et al.*, 2004; Turpin and Liu, 2000; Yang, 2003). The Chinese Academy of Science contains the most important set of R&D institutions in the Chinese innovation system and has been an 'important stakeholder in the Chinese innovation policy framework' (Huang *et al.*, 2004, p. 369). Its main responsibility is to carry out basic scientific research and support major mission-oriented projects (Turpin and Liu, 2000). A second category of R&D institutions are those that are attached to universities, which have the responsibility of combined research and education (Turpin and Liu, 2000). The third category of R&D institutions are those that are housed within the industrial sector, often at enterprise level. Their primary function is to solve R&D problems within specific sectors. The activities of these institutions are coordinated by the government (Turpin and Liu, 2000). This centralized system dominated by state institutions carries the inherent problem of being inflexible, distanced from the market and industrial needs and a bureaucratic culture that does not engender openness and entrepreneurship.

Whilst China has a relatively poor record of R&D and innovation to date, a considerable amount of effort has been made by the government to address the problem. In particular, a number of policies and action plans have been introduced since the 1980s that are aimed to promote innovation (Huang *et al.*, 2004). These include: finance policy in the form of funding and tax relief policy; HR policy in the form of educational and training programmes; support of business innovation through the establishment of science parks and incubators, high-tech fairs and productivity promotion centres; legislative actions; and reform of public S&T institutions (Huang *et al.*, 2004, see Figure 2.2). These

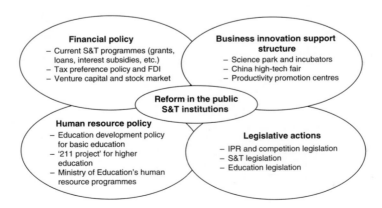

Figure 2.2 Chinese innovation policy
Sources: Huang *et al.* (2004, p. 370).

policies and actions have had a tangible effect in that both the input and output of R&D in China has been increasing steadily in recent years.

Investment in R&D

R&D and technological innovation are expensive activities that take a long time and heavy investment to accumulate the knowledge base. China started from a low base. The overall investment in R&D in China remains relatively small in comparison with that in developed countries (see Table 2.6). For example, in 1999, China's R&D investment consisted of only 0.83 per cent of its GDP, whereas the United States had 2.65 per cent, Japan had 2.93 per cent and South Korea had 2.47 per cent.

It must be noted, however, that the level of R&D spending in China has been increasing in recent years. In 1978, the overall government expenditure for science and research was only 5.29 billion yuan. This was increased to 133.49 billion yuan in 2005 (see Table 2.7). In 1999, the gross expenditure of R&D was only 0.76 per cent of the GDP. This was increased to 1.23 per cent in 2004 (see Table 2.8), in spite of the fact that the gross expenditure on R&D now formed a smaller percentage of the total government expenditure.

Investment in the R&D infrastructure and activities in China comes from four main sources: the government, enterprises, bank loans and others (see Tables 2.9 and 2.10). Enterprises are the largest funding source by far, making up 65.52 per cent of the total S&T funds in 2005. The government is the second-largest funding source, contributing to just less than a quarter of the total fund. There is a continuous, albeit small, increase in R&D investment from enterprises. While funding from enterprises flows mainly back to enterprises, research institutes and higher education institutions are the major recipients of the government's R&D funds (see Table 2.10). This pattern of funding source and flow is broadly similar to that in other countries (see Figure 2.3). However, compared with their counterparts in developed countries, the higher education institutions in China receive a small percentage of the gross expenditure on R&D. This is in part due to the traditional functional separation between research institutes (research oriented) and universities

Table 2.6 Ratio of R&D investment to GDP of selected countries

Country	China	USA	Japan	Britain	France	Germany	South Korea	Turkey	Czech	Mexico
Year	1999	1999	1999	1999	1999	1999	1999	1999	1999	1999
R&D/ GDP	0.83	2.65	2.93	1.87	2.19	2.44	2.47	0.63	1.25	0.4

Figures in %
Source: adapted from *China Science and Technology Statistics Yearbook* (2002).

Table 2.7   Government expenditure for science and research

Year	Total	Expenditure on science and technology promotion	Expenditure on science	Expenditure on capital construction of S&T institutes	Other science and technology operating expenditure
1978	5.29	2.55	1.55	0.67	0.53
1980	6.46	2.76	1.96	1.13	0.61
1985	10.23	4.44	3.20	1.88	0.74
1989	12.79	5.91	3.85	1.79	1.24
1990	13.91	6.35	4.44	1.75	1.37
1991	16.07	7.33	5.42	1.84	1.48
1992	18.93	8.94	5.72	2.46	1.81
1993	22.56	10.66	6.56	3.40	1.95
1994	26.83	11.42	8.79	3.61	3.01
1995	30.24	13.60	9.69	3.80	3.15
1996	34.86	15.50	10.97	4.86	3.54
1997	40.89	19.00	12.71	4.27	4.90
1998	43.86	18.99	15.19	4.73	4.95
1999	54.39	27.28	16.81	5.29	5.01
2000	57.56	27.72	18.90	6.15	4.79
2001	70.33	35.96	22.31	6.34	5.72
2002	81.62	39.86	26.99	7.00	7.78
2003	97.55	41.66	30.08	11.11	14.71
2004	109.53	48.40	33.60	9.60	17.95
2005	133.49	60.97	38.91	11.25	22.36

Figures in billion yuan
Source: adapted from China Statistical Yearbook (2006, p. 284).

(teaching oriented) in China, although these two have become more integrated in recent years. It is interesting to note that Russia has a similar pattern to China.

Compared with other countries such as Korea, Russia, France, Japan and the United States, China spends a much smaller proportion of its R&D fund on basic research and a considerably higher proportion on experimental development (see Figure 2.4). China also has a much smaller ratio of R&D personnel per 10,000 labour force. For example, China had 15 R&D personnel (including R&D scientists and engineers) per 10,000 labour force in 2004. By contrast, Japan had 132, Germany had 122, France had 127, and Russia had 135 in 2003 (see Figure 2.5). What is promising though is that the number of R&D personnel in China has continued to grow in recent years. For example, in 1999, there were a total of 821,700 R&D personnel in full-time employment, and there were on average 7.3 R&D scientists and engineers per 10,000 labour force in full-time employment. These figures

Table 2.8 National science and technology financing indictors (1999–2004)

	1999	2000	2001	2002	2003	2004*
Gross expenditure of R&D (100 million yuan)	678.9	895.7	1,042.5	1,287.6	1,539.6	1,966.3
As percentage of GDP (%)	0.76	0.90	0.95	1.07	1.13	1.23
Government S&T appropriation (100 million yuan)	543.9	575.6	703.3	816.2	944.6	1,095.3
As percentage of total government expenditure (%)	4.1	3.6	3.7	3.7	3.8	3.8

* Data for 2004 are calculated by the adjusted GDP based on the National Economic Census in 2004. Data in previous years are calculated based on the revised GDP data for each year (original note).
Source: The Ministry of Science and Technology (MOST) of the People's Republic of China (2005), 'Outline of S&T activities'.

Table 2.9 Structure of source of funding for scientific and technological activities in China

Source	Year							
	1998	1999	2000	2001	2002	2003	2004	2005
Total of S&T fund (billion yuan)	128.98	146.06	234.67	258.94	293.80	345.91	432.89	525.08
Of which: Government fund (%)	27.43	32.38	25.29	25.35	26.42	24.26	22.77	23.10
Enterprise fund (%)	50.79	51.07	55.24	56.32	57.07	59.37	64.03	65.52
Bank loan (%)	13.26	8.42	8.36	7.37	6.87	7.50	6.12	5.27
Others (%)	8.53	8.13	11.11	10.96	9.64	8.88	7.08	6.11

Sources: adapted from *China Statistical Yearbook* (2002, p. 703) and (2006, p. 825).

Table 2.10   Gross expenditure of R&D by source of funds, flow of funding and sector of performance in 2004

Source of funds	Performance sectors receiving the funds					
	Research institutes amount	Enterprises amount	Higher education amount	Other organizations amount	Total Amount	%
Government	344.3	62.6	108.8	7.8	523.6	26.6
Enterprises	22.4	1,189.3	74.5	5.1	1,291.3	65.7
Abroad	2.6	19.8	2.6	0.1	25.2	1.3
Others	62.4	42.3	14.9	6.6	126.2	6.4
Total	431.7	1,314.0	200.9	19.7	1,966.3	100

Figures in 100 million yuan and %
Source: adapted from the Ministry of Science and Technology (MOST) of the People's Republic of China (2005), 'R&D activities'.

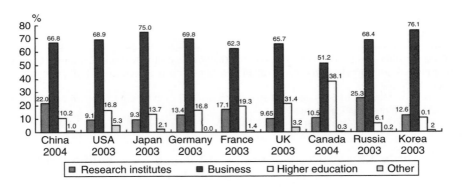

Figure 2.3   Gross expenditure on R&D in selected countries by sector of performance
Sources: The Ministry of Science and Technology (MOST) of the People's Republic of China (2005), 'R&D activities', http://www.most.gov.cn/eng/statistics/2005/t20060317_29724.htm.
MOST's source: OECD, Main Science & Technology Indicators 2005/1, except the data on China.

rose to 1,152,600 and 12.1, respectively in 2004 (see Table 2.11). In 1985, China trained only 115,287 first university degree students in sciences and engineering (S&E) disciplines whereas Japan, the United States, the United Kingdom and Germany trained 247,258, 332,273, 40,550 and 71,540, respectively. In 2002, China trained 384,529 S&E first university degree students, approaching the United States who trained 415,611 and overtaking Japan who trained 357,282. In 1985, China trained only 140 PhD students in natural sciences and engineering subjects, whereas Japan, the United States, the United

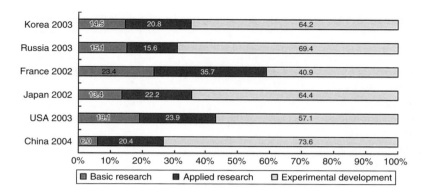

Figure 2.4 R&D expenditures in selected countries by type of activity
Sources: The Ministry of Science and Technology (MOST) of the People's Republic of
China (2005), 'R&D activities',
http://www.most.gov.cn/eng/statistics/2005/t20060317_29724.htm.
MOST's source: Ministry of Science & Technology of China, Eurostat, Research &
Development Statistics 2004 (OECD).

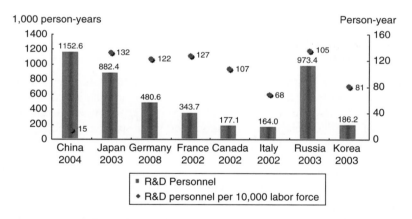

Figure 2.5 R&D personnel in selected countries
Sources: The Ministry of Science and Technology (MOST) of the People's Republic of
China (2005), 'R&D activities',
http://www.most.gov.cn/eng/statistics/2005/t20060317_29724.htm.
MOST's source: OECD, Main Science & Technology Indicators 2005/1, except the data on
China.

Kingdom and Germany trained 2960, 13,330, 3920 and 4770, respectively.
In 2001, China produced 7530 PhD students in the same fields, whereas
Japan, the United States, the United Kingdom and Germany trained 6790,
19,640, 7340 and 9620, respectively (Science and Engineering Indicators,
2006).

Table 2.11 National R&D personnel indicators (1999–2004)

	1999	2000	2001	2002	2003	2004
R&D personnel (1,000 full-time employees)	821.7	922.1	956.5	1035.1	1094.8	1,152.6
Of which scientists and engineers (1,000 full-time employees)	531.1	695.1	742.7	810.5	862.1	926.3
Scientists and engineers engaged in R&D per 10,000 labour force (in full-time employment)	7.3	9.4	10.0	10.8	11.3	12.1

Source: The Ministry of Science and Technology (MOST) of the People's Republic of China (2005), 'Outline of S&T activities'.

Government-sponsored programmes and Sino-foreign collaborations

While industrial investment in R&D is growing, the Chinese government remains an important decision maker and sponsor in shaping the country's research agenda. More notably, the Chinese government has been funding a series of S&T development programmes with specific objectives. These include:

The Key Technologies R&D Programme It was launched in 1982, covering agriculture, electronic information, energy resources, transportation, materials, resources exploration, environmental protection, medical and health care and other fields. It is the largest national programme and funds research at more than 1000 scientific research institutions (Yoshida, 2005, p. 3).

The 863 High-tech R&D Programme It started in 1986 with the aim to be a pioneer country in selected applied research areas, including biotechnology, space technology, information, laser technology, automation, energy and advanced materials (Yang, 2003, p. 143, see Box 2.1 for more details of this programme as an example of these high-profile government-funded R&D programmes).

The Spark Programme It was set up in 1986 with the aim of diffusing technology appropriate for TVEs and farming in order to revitalize the rural economy (Yang, 2003, p. 144; Yoshida, 2005, p. 3).

The Torch Programme It was established in 1988 with the aim of commercializing discoveries from institutes and universities and to create new high-technology enterprises. It was a key initiative in providing technological links for the establishment of 53 national-class New High Technology Zones across China. By the end of 1997 these zones housed 13,681 new high-tech enterprises and realized a total output of 338.7 billion yuan (CSIESR, 1999, p. 56, cited in Yang, 2003, pp. 143–4).

The 973 Programme It began in 1998 and is directed at basic research. It represents China's increasing support for basic knowledge creation and focuses on interdisciplinary scientific research in areas such as agriculture, energy, information, environment and resources, population and health, and materials (Yoshida, 2005, p. 3).

BOX 2.1

The National High-Tech R&D Programme of China (The 863 Programme)

Background The National High-Tech R&D Programme of China (more widely known as the 863 Programme named after the time when it was officially approved in March 1986) was launched by the Chinese government with the aim of enhancing China's international competitiveness and improving China's overall capability of R&D in high technology. Based on the successful implementation during the seventh, eighth and ninth five-year plan periods, it was officially approved by the State Council in April 2001 that the programme should continue to be carried out during the tenth five-year plan period.

Main mission The 863 programme focuses on the strategic, forefront and forecast high technology that benefits China's long and medium-term development and security needs. It promotes the development of high technologies and fosters new growth areas of high-tech industry.

Objectives The 863 Programme has the following objectives:

- To promote the development of key supporting technologies for the construction of national information infrastructure;
- To promote the development of key biological, agricultural and pharmaceutical technologies for improving the quality of life;
- To promote the development of key novel materials and advanced manufacturing technologies for raising industry competitiveness;
- To promote the development of key resource, environment protection and energy technologies beneficial to social sustainable development.

Priorities Nineteen Priorities have been identified in the six fields of the 863 Programme: IT, biological and advanced agricultural technology, advanced materials, advanced manufacturing and automatic technology, energy technology and resource and environment technology. Priority Projects are guided by encouraging innovation, obtaining IPR proprietorship and addressing key technological issues. Priority Projects conduct R&D in the 19 selected subjects which are deemed to impose the most significant impact on enhancing China's overall national strengths. The R&D projects to be supported in the Priorities are oriented to stimulating original innovation, tackling major key technological issues and forming IPR. In addition, several Key Projects are selected. Hundreds of scientists are involved in the projects promoted by the 863 Programme. The projects are believed to have significantly narrowed the gap between China and the rest of the world in a wide range of research areas.

Funding Priority Projects are mostly financed by the government and adopt a project budget system. Meanwhile, local governments, industries, enterprises and the whole society are encouraged to increase input into high-tech R&D.

International cooperation International cooperation and exchange in various forms are encouraged so long as domestic R&D activities are integrated with the importation, assimilation and absorption of foreign technologies. Foreign scientists are encouraged to take part in the projects under the 863 Programme in their personal capacity, and foreign research institutions can apply for projects sponsored by the 863 programme jointly with domestic institutes, and share the cost and research outcomes.

Source: compiled from the Ministry of Science and Technology (MOST) of People's Republic of China (2001), 'Overview of 863 Programme in the Tenth Five-Year Plan period'; MOST (2006), 'National High-Tech R&D Programme (863 Programme)'; and *China Daily Online* (31 August 2002).

In recent years, the Chinese government has demonstrated a stronger commitment to promoting innovation. In addition to sponsoring S&T programmes as mentioned above, the government has been making efforts to forge stronger R&D partnership with foreign governments and institutions and to encourage technology transfer, spin-off companies and science parks.

In the China-Germany Hi-Tech Dialogue Forum held in Beijing in 2001, the Chinese government stated that it is important for China to develop its hi-tech industries in the coming years and that the development of high-tech industries should be given top priority in key areas of the national economy in the next five to ten years. The government also revealed that the high-tech industry has taken the place of traditional industry as China's most vigorous sector (http://www.edu.cn/20011102). According to official statistics,

From 1996 to 2000, the high-tech industry grew at an average annual rate of 21.2 per cent, 11 percentage points higher than that of the industrial sector in the same period. The exports of high-tech products grew by 38.4 per cent on average annually, 28 percentage points higher than the country's total exports. The proportion of high-tech exports among total exports rose from 8.4 per cent to 14.9 per cent.

(http://www.edu.cn/20011102)

In 2000, the output value of the electronic and information products manufacturing sector reached 1000 billion yuan (about US$120.9 billion), four times the figure five years before (http://www.edu.cn/20011102).

Box 2.2 is an example that the Chinese government and foreign governments have begun to join forces to help innovation and business growth for mutual benefit. It is worth noting that an increasing number of foreign-based non-governmental organizations (NGOs) have also started to play the brokering role in bridging the R&D links between foreign and Chinese partners (see Chapter 9 for more details).

China now houses an increasing number of science parks or high-tech zones, many of them JVs with foreign partners. The largest and strongest one is perhaps the Zhingguancun Haidian Science Park in Beijing, in which China's largest PC maker Lenovo is located. The Park's total annual income is expected to hit 366 billion yuan (about US$44 billion) by 2008, the greatest of all of China's 53 high-tech zones (*China Daily Online*, 6 January 2005, also see Chapter 6). Foreign firms are turning their attention to China for its low-cost R&D talent,

---

BOX 2.2

Finland-China Innovation Centre

The Ministry of Trade and Industry of China, together with Finpro and Tekes, opened Finland-China Innovation Centre (FinChi) in Shanghai in the spring of 2005. FinChi is a new service concept for innovative, growth-oriented companies. The innovation centre will support the operations of growth-oriented Finnish companies and organizations in the Chinese market. Reciprocally, it will serve as a service centre for Chinese companies, research institutes and authorities, presenting Finnish know-how to the Chinese.

The Centre will begin its operations as a two-year pilot project. During this time, operational models will be created with the purpose of bringing added value to the participants by helping innovative operators to form networks both in China and in Finland.

FinChi is a publicly funded, non-profit organization operating in the Zhangjiang Technology Park. The innovation centre boasts a full-service office hotel with exhibit space, provides technology services essentially geared for small- and medium-sized companies and helps them enter the market. The services are designed to help in recognizing business opportunities, starting operations and lowering the risks of operating in a new market environment. The centre aims to establish networks with businesses, authorities and individuals, all of which are important for successfully operating in China. In addition, the centre will offer business services provided by both Finnish and Chinese companies.

FinChi will serve large companies and their subcontractors by speeding up the establishment of new contacts and cooperation with Chinese universities and research institutes. The innovation centre will strengthen the companies' visibility and position with the local authorities and other actors. Finnish universities and research institutes will benefit from FinChi's Services when searching for high-quality partners. FinChi will also help them to find buyers for research services and assistance in commercializing their innovations. FinChi will utilize the S&T agreement between Finland and China and support educational and researchers' exchange between the two countries.

Source: adapted from the Ministry of Trade and Industry (2005), 'Finland-China innovation centre'.

proximity to the market and market-specific knowledge. For example, IT giant Microsoft has established Microsoft Research Asia (MSRA) in Beijing as one of five Microsoft research laboratories around the world which carries out research for the use of the company's global operations (Fiducia Management Consultants, 2004a). By the early 2000s, there were more than 130 foreign-owned R&D facilities in Shanghai (Fiducia Management Consultants, 2004a). One of the examples is the Pan Asia Technical Automotive Centre (PATAC). It is a 50/50 JV between one of the world's largest automobile manufacturers, General Motors, and Shanghai Automotive Industry Corporation Group. PATAC is responsible for automobile designs and validating parts and vehicles as well as for the engineering, development and testing of vehicles that meet the specific requirements of roads and drivers in China. PATAC's workforce is expected to grow from 770 to 1200 by 2010 (Fiducia Management Consultants, 2004a). In April 2003 General Electric (GE) opened its China Technology Center (CTC) – one of its four international R&D centers around the world – in the Zhangjiang High-Tech Industrial Park in East Pudong District to undertake GE's large projects. GE's R&D workforce has grown very rapidly in part because of its aggressive expansion in China (Fiducia Management Consultants, 2004a). According to a survey of the world's largest R&D spenders conducted by UNCTAD during 2004–5, 69 per cent of the firms stated that the share of foreign R&D was set to increase. While over 35 per cent of these transnational firms surveyed already have R&D sites in China (after the United States 58.8 per cent and United Kingdom 47.1 per cent), 61.8 per cent reported that China would be the most attractive prospective R&D location in the next few years (*World Investment Report*, 2005). This finding suggests that there is enormous opportunity for Chinese firms to collaborate with foreign partners in R&D activities.

S&T output

The continuous rise in the level of R&D investment and activities in recent years has seen a corresponding growth in the S&T output. For example, there was an increase of 15 per cent in the total number of patent applications in 2004 from 2003 (see Table 2.12). It must be noted, however, that there was a slight drop in the proportion of domestic applications, that is, from 81.4 per cent in 2003

Table 2.12 Number of patents applied for and granted by the State Intellectual Property Office of (SIPO) the People's Republic of China (2003–4)

	2003				2004			
	Total (cases)	Domestic (cases)	% of total	Foreign (cases)	Total (cases)	Domestic (cases)	% of total	Foreign (cases)
Patent applications	308,487	251,238	81.4	57,249	353,807	278,943	78.8	74,864
Invention	105,318	56,769	53.9	48,549	130,133	65,786	50.6	64,347
Utility model	109,115	107,842	98.8	1,273	112,825	111,578	98.9	1,247
Design	94,054	86,627	92.1	7,427	110,849	101,579	91.6	9,270
Patent granted	182,226	149,588	82.1	32,638	190,238	151,328	79.5	38,910
Invention	37,154	11,404	30.7	25,750	49,360	18,241	37.0	31,119
Utility model	68,906	68,291	99.1	615	70,623	70,019	99.1	604
Design	76,166	69,893	91.8	6,273	70,255	63,068	89.8	7,187

Source: adapted from the Ministry of Science and Technology of the People's Republic of China (2005), 'Output indicators'.

Table 2.13 Domestic service invention patent applications filed and patents granted by SIPO by sector (2001–4)

	Patent applications (cases)				Patent granted (cases)			
	2001	2002	2003	2004	2001	2002	2003	2004
Total	14,815	22,668	34,731	41,750	2,614	3,144	6,895	12,176
Universities and colleges	2,636	4,282	7,704	9,683	579	697	1,730	3,484
Scientific research institutions	2,659	3,429	4,711	4,543	800	907	1,677	2,406
Enterprises	9,371	14,657	21,858	27,029	1,089	1,461	3,382	6,128
Government and social organizations	149	300	458	495	146	79	106	158

Source: The Ministry of Science and Technology of the People's Republic of China (2005), 'Output indicators'.

to 78.8 per cent in 2004. In addition, the majority of domestic cases of patent applications were for utility model and design instead of invention. By contrast, 86 per cent of the foreign cases were for invention in 2004. Within the domestic sector, enterprises are again well ahead in the applications of service invention patents, compared with universities/colleges, scientific research institutes and government and social organizations (see Table 2.13).

China has attracted much criticism on the international stage for its lax attitude towards IPR. On the one hand, the Chinese fail to give due respect to the IPRs of others. On the other hand, they are not aware of the need to protect their own IPRs (also see Chapters 3 and 5). Nevertheless, there is now a growing awareness of the need to use IPRs to protect firms' asset and competitive advantage. For example, when the trade mark system was first resumed in 1978 in China, there were a total of fewer than 20,000 registrations of trade marks. This had risen to 2.24 million by 2004 and the figure is continuing to grow at an annual rate of 27 per cent (*China Business*, 17 October 2005). It is reported (e.g. Boyarski *et al.*, 2001) that some Chinese firms are waking up to the use of IPRs as a tool to develop their businesses and protect themselves from foreign exploitation, especially in controversial areas of scientific research where China has the freedom to explore (e.g. research in human genomes). The Chinese government has also recognized the need to develop 'an intellectual property system and intends to heighten protection for intellectual property by improving the country's legal and judicial systems' through which to develop its S&T (Boyarski *et al.*, 2001, p. 28).

Exports of high-tech products is another indicator of S&T output. There has been a continuous growth in China's exports of high-tech products in both value and their share in the total exports (see Table 2.14). In particular,

Table 2.14   National imports and exports of high-tech products (1999–2004)

	1999	2000	2001	2002	2003	2004
Exports of high-tech products (billion US$)	247.0	370.4	464.5	678.6	1,103.2	1,653.6
Share in total exports (%)	12.7	14.9	17.5	20.8	25.2	27.9
Share in exports of industrial manufactured products (%)	14.1	16.6	19.4	22.8	27.3	29.9
Imports of high-tech products (billion US$)	376.0	525.1	641.1	828.4	1193.0	1613.4
Share in total imports (%)	22.7	23.3	26.3	28.1	28.9	28.7
Share in imports of industrial manufactured products (%)	27.1	29.4	32.4	33.7	35.1	36.6

Source: The Ministry of Science and Technology of the People's Republic of China (2005), 'Output indicators'.

computers and telecommunications and electronics products are the major export products (see Table 2.15). It needs to be pointed out that a large proportion of the high-tech exports are produced by foreign, Hong Kong or Taiwan invested companies in the industries that have a high share of exports. It must also be pointed out that the high-tech export products are mainly to do with the manufacturing or assembling of final products rather than the design or manufacturing of core product components. In other words, they are not the most value-added part of the production process. At the same time, the level of imports of high-tech products into China remains constant at just below 30 per cent of the total value of national imports. A majority of these imported high-tech products are related to the core technology, such as electronics, computer-integrated manufacturing and aerospace, in which China is not yet self-sufficient. This indicates China's continuous reliance on foreign technology for its industrial production. The lack of technical competence of the Chinese manufacturing industry means that key components of the products (e.g. vehicles and electronic goods) have to be imported or supplied by the foreign partners of the JVs. This exposes the Chinese partners to a heavy financial burden (e.g. paying for patent rights), increased business risk

Table 2.15 National imports and exports of high-tech products by field (2004)

	Exports	Imports	balance
Total	1653.64	1613.45	40.19
Computers and telecommunications	1362.15	506.95	855.21
Life science technologies	32.37	37.93	−5.56
Electronics	184.30	771.49	−587.19
Computer-integrated manufacturing	14.96	174.02	−159.06
Aerospace	9.96	63.66	−53.70
Opto-electronics	37.97	32.16	5.80
Biotechnology	2.19	1.08	1.11
Materials	6.70	22.94	−16.24
Other technologies	3.04	3.22	−0.18

Figures in billion US$
Source: The Ministry of Science and Technology of the People's Republic of China (2005), 'Output indicators'.

and constraint in developing its own technical competence (see Chapter 4 for more details). To make matters worse, there seem to be few incentives for the Chinese enterprises to carry out their own innovation or adaptation on the basis of the imported technology (Yang, 2003).

Human capital of China

Technological competence and innovativeness of a nation depends heavily on the education and skills level of its workforce. Investment in education and training and creating a learning environment and an innovative culture are seen as crucial means to foster an innovative workforce that will enhance a nation's competitive advantage (Hamel and Prahalad, 1993; OECD, 1992; Porter, 1990). Human capital, as its proponents (Becker, 1964; Lucas, 1988; Romer, 1990; Schultz, 1961) argue, is the most valuable of all capital and a major ingredient for high productivity and quality performance. The most important investments in human capital are education and training.

China, which possesses one of the largest labour forces in the world, has often been criticized for the low quality of its labour supply. Its perceived competitive advantage lies in its abundance of low-cost unskilled labour. According to the China 2003 Survey as part of the Investment Climate Surveys conducted by the World Bank, tax rates, economic and regulatory policy uncertainty, as well as the low skill and education level of the workforce are identified by the firms surveyed as the three biggest constraints of the top ten constraints of operating in China. More specifically, over 30 per cent of the firms surveyed felt that labour skill level was a major constraint for investing in China (The World Bank, 2005b).

Education and skill levels of the workforce

It is true that the vast majority of Chinese workers have relatively low education levels and aggregate at the lower end of the skill level, even after taking its vast force of rural workers out of the equation. In 2004, one-third of its workforce had only primary school education level or less. Just over 7 per cent of the workforce were educated to the college or university level (see Table 2.16). In general, less than 30 per cent of the staff and workers in formal urban units are classified in the scientific and technical category (Table 2.17). It needs to be pointed out that the overall education and skill levels of the workforce in these units are higher than that of other units such as private enterprises and TVEs (see note of Table 2.17). In addition, the education and skill levels of the workforce are not evenly spread across industrial sectors, making some sectors (e.g. manufacturing and wholesale and retail trade) even less competitive than others (see Chapters 4, 5, 6 and 7 for further discussion).

By the mid-2000s, approximately 23 per cent Chinese workers were classified as skilled or professional. Among them, only about 1.5 per cent were

Table 2.16   Educational attainment composition of employment (total and by selected sectors)

Educational level	Total (%)	Manufacturing	Information transmission, computer service and software	Wholesale and retail trade
Illiterate and semi-illiterate	6.2	1.2	0.2	1.9
Primary school	27.4	14.3	2.1	14.4
Junior secondary school	45.8	54.9	23.1	53.3
Senior secondary school	13.4	22.9	33.3	25.5
College	5.0	4.8	24.6	3.9
University graduate	2.1	1.8	15.1	1.0
Postgraduate level	0.13	0.1	1.6	—
Total	100 (proportion of male: 55.2%)	100	100	100

Data source: 2004 population change sampling survey (original note).
Source: adapted from *China Labour Statistical Yearbook* (2005, p. 62).

Table 2.17 Number of staff and workers* and number of scientific and technical personnel in urban units by sector at the year-end

Industry	2003			2005		
	Staff and workers	Scientific and technical personnel	Percentage of scientific and technical personnel to staff and workers	Staff and workers	Scientific and technical personnel	Percentage of scientific and technical personnel to staff and workers
Farming, forestry, animal husbandry and fishery	4,597	782	17.0	4,142	705	17.0
Mining and quarrying	4,810	665	13.8	4,976	650	13.1
Manufacturing	28,989	4,316	14.9	30,965	4,495	14.5
Electricity, gas and water production and supply	2,923	683	23.4	2,937	683	23.3
Construction	7,735	1,609	20.8	8,543	1,784	20.9
Transport, storage, post and telecommunication services	6,097	900	14.8	5,792	819	14.1

Information transmission, computer service and software	1,040	411	39.5	1,168	468	40.1
Wholesale and retail trade	5,920	1,010	17.1	5,083	860	16.9
Hotels and restaurants	1,594	175	11.0	1,665	193	11.6
Finance and insurance	2,862	1,595	55.7	2,950	1,562	52.9
Real estate	1,083	293	27.1	1,327	335	25.2
Leasing and business services	1,676	364	21.7	1,988	383	19.3
Scientific research, technical services and geological prospecting	2,063	1,128	54.7	2,127	1,135	53.4
Management of water conservancy, environment and public facilities	1,639	263	16.0	1,703	277	16.3
Services to households and other services	475	71	14.9	472	65	13.8
Education	14,017	11,542	82.3	14,447	12,009	83.1

Table 2.17 (Continued)

Industry	2003			2005		
	Staff and workers	Scientific and technical personnel	Percentage of scientific and technical personnel to staff and workers	Staff and workers	Scientific and technical personnel	Percentage of scientific and technical personnel to staff and workers
Health care, social securities and social welfare	4,717	3,493	74.1	4,914	3,641	74.1
Culture, sports and entertainment	1,220	601	49.3	1,170	544	46.5
Public management and social organization	11,463	1,228	10.7	12,135	1,403	11.6
Total	104,920	31,130	29.7	108,503	32,010	29.5

Figures in 1000 persons and %

* Staff and workers refer to persons working in, and receive payment from units of state-ownership, collective ownership, joint ownership, sharing holding ownership, foreign ownership and ownership by entrepreneurs from Hong Kong, Macao, and Taiwan, and other types of ownership and their affiliated units. They do not include (1) persons employed in township enterprises; (2) persons employed in private enterprises; (3) urban self-employed persons; (4) retirees; (5) re-employed retirees; (6) teachers in the schools run by the local people; (7) foreigners and persons from Hong Kong, Macao and Taiwan who work in urban units; and (8) other persons not to be included by relevant regulations (original note from *China Statistical Yearbook*, 2006, p. 183).

Source: compiled from *China Statistical Yearbook* (2006, pp. 137–9, 149–51).

at the most senior level (senior technicians), 3.5 per cent were senior skilled workers, 35 per cent were mid-ranking skilled workers and the remaining 60 per cent were skilled workers at junior level (Pan and Fang, 2005; Pan and Lou, 2004). In 2003, China had 2.7 million university graduates and 0.27 million postgraduates. However, there were only a total of 28,173 senior technicians (Pan and Fang, 2005). According to a survey conducted by the Ministry of Labour and Insurance in 2004, the most needed skills reported by enterprises surveyed in 40 major cities included technicians, technical engineers, marketing personnel and managers (see Table 2.18).

Shortages of technicians and senior technicians are more pronounced in cities with well-developed manufacturing sites. For example, in the second quarter of 2004, manufacturing enterprises in Wuxi City, an economically developed city of Jiangsu Province, registered that they needed 275 senior technicians and technicians. Unfortunately, nobody applied for the jobs (Mo, 2004, p. 270). Enterprises in Guangdong Province encountered similar skill shortage problems. A survey of 306 enterprises in several developed cities in the Province revealed that 128 of the enterprises needed a total of 18,000 skilled workers urgently, but few applicants met the recruitment criteria (Mo, 2004, p. 270). There was a shortage of over 600,000 skilled operators of computerized numerical controlled (CNC) machines nationwide in 2004. In Beijing, there was a shortage of 159,000 skilled workers and in Shenzhen, there were only 2040 senior skilled workers, making up only 0.155 per cent of the total skilled workforce in the city (*Workers' Daily*, 5 December 2004). This is a major threat to the manufacturing industry.

Table 2.18   Most needed skills in enterprises in China

Types of skills needed	Ratio
Marketing	14.4
Senior technician	12.1
Technical engineer	10.9
Mid-ranking manager	10.6
Senior manager	9.1
Ordinary technician	8.9
Construction engineer	6.8
R&D engineer	5.9
Public relations	4.0
Accountant	4.0
IT	3.9
Machine maintenance	3.7
Clerk/secretary	2.3
Interpreter	1.0
Total	100.0

Source: Survey on enterprises in 40 cities conducted by the Ministry of Labour and Insurance in April (2004), cited in Mo (2004, p. 269).

The shortage of skilled workers causes one of the biggest bottlenecks in production expansion in many economic zones. For example, it was reported (C. S. Wang *et al.*, 2004) that Haining City in the Yangzi River Delta Area (one of the economically most developed manufacturing zones in China) lost about US$1 million sales revenue each day due to the shortage of sewing operatives. Haining City is renowned for leather jacket manufacturing, with over 2000 factories in the City and a production capacity of over 60,000 jackets per day. In terms of managerial skills, the lack of managerial talent has been widely noted to have negative effects on China's economic development (e.g. Branine, 1996; Child, 1994; Ralston *et al.*, 1997; Smith and Wang, 1997; Warner, 1992). This is in spite of the fact that considerable amounts of effort and resources have been invested in the training and development of management and professional workers in the last two decades (Cooke, 2004). Not only are state-owned sector organizations short of managers with modern management knowledge and mindsets, but also entrepreneurs in private enterprises suffer from a relatively low level of education. For example, Zhejiang Province is well known for its strong private economy. Most of the private enterprises grew up during the early period of marketization and industrialization of the 1980s and 1990s. Private enterprises deliver some 70 per cent of the total output value and 60 per cent of the tax of the Province. In addition, 183 of the Top 500 Private Enterprises in 2004 came from the Province, with three of them in the Top ten. However, nearly 80 per cent of the entrepreneurs came from farmers' background with low levels of educational attainments. Over 70 per cent of them had only junior secondary school education or below. Among the 1.52 million managerial employees, only 0.88 per cent had postgraduate degree qualifications and 11.4 per cent had bachelor degree qualifications (*Workers' Daily*, 17 November 2005).

Reasons for skill shortages

To some extent, China's skill shortage problem is a result of its unprecedented rapid economic development at a pace that is faster than its speed of skill development. However, insufficient investment in enterprise training and inadequate provision of vocational training are two major contributing factors to the problem[3] because enterprises and vocational training are the two main sources of developing the skills of the workforce. Many enterprises ignore the importance of investment in human capital and do not invest sufficiently in training. According to a survey conducted by the Ministry of Labour and Insurance on enterprises in 40 cities, the overall investment in enterprise training was reported by the employers to be 1.4 per cent of the total wage bill, slightly below the state requirement of 1.5 per cent which is already lower than the 2–4 per cent level of the developed countries. Nearly 60 per cent of the employers reported that less than 20 per cent of the investment was spent on the training of skilled workers (Mo, 2004). The same survey also showed that at least 30 per cent of the enterprises paid only lip service to employee education and training, with an annual training budget of less than 10 yuan per person. Another 20 per cent of enterprises spent between 10 and 30 yuan per person annually, well below the state requirement of an annual training budget (*Workers' Daily*, 3 November 2004). Some organizational leaders may not even be aware of what an employee training budget is for, let alone delivering the training function. This is evidenced in an interview I conducted with a general manager of a large state-owned transport company in late 2005. During the interview conversation, the General Manager admitted that he did not know what the item 'Employee Education Budget' in the monthly management account stood for even though he had to review and approve the account each month. Since it was only a very small amount in the account, he never bothered to inquire about it but assuming it was some sort of employee welfare activities. More broadly, there is a lack of skill assessment and reward systems to attract, develop, motivate and retain skilled staff in many enterprises. Poaching becomes a serious problem in some skill areas. Increasingly, employees jump ship collectively, led by a group leader.

Equally, vocational training in China receives a relatively low level of investment and attention from the government. In general, vocational schools and technical colleges in China suffer from a number of related problems, including being small-sized, under resourced, technologically outdated, shortage of competent trainers and failure to match skill supply with market demand (Cooke, 2004). In the 20 years between 1985 and 2005, the total number of technical colleges has been reduced through closures and mergers in order to gain economies of scale (see Table 2.19). The total number of teachers and staff has also been reduced slightly as a result of efficiency drives. In the meantime, the total number of students graduating from these schools has tripled. Many of them are not able to find satisfactory employment due to the poor quality of training and a mismatch of skill supply and demand (Cooke, 2004).

In comparison, China's higher education sector has expanded far more dramatically, especially since the early 2000s. In 2001, there were a total of 1225 higher education institutions (*China Statistical Yearbook*, 2002). By 2005, the number had risen to 1792 (*China Statistical Yearbook*, 2006). In 2000, a total of 2.2 million students (full-time) were enrolled for university bachelor degree and diploma courses (1.16 million were for bachelor degree courses) (*China Statistical Yearbook*, 2002). In 2004, nearly 4.5 million (full-time) students were enrolled for bachelor degree and diploma courses. Over 326,000 (full-time) postgraduate students were enrolled, 84 per cent of them studying for a Masters degree, the remaining for a doctoral degree. In the same year, 2.4 million (full-time) students graduated with a bachelor degree or diploma and another 150,777 graduated with postgraduate qualifications (84 per cent at Masters level) (*China Statistical Yearbook*, 2005, p. 695). This trend is set to continue. In 2005, 5.04 million students were enrolled for university bachelor degree and diploma courses (2.36 million were for bachelor degree courses) (*China Statistical Yearbook*, 2006).

However, the rapid expansion of higher education at the expense of vocational training creates a paradoxical situation in the labour market in China. On the one hand, there is an increasingly severe shortage of skilled workers and managerial talent. On the other hand, there is mounting pressure for graduate

Table 2.19   Number of technical colleges, students, teachers and staff (1985–2005)

Year	No. of colleges	New enrolment (1000 persons)	Total enrolment (1000 persons)	Graduates (1000 persons)	Teachers and staff (1000 persons)
1985	3,548	355	742	226	215
1986	3,765	394	892	233	244
1987	3,952	423	1,031	265	262
1988	3,996	461	1,161	311	280
1989	4,102	470	1,258	368	296
1990	4,184	506	1,332	413	308
1991	4,269	544	1,422	454	325
1992	4,392	602	1,556	457	336
1993	4,477	664	1,717	497	335
1994	4,430	714	1,871	557	340
1995	4,521	740	1,886	681	337
1996	4,467	727	1,918	681	335
1997	4,395	734	1,931	699	310
1998	4,362	594	1,813	682	310
1999	4,098	515	1,560	662	269
2000	3,792	504	1,401	646	240
2001	3,470	551	1,347	477	220
2002	3,075	733	1,530	454	203
2003	2,970	916	1,931	453	202
2004	2,884	1,097	2,345	535	205
2005	2,855	1,184	2,753	690	204

Source: adapted from *China Statistical Yearbook* (2006, p. 809).

employment. With 2.12 million graduates in 2003, 2.8 million in 2004 and 3.38 million in 2005, there is an over-supply of graduates (*China Business*, 17 January 2005). In 2004, less than 70 per cent of the 2.8 million graduates have found employment (*The Epoch Times*, 8 June 2006). Worse still, the most highly qualified graduates are lost due to a brain drain to overseas, adding further to the skill shortage problem. It was reported that 80 per cent of the graduates in high-tech related subjects from Tsinghua University have gone to the United States since 1985. A similar proportion (76 per cent) have done the same from Beijing University (Pan and Lou, 2004). Tsinghua and Beijing universities are the two best universities in China. Other premium universities encounter similar trends albeit in less numbers.

In the meantime, the cost of university education and vocational education is increasingly born by individuals, or more precisely, their families. The state fiscal fund which in 1995 supplied 81.4 per cent of the total fund for higher education had by 2001 reduced its contribution to 53.4 per cent, while individual finance had increased from 17.4 per cent to 43.2 per cent in the same years. Similarly, in 1995, nearly 70 per cent of the total fund for senior school and vocational school education came from the state fiscal fund. This was reduced to 54.4 per cent in 2001 (Pan and Lou, 2004). In 1995, individual finance made up 23 per cent of the total funding structure. In 2001, it made up 38 per cent.

State initiatives to combat skill shortages

Realizing the implications of skill shortage for its economic development, the Chinese government has taken a series of measures to combat the problem and to raise the skill standard of its workforce. These range from attracting overseas graduates to return home to initiating a number of state-sponsored skill development programmes.

Favourable conditions are offered to attract Chinese overseas scholars and graduates to return home to take up employment and develop their careers. According to the Ministry of Education (cited in *People's Daily Overseas Edition*, 30 May 2006), 97 per cent of the 22,031 scholars sent abroad to study by the state during 1996–2005 had returned to China. Some 55 per cent of them had obtained a PhD degree and many became experts in key fields of S&T research. To encourage the return of talented expatriates, the Chinese government initiated a programme to develop its 100 top universities into world-class institutions which not only provide top quality higher education training, but also offer attractive academic employment and research opportunities (OECD Observer, 2003). In addition, an increasing number of science parks are developed with the support of local governments to attract expatriates to develop their R&D and entrepreneurial projects in these incubators. In recent years, some local governments have begun to launch overseas recruitment drives to attract talent. For example, since 2001, Shenzhen City government has been sending out overseas recruitment teams to entice overseas Chinese scholars and students back to Shenzhen. Each year, over 1000 talented personnel are attracted, about 10 per cent of them hold a doctoral degree and the remaining a Masters degree (Chen, 2005). Prestigious MNCs operating in China are another major source that attracts repatriation of talent by offering attractive employment package and career prospects.

However, significant repatriation of highly skilled Chinese requires time (OECD Observer, 2003). Between 1978 and 2003, a total of 700,200 people went abroad to study, 172,800 of them had returned to China. In 2003, some 117,300 people went abroad to study, 109,200 of them self-funded. In the same year, over 20,000 returned to China after completing their study (The Ministry of Education, cited in Pan and Fang, 2005). It must be noted that not all the overseas graduates who choose to return home are attracted by promising career prospects or are in the category of highly sought-after talent. Some of them return because of the difficulty in gaining employment in their host countries. Not all of those who return have found employment for various reasons. This adds further pressure to the problem of graduate unemployment.

In addition to the above initiatives to repatriate overseas talent, a number of state-sponsored skill development programmes have been launched since the 2000s to train up skills. Below are a few examples.

The 'Five hundred thousand in three years' programme and the eleventh five-year plan In order to combat the skill shortage problem at the senior level, the Ministry of Labour and Social Insurance launched an initiative in 2004 – The '500,000 Senior Technicians in Three Years' training plan. The plan aims to train up 500,000 new technicians at senior level ('golden blue collar workers') in three years between 2004 and 2006, with a focus on the manufacturing and service industry (*Workers' Daily*, 3 November 2004). During the eleventh five-year plan period (2006–10), the Chinese government plans to train up 1.9 million technicians (*jishi*) and senior technicians as well as 7 million technical workers (*jigong*) at senior level (*People's Daily Overseas Edition*, 13 February 2006).

Professionalization of occupations A number of initiatives have been launched that are aimed to professionalize occupations in China. For example, the 'National vocational qualification training system for enterprise trainers' was implemented by the Ministry of Enterprise Training in 2003. It is an initiative to train the trainers in order to raise the quality of vocational training. Over 4000 people had obtained the enterprise trainer qualification in two years (*Workers' Daily*, 27 December 2005). Professional bodies are set up and stipulate professional qualification requirements for practitioners. For example, the first national standard for professional managers – 'Qualification Requirements for Practising Professional Managers in the Hotel Industry' was promulgated in 2004. Within a year, over 5000 senior and mid-ranking managers had obtained the qualification, according to the Chinese Hotel Association Professional Management Specialist Committee (reported in *Workers' Daily*, 29 October 2005).

Chuangzheng programme Perhaps the most widespread and influential initiative is the chuangzheng initiative: 'to build' ('chuang') a learning organization, to be ('zheng') a knowledge worker. It is a nationwide and state-led initiative launched in December 2003 to promote learning, skill enhancement and innovation. In February 2004, an administrative policy document, the 'Recommendations on the Nation-Wide Implementation of the Initiative "To build a Learning Organization, To Be a Knowledge Worker"', was issued jointly by nine ministries of China, including the ministries of education, labour and social insurance. The document provides recommendations that are aimed to promote and implement the initiative rapidly throughout the whole country (*Workers' Daily*, 19 October 2004). Further administrative regulations have been promulgated in order to tackle the skill shortage problem. Emergency training plans have been formulated for those industries, for example, the manufacturing industry and the modern service industry, which suffer the most severe skill shortages.

Enterprises are encouraged to adopt a wide variety of forms of learning and practising, including self-study, technological innovation, skills and performance contests, on-the-job training and problem-solving teams. It is hoped that these mechanisms will provide a learning environment to motivate employees to acquire new knowledge and skills (*Workers' Daily*, 19 October 2004). These activities share two similar characteristics: to raise employees' skill level through training and competition and to harness employees' innovative ideas through participation and suggestion schemes. The objective is to increase productivity and organizational competitiveness. This has resulted in a renewed enthusiasm in skill competitions and employee participation schemes in innovations in enterprises in China. New role model enterprises and workers were selected. Competition winners were rewarded with prizes and promotions. Their achievements serve as examples to help organizations promote the chuangzheng initiative further. The chuangzheng initiative is aimed to help achieve the 'National Training Programme for Advanced Technical Talents' and the '500,000 New Technicians in Three Years Training Plan' promulgated by the Ministry of Labour and Social Insurance. Life-long learning, knowledge management, organizational learning and HR development are now some of the topics that feature prominently in management literature and organizational policy statements in China, as well as other Western-imported management jargon that are perceived to be modern and innovative in management thinking. Whether life-long learning and creativity is now embedded at workplaces remains debatable.

Summary

In recent decades, China has transformed itself from being an agricultural economy to an industrialized country with a continuously high growth rate. Its R&D investment and stock of human resources have both improved significantly. Much of this achievement has been an outcome of investment and policy interventions from the state. It is true that China's national system of innovation is now experiencing a greater level of interaction between business enterprises and R&D organizations 'on the creation, transfer and absorption of technology, knowledge and skills' (Huang *et al.*, 2004, p. 368; also see Chapter 3). However, innovation is still a relatively new concept in China. Few firms adopt an innovation policy driven by R&D. Effective management and exploitation of innovation through commercialization remains scarce (De Meyer and Garg, 2005). Most firms adopt an adaptor's approach to product innovation rather than being the innovator to minimize cost. This is in part because they have neither the in-house expertise for R&D nor the spare financial resource to develop joint activities with research institutes (White and Liu, 2001). It is also in part because patent laws and intellectual copy rights are not well established and even less effectively enforced in China. There was, and still is, a significant gap between China and the developed world, and the quickest way for it to reduce the gap was, rightly or wrongly, by imitation and adaptation. It should be noted that the government has been under pressure, and is now making efforts, to clamp down on piracy and introduce laws to protect innovations. And it is 'important to understand that the evolution of China's legal environment in regard to competition and IPR protection has been both recent and rapid' (Huang *et al.*, 2004, p. 376).

Similarly, China is making significant progress in developing its human resources through education and skill training. Raising the nation's education and skill level has been increasingly high on the Chinese government's agenda. It is increasingly recognized that the worsening skill shortage is causing bottlenecks in production and innovation and that this problem must be addressed urgently for China to compete at international level and to become an integral part of the global economy. The government's growing effort in reversing the skill shortage problem is evidenced in the promulgation of a series of training regulations and initiatives in the last decade, although the effectiveness these interventions remain to be seen. It is also evidenced in the fact that HR development has been enlisted as one of the key components of its tenth five-year plan (2001–5) and eleventh five-year plan (2006–10). What seems to be problematic is that the rising stock of university graduates is misaligned with the skill needs of the labour market, creating employment pressure for graduates on the one hand but unable to fill the vacancy of thousands of skilled and technical posts on the other. It begs the question as to whether it is better to invest the valuable fund in vocational training or to expand the higher education. This is a problem some developed countries such as Britain are also facing.

In short, this chapter has outlined the macro business environment of China, an environment that is heavily influenced by political and regulatory frameworks. The chapter serves as the backdrop against which more detailed analysis is to be carried out at industry and firm level in the following chapters, beginning with an analysis of competition strategy at firm level in Chapter 3.

Recommended readings

R. Garnaut and Y. P. Huang, *Growth without Miracles – Readings on the Chinese Economy in the Era of Reform* (Oxford: Oxford University Press, 2001).

P. Nolan, *Transforming China: Globalisation, Transition and Development* (London: Anthem Press, 2004).

T. Saich, *Governance and Politics of China* (Basingstoke: Palgrave Macmillan, 2001).

V. Shue and C. Wong, *Paying for Progress in China: Public Finance, Human Welfare and Changing Patterns of Inequality* (London: Routledge, 2007).

CHAPTER 3

Competition Strategy of Leading Chinese (Private) Firms

Introduction

An important outcome of China's 'open door' policy and continuing marketization of its economy since 1978 has been the growth of firms in a diverse range of business ownership forms outside the state-owned sector. In particular, the domestic private sector has grown significantly in both the number of firms and the number of employed. This growth has taken place in parallel with the contraction of the state-owned sector through downsizing and privatization (see Tables 2.3 and 3.1). The growing strength and importance of private enterprises in China's economic development is well recognized (e.g. Child and Tse, 2001; Cooke, 2005b; Garnaut and Huang, 2001; Parris, 1999; Saich, 2001), although their business strategy remains under-explored. In the past 25 years, this sector has been growing steadily in terms of the number of entities, size of the workforce and industrial output. Its scope of business has been expanding into a diverse portfolio, despite the fact that commercial services and labour-intensive light manufacturing industries remain its main territory. While small businesses make up a large proportion of private businesses, the size of firms appears to be growing. Their organizational structure is becoming increasingly formalized, with limited and share-holding entities becoming the main stake of private businesses. Compared with SOEs and larger firms in other ownership forms (e.g. foreign-owned firms and international JVs), Chinese private businesses tend to have stronger adaptability to market trends in part because of their relatively simple product structure and technology. They mainly operate in the gaps which larger enterprises have not explored. They are highly profit driven and therefore more adventurous and opportunistic, but with a relatively lower level of investment risk. In recent years, they have been playing an increasingly important role in the export of industrial products (Chen, 2003).

The growing level of freedom to operate, the abundant availability of cheap labour, the enormous market potential, the rapid advancement of technology and the emergence of a force of Chinese entrepreneurs have led to the rise of a number of strong private firms that are highly competitive in the domestic market, if less so in the international arena. Charisma of CEOs, strong domestic brand, deployment of modern management techniques, mobilization of capital through the stock market and motivation of staff through performance-related

Table 3.1   Industrial enterprises of state-owned and non-state-owned above designated size*

Industrial enterprises by size and ownership	2003	2004	2005	Increase rate in 2005 over 2004 (%)
Total	196,200	276,500	271,800	−1.7
Large industrial enterprises	2,000	2,100	2,500	17.2
Medium-sized industrial enterprises	21,600	25,600	27,300	6.7
Small industrial enterprises	172,600	248,800	242,100	−2.7
State-owned and state-holding enterprises	34,300	35,600	27,500	−22.8
Collectively owned enterprises	22,500	18,100	15,900	−11.9
Enterprises with funds from Hong Kong, Macao, Taiwan and foreign countries	38,600	57,200	56,400	−1.4

* Enterprises of 'above designated Size' are those with annual sales income of over 5 million yuan (original note from *China Statistical Yearbook*, 2005, p. 488).
Source: adapted from *China Statistical Yearbook* (2005, p. 23) and (2006, p. 23).

incentive schemes appear to be the major contributing factors to their success (Nolan, 2004). Nevertheless, it needs to be noted that institutional constraints (see below for further analysis) and the guarded freedom granted by the state to the private sector during the earlier years of economic reform constrain the ability of private firms to grow and gain competitive advantage through economies of scale. Consequently, most Chinese firms are relatively small in scales and compete intensely on the basis of price (Steinfeld, 2004).

This chapter aims to analyse the key elements in the competition strategy adopted by top-performing Chinese firms, drawing on empirical data from secondary sources. In particular, the analysis relies heavily on the data contained in the self-reports from 30 of the Top 50 Chinese private enterprises of 2004 included in Liu and Xu (2004, pp. 197–320), to whom I am very much indebted. Each self-report contains two to four pages in Chinese which provides a brief description of the history and product market of the firm, and key strategies that are perceived to be related to the company's success. These include business strategy, innovation strategy, product and production strategy, marketing strategy and HR strategy. In addition, most cases also include some background information on the CEO responsible for the company's success. In analysing the cases, I have compiled a table (Appendix 3.1) that records the name of each case study firm, nature of its businesses, its ranking in the Top 50 in 2004, background of the owner entrepreneur/CEO, history of the firm and key elements of its strategy. It must be noted that not all this information was supplied or covered to the same extent in each report. For example, a small number of reports did not contain any information about their CEOs. A few others did not report anything on their HR policy and practice. Whilst missing data does not necessarily mean that it does not exist, it does present a gap in the data which makes it more difficult to outline a full profile of these firms. The missing data may also lead to less reliable conclusions. For example, it is tempting to conclude that HRM may not be considered an important part of the strategy for firms that did not report their HR policy and practice.

Hence, a major drawback of using secondary data is that information needed may not be available as the data was collected primarily for the purposes of other research. Another drawback of self-reporting is that it may contain a strong bias from the reporting person, as do other forms of data collection methods such as interviews and questionnaire surveys (Shipman, 1988). The information made available should therefore be treated with caution. Nevertheless, these self-reports do reveal some valuable insights into the mindset of Chinese senior managers in terms of what they believe to be the most important elements as part of their corporate strategy that give them the competitive edge.

The data of the 30 of the Top 50 private enterprises is supplemented by that from other studies conducted by leading international consultancy firms (e.g. Accenture, 2003; Deloitte, 2004; Hill and Knowlton, 2004) as well as Chinese institutions. These studies provide further examples of leading Chinese firms of various ownership forms primarily in the non-state sector. Domestic non-state-owned businesses are the focus of analysis in this chapter because they are less controlled and less supported by the state compared with their state-owned counterparts. As a result, management has a stronger influence in shaping their corporate strategy than their counterparts in SOEs.

The analysis of these firms' competitive strategy uncovers a number of common characteristics. These include: firm growth through business diversification, mergers and acquisitions (M&As) and internationalization, strong emphasis on product innovation and quality enhancement, strategic marketing and product branding, and importantly, the entrepreneurship of owner managers/CEOs and reform of corporate governance. Apart from these interrelated factors associated with the enterprises' success, the findings of these studies also reveal some significant gaps in the strategies adopted by the leading Chinese firms, such as the relatively insignificant role afforded to HRM and technology as part of the overall management strategy. In addition, Chinese managers seem to be less concerned about corporate social responsibility (CSR) and the way they interpret the notion reflects strong personal as well as societal values. These are the issues that we will discuss in this chapter, followed by a brief summary of literature on factors influencing competitiveness of firms.

Factors influencing firms' competitiveness

Competitiveness at micro level 'refers to the capacity of firms to compete, to increase their profits and to grow. It is based on costs and prices, but more vitally on corporate organization, the capacity of firms to use technology and the quality and performance of products' (OECD, 1992, p. 237). Innovation, technological advancement, effective management of organizational activities, brand, quality of products and services and human capital are now widely recognized as vital sources of competitiveness for firms (Johnson and Scholes, 2002). Innovation includes product and production innovation, business and management innovation and service innovation. These are achieved through in-house development as well as strategic alliances across organizational boundaries. There is a general consensus in strategic management thinking that the ability of an organization to develop and exploit knowledge faster than its competitors is a key component of its competitive advantage (Leonard-Barton, 1995; Nonaka and Teece, 2001; Porter, 1980; Prahalad and Hamel, 1990). Writers on strategic management have also accentuated the importance of embracing and exploiting externally held knowledge through organizational networks and inter-firm relationship (e.g. alliance and partnership) in a context of accelerating global competition (Castells, 1996; Child and Faulkner, 1998; Powell et al., 1996; Pucik, 1988). According to Davies et al. (2003), brand is a valuable asset that differentiates one product or company from the others. Brand management is considered to be essential to sustain and enhance organizational competitiveness especially in a highly competitive environment where product differentiation is not easy to achieve (Lasserre and Schütte, 2006). This is particularly relevant to the Chinese product market. Similarly, it has been increasingly recognized that competitive advantage is more likely to be achieved through effective development and deployment of human resources (e.g. Drucker, 1988; Kanter, 1989; Peters, 1989). This includes heavy investment in training and development, implementing motivation mechanisms to cultivate and harness employees' innovativeness and attracting talent to work for the firm through employer branding.[1]

It has been observed that 'the competitiveness of [Asian] firms is increasingly reflecting their willingness and capabilities, first to engage in product improvement and innovation, and second, to harness resources and capabilities from throughout the world and to integrate these with their home-based competencies' (Dunning and Narula, 2004, p. 246). It has also been noted that diversification and internationalization have been some of the new corporate strategies pursued by an increasing number of Chinese firms (Benson and Zhu, 1999; Zhang et al., 2006). The relationship between product diversification and firm performance has been an important topic in strategic management literature (Zhao and Luo, 2002). Influential authors (e.g. Ansoff, 1965; Chandler, 1962; Hoskisson and Hitt, 1990) have argued that firms adopting a diversification strategy in related businesses are able to achieve better economic performance through the synergy of sharing resources and skills across multiple businesses. This is in spite of the fact that research studies so far have failed to provide conclusive evidence to support this argument (Li and Wong, 2003; Zhao and Luo, 2002). It has been argued that diversification is a useful business strategy for firms operating in emerging economies in order to overcome deficiencies in the institutional environment

(Li and Wong, 2003). According to Khanna and Palepu (1997), emerging economies suffer from a number of institutional weaknesses. These include: the lack of well-established product markets, capital markets and labour markets, the lack of an independent and fully functional regulatory system and the ineffective enforcement of contracts. Diversified business groups may be well suited to the institutional environment of the developing economies, because they can add value by carrying out some of these institutional functions internally which would have been performed by the institutions in advanced economies.

What then, are the strategies that top-performing Chinese firms pursue in order to gain competitiveness?

Diversification as a growth strategy

Business diversification has certainly been a strategy adopted by the majority of the Top 50 private enterprises in 2004 (see Appendix 3.1). The majority of firms have grown from very small businesses into large or super-large group corporations employing several thousands of employees. This is often achieved through business diversification. Seven firms reported that they have diversified into related businesses as a result of the corporations' identification and strategic exploitation of their core competence and organizational resources for corporate growth. While a significant proportion of the enterprises (16 cases) have diversified into a number of less-related or unrelated businesses, they seem to have maintained a core business/product line from which the company had initially grown (e.g. Cases 7, 15, 18 and 19). Although detailed information on why these firms have diversified into these particular unrelated businesses is unavailable, it seems that they have diversified into these businesses because of the perceived attractive business opportunities rather than the need to build internal competence to overcome institutional and market deficiency. Estate, IT and education are amongst the popular business areas for investment in China. Another reason may be that diversifying into unrelated businesses offers an opportunity to expand regionally and nationally through gaining market in new geographical areas, that is, from being a local to a regional and national firm.

To a large degree, the diversification strategy adopted by these top enterprises reflects the business growth pattern in China. According to Fang (2004), Chinese enterprises have been through four stages of development in the last 20 years: capital accumulation, full development of core businesses, diversification and internationalization. As we can see from Appendix 3.1, the vast majority of the case study firms were initially formed as very small business entities in order to make a basic living. Some were family businesses or TVEs with only primitive production equipment and management structure (e.g. Cases 10, 13, 18, 24 and 28).

There are several reasons why firms choose to diversify 'in order to provide channels for growth, profits and employment' (Nolan, 2004, p. 207). These include: the need for financial resources (Li and Wong, 2003), limited capability to compete in export markets, high transactional cost due to the underdevelopment of infrastructure, and most importantly, the Chinese 'government's support for the idea of a "business group" with a core firm at its centre' (Nolan, 2004, p. 207). Private businesses in China generally do not enjoy the sort of privilege and favourable treatment (e.g. bank loans and other resources) from the central and local governments like their state-owned or state-affiliated counterparts do (Lau *et al.*, 1999). Private businesses have to develop their own social network to obtain necessary resources for them to survive and compete in the market. A particularly important aspect of this includes building a strong network relationship with the local authorities (Tsang, 1994; Young, 1989, cited in Lau *et al.*, 1999). Another important practice is to diversify into unrelated businesses in order to gain access to resources necessary for the firm to perform which are otherwise difficult to obtain due to the deficiency of the market system and insufficient government support (Li and Wong, 2003; Zhao and Luo, 2002). Consequently, even the largest firms may consist of a small core business and numerous even smaller non-core subsidiaries in unrelated businesses (Nolan, 2001; Steinfeld, 2004).

While we do not have detailed information that explains why these case study firms have adopted their business diversification strategy in the way they did, what is certain is that their strategic intent differs. Those that stick to their core products or diversify into closely related products appear to have taken a more cautious approach to growth. To some extent, their firm's growth is the result of their business success and to gain economies of scale. For those that have diversified into unrelated businesses, they did so in order to grow, to venture into the unknown, to explore the market, to exploit perceived opportunities and to test their corporate strengths. By comparison, the latter are far more adventurous than the former. Given the fact that only a small number of firms that are engaged in a wide network of diversified second and third tier businesses are 'able to benefit from economies of scale' (Nolan, 2004, p. 207), it would be worthwhile to follow the development of these firms and investigate the extent to which their non-core businesses contribute to the firms' success.

Firms might expand into related businesses in order to enhance their organizational resources and competitive advantage of a higher order. Zhongtian Construction Group (Case 9) is a case in point. This construction group was rooted in housing construction. It expanded its businesses into estate development and then through the acquisition of two road and bridge building firms. More recently, it acquired shares of two top-class construction design institutes in China in order to enhance the firm's total capacity in winning business contracts. Similarly, firms may expand their businesses by developing their own industrial cluster to overcome bottlenecks in the market. Tongwei Group (Case 18) is a case in point. Established in the early 1990s with only 500 yuan, Tongwei is now one of China's largest enterprises in animal feeds and aquatic products. It is also a pioneer firm in developing animal feeds products. In order to maintain and enhance its competitive position in the product market, Tongwei invested heavily in new product development. Animal and fishery test farms were developed to facilitate R&D activities. The development of new feeds also goes hand-in-hand with the development of new types of fishery products, for example, by growing fish that have reduced fat and smaller bowels in proportion to the fish body. In the last decade, Tongwei has developed an extensive industrial cluster including feed production, animal and fishery farming and product processing to streamline its business.

One major channel for Chinese firms to diversify and grow is through M&As, often under pressure from the government to consolidate and compete. Peng *et al.* (1999) highlighted the growing importance of M&As as a firm growth strategy in China. M&As were used as the 'third wave' to restructure poor-performing SOEs during the 1980s and 1990s, often through the 'forced marriage' between a strong and a weak SOE arranged by the government (Peng *et al.*, 1999, also see Chapter 8 for further discussion). Since the 1990s, M&As in China have taken a diverse range of forms, 'within and across industrial, regional, ownership, and national boundaries' (Peng *et al.*, 1999, p. 82). This was facilitated by the establishment of the stock market and the emerging legal and regulatory framework (Peng *et al.*, 1999). It is believed 'bigger is stronger', and 'to become bigger and stronger' is one of the Chinese government's latest slogans to encourage firms to grow and compete – internationally.

Internationalization as a competition strategy

Encouraged by another slogan of the Chinese government – 'Go Global' (also see Chapter 9), internationalization is another strategy adopted by leading Chinese firms to grow and compete. They do so through the expansion of product market overseas, acquisition of technological and managerial competence, brand image and distribution networks from foreign firms and obtaining funds from the international capital markets (also see Chapter 9 for more detailed discussion). Whilst domestic M&As have been the main mode of expansion for the Top 50 private enterprises of 2004, a small but significant number of them (e.g. Cases 8, 10, 11, 12, 21, 22, 23, 24, 25 and 29) have also adopted an internationalization strategy to grow and compete. Some of the firms also built their international industrial cluster in the form of international JVs to ensure the smooth supply of parts needed for the main production because of the bottlenecks in the domestic supply chain. For example, high-quality garment manufacturer Youngor (Case 23) not only established international JVs to provide in-house textile materials and accessories for shirt production, but also set up brand-name high street chain stores to retail its shirt products. Similarly, Nanshan Group (Case 24) sought its international expansion to secure supplies of raw material, for example, by establishing bases in Australia for wool and bauxite supplies for its core businesses in aluminium and fine textile products. Other well-known examples include Lenovo's acquisition of IBM's PC business, TCL's acquisition of Thomson's DVD player manufacturing business and Alcatel's mobile phone business, Haier's (white goods manufacturer) aggressive expansion in different parts of the world and Huawei's strategic global expansion in the ICT market (also see Chapter 9).

Whether a company is expanding internationally or not is to some extent defined by the product/business nature and the stage of development of the firm and industry. For example, Chinese estate businesses are largely confined to China (e.g. Cases 1, 3, 7, 9, 20 and 25) because of the bourgeoning domestic market and the lack of international competitiveness of these firms. Similarly, domestic retail businesses, for example, Jiashijie Commercial Chain Shops Group (Case 30), are generally small in scales by international standard. They find it hard to survive the strong competition from foreign retail giants operating in China, let alone compete against them internationally.

The findings of two major studies further reveal a broader trend that a growing number of Chinese firms are aspiring to become global players by investing and operating abroad. According to a survey conducted by the Academy of International Trade and Economic Cooperation of the Ministry of Commerce on CEOs from 102 internationally active Chinese companies in 14 provinces and cities in China in 2005, nearly 50 per cent of them reported that they were planning to invest overseas in the next two years as part of their globalization and internationalization process. Seventy per cent reported that they would be well prepared for the expansion of overseas business in four years and 20 per cent predicted that their overseas investment would exceed US$10 million. The survey, sponsored by the Welsh Development Agency (UK), revealed that the majority of participants would take the United States, Germany and the United Kingdom as their first choices of investment. The same survey also found that the primary motivation for Chinese companies' investment in Europe and North America is market expansion, followed by development strategies and partnership seeking. The establishment of agencies and representative offices appears to be the predominant investment model (favoured by 70 per cent respondents). Almost half of the companies surveyed would like to form JVs or set up wholly funded companies in Europe and North America, while 34 per cent intend to acquire local firms. Acquisition is mostly favoured by home appliance manufacturers as 46 per cent of the companies in the industry revealed that they would acquire foreign counterparts. Respondents cited low taxes and subsidies as the policies most likely to make them choose an investment destination (*China Daily Online*, 1 March 2005).

Similar findings are reported in a survey and interview study conducted by Roland Berger Strategy Consultants (2003) on 50 leading Chinese firms (China's Top 50) on the four major decision points: the Whether, Why, Where and How of globalization. The study found that seeking new markets is the strongest motivation for internationalization for 60 per cent of China's Top 50 firms, whereas obtaining natural resources is the main motive for 20 per cent of the firms. This is characterized by the large energy acquisitions of China National Offshore Oil Corporation (CNOOC) and China National Petroleum Corporation (CNPC). For 16 per cent of the firms, obtaining advanced technology and related brand equity is the strongest motivation. An example in this category is Shanghai Electronic Group's acquisition of the bankrupt Akiyama Publishing Machinery Company in Japan (Roland Berger Strategy Consultants, 2003).

Whilst some of the leading Chinese firms may have been successful in their business diversification and international expansion, Fang (2004) believes that the diversification and internationalization stages have not been that successful for many firms and were characterized by unfulfilled expectations and reduced corporate profits. For example, it has been widely reported that TCL's international acquisition moves had not been successful, with a significant drop in net profit which included a loss of 0.69 billion yuan in the first six months of 2005 (*Workers' Daily*, 7 September 2005).

There are many reasons for the limited success in the international expansion of Chinese firms (see Chapter 9 for more detailed discussion). Poor image of Chinese firms in terms of product quality and social responsibility, and lack of innovation capacity and marketing/product branding competence are some of the factors. In the next sections that follow, we will investigate how Chinese firms are doing on these issues and what strategies leading firms adopt.

Product innovation and quality enhancement

On the innovation and quality front, Chinese firms have been widely criticized internationally for their low level of technological competence and innovation capacity and their poor attitude towards IPR. They rely on their low cost advantage and mass production mode as their main competitive advantage instead of product innovation and quality of products and services. Indeed, the low level of technology and quality of products has been the major cause of China's low production efficiency. As a result, producers compete on price to grab market share (*People's Daily Online*, 26 July 2004). If a 'make-do' attitude instead of lack of capability is seen as the root of the low quality problem (*People's Daily Online*, 26 July 2004), then this is a problem that the leading Chinese firms have tackled successfully.

A common feature that emerges in the self-reports of the 30 top-performing private firms is their strong emphasis on innovation and quality of products and services. Innovation in these firms takes two forms: innovation in products and services and innovation in production technology and techniques. At least 16 firms reported that product and service innovation were a key part of their strategy. They strived to be the market leaders in exploring new markets and compete at the upper end of the product market. Many of them have in-house R&D functions and collaborate with universities and research institutions for their product development. Some of them have even developed international collaboration. For example, Wanxiang Group (Case 22) has an R&D centre in the United States and R&D relationships with premium universities in China and overseas auto research firms and associations. Quite a few of these 16 firms have been winners of national innovation awards (e.g. Case 1) or are patent holders (e.g. Cases 4 and 17).

Furthermore, these firms see investment in advanced technology and quality assurance as the key to competitiveness. At least eight firms stated that they invested heavily to upgrade their production technology/equipment by importation. For example, Nanshan Group (Case 24) imported advanced textile production technology from Britain, France, Germany and Italy to become one of the largest and most advanced textile producers in China. Similarly, Baoye Group (Case 25) pursued its continuous technological innovation through the importation of Western advanced construction technology, techniques and materials. At least 18 firms reported that quality was an extremely important issue. Many of them have achieved quality awards or accreditations such as ISO 9000 series (e.g. Cases 3, 6, 7, 17, 23 and 28). They adopted a quality management approach to their production and service activities. For example, Hailiang Group (Case 7) adopted a zero tolerance approach to quality defects as well as other operations management initiatives including ISO 9001, ISO 9002, ISO 1400, OHSA18000 and 5S. In light of the prevailing fake and shoddy products in China that have become a serious issue, these top-performing privately owned enterprises have captured the consumers' anxiety and developed a strategy that builds their reputation on quality, honesty and trustworthiness in conducting business. Quality assurance is emphasized as a key differentiating factor in their competitiveness.

The finding that top private enterprises pay more attention to innovation is in line with the national picture. It is now clear that Chinese privately owned enterprises are the main driver of technological innovations. Over 80 per cent of the enterprises in the 53 high-tech zones in China are privately owned; privately owned enterprises hold 66 per cent of the patents, 74 per cent of the technological innovations and 82 per cent of the new product developments in China (*People's Daily Overseas Edition*, 13 January 2007).

It needs to be pointed out, however, that adaptation seems to be the main characteristic of the Top 50 private firms' innovation and technological upgrading drive. This is in line with the Country's practice. More radical innovation of technology comes mainly from the importation of advanced technology, mostly from developed countries. There has been a surge in the import of 'Western' products and production equipment in China throughout the 1980s and 1990s. 'Many Chinese enterprises rely too much on imports of core technologies and equipment. Imported equipment costs more than 60 per cent of China's input in equipment every year' (*People's Daily Online*, 26 July 2004). One implication of this mode of technological change is the difficulty for the workforce to acquire skills to operate and maintain this equipment, which in turn influences its effective utilization.

Taking a wider view, major gaps in R&D funding and activities exist amongst the leading Chinese enterprises. According to a survey study (Li and Li, 2004) conducted by the Ministry of Statistics of China on the innovation capacity of 4223 firms that were classified by the state as 'key enterprises' at national and provincial level, 59.6 per cent of the enterprises had established a technology centre by the end of 2003. Nearly 86 per cent of the centres were more or less sufficient in R&D facilities, funding and staff. Among the 4223 enterprises, a total of 63.7 billion yuan was invested in R&D, making a 20.5 per cent increase from the previous year. More specifically, Sino-foreign JVs and Hong Kong and Macao funded enterprises had bigger increases of 68.1 per cent and 44.4 per cent, respectively. Some 65 per cent of the enterprises developed their innovation projects independently as the main mode of R&D,

while 48.8 per cent of all firms also adopted a joint R&D mode in collaboration with universities, and research institutions. By the end of 2003, there were a total of 570,000 R&D staff in the 4223 enterprises, an increase of 3.5 per cent from the previous year. In 2003, the average wage increase of the 570,000 R&D staff was 20.3 per cent, more than 5 per cent higher than that of the whole workforce. Over 57 per cent of the enterprises had established a reward incentive mechanism to retain and motivate R&D staff. In addition, 70 per cent of the enterprises had obtained the ISO9000 accreditation and 19 per cent had ISO14000 accreditation, even though the motive and effect of these accreditations in China is debatable (Cooke, 2002). In spite of these improvements, there are still major gaps in the R&D activities of these enterprises. For instance, three-quarters of the enterprises had an R&D budget of less than 1 per cent of their sales revenue in 2003, including 46 per cent of the enterprises that had no R&D budget at all due to financial constraints. In 2003, the sales revenue from new products made up only 11.6 per cent of the total sales revenue of all 4223 firms, and only 16.3 per cent of firms which had set up a technology centre. Nearly two-thirds of the firms had no sale revenue from new products. This suggests that a majority of the Chinese key enterprises have only a very weak ability to accumulate their R&D capacity and that their competitive strength is not yet based on their innovativeness.

Product branding as a success factor

Effective product branding is increasingly seen as a strategic success factor in gaining competitive advantage (Davies *et al.*, 2003; Fuchs, 2003; Kotler *et al.*, 2005; Lasserre and Schütte, 2006).[2] Despite their relatively limited purchasing power, Chinese consumers are highly conscientious, even obsessed, with brand-name products, especially for goods that are visible to others when used (De Meyer and Garg, 2005) to enhance their social status. Brand names are seen as a symbol of high-quality production, effective sales management, scientific marketing techniques, as well as having good reputations among consumers (Zhang and Cheng, 2002). Brand-name products are therefore highly aspirational and can command premium brand equity – a niche that has been dominated by Western products. Chinese consumers have also become better informed and more sophisticated in product choice. Quality, service and choice are now the top criteria in their purchasing decisions instead of price. They have also developed loyalty to their preferred brands (Fan, 2005).

Yet, Chinese companies are lagging behind in their understanding of the concept of brand and in formulating a brand management strategy. The notion of brand is often used as a synonym of enterprise trademark and advertisement. Chinese firms generally lack professional brand knowledge and skills required to enhance the visibility of their brands and brand values. When promoting their products in advertisements, they often focus on the company rather than the brand values, for example, the firm's history, its production capability and technological competence, its position as a leader and how many prizes it has won (Fan, 2005). Product competition commonly takes the form of price competition instead of brand value which takes time and strategic planning to achieve. Attempts to establish nationwide brands and distribution channels may be hampered by the geographic dispersion, persisting regional protectionism, deep-rooted cultural variance, rising disparity in income and purchasing power and heterogeneity of the market – a direct consequence of the liberalization of China's economy has been the fragmentation of China's huge market.

Even when domestic brands are well-established, few of them have successfully entered the international market. This is in part because Chinese firms often do not have a clear marketing strategy that is targeted at retailers and customer segments in the host country and neglect the after-sales services (*China Business*, 31 October 2005). Another barrier is trademark protection. With China's accession to the WTO and domestic firms encouraged to 'Go Global' by the government, opportunistic enterprises and individuals overseas are pre-empting Chinese firms' internationalization move and profit from it. They register China's well-known brands pre-emptively, creating new barriers for Chinese products entering host markets (*China Economic Net*, 13 September 2004). For example, The 'Hero' brand gold pens (one of the most famous Chinese brands) are believed to be very popular among Japanese consumers. A Japanese businessman pre-emptively registered the trademark and demanded a 5 per cent sales commission from the sale agents in Japan. This has led to the withdrawal of the agency contract because of the non-profitability of the sales after the commission (*China Economic Net*, 13 September 2004). These incidents suggest that many Chinese firms not only have not developed their brand-name products, but also failed to recognize and protect their established brands strategically.

Nevertheless, Chinese companies are now more proactive in introducing their own brands to the market and competing with major MNCs (Melewar *et al.*, 2004). An increasing number of Chinese companies have successfully created strong local brands through strategic brand management (see below for examples). Some have even started to taste success in the highly competitive international markets. For example, Haier (white goods manufacturer) is one of the few Chinese firms that have been able to establish themselves in the developed markets and demonstrate 'a thorough understanding of customers and their behaviour patterns, commanding high prices and loyalty' by 'offering design and value to the customers' (De Meyer and Garg, 2005, pp. 49–50). The Chinese government is also making an effort to foster top brand-name products in order to sharpen the competitive edge of Chinese firms in both the domestic and international market and promote economic growth (Zhang and Cheng, 2002). The China Promotion Committee for Top Brand Strategy was set up in Beijing in 2001 to promote the implementation of the Top Brand Strategy in enterprises and direct them to improve product quality (Zhang and Cheng, 2002).

Even when local brands do not have the global reach and reputation of the foreign ones, some of them do have local roots and loyalty that are unrivalled by foreign brands in the home market. For example, the massive advertising expenditure of foreign beer manufacturers in China did nothing to dampen Tsingtao Brewery's dominant market share (Tsingtao beer is arguably the most famous brand of beer and one with the longest history in China). Similarly, the unparallel marketing and branding power of Dell has not been able to undermine the dominance of Legend (now Lenovo) in the IT industry (French, 2003).

As mentioned in the earlier section, high-quality products and services and good business ethics are seen as two of the important elements in the top-performing Chinese private firms' strategy. Some of them are beginning to embrace the concept of product and corporate branding more strategically (e.g. Cases 4, 7, 8 and 9). Kangna Group (Case 8) won the title of 'Best Chinese Shoe Maker' in 1993 and has been working hard to maintain this reputation. Hailiang Group (Case 7, core business in copper processing) was awarded SA8000 (social accountability) accreditation in 2004. Product and corporate branding is essentially part of their strategy to attract customers as well as talented employees. For example, Zhongtian Construction Group (Case 9) stated that it endeavoured to establish itself as one of the most reputable construction contractors and developers in China and attracted talent to do so.

Marketing and branding is a form of business innovation that may lead to the creation of new products. In general, leading Chinese enterprises adopt one or more of the following three strategies to establish and enhance their brand identity and develop new products and markets:

1. Brand acquisition – Acquisition of foreign firms to acquire brand names and distribution channels (e.g. TCL's acquisition of the TV business of Thomson of France) (see Chapter 9 for further discussion);

2. Brand extension – Exploitation of established national brand by diversifying into other related businesses targeted at specific market segments (e.g. Wahaha, meaning 'Baby Laugh' in Chinese, exploits its reputation as a health drink manufacturer for children and expands into children's clothing. It focuses on less developed cities to avoid direct competition with prestigious international brands) (Fiducia Management Consultants, 2004b);

3. Brand revitalization – Revitalization of time-honoured brand (e.g. Beijing Tongrentang, a traditional Chinese medicine manufacturing and retail enterprise that enjoys a 300-year history, revitalizes its brand name by developing new products and international product markets, see Chapter 5 for more details).

It is worth noting that a common misconception is that China has few brands to showcase due to its communist background and its former closed market economy. In fact, China is home to thousands of home-grown brands, with some centuries old. However, many are in danger of disappearing from the market forever due to the outdated management structure and practice of the enterprises and limited product range that may no longer be relevant to consumers today despite their glorious brand histories in their time (Ho, 2005).

What type of product branding strategy to adopt is dependent not only on the nature of the competition of a specific industry but also the preference of enterprise leaders. For example, in the wine-making industry, one of the key elements in an enterprise's business strategy is the product positioning strategy. More specifically, it is a choice between specialization and diversification in its product range. The competition between Maotai and Wuliangye, the two top-brand rice wine makers in China, is a classic example. The dual pressure of increasing control from the state on quality and production standard and the accelerating market competition based on price has led to the dramatic decline in profit margins in the industry. While many smaller wine/spirit producers have gone into liquidation, others have opted for a product diversification route that incorporates non-wine/spirit products in order to survive. Maotai chooses to pursue a single brand strategy to defend its 'premium product for premium price' position. By contrast, Wuliangye goes for product diversification by launching a succession of new products in the upper and mid-range that are developed to suit local tastes, customers' consumption tradition and affordability (see Box 3.1 for more details). As a result, the sales revenue of new products made up 50 per cent of the enterprise's total sale revenue of 2001 (Q. Z. Zhang, 2004). Compared with Wuliangye Group's adventurous approach to product and product market development, Maotai Corporation appears to be far more conservative and is firmly located in the top product range as its market positioning. It differentiates its product by year of production and by degree of alcohol strength in the same product range. Nevertheless, in recent years, it began to launch a small number of Maotai products in the lower price range, although these new products have yet to gain popularity among consumers (Q. Z. Zhang, 2004). An interesting turning point is that Wuliangye has become aware that its strategy in product development may lead to mass customization of its products and dilution of its brand position as a premium wine maker. It is refocusing on its core product Wuliangye by developing vintage brands.

Below are further examples of how three leading Chinese enterprises in different industries craft their business success through brand-building and creating access to distribution networks (see Boxes 3.1, 3.2 and 3.3).

BOX 3.1

Brand management of a top rice wine company – Wuliangye Group

The Chinese rice wine making industry is a highly competitive market based on price and product branding. Wuliangye's (Five Grain Fluid) success is an example of product market positioning and product innovation (P. Jin et al., 2003).[3] There are eight major brands of Chinese rice wine with Maotai being the most famous brand. Good quality rice wines are often purchased for gifts or consumed in restaurants (often paid for by the company). Chinese consumers tend to choose the more expensive product from the same product range as gifts or to consume in public in order to gain face. In the late 1980s and early 1990s, there was a price war among the eight major brands of rice wine products. Most of them chose a low price strategy in order to increase sales volume. Wuliangye chose to increase its price to be on par with Maotai and so differentiate itself from the rest of the market as being the higher quality product (reflected in price). From 1994 onwards, Wuliangye has been the country's highest payer of sales tax on this type of products. Until 1996, Wuliangye Group had only two products brands: Wuliangye at the higher end of the market and Jianzhuang at the lower end. There was no product at the upper-middle or lower-middle end of the market where profits are more lucrative. In 1997, Wuliangye Group launched three brand series Wuliangchún (Five Grain Spring), Wuliangchún (Five Grain Mellow) and Wuliangshen (Five Grain God) in the mid-range market. However, these three brand series did not bring the anticipated sales volume (only 1000 tons were sold in 1997) for Wuliangye Group initially due to strong competition from other brand competitors. Two strategies were then deployed by the Group. One was to use local agencies, wholesalers and retailers to promote its products in different regions. Another was to develop and produce wine products branded and registered by local agencies, wholesalers and retailers to avoid direct competition with local brand products and to tap into local distributors' brand name and markets. Jingjiu (Beijing Wine), registered and promoted by Beijing Confectionary, Cigarette and Wine Products Corporation, is an example of such success. Over 8500 tons of Jingjiu was sold within a year. Through the strategic alliance with local distributors, Wuliangye Group expanded its distribution channels dramatically and became the national leader in the rice wine making industry. By the end of 2002, Wuliangye Group had a portfolio of over 100 brand products, 67 of them were branded products developed in-house, flag-shipped by the Wuliangye brand.

Source: adapted from P. Jin *et al.* (2003).

BOX 3.2

Product branding strategy of a leading Chinese tourist firm

Shenzhen Huaqiaocheng (China Town) was ranked No.1 in the tourist industry in the China Business Competitiveness Index (P. Jin *et al.*, 2003). The Company's core business is tourism based on natural scenic spots, mostly famous mountains in China. It has the advantage of geographical monopoly on the one hand but has a limited expansion capacity, constrained by traffic and accommodation capacity on the other. The company focuses on theme parks and historical sites as its core business and branding. It has successfully developed itself from being a regional to a national brand by developing tourist businesses at historic sites, including the Confucius Temple and the Three Gorges Reservoir of Yangzi River. In addition, Huaqiaocheng Corporation expanded into the estate businesses by developing luxury housing estates that model theme park environments. Its environment-friendly housing estates in Shenzhen are among the most desirable housing estates in the City.

Source: adapted from P. Jin *et al.* (2003).

BOX 3.3

Xinfei – Creating brand competitiveness in the refrigerator industry

Xinfei Refrigerator Series won the top prize in the 'Brand China' national competition in 2004. Xinfei's achievement is the result of a comprehensive business strategy that aims to establish a brand that is built on product innovations and customer services. In light of strong competition in the white goods industry, Xinfei has been investing heavily on in-house product development for the last 20 years. It has a strong team of R&D engineers who are well rewarded for their innovations. For example, those who have made special contributions will be rewarded with bonuses that are 10 to 14 times that of an average worker. Talent is promoted rapidly. Since 1989, Xinfei has been introducing a new model of refrigerator to the market every two and a half months on average. In its first generation, there was only one series with three models. By the fourth generation, there are four series with over 30 models.

Xinfei pays special attention to its customer services and improvizes its products based on customers' feedback. Its motto is 'customer service first, sales second'. Xinfei has a strong customer services section with expanded customer services both in the range of services and length of guaranteed period provided. More importantly, collecting customers' feedback on Xinfei products has become part of the sales and services teams' routine function. In addition, managerial staff in the factories are required to work for two to three months each year behind the sales counter to listen to customers' comments and to compare their products with imported ones for quality and design. This, it is believed, will stop managers being complacent and make them more open-minded to market changes.

Source: adapted from *China Business* (31 January 2005).

Strategic human resource management

Human resource management is another important aspect of the strategy adopted by leading Chinese enterprises to gain competitive advantage. This is the case with a number of the 30 top-performing private enterprises. However, it is worth noting that not all firms saw the strategic importance of HRM, judging from the way it was reported in the self-reports. While 15 firms have provided a detailed account of their HR policy and practice, five firms only mentioned HRM briefly. Another ten firms did not mention anything related to their HR policy and practice. While it may be misguiding to conclude that these ten firms failed to see the strategic importance of HRM, it does beg the question why these firms have not reported anything on it, if human resources were treated as an important aspect of their competitiveness.

For those that have provided information about their HR policy and practice, several main characteristics emerge. One is that they tended to adopt a high commitment model of HRM that emphasizes employee training and development, cultivation of innovativeness, performance-related reward to incentivize individual performance, promotion by competence and extensive employee welfare provision. In particular, talent management was an important part of their HRM (e.g. Cases 10, 16, 17, 21, 25, 27 and 30). This is not surprising given the fact that many of these firms invest in R&D and innovation activities, with a large proportion of their employees being highly qualified (e.g. Cases 18 and 26). A number of firms also clearly stated that they adopted a humanistic approach to HRM (e.g. Cases 14, 15 and 16). They emphasized the need to nourish employees in order for them to unleash their talent and productivity, although whether these HR schemes are genuinely implemented to good effect or not remains unknown without obtaining the views of their employees. For instance, the HRM philosophy and strategy of Shanghai Fuxing High-tech Group (Case 14) was:

- To attract talent with organizational development, to retain talent with career prospects, to develop staff with work opportunities, and to appraise staff with performance;

- Harmonization and unification of the development of the organization and individuals;

- Development of core enterprise values that was heavily influenced by the Chinese philosophy;

- Promoting concepts of learning organization and innovative teams; and

- Enhancing employees' satisfaction with a humanistic approach to management.

Another unique feature in the approach to HRM adopted by some of the firms is the paternalistic style with typical Chinese cultural values that emphasize unification, integrity, harmonization, moral teaching and role model setting (e.g. Cases 8 and 14). At the same time, they also adopted a normative approach to systematic management that focuses on procedures and impartiality. This was exemplified by putting a full set of company policies and procedures in place so that organizational behaviour was guided by pre-specified rules and norms (e.g. Cases 5, 6, 10, 18 and 20). Tongwei Group (Case 18) is perhaps one of the most informative examples of how a leading Chinese firm configured its HR policy that combined modern Western notions of HRM, the Japanese approach to systematic management and the Chinese traditional value of employee care and development (see Appendix 3.1).

Indeed, performance management, with performance-related pay and competence-based promotion as key features, is one of the HRM areas in China that has experienced new dynamics that departs from traditional practices that were egalitarian and seniority oriented. For example, Ding *et al.*'s (1997, p. 611) study of 158 foreign-invested enterprises in southern China showed that 'regular evaluation of individual employee performance and setting employee pay levels based on individual performance have become organizational norms'. They also found that workers were receptive of individual-oriented performance measurement and reward in order to maximize their income. Lindholm's (1999) survey of 604 Chinese managerial and professional employees from MNCs in China found that they were satisfied with the Western-styled performance management system adopted in their company. They particularly liked the developmental approach in the system and were keen to participate in setting their performance objectives and to receive formal performance feedback. Bai and Bennington's (2005) more recent study of the Chinese SOEs in the coal mining industry also revealed that as a result of increasing pressure from intensified market competition, Chinese SOEs were utilizing modern performance appraisal measures as effective tools to enhance their management efficiency and productivity. Their study showed that whilst differences from Western performance appraisal practices persist, significant changes were taking place in performance appraisal practices in China that depart from its traditional form.

It needs to be noted that strategic HRM is not yet adopted by the majority of Chinese firms, even though its importance to enhancing organizational competitiveness is increasingly emphasized in popular management writings. By contrast, CSR as a new focus in strategic management appears to have received increasing attention amongst leading Chinese enterprises.

Corporate social responsibility

The plausibility of spending corporate funds on social responsibility activities has been a subject of academic debate for some time (Baron, 2001; Freeman, 1984; Friedman, 1993; Rodriguez *et al.*, 2006). The topic of CSR now features even more prominently in strategic management literature as business competition intensifies globally. Writers on CSR have identified two approaches adopted by firms to CSR. They are what Hillman and Keim (2001) called the stakeholder approach versus the social approach, or what Baron (2001) labelled the strategic approach versus the altruistic approach (Rodriguez *et al.*, 2006). They argue that strategic stakeholder management will contribute to the financial performance of the firm whereas social issue participation does not (Hillman and Keim, 2001). More specifically, they argue that building good relationships with key stakeholders (e.g. employees, customers, suppliers, communities, government and investors) will help enhance the company's reputation and product differentiation, which will lead to greater customer and supplier loyalty and greater ability to attract and retain talented employees. These intangible and valuable assets will in turn contribute to the company's financial performance and shareholder values (Baron, 2001; Freeman, 1984; Hillman and Keim, 2001; McWilliams and Siegel, 2001; Pfeffer, 1998).

Corporate social responsibility is a relatively new concept in China, but is one that is gaining attention from organizational leaders. At least 11 of the 30 top-performing private enterprises reported that they had adopted the notion of CSR (see Cases 5, 7, 10, 11, 14, 16, 20, 21, 22, 27 and 29). Their CSR activities mainly involved sponsoring social events, taking part in charity actions and supporting the development of the western region of China. For example, Jinzhou Group's (Case 10) CSR practices included being environmentally responsible, encouraging employee participation in community and charity events, providing jobs to disabled workers in 1980s and laid-off workers in 1990s, donations to education and donation of pig farms to local army camps. Similarly, the CEO of Xinxiwang Group (Case 29) was one of the national private entrepreneurs who championed the cause of investing in the western region of China to help its economic development. The company has invested a total of 200 million yuan to build 14 factories in the western region and provided skill training to the workforce. These CSR activities were often described as gestures 'to reciprocate the society', although other intentions may include corporate image and reputation building. In some ways, their support of the study of the Top 50 Chinese private enterprises of 2004 was a demonstration of their commitment to sharing the social responsibility (Liu and Xu, 2004).

The approach to CSR adopted by some of these top-performing Chinese private enterprises appears to share much similarity with that revealed in Hill & Knowlton's Annual Global Survey of Senior Executive Opinions on Corporate Reputation Management (Hill and Knowlton, 2004). Hill and Knowlton's survey shows some interesting differences in the views on corporate reputation, corporate responsibility and corporate governance between the Chinese CEOs and their counterparts outside China. In particular, the survey findings suggest that Western CEOs adopt a broader and more complex approach to CSR than the Chinese CEOs. Human rights and environmental issues, employer branding, identification of national and local culture and community projects may all be part of Western firms' CSR concerns. By contrast, Chinese CEOs tend to focus on employment creation, charity actions and their influence in local communities as the key indicators of their CSR achievements. They take more seriously the influence of the government and are much less concerned about litigation and criticism from pressure groups such as NGOs.

To a large extent, the CEOs' views on CSR are a reflection of not only their recent corporate experience but also wider societal concerns that are culturally sensitive (Hill and Knowlton, 2004). For example, litigation and law suits in China may not be as stringently handled as they are in the West due to the less vigorous legal system in China. Similarly, shareholders' views may not be taken seriously because the stock market system is not yet fully developed or functioning properly. The same goes for NGOs and other social groups that have yet to find their voice in China. As Zinkin (2004, p. 80) observed, 'CSR is a moving target and difficult to define'. Whereas the basic principles of CSR are the same, how they are applied in specific societal context differ according to the priorities of the country and the company concerned.

What is clear is that Chinese firms are lagging behind their counterparts in developed countries in their strategic management of CSR. The lack of social environment and supporting structures presents further barriers to CSR activities, although firms should not rely solely on external support systems to implement their CSR initiatives. According to the official record, 99 per cent of the 10 million registered Chinese enterprises have never donated any monies to charity organizations, in part due to the lack of government policy support (e.g. tax relief) and in part because of the underdevelopment of the Chinese charity sector. There are just over 100 charity organizations in China, consisting of only 0.1 per cent of GDP, compared with the 9 per cent of GDP in the United States (*Workers' Daily*, 17 November 2005). If it is true that a stakeholder-oriented CSR is positively associated with the financial performance of the firm (Hillman and Keim, 2001; Rodriguez *et al.*, 2006), then Chinese firms in general may have a long way to go in developing a strategic approach to CSR in order to enhance their corporate image and gain competitive advantage.

Entrepreneurship of CEOs and reform of corporate governance

In addition to the above key elements of corporate strategy, entrepreneurship of the CEOs and managerial foresight from elite managers is an important factor contributing to the success of leading Chinese enterprises. An interesting feature to note from the analysis of the self-reports is that the shaping of corporate strategy (including business and HR strategies and CSR activities) seems to have been heavily influenced by the background of the CEO. For example, the CEO of Jinzhou Group (Case 10) was an ex-army officer. He had a strong affinity with the army and was keen to build a relationship with the local army units, hence the firm's donation of pig farms to the local army camps. Similarly, the CEO of Jiangsu Yonggang Group (Case 13, steel making) was a village Communist Party secretary with limited level of education. The Enterprise operates in mass production of basic steel products (but with high quality as its product differentiation) and few HRM practices reported. By contrast, the CEO of Shanghai Fuxing High-tech Group (Case 14) was a graduate of philosophy and an MBA. He took a philosophical approach to justify the existence of the enterprise – to reciprocate the society.[4] The influence of his MBA training was also evident in the Company's comprehensive HR philosophy and business strategy. More broadly, the enterprises led by younger CEOs who have received higher education tended to have more articulate and comprehensive strategies informed by management theories, whereas those led by older CEOs, particularly those from TVEs seemed to have less focus on HRM. CEOs in the relatively more high-tech firms generally possess a higher level of educational qualifications than those from ex-SOEs and ex-TVEs. It must be noted that external opportunities, as well as the strategic foresight of CEOs, play an important role in these firms' success. In particular, the success of some of the ex-SOEs and ex-TVEs seems to be facilitated by locational advantage (e.g. having their own ports or having access to special raw materials) and being the first mover to occupy the market where entry barrier is relatively high. The risk is that these advantages may be eroded and without unique internal competence, the competitiveness of these firms may be under threat.

Finally, reform of corporate governance is another important factor attributed to these firms' success.[5] As discussed earlier, the majority of these 30 top-performing firms have grown from very small businesses into large or super-large corporation groups. Some of them were initially set up as small family-owned or TVEs to make a basic living. A small number were collapsed SOEs or collectively owned enterprises (COEs) that were turned round through privatization. As the small private firms grew, they have all been through ownership reform and organizational restructuring to improve the structure of corporate governance. A number of them have changed from TVEs and SOEs/COEs to share ownership or stock-listed firms. Some family-owned enterprises also deliberately got rid of family control and adopted modern management techniques. For example, Delixi Group (Case 19), led by its current CEO who holds a PhD, has moved away from a family-business management to a professional corporate management structure. With industrial electrical equipment as its core products, the firm is now a key supplier for China's state-controlled astronomy projects. Similarly, Jiangsu Yuandong Group (Case 27) has been through four rounds of ownership reforms in the last 12 years to improve its corporate governance structure.

According to Oliver (1997), an organization's business strategy may be profoundly influenced by a complex institutional context of resource decisions and not just by strategic factors such as the nature of the product (market). This institutional context includes decision makers' norms and values, corporate history, organizational culture and politics, public and regulatory pressures and industry-wide norms (Oliver, 1997). In other words, an organization's resource selection and sustainable competitive advantage may be shaped by the social as well as economic context of the firm in which firms may be the captives of their own as well as that of their clients. It is clear here that the selection of organizational resource and business strategy of the top-performing Chinese private enterprises is influenced by the CEOs' personal values. It is also clear that the organizational leaders of the ex-SOEs and ex-TVEs among the Top 50 Chinese private enterprises have been able to overcome their enterprise's past and transform the business successfully. This transformation gives these firms competitive advantage over the thousands of SOEs that have not managed to do so.

This chapter has so far documented the key elements in the business strategy adopted by leading Chinese enterprises, using a sample of 30 of the Top 50 Chinese private enterprises of 2004 as the main data for analysis. These findings are supported by that from a number of surveys conducted by leading international consultancy firms (e.g. Deloitte, 2004; Accenture, 2003; Roland Berger Strategy Consultants, 2003) that have captured the changes and new foci in the business strategy of Chinese firms. These surveys deserve further discussion here.

New strategic orientations of Chinese firms – some survey findings

The surveys conducted by Deloitte (2004), Accenture (2003) and Roland Berger Strategy Consultants (2003) have revealed some new strategic orientations of Chinese firms. For example, the Deloitte (2004) survey on new business strategies of Chinese firms found that competition is becoming a top priority in the Chinese companies. Over 75 per cent of Chinese companies surveyed reported that they are now concerned about competition, whereas only 25 per cent of firms felt so in the survey in 2002. Senior executives in Chinese companies are becoming more aware of the need to adopt new strategic tools. Corporate governance, brand-building and intellectual property protection appear to be the three most important strategic issues of Chinese companies interviewed, although how to implement good practices in governance effectively is another issue to be addressed. Branding is now regarded by Chinese companies surveyed as being important and they are grasping the branding proposition to build competitiveness. This has been demonstrated by the growing success of Chinese household names such as Haier, TCL and Lenovo. The challenge is to recognize that brand-building is a total concept that addresses and integrates all aspects of a business' marketing, operations and service delivery. Leading Chinese companies also demonstrate a higher level of investment in R&D and are more aware of the need to protect their intellectual property. By comparison, human capital is not explicitly a top priority for Chinese companies, although there is an implicit awareness of the need to invest in human capital development in the context of war for talent (Deloitte, 2004).

These findings mirror that from 'The Global Accenture study' (Accenture, 2003). This survey of nearly 600 senior executives in 18 countries conducted by Accenture in 2002 revealed that Chinese business organizations are becoming more competitive and efficiency-driven, as well as seeking to maintain growth by entering new markets and diversifying their product ranges. Workforce performance was by some distance their most important strategic priority, followed by customer acquisition and retention and increasing sales volumes. More than two-thirds of the organizations surveyed had changed their company strategy during the past year, with significant change in every aspect of their operations, including manufacturing, marketing and sales, human resources, procurement and R&D. Over 80 per cent of the companies surveyed had expanded into new geographic and product markets in the last year in order to acquire and retain customers. This expansion strategy was facilitated by technology investment such as a sales system, a customer relationship management system and a supply chain management system.

In addition, the Accenture's (2003) survey found that a majority of the senior executives surveyed identified workforce performance as their most important strategic priority. They believed that the workforce needs to be more responsive and flexible in the current economic climate. Technology investments reflect these beliefs – just under a third of respondents have installed collaborative technology and e-learning systems. Nearly 20 per cent have also implemented a business intelligence system in the past two years, with another 38 per cent indicating that they plan to install a business intelligence platform in the near future. Despite this, China's business community is still unsure about the strategic importance of IT systems. Only 10 per cent of executives – less than in any other Asian country Accenture surveyed – believed that IT systems have a central role to play in developing new products and services, ways of working or insights into customer requirements. It appears that Chinese executives tend to have low expectations of IT, seeing it as a day-to-day rather than a strategic tool. Relatively few executives in China said that their organizations were innovative, although 70 per cent of those surveyed indicated a desire to become more so and 90 per cent felt that their industry had become more innovative in response to the economic downturn (Accenture, 2003).

Accenture's (2003) survey finding of the low significance of business intelligence afforded by the Chinese executives is reflected in Roland Berger Strategy Consultants' (2003) survey. This survey shows that even the top Chinese companies do not devote sufficient attention to competitive intelligence and strategy. This weakness is compounded when applied to less familiar foreign markets. A reason for this deficiency may be the legacy of the state planned economy (Roland Berger Strategy Consultants, 2003). Another reason may be to do with the fact that Chinese managers have still to become more competition oriented and to equip themselves with more modern management techniques that are new to China.

Summary

This chapter has analysed key elements of leading Chinese firms' strategy, drawing on secondary empirical data as the basis for analysis. Key success factors of these firms appear to be associated with firm growth through business diversification, internationalization, strong emphasis on product innovation and quality enhancement, strategic marketing, product and corporate branding, and importantly, entrepreneurship of owner managers/CEOs and reform of corporate governance. Indeed, diversification and internationalization has been a key part of the new corporate strategies pursued by many Chinese firms

(Benson and Zhu, 1999, cited in Zhang *et al.*, 2006). However, managerial foresight from elite Chinese managers is one of the driving forces for Chinese firms' international expansion. The motives of Chinese outward investment will be further explored in Chapter 9.

It is evident that leading Chinese firms are making a greater effort than their less well-performing counterparts in innovation and strategic marketing, including product and corporate branding. Nevertheless, significant gaps remain compared with leading international firms. The ability to innovate is a key to sustaining a firm's competitiveness. This poses an important challenge to the sustainability of the competitiveness of Chinese firms who face unique challenges and barriers to innovation due to institutional deficiencies and the imitative culture. The concept of branding represents a specific corporate culture, an intangible value unique to the enterprise, an ultimate demonstration of its product development capability and a reflection of the overall strength of the enterprise. While a small number of leading Chinese firms are beginning to take a strategic approach to brand management, the majority of Chinese enterprises have yet to fully grasp the concept of branding.

In addition, well-performing Chinese firms tend to adopt a high commitment model of HRM which emphasizes training and development, promotion by competence, extensive employee welfare provision and enterprise culture development and management. However, their HRM configuration is largely of the paternalistic nature, with enterprise culture typical of that of Chinese values. This is coupled with a normative approach to management. A major weakness in these well-performing firms' strategy is that HRM is not necessarily placed in an important strategic position in the corporate strategy, judging from the noticeable absence in the self-report or the brief mentioning of HRM by a large proportion of the top-performing firms. Given the fact that human resources are the key resource that can enhance an organization's competitive advantage, this remains a serious challenge for Chinese firms.

Finally, Chinese firms are beginning to pay attention to their corporate image and the social impact of their organization – notably through their activities related to social corporate responsibility. Again, the configuration of CSR appears to be of Chinese characteristics, with sponsoring social events and charity actions being the main activities. Stakeholder values and environmental issues rarely feature as part of the CSR in China, as they tend to do in Western countries.

To conclude, this chapter does not claim to have found the definitive factors that have contributed to the success of the top-performing Chinese (private) firms. Rather, it is an attempt to analyse what were reported as the key elements in their corporate strategy that are associated with their competitiveness. The secondary data came from company self-reports and survey findings. They were snapshots and anecdotal instead of longitudinal studies. These methodological drawbacks mean that the findings need to be interpreted with caution and that new empirical research is needed to shed light on the subject that is of growing importance in understanding Chinese business and management.

Appendix 3.1 Key success factors: A summary of 30 of the top 50 Chinese private enterprises of 2004

Case	Name of the firm	Nature of business	Ranking in top 50	Background of the owner entrepreneur/CEO and firm	Key elements of strategies
1	Zhejiang Zhongcheng Ltd	Construction and related business	2	■ Male, born in 1949, senior engineer, national model entrepreneur	■ Steady growth based on one main industry – construction ■ Prudent diversification into businesses related to construction (e.g. estate, tourism) ■ Product branding to create company brand image ■ Innovations – won 25 national innovation awards ■ Quality management – 11 projects received quality excellence award ■ Systematic HR policies and practices – no family control; a strong enterprise culture that is based on innovation, participation, employee care and employee entertainment programmes
2	China-People Electrical Group	Production and sales of industrial electrical equipment	3	■ Male, born in 1958, senior economist ■ Established in 1988 with 12 employees; now over	■ Innovation – in-house R&D centre and post-doctoral research centre ■ Importation of advanced technology (e.g. ABB technology)

Appendix 3.1 (Continued)

Case	Name of the firm	Nature of business	Ranking in top 50	Background of the owner entrepreneur/CEO and firm	Key elements of strategies
				18,000 employees; products sold to 27 countries; total industrial output 8.6 billion yuan in 2003	■ Role models to set examples for employee commitment ■ Recruitment of talent at postgraduate level
3	Zhejiang Nanfang Group	Textile production and estate	5	■ Established in 1979; now over 3500 employees, 580 engineers and technicians; 2.1 billion yuan sales revenue in 2002	■ Innovation ■ Advanced production technology imported from developed countries ■ Quality assurance (e.g. ISO 9000) ■ Strategic development of international market (e.g. registered company in Brazil) ■ HRM practices not reported
4	Zhejiang 001 Electronics Group	Electronic products (specialized in aerials TV)	6	■ Male, born in 1958; innovator of one of the products which led to the establishment of the company	■ 'Small product, large market' business philosophy ■ Product innovations and technology upgrading – with over 130 patents ■ Utilizing universities as its R&D source

No.	Company	Sector		Description	Key factors
				■ Established in 1988; now the largest aerial producer in China occupying 60% of the market; 5.5 million sets of aerials sold in 2003	■ Diversification and expansion of products related to electronic technology ■ Quality assurance and customer services orientation ■ Innovation in management process (e.g. e-administration process to process business information with high efficiency) ■ Branding of key products ■ Competence management – building a young, professional and competent management team with innovative management concepts
5	Jiangsu Suning Electronics Group	Electronic products (household electronic goods, PCs and telecom equipment)	8	■ Established in 1990 as a retailer of air conditioning equipment; expanded into a variety of electronic products chain shops in early 2000s with 5% market share by 2004	■ A genuine approach to relationship management with stakeholders (e.g. win-win style of collaboration with suppliers; customer satisfaction-oriented service policy that differentiate Suning with competitors) ■ Chain shop approach to deal with competitive pressure – with the corporate ambition of being the Chinese 'Wal-Mart'

Appendix 3.1 (Continued)

Case	Name of the firm	Nature of business	Ranking in top 50	Background of the owner entrepreneur/CEO and firm	Key elements of strategies
					■ HRM: A systematic approach to organizational management and HRM – no nepotism and a cultivation of a 'can do' culture
					■ CSR approach (e.g. donation to set up Suning Hardship Fund to support education, recruiting laid-off workers for re-employment)
6	Guangdong HengXing Group	Animal feeds development and production and pilot sites for new fishery products	9	Established in 1996, now has over 4000 employees, with 35% of them with educational qualifications of diploma or above	■ Strict quality control in recipe, raw material, production process and final product – obtaining ISO 9001 recognition in 2000
					■ Product development with in-house laboratory farms
					■ Market research to develop products to match new market demand (e.g. developing prawn feeds to meet the growing market for prawn products)
					■ Utilization of universities and research institutes for product development

- HRM: A systematic approach to HRM that emphasizes on learning and development, competence based promotion, performance-related reward, sophisticated recruitment selection process, internal succession planning and management development as well as recruiting talent externally to fill gaps (i.e. high commitment model of the HRM)

| 7 | Hailiang Group | Copper processing as the main business, plus estate, trading and education | 10 | ■ Male, born in 1960, senior economist ■ Established in 1989, now has over 3000 employees; 3.1 billion yuan sales revenue in 2003 | ■ Focusing on high-tech, high value-added and precision products ■ Rapid expansion of production capacity to gain economies of scale ■ Branding of product for quality and corporate for trustworthiness ■ Development of international market through strong market (trading in over 60 countries) ■ Zero tolerance of quality defects and adoption of quality and operations management initiatives (e.g. ISO 9001, 9002, 1400; OHSA18000; 5S) |

Appendix 3.1 (Continued)

Case	Name of the firm	Nature of business	Ranking in top 50	Background of the owner entrepreneur/CEO and firm	Key elements of strategies
					▪ Good HRM practices (e.g. high level of investment in employee training and development, high level of investment to improve employees' living environment and social life)
					▪ Emphasis of CSR (e.g. SA8000 accreditation in 2004)
8	Kangna Group	Kangna brand of upper range leather shoes	11	▪ Male, born in 1967, economist, MBA	▪ Branding of products and corporation (Best Chinese Shoe Maker)
				▪ Established in early 1980s and won the title of 'Best Chinese Shoe Maker' in 1993	▪ Achieving high-quality products by importing advanced production equipment
					▪ Frequent product innovations by employing in-house designers who analyse and keep up with international fashions
					▪ Development of international markets (over 80 shops in the United States, Europe and other developed countries, with the first one in France in 2001)

| 9 | Zhongtian Construction Group | Housing construction, estate development and road/bridge building | 12 | ■ Male, born in 1954, senior engineer CEO of Zhongtian since 1993
■ A bankrupting old enterprise reborn in the 1993; now has over 2000 employees with total asset of 3 billion yuan and sales revenue of 4.8 billion yuan in 2003 | ■ HRM: Full range of HRM policies tailored for an enterprise culture that emphasizes on employee development, employee care, trust, integrity, harmony, diligence, corporate value and business ethics
■ Quality assurance (e.g. winning the national quality management award in 2004)
■ Expansion of business through acquisition of two road and bridge building firms
■ Enhancing the corporation's total contracting capacity by acquiring shares of two top-class construction design institutes
■ Establishing itself as one of the most reputable construction contractors and developers in China and attracting talent
■ HRM practices not reported |

Appendix 3.1 (Continued)

Case	Name of the firm	Nature of business	Ranking in top 50	Background of the owner entrepreneur/CEO and firm	Key elements of strategies
10	Jinzhou Group	Metal piping manufacturing and environmental tourism (to develop southwest of China)	14	■ Male, born in 1957, ex-army officer ■ Established in 1981 as a TVE; now has over 2800 employees; 2.1 billion yuan sales revenue of piping products in 2003; 1.6 billion yuan total asset	■ Quality assurance – pursuit of zero tolerance to defects and total satisfaction of customer ■ Product development in collaboration with R&D institutions and universities (e.g. development of 'green products' and non-corrosive piping products) ■ Development of international market (exporting to the United States, Europe etc.) ■ HRM practices: target recruitment of talent (e.g. from universities and research institutes, governmental and public sector organizations), full set of management policy and procedure, frequently organizing employee training and development ■ CSR: environmentally responsible, employee participation in community and charity events, providing jobs to disabled workers in 1980s and laid-off workers in 1990s, donations to education and donation of pigs farms to local army camp

11	Kasen Industrial Ltd	Leather goods design and production	15	■ Male, born in 1965, senior economist ■ Established in 1988, 3.6 billion yuan sales revenue in 2003	■ Expansion of business through M&As and alliances ■ Establishing competitive advantage through economies of scale, high efficiency, high quality and low cost ■ Continuous increases in R&D investment ■ International market with regular customers from the United States and Europe ■ CSR: donations to education and other charity causes ■ HRM practices not reported
12	Huali Group	Manufacturing of electrical meters as core business and diversification into others	16	■ Male, born in 1960 ■ Established in 1970 as an SOE, privatized in 1990s; nearly 10,000 employees; over 6.7 billion yuan sales revenue in 2003; over 6 billion yuan total asset; factories and R&D centres in Thailand, Canada, Argentine and Israel	■ Quality assurance – electrical meter products ranked first in China since mid-1990s ■ Diversification into IT and other high-tech industries to update its traditional electrical meter products ■ International expansion to gain market and technology

Appendix 3.1 (Continued)

Case	Name of the firm	Nature of business	Ranking in top 50	Background of the owner entrepreneur/CEO and firm	Key elements of strategies
					▪ Product branding – aiming to build a reputation as a high-tech and high-quality product producer in the global market
					▪ HRM practices: encouraging creativity and innovation; enterprise culture remodelling – from SOE to a high-tech international player
13	Jiangsu Yonggang Group	Steel making	17	▪ Male, born in 1936, ex-Party Secretary of the village, founder of the village company	▪ Mass production of basic steel products, but with high quality as its product differentiation
				▪ Established in 1984; over 5.3 billion yuan sales revenue and nearly 6 billion yuan total asset in 2003	▪ Competitive advantages: located in Yangzi River Delta Area as one of the economically most developed areas in China, possessing its own dock for transportation
					▪ Enterprise value: stakeholder perspective that aims to create value for customers, profit for shareholders, future for employees and prosperity for the society

| 14 | Shanghai Fuxing High-tech Group | Pharmaceutical, estate, steel, commercial and finance businesses | 18 | ■ Male, born in 1967, BA in Philosophy and MBA from Fudan University, Shanghai
■ Established in 1992; 27 billion yuan sales revenue in 2003 | ■ Business strategy: diversification of investment, professionalization in operations and investment
■ HRM philosophy and strategy: to attract talent with development, to retain talent with career, to develop staff with work opportunity and to appraise staff with performance; harmonization and unification of the development of the organization and individuals; development of core enterprise values that is heavily influenced by the Chinese philosophy; promoting concepts of learning organization and innovative teams; enhancing employee satisfaction with humanistic approach to management
■ CSR: generous charity donation to support poverty elimination, health and educational projects and renovation of famous historic sites |

Appendix 3.1 (Continued)

Case	Name of the firm	Nature of business	Ranking in top 50	Background of the owner entrepreneur/CEO and firm	Key elements of strategies
15	Tongkun Group	Chemical fibre as core business and diversification into estate, trading, finance and IT	20	■ Male, born in 1963, senior engineer ■ Established in 1981 as a township and village enterprise; now over 7000 employees; 2.3 billion yuan total asset	■ Heavy investment in technological innovation and product development ■ Enterprise values: high-quality employees to produce high-quality products; humanistic approach to management
16	Zhengtai Group	Low voltage electrical products	21	■ Male, born in 1963, senior economist ■ Established in 1984 with eight employees; over 14,000 employees, 3.1 billion yuan total asset and 10.1 billion yuan sales revenue in 2003; product sold to more than 70 countries	■ Core value: honesty and trustworthiness in conducting business ■ Emphasis on technological innovation and product development, with some innovations awarded national patents ■ HRM philosophy: humanistic approach to managing employees; heavy incentives to attract and motivate key talents to enhance corporate competitiveness ■ CSR: unitarist approach to individual, organizational and social development; donations to poverty relief and education projects and participation in charity projects

| 17 | Xilinmen Group | Furniture making (especially beds) as core business and diversification into estate | 23 | ■ Male, born in 1962, senior economist
■ Established in 1984; now over 2000 employees and 0.8 billion yuan total asset | ■ Technology focused – importation of advanced production technologies; collaboration with Beijing University in R&D centre
■ Product development oriented – over 200 new products developed in-house, 15 awarded national patents
■ Quality assurance – ISO9001 and ISO14001 accreditations
■ International expansion through joint venture with reputable Western furniture giants (e.g. Ikea); products sold to more than 12 countries
■ HRM practices: talent management – over 20% of employees possessing diploma or above qualifications or professional qualifications; heavy investment in training – 1 million yuan annual training budget (sending key employees overseas or to premium universities in China for training and development) |

Appendix 3.1 (Continued)

Case	Name of the firm	Ranking in top 50	Nature of business	Background of the owner entrepreneur/CEO and firm	Key elements of strategies
18	Tongwei Group	25	Animal feeds and aquatic products as core business and diversification into pets feeds, estate, IT and international trade	■ Established in the early 1990s with 500 yuan; now one of China's largest enterprises in animal feeds and aquatic products, possessing an extensive industrial cluster including feeds production, animal and fishery farming and product processing	■ Perceived importance to corporate competitiveness: corporate branding characterized by good prices, quality and after sales services to gain customers' trust and corporate image ■ Heavy investment in R&D with in-house R&D centre ■ HRM practices: comprehensive set of staff manual to define behavioural norms and management practices; advocate of learning organization and encouraging employees for self-development – two-thirds of staff with university or professional qualifications; adoption of western management practices such as flat organizational structure and team working; a unitarist but humanistic approach to HRM that is open, transparent, fair and participative; effective scheme of performance assessment and reward; regular two-way communications, encouraging employees to participate in the enterprise management in order to motivate staff and harness their innovative ideas; annual staff turnover less than 1%

19	Delixi Group	Industrial electrical equipment as core business, diversification into estate, distribution	26	■ Male, born in 1961; PhD ■ Established in 1984 as family business; now over 13,000 employees and 3 billion yuan total asset; a core supplier for China's astronomy projects	■ Management strategy – from family-business management to professional corporate management ■ Heavy investment in technology and quality – 5% of annual sales revenue as technological innovation fund, with R&D centres in Wenzhou (HQ), Shanghai and Germany ■ HRM practices not reported
20	Guangxia Group	Estate, investment, tourism as core businesses and diversification into other businesses	28	■ Over 50,000 employees and 14 billion yuan total asset	■ Business expansion through acquisitions of businesses in various industries (e.g. utilities, education, hospital and media); corporate slogan – 'to do construction business outside the construction industry' ■ HRM: devolution of management responsibilities, strict management procedures and behavioural norms, clear management responsibilities, strict performance assessment and reward/punishment scheme ■ CSR: donation to public causes and education, participation in charity causes

Appendix 3.1 (Continued)

Case	Name of the firm	Nature of business	Ranking in top 50	Background of the owner entrepreneur/CEO and firm	Key elements of strategies
21	Lilian Group	Estate, manufacturing, finance and media	31	■ Male, writer and editor by trade ■ Established in 1994; now 3000 employees and over 10 billion yuan sales revenue	■ Core values: sincerity and 'win-win and mutual development' principles ■ Internationalization through joint ventures with world class businesses, such as GE (USA), and overseas subsidiaries ■ HRM practices: talent management; extensive employee welfare schemes ■ CSR: donation to public causes and education – with over 40 million yuan donation since 1996
22	Wanxiang Group	Manufacturing of auto parts	33	■ Established in 1969; over 15 billion yuan sales revenue in 2003	■ Expansion through M&As of other auto manufacturing companies in various locations in China and partnership with local whole-car manufacturing companies to supply parts locally ■ Investment in advanced technology and quality assurance as the key to competitiveness – R&D centre in the United States and R&D relationships with premium universities in China and auto research firms and associations overseas

					■ Internationalization: M&As of firms in eight countries including: the United States , Britain, Germany, Canada and Australia, with 31 overseas subsidiaries
					■ HRM practices not reported
23	Youngor	Textile and garment as core businesses, estate and international trade as supplement businesses	34	■ Male, born in 1951 ■ Established in 1979 as a TVE; over 10 billion yuan sales revenue and 20,000 employees in 2003	■ Business market: upper end of products (shirts) aimed for domestic and international market
					■ Continuous development of production and product technology
					■ Quality assurance: ISO9001, ISO9002 and ISO14000 accreditation
					■ International joint venture to provide in-house textile materials and accessories for shirt production, brand-name high street chain shops to retail shirt products
					■ CSR: donation to public causes and charity events – with a total of 80 million yuan donated so far
					■ HRM practices not reported

Appendix 3.1 (Continued)

Case	Name of the firm	Nature of business	Ranking in top 50	Background of the owner entrepreneur/CEO and firm	Key elements of strategies
24	Nanshan Group	Aluminium and fine textile as core products in addition to more than ten different lines of businesses	35	■ Male, born in 1947, Party Secretary of Nanshan Village ■ Established in 1978 as a small village enterprise; over 6.6 billion yuan sales revenue, over 36,000 employees and total asset of 12 billion yuan in 2003	■ Import of advanced textile production technology from Britain, France, Germany and Italy to become one of the largest and most advanced textile producers in China ■ Continuous enhancement of product quality and level – winner of a succession of national product quality awards ■ International expansion to secure raw material supply, for example, establishing bases in Australia for wool and aluminium ore supply ■ HRM practices not reported
25	Baoye Group	Construction and estate developer	36	■ Male, born in 1957 ■ Established in 1970s as a small construction company; now employing 47,000 employees and worth over 2 billion Hong Kong dollar in the stock market	■ Developing luxurious and environment-friendly housing estate ■ Using modern technology and materials to replace traditional construction methods and materials ■ Continuous technological innovation through importation of western advanced construction technology, techniques and materials

26	Hengdian Group	Electronics, pharmaceutical, media and entertainment and high-tech agricultural products	38	■ Male, founder of the firm ■ Established in 1975 as a silk-producing TVE; over 12 billion yuan sales revenue and over 30,000 employees in 2003 ■ HR Strategy: team-working culture; promotion through training and developing its own employees as well as recruiting talents from the market; employee profit-sharing schemes to retain key talents
27	Jiangsu Yuandong Group	Electrical wires and cables, medicine and new materials	39	■ Male, founder of the firm ■ Established in 1990; over 3200 employees and 3.6 billion yuan sales revenue in 2003 ■ Strategic approach: outward looking in attracting talents, capital and profit; internationalization of all processes of the businesses; innovations in product, production, service and management processes ■ HRM: highly qualified employees – 18% of employees with university diploma or above qualifications, including 58 PhD graduates and 315 postgraduates by the end of 2003 ■ Four rounds of ownership reform in 12 years to improve corporate governance ■ Innovations in marketing and sales strategy to gain competitive advantage in the market – identifying new markets, new customers and new sales methods

Appendix 3.1 (Continued)

Case	Name of the firm	Nature of business	Ranking in top 50	Background of the owner entrepreneur/CEO and firm	Key elements of strategies
					■ Performance management – management by objectives and sales targets ■ Strategic HRM: attracting talent from international pool; alignment of job and person characteristics; annual employee opinion pole on their managers, investing in training and promoting life-long learning; extensive welfare benefits for employees; lucrative welfare package to attract key talents; harmony as the core corporate value and agility as the key business sense to develop ■ Stakeholder value – striving to satisfy all parties concerned
28	Baosideng Ltd	Garment manufacturing (jackets as core product)	42	■ Male, born in 1952, created the product brand worth of 4.2 billion yuan ■ Established in 1976 as a sewing group with eight sewing machines in a village; now employing 11,000 employees	■ Advanced production technology – importation of advanced manufacturing technology from the United States, Germany and Japan ■ Continuous product development and fashionable product design – with over 200 new designs in each season

No.	Business	Founder	Age	Strategic practices
				■ Quality assurance – ISO9001 and ISO14001 accreditation ■ Core products (jackets) occupying 50% of the domestic market share and worn by sportspersons in world class sports events ■ International expansion through product market development ■ HRM practices not reported
29	Xinxiwang Group	Animal feeds, dairy products as core businesses and diversification into chemicals, investment and estate development	43	■ Male, founded the firm with three brothers ■ Established in 1982; now over 15,000 employees ■ Expansion through diversification of businesses ■ Internationalization through building subsidiaries in east Asian countries ■ Product development through in-house R&D centre and collaboration with universities ■ CSR: CEO was one of the national private entrepreneurs who championed the good cause of investing in the western region of China to help its economic development. The company has invested a total of 0.2 billion yuan to built 14 factories in the western region and carried out skill training ■ HRM practices not reported

Appendix 3.1 (Cotinued)

Case	Name of the firm	Nature of business	Ranking in top 50	Background of the owner entrepreneur/CEO and firm	Key elements of strategies
30	Jiashijie Commercial Chain Shops Group	Supermarket	47	■ Male, born in 1948, MSc in Economics ■ Established in 1996 with 650 employees; with 15,000 employees and 5.3 billion yuan sales revenue in 2003	■ Business strategy: one-stop shop that offers comprehensive range of commercial goods; economies of scale with large-scale shopping sites; low-cost based operation; excellent shopping environment and after-sales services; streamlining supplier chain to ensure quality, efficiency and low cost ■ HRM practices: increasing investment in human resources; extensive training provision and management development programmes, including in-house management training college and sending managers abroad for training; competing with competitors through higher level of human capitals

Note: Top 50 here refers to their overall competitiveness that was calculated and ranked based on each firm's total asset, sales revenue and net profit. All Top 50 Chinese private enterprises were approached by the authors through postal mail. The 30 cases reported in the book were those who were willing to participate in the study by the deadline set by Liu and Xu. The self-reports from participant companies have been edited by Liu and Xu (2004) in order to maintain a broadly consistent presentational format across the 30 reports. I am indebted to Liu and Xu (2004) for the empirical data which serves as the basis for the analysis of firm's strategy in this chapter.

Source: analysed and summarized by the author based on the self report description from the 30 case studies reported in Liu, Y. Q. and Xu, Z. X. (2004, pp.197–320).

Recommended readings

G. Davies, R. Chun, R. V. da Silva and S. Roper, *Corporate Reputation and Competitiveness* (London: Routledge, 2003).

L. Kelley and Y. Luo (eds), *China 2000: Emerging Business Issues* (London: Sage Publications, 1999).

P. Lasserre and H. Schütte, *Strategies for Asia Pacific: Meeting New Challenges* (3rd edition) (Basingstoke: Palgrave Macmillan, 2006).

Y. Yu, *Comparative Corporate Governance in China: Political Economy and Legal Infrastructure* (London: Routledge, 2007).

Analysis of Selected Industries

CHAPTER 4

Automotive Industry

Introduction

'Producing automobiles has often been a symbol of economic prestige in the developing world' (Francois and Spinanger, 2004, p. 85). With the introduction of the Automotive Industrial Policy by the State Council in 1994, the automotive (auto) industry is regarded by the government as one of the 'pillar industries' in China's economy to be developed strategically. The auto industry consists of whole-vehicle manufacturing (including trucks, buses and cars), component parts manufacturing, motorcycle manufacturing and so on. This chapter focuses mainly on car manufacturing, because it is the newly developing part of the industry where the potential market is and the future of the industry lies, if the industry were to truly become one of the pillar industries in China's economic and technological development. It is also where government protection is high on the one hand but foreign competition is intensive on the other.

Due to space constraint, this chapter will not cover in detail foreign auto firms in China; websites offer rich sources of factual information and up-to-date news on the development of their business activities. Instead, this chapter focuses on the historical development and structural problems of the Chinese auto industry as well as competition, pressure and strategic implications at industrial level.

As mentioned in Chapter 1, the analysis of the selected industries in this part of the book will mainly focus on issues and problems that have a direct impact at the industry and organizational level instead of the national level. For example, this chapter deals with competition problems and strategic implications at industrial and firm level. It does not deal with wider problems at the societal/macro level that are associated with the development of the auto industry. These problems include, for instance, environment, fuel, transport and the road system,[1] the structure of consumption, the imbalanced structure of the industry, the imbalance of export and import of vehicles and its negative impact on national foreign exchange.

This chapter consists of six main sections. The first two sections provide a brief overview on the development of the Chinese auto industry as well as the structure of its products, production outputs and sales volumes. The next two sections analyse its patterns of investment as well as problems and competitive pressures experienced by auto firms in China, especially the domestic firms. The fifth section explores opportunities and strategic implications faced by the industry. This is followed by a summary of major HR issues, including low educational attainment and skill level, skill shortage, low wage and recruitment and retention problems.

History of the industry

The development of China's auto industry under the socialist China can be broadly divided into three stages (Qian, 2004). The first stage was the start-up period from 1953 to 1958 when the first auto factory – *Changchun* First Automotive Works (FAW) – was established in northern China with the full technical support from the then Soviet Union. In 1958, the factory produced 16,000 trucks and jeeps. Soviet Union provided not only all the technical information needed to build the factory, but also the training for over 500 Chinese technical staff and managers in the Soviet Union. This support, however, was provided in exchange for agricultural produces from China (Qian, 2004).

The second stage was the independent development period from 1958 to 1984 after the Sino-Soviet Union relationship went sour in the late 1950s. A second auto factory – Second Automotive Works (SAW) – was built in Hubei Province with the support from the *Changchun* Factory. SAW had an annual production capacity of 100,000 automobiles and became the largest auto factory by the late 1970s when China started to open up its economy. It was also during the late 1970s when FAW designed and produced China's first home-made model of indigenous trucks – the *jiefang* ('Liberation') brand. In 1984, China produced 316,000 vehicles, most of them trucks and buses, and became one of the largest commercial vehicle producers in the world. However, China was still lagging behind in the design and manufacturing technology despite substantial investment in importing technologies (Qian, 2004).

The third stage began in the mid-1980s and was characterized by the industry's opening up to foreign firms through JVs. During the mid-1980s, there was a debate in China as to whether it should develop a domestic market for car production and consumption. Up till then, only a few thousand cars were produced annually for government departments. As it stood, the low level of technology and production capacity in car manufacturing made the industry unable to cope with the development of the car market. It was then decided that China should develop its car production as an important part of the development of the auto industry. In 1984, the first Sino-foreign JV was established in Beijing between Beijing Automotive Industry Corporation, one of the largest auto firms in China, and the then America Motor Company (AMC). This was followed by a succession of other JVs (Qian, 2004). During the 1990s, the auto industry received much attention from the government (see Box 4.1).[2]

BOX 4.1

The 1994 auto sector industrial policy of China
Objectives

The state will promote the development of two or three large automotive groups, six or seven key auto plants and eight to ten major motorcycle plants. In the longer term, to 2010, the state will promote agglomeration among the enterprises, so that there would be three or four auto groups that are internationally competitive.

Target enterprises for promotion

The state will give special support to auto enterprises which, as of end-1995, meet one of the following criteria:

- Annual production of at least 100,000 vehicles and sales of at least 80,000.
- Annual production and sales of at least 20,000 heavy-duty vehicles.
- Annual production of at least 1500 large/medium buses, sales of at least 1000.

Policy tools

State support for companies meeting the above criteria and investing in priority projects will include fast-track approval for issuance of stocks and bonds, loan support from state banks including policy loans, access to overseas funds and greater freedom for finance company subsidiary of an auto enterprise.

Others

No new small-scale auto production plants will be approved. Foreign companies may not have more than one JV making the same type of vehicles.

Source: Government Policies on the Automotive Industry (1994), cited in Eun and Lee (2002, p. 9).

Structure of products, production outputs and sales volumes

The JVs with brand-name foreign auto manufacturers have injected the much needed technology and management know-how into the Chinese auto industry for its car manufacturing and have increased its production capacity significantly (Qian, 2004). For example, in 1985, only 900,000 cars were produced. In 2004, over 2.3 million were made (see Tables 1.2, 4.2) In 1992, China's automotive industry reached the production output of 1 million vehicles for the first time, and in 2000, it reached a record of 2 million for the first time (Tian, 2003).

However, the development of the auto industry was relatively slow during the two decades before 2002. During 1996–2000 (the ninth five-year plan), automotive manufacturing was only using about 50 per cent of its production capacity largely due to insufficient market demand (see Table 4.1). The total number of all vehicles produced during this period was significantly lower than the anticipated figure (Fu, 2005).

Table 4.1   Possession of civil vehicles and private vehicles in China (1985–2004)

Year	Possession of civil vehicles				Possession of private vehicles			
	Total	Passenger vehicles	Trucks	Other vehicles	Total	Passenger vehicles	Trucks	Other vehicles
1985	3,211.2	794.5	2,232.0	–	284.9	19.3	264.8	–
1989	5,113.2	1,464.3	3,463.7	–	731.2	202.8	525.0	–
1990	5,513.6	1,621.9	3,684.8	–	816.2	240.7	574.8	–
1991	6,061.1	1,852.4	3,986.2	–	960.4	303.6	656.1	–
1992	6,917.4	2,261.6	4,414.5	–	1,182.0	417.8	761.5	–
1993	8,175.8	2,859.5	5,010.0	–	1,557.7	598.5	940.0	–
1994	9,419.5	3,497.4	4,603.3	–	2,054.2	786.2	1,232.9	–
1995	10,400.0	4,179.0	5,854.3	–	2,499.6	1,141.5	1,318.3	–
1996	11,000.8	4,880.2	5,750.3	–	2,896.7	1,430.4	1,427.8	–
1997	12,190.9	5,805.6	6,012.3	–	2,353.6	1,912.7	1,631.9	–
1998	13,193.0	6,548.3	2,678.9	–	4,236.5	2,306.5	1,920.3	–
1999	14,529.4	7,402.3	6,769.5	–	5,338.8	3,040.9	2,286.8	–
2000	16,089.1	8,537.3	7,163.2	–	6,253.3	3,650.9	2,590.9	–
2001	18,020.4	9,939.6	7,652.4	–	7,707.8	4,698.5	2,989.5	–
2002	20,531.7	12,023.7	8,122.2	385.8	9,689.8	6,237.6	3,412.9	39.4
2003	23,829.3	14,788.1	8,535.1	506.1	12,192.3	8,458.7	3,673.5	60.0
2004	26,937.1	17,359.1	8,930.0	648.0	14,816.6	10,696.9	4,028.2	91.5

Figures in 1000 vehicles
Source: adapted from China Statistical Yearbook (2005, pp. 567–70).

In 2002, over 3.25 million vehicles were produced in China, consisting of approximately equal proportions of cars, trucks and buses (see Table 4.2). In 2004, a total of 5.07 million vehicles were produced and a similar number were sold in China (see Table 4.2). In 2004, China was the fourth largest auto manufacturing country in the world, after the United States, Japan and Germany (see Table 4.3) and ranked third in sales (see Table 4.4). In 2005, China closed its gap with Japan and tied in a second position, making up 10 per cent of the world's auto sales volume (see Table 4.4). This was a significant growth from 5 per cent in 2001 (see Table 4.4) and 8.06 per cent in 2004 (Fu, 2005).

However, China's share of the world market remains comparatively small in relation to its population. For example, only 4.5 million vehicles were purchased in the domestic market in the year 2003 (Zhang, 2005). Almost 90 per cent of passenger cars made and sold in China are brands from foreign automakers, including Volkswagen, General Motors (GM), Honda, Citroën, Toyota, Ford and BMW (*China Daily Online*, 2004a). It is estimated that there are some 120 major brands of car in the Chinese market, with the top ten brands controlling 70 per cent of the market (*China Business*, 7 April 2004). According to statistics from the China Automotive Industry Association, only nine of the 15 largest automobile enterprises had increased their sales revenue in 2004 from the previous year. The remaining six enterprises suffered a drop to varying degrees.

Table 4.2 Vehicle production by types in China (2002–4)

Type		2002		2003		2004	
		Output	Sales	Output	Sales	Output	Sales
	Total	3,251	3,248	4,444	4,391	5,071	5,071
	Cars	1,091	1,164	2,019	1,972	2,316	2,327
Trucks	Sub-total	1,096	1,077	1,230	1,211	1,455	1,526
	Heavy trucks	253	245	262	255	369	371
	Medium-sized trucks	164	165	136	136	173	176
	Light trucks	531	520	689	682	806	808
	Mini-trucks	148	983	143	137	167	172
Buses	Sub-total	1,064	1,046	1,195	1,201	1,240	1,219
	Large buses	17	17	20	19	26	261
	Medium-sized buses	65	65	54	53	53	527
	Small buses	328	333	443	440	403	398
	Mini-buses	654	631	679	695	758	742

Figures in thousand
Source: Fu (2005, p. 186), who sourced it from the China Automotive Industry Association.

Only five enterprises had increased profit from 2003, whereas in the remaining two-thirds of the enterprises profits declined. In fact, three of them made a loss (*China Business*, 28 February 2005). In addition, China's international auto sales volume was equivalent to only 2.7 per cent of that of the domestic market in 2004 – a trading pattern in sharp contrast to that of the top automotive manufacturing countries in the world (Fu, 2005). It was reported that Chinese auto manufacturing firms are inexperienced in operating in global markets on a large scale and have opted to focus primarily on the domestic market (Sun, 2006).

On the auto component parts manufacturing side, according to the *China Auto Industry Yearbook 2000*, by the end of 1999, there were a total of 1452 auto parts suppliers in China. They employed a total of 709,000 employees – 63,000 of them were engineers and technicians (cited in Council for the Promotion of International Trade, 2002). The industry is dominated by a relatively few large enterprises, with the Top 50 auto parts manufacturing enterprises accounting for 45 per cent of the market in 1999. The total sales value of the ten largest auto parts and accessories manufacturing enterprises was US$1.38 billion, taking 18.2 per cent of the domestic market share (Council for the Promotion of International Trade, 2002). According to the China Association of Automobile Manufacturers, auto parts makers in China could more or less satisfy market demands for components of imported cars. The total sales of auto parts in 2003 were reported at 264 billion yuan (approximately US$31.9 billion). By mid-2004, China was home to 4413 auto parts manufacturers,

Table 4.3   World motor vehicle production by country 2003–4, OICA correspondents survey

Motor vehicle	2003	2004	Percentage of change (%)
Europe	20,000,286	20,829,774	4
France*	3,620,066	3,665,990	1
Germany**	5,506,629	5,569,954	1
Italy	1,321,631	1,141,944	−14
Spain	3,029,826	3,011,010	−1
UK*	1,846,429	1,856,049	1
NAFTA (Canada, Mexico and US)	16,243,280	16,264,886	0
US	12,114,971	11,989,387	−1
South America	2,037,032	2,562,058	26
Brazil	1,827,791	2,210,062	21
Asia-Oceania	21,986,694	24,086,520	10
China	4,443,686	5,070,527	14
India	1,161,523	1,511,157	30
Japan	10,286,218	10,511,518	2
South Korea	3,177,870	3,469,464	9
Africa	395,933	422,017	7

Figures in units
* All manufacturers.
** Official figures include Belgian GM assembly (original notes).
Source: adapted from Organization Internationale des Constructeurs d'Automobiles (OICA) (2005).

Table 4.4   Country share in percentage of automotive sales (units)

	2001	2005
US	33	28
China	4	10
Japan	11	10
Germany	7	6
UK	5	5
France	5	4
Italy	5	4
Other	30	33

Source: Sun (2006, p. 38).

more than 800 of which were Sino-foreign JVs, employing nearly 700,000 persons in total (*China Daily Online*, 2004b).

Investment in production capacity

Generally speaking, the investment level of the auto industry has been low, as was the case with the majority of industries in China. During the period of 1949–80, the total investment in the automotive industry in China was no more than 6 billion yuan. According to Xing (2002, p. 9), there have been four waves of investment in the Chinese auto industry. The first wave began in 1984 which included the establishment of Beijing Jeep Corp. Ltd and Shanghai Volkswagen. The second wave came in the early 1990s which saw the establishment of the First Automotive Works-Volkswagen Automotive Co Ltd and Dongfeng-Citroën Automobile Co Ltd. This was followed by the third wave in the late 1990s when GM, Honda Motor Co Ltd, Toyota Motor Corp and Ford secured their respective car assembly deals at Shanghai GM automobile Co Ltd, Guangzhou Honda Automobile Co Ltd, Tianjin Toyota Motor Co Ltd and Chang'an-Ford. The fourth wave began in 2001 which saw intensifying negotiations between foreign MNCs and Chinese automakers. Xing (2002) believes that the key difference between the fourth wave of investment and the first three waves is the emergence of significant domestic investment that came from private investors and regional governments in the fourth wave instead of from the central government.

The years of 2002 and 2003 saw another round of enthusiasm in plant investment in the auto industry in China, lured by the rapid growth of the auto market. Investment came from both the state-owned funding as well as private capital. By 2004, a total of 11.7 billion yuan of domestic private funds had been injected into the automotive industry in China (Fu, 2005). Many municipal governments were keen to develop auto production clusters in their cities. It was estimated that a total of 200 billion yuan were to be invested in the industry from the period between 2003 and 2007 and by the end of 2007, the industry would have a total production capacity of 11–12 million vehicles. A large proportion of this capacity would not be utilized due to over-capacity. In fact, it was estimated that about one-third of the production capacity would not be utilized due to over-capacity in the industry (Fu, 2005). It was predicted that the by 2007, only about 7 million vehicles would be produced and sold (C. S. Wang *et al.*, 2004). In 2005, only 55 per cent of the total automotive production capacity was utilized and 5.5 million vehicles were sold (*China Business*, 12 December 2005).

Problems and competitive pressure

The Chinese auto industry suffers from a number of problems that constrain its performance and international competitiveness. These problems include: the lack of economies of scale, inadequate R&D and technology level, lack of domestic brand-name products, lack of integration due to local protectionism and geographical dispersion and the threat of gradual removal of government protection to the industry.

Lack of economies of scale About 90 per cent of the total production of the Chinese auto industry is yielded by the Top 15 manufacturers (Tian, 2003). In fact, over 68.8 per cent of the sales in 2004 were achieved by the top five manufacturers (Fu, 2005). The majority of the auto manufacturers are operating on a small scale (Chen *et al.*, 2004; Qian, 2004; Zhao, 2004). This is in spite of the fact that the government has been trying to control the number of enterprises. In 1980, there were some 56 manufacturers, 192 modification factories and over 2100 component manufacturers (Rui and Tao, 2004). In 2002, there were a total of 2401 enterprises in the whole country, employing more than 1.38 million workers. One hundred and seventeen of the enterprises were whole-vehicle manufacturers, compared with 56 in 1980. Among the 117 whole-vehicle manufacturers, 22 were Sino-foreign JVs mainly engaged in car production (Qian, 2004). In 2002, 60 of the 117 whole-vehicle manufacturers (51 per cent) had a production capacity of less than 1000 vehicles. Only seven manufacturers produced more than 50,000 vehicles. In addition, these manufacturers produced 70 per cent of the components in-house, compared with about 30 per cent in international auto manufacturers (Chen *et al.*, 2004). The majority of auto manufacturers in China, of whatever form of ownership, have their own component manufacturing plants. For example, in 2003, Shanghai Auto Industry Corporation (SAIC) owned 43 component enterprises and *Tianjin* Auto Company had 52. Such an in-house 'full-house' arrangement heavily constrains the specialization of auto production and prevents them from gaining economies of scale (Chen *et al.*, 2004). In short, despite the Chinese government's intention since the late 1980s to rationalize the industry by limiting the entry of more auto firms and by growing the size of existing ones through M&As, for example, the actual number of auto firms has grown. A main reason for the growth of the relatively small-sized firms was that projects below 50 million yuan did not require the approval of the central government. Therefore, a large project may be carved into several smaller ones to get the approval from a local government (Eun and Lee, 2002), which often has a vested interest in these projects.[3]

Low R&D and technology level For 20 years, the development of the Chinese auto industry has been following a JV route which allows foreign firms to enter the domestic market in exchange for advanced technology and the know-how they bring into China. However, the industry is increasingly facing the risk of losing the market and not gaining any technology and know-how. Even where JV partners hold 50 per cent of the shares each, the foreign partner tends to control key business processes including patent, brand, technology, management, supply chain, distribution and after-sales services. By contrast, the Chinese partner appears to play a passive role in most of these aspects (H. L. Zhang, 2004).

On average, the R&D investment in the Chinese auto industry accounts for only '1.44 per cent of the total sales revenue, much lower than the world average level of 5 per cent' (Council for the Promotion of International Trade, 2002, p. 4). In addition, technical workers make up less than 10 per cent of the total workforce in the industry, with fewer than 20,000 working in the R&D field. The lack of technical expertise in R&D has been a major constraint in the development of the Chinese auto industry (Qian, 2004). Although the foreign partners of auto JVs brought into the Chinese auto industry much of the technological know-how which have reduced its technological gap significantly, these technologies were mainly imported from the foreign parent corporation instead of being developed in China. The overall technical competence of the Chinese auto industry thus remains very low. Low technological capacity and dependence on a foreign supply of technology confines the Chinese auto industry to producing lower-end and low value-added whole-vehicle products and component products (Zhao, 2004). In recent years, many Chinese car manufacturers have taken short cuts by adopting the CKD ('completely knocked down' or whole-car assembly) and SKD ('semi-knocked down' or partial assembly) production modes. Since the vehicle components are imported, this production mode increases the R&D gaps further and subjects the industry to a deepening dependence on foreign technology (Fu and Zhang, 2003). It forms a vicious circle of 'importation of technology – lagging behind – further importation' for the Chinese auto industry (H. L. Zhang, 2004, p. 173).

As a result, the majority of local original equipment manufacturers (OEMs) lack significant product development capability. For a long time, most of the new products launched in China were simply local versions, or even copies, of existing models from outside China. While the 'trading market for technology' policy has successfully attracted investment from almost all the top ten global auto giants, who have also committed to introducing the latest models into the market, the drawback of this policy is that it has discouraged local OEMs from developing new products on their own. While it has taken Chinese OEMs a relatively short period of time to learn how to assemble vehicles, it is going to take them much longer to fully develop their own products (Sun, 2006).

The same is true for auto parts development which requires a high level of technological competence. As discussed above, the investment in China's auto industry appears to focus on assembly, production capacity, whole-vehicle production and the core part of the industry, ignoring R&D and manufacturing of parts and other accessory components. In recent years, the supply of car components has been sourced from the global market in the new modular mode. Traditional Chinese automotive component manufacturers encounter difficulties in keep up with the speed of technological innovation and the introduction of new models due to their small scale in production capacity and low level of R&D. The combined deficiency in technology, system and production knowledge, and management skills and know-how inevitably lead to inferiority of product quality, a problem that discourages foreign auto firms from sourcing their supplies from Chinese auto parts manufacturers.

Lack of domestic brand-name products A lack of domestic brand-name product is another major barrier for Chinese car manufacturers seeking to establish themselves in the market (Li and Zhang, 2005; C. S. Wang *et al.*, 2004). This is a problem more prominent in the car market than in other types of vehicles. For example, 69 per cent of the brands of commercial vehicles were owned by

Chinese manufacturers whereas the rest were owned by foreign firms in 2005. By contrast, only 37 of the 107 brands of cars were developed by Chinese manufacturers, the remaining were owned by foreign firms (*China Business,* 23 November 2005). This is a problem that is related to the low level of R&D and technological competence. This problem prevents the Chinese auto firms from moving their products up the value chain to gain premium pricing. While a few Chinese car manufacturers are beginning to develop their brand products, they face strong competition from foreign firms and products from JVs. Chinese consumers have a long-held perception that foreign brands are better than domestic ones for a number of reasons. This view is unlikely to be changed in a short term until domestic products can demonstrate clear advantages (e.g. price, style, quality and after-sales service). In addition, Chinese brands will have a tough battle in establishing their brand prestige amongst the crowd of auto models already existing in the market. As Sun (2006, p. 38) noted, 'there are more brands or models in the Chinese auto market than in any other global market. Over 100 registered vehicle makers in China launched 104 new vehicle models in 2005 alone' (Sun, 2006, p. 38).

Dispersed geographical location To exacerbate the small-scale problem of the industry, auto factories in China are located far apart, often hundreds of kilometres from each other and are shackled by local administrative regulations and parochial protectionism. This geographical distance serves as a barrier to the restructuring of the industry through M&As to gain economies of scale. It also prevents them from developing collaborative relationships through knowledge sharing and through subcontracting between each other in order to become more specialized in auto manufacturing and thus gain economy of scale. For example, according to the statistics revealed by the Chinese Automotive Association, three-quarters of the 230 foreign and JV car component manufacturers operated within an agreement sum of between US$1–10 million (Fu and Zhang, 2003). In other words, car component manufacturing operates on a small scale and in a scattered mode with a low level of technical capacity.

Limited scale of JVs A related problem to the geographical dispersion and local government protectionism is that foreign firms have to establish JVs with different Chinese auto enterprises in different regions and have to adapt to their different customs and practice. This reduces the scope for synergies and dilutes the resources of the foreign partners. As a result, existing JVs in China are relatively small in scale, most of them with an annual production capacity of below 300,000 vehicles (Qian, 2004). They lack variety in their products, mainly producing one or two brands. Technological capacity is also relatively weak in these JVs, with most of them unable to develop whole new cars (Qian, 2004). JVs also encounter other problems in their business management. For example, the foreign partners felt that their Chinese partners over-interfere with the business, whereas the Chinese partners felt that their rightful interests have not been guaranteed. It was also reported that the Chinese partners are not keen to reinvest the profit into their JV businesses because they lack enthusiasm to sell more products that carry the foreign partner's brand name instead of the Chinese one. The forced marriage between foreign and Chinese auto firms by the Chinese authority was in part responsible for the failure of a number of JVs including Guangzhou Peugeot Automobile Co Ltd (*China Business*, 29 May 2005).

Removal of protection For a number of years, the Chinese government had set up barriers to protect the domestic Chinese auto firms against foreign competition. These include restricting the mode of entry of foreign auto giants (through JVs only) and high import taxes. As the industry grows and China becomes one of the largest auto manufacturing countries in the world, it becomes increasingly difficult for the Chinese government to maintain these barriers. They are being removed gradually in any case, in part as a result of trade negotiations between China and individual countries but more so because of China's accession to the WTO. For example, tariffs were to be reduced from the current 80–100 per cent level to 25 per cent by 2006, import quotas were to be phased-out by 2005, and prevailing technology transfer and local content requirements imposed upon foreign automakers were to be eliminated (Zhang, 2001a). More specifically, firms producing sedans and car components will be more affected by China's WTO accession than manufacturers of lightweight automobiles, buses and heavy-duty tractors. By contrast, agricultural vehicle and motorcycle manufacturers are most likely to benefit from greater access to foreign markets (Zhang, 2001a).[4]

In 2004, the National Development and Reform Commission launched a new policy for China's auto industry which replaced the old one introduced in 1994 by the State Council. Under the new policy, foreign investors will be allowed to control stakes of more than 50 per cent in automobile and motorcycle JVs with Chinese partners if their JVs are built in China's export processing zones and target the overseas market. For example, Japan's Honda Motors has a 65 per cent share in a JV with China's Dongfeng Motor Corp and the Guangzhou Automobile Group (*China Daily Online*, 2004c).

The removal of barriers to foreign products and foreign firms operating in China means the end of the era of high profit growth through heavy government protection for China's auto industry. Instead, it will be exposed to the full force of global competition (Zhang, 2001a). Domestic products will need to compete directly with foreign products at home while trying to develop its overseas markets. Productivity rate, technological innovation and management standard are becoming the most important factors that determine the competitive advantage of the industry and firms.

Strategic implications

Against the context of low technical competence and intensifying global competition on the one hand and a growing domestic market on the other, there are several strategic implications for the Chinese auto industry if it were to fulfil its pillar industry role.

Opportunities The Chinese auto industry is situated in a geographical area with a huge potential market both at home and overseas. Within China, it has a growing auto market, especially in vehicles for private use, as a result of the rising middle class population and the growth of private and individual economy. For example, only 284,900 vehicles (8.1 per cent of total vehicles) were privately owned in 1985, 19,300 of which were passenger vehicles. By the end of 2004, over 14.8 million vehicles (35.5 per cent of total vehicles) were privately owned, 10.7 million of which were passenger vehicles (see Table 4.1). This is an increase of more than 52 times in the total of private vehicles and an increase of 554 times in private passenger vehicles from 1985. In addition, the government's strategic investment in developing the western region of China means that more vehicles will be needed for construction, transportation and economy development (Rui and Tao, 2004). For the markets abroad, China has a large and lucrative car market at its own Asian doorstep. This is in spite of the fact that competition against Japan and Korea on quality, style and technology to satisfy the customers is a major challenge for the Chinese auto firms. Challenges to develop markets in other continents are likely to be stronger where differences in legislation and government policy, economic condition, social culture and consumers' expectation are even more prominent.

Development of domestic brand products As the Chinese car consumers are becoming increasingly knowledgeable about car products and sophisticated in their choice, car manufacturers in China cannot depend solely on foreign imports of models but need to develop new product models at home to satisfy the demands of their domestic consumers. As cars are often purchased as a luxury commodity, auto firms should prioritize the development of medium and premium range car products where the profit margin is more significant, in addition to developing niche products that can be tailored to the consumers' taste and to reflect the production strengths of individual manufacturers. Without its own brand-name products, the manufacturers will be technologically constrained by its foreign JV partner and pay a heavy proportion of its profit to foreign firms for supplying the technology (Li and Zhang, 2005).

Since the majority of Chinese car consumers are first time buyers and have little knowledge about vehicles, designing customer services, including advice tailored to these consumers, should be an integral part in the development of brand-name products. Needless to say, the development of domestic brand products requires not only higher levels of R&D and technological competence, but also the development of marketing and sales skills from the Chinese auto industry. As Hoffe *et al.* (2003, p. 1) pointed out,

> Chinese car buyers have strong emotional preferences, are extremely brand conscious, and place great importance on industry leadership. Therefore, automakers must develop and maintain strong emotional and intangible associations between their brands and the customer not only on the level of individual models but also on the corporate, or umbrella, brand level.

Nonetheless, domestic Chinese auto firms are beginning to develop new products that are aimed at the domestic market as part of their business strategy to create and satisfy customer demands. For example, 97 new products were introduced in 2002, including 29 products that were developed in-house (Zhao,

2004). In the first six months of 2003, more than a dozen new models were introduced to the market. As Gan (2003) noted, market competition was one of the major driving forces behind the energy efficiency of newly produced cars. Price reduction is another important part of the strategy to increase sales. In the first six months of 2003, more than 30 different models were on sale, with up to 10 per cent price reductions (Zhao, 2004).

Development of strategic alliance with MNCs In spite of all the weaknesses identified above, the competitiveness of the auto industry of China is gradually increasing, mainly with its rising technological competence. This is a major beneficial outcome of JVs with foreign auto manufacturers (Tian, 2003). It is estimated that more than 1000 technologies have been transferred to China from the foreign partners, including component and whole-car technology (Qian, 2004). This technology transfer is continuing at an increasing speed and technology level, through JVs in China and through outward investment of Chinese firms which the aim to develop their international presence.

Therefore, developing strategic alliances with foreign firms through JVs and international collaboration will help Chinese auto firms to acquire technological know-how and to develop markets. It will also enable the Chinese auto industry to integrate with and become part of the global auto industry. However, it must be noted that there is divergence between the business objectives of the foreign MNCs in China and that of the Chinese firms (see Box 4.2). JV in China forms only a small part of the MNC, the performance of the JV may not be vital to the overall strategy of the MNC as a whole, whereas forming JV may be a significant pathway for the development of the Chinese partner.

BOX 4.2

Market entry strategy of foreign auto firms in China

In terms of market entry strategy, automakers in China can roughly be divided into two groups. The first group includes Volkswagen, General Motors (GM), Toyota, Ford, Peugeot Citroën, Nissan, Daimler-Chrysler, and Suzuki. This group of enterprises is attempting to establish themselves in the Chinese market mostly through JVs with Chinese counterpart companies. Their strategy is to maximize their domestic market shares. By utilizing the skilled and cheap labour force in major Chinese automakers, these foreign companies can reduce production costs and maximize profits . . . . The strategy of the second group of automakers is to first export their products to China. This group includes primarily luxury automakers, such as Volvo, BMW, and Mercedes-Benz. These manufacturers are taking a cautious approach in their market entry strategy, but they remain open to large-scale engagement in the future.

Source: Gan (2003, pp. 541–2).

MNCs enter partnerships with Chinese firms in order to develop markets in China and therefore export is often not their primary concern. This is evidenced in the fact that existing auto JVs in China mostly lack export capacity. By contrast, developing an international market for their products should be a top strategic priority for Chinese auto firms to materialize their cost advantage and other potentials, including the utilization of their production over-capacity.

Acquiring brand-name international auto firms If forming strategic alliances with foreign auto firms took place mainly in China through JVs with MNCs in the 1980s and 1990s, then the 2000s is witnessing leading Chinese auto firms venturing abroad through acquisitions of collapsing Western auto plants. Their motives are to acquire advanced technology, brand names and markets (see Chapter 9 for a more detailed discussion of Chinese firms investing abroad). Case Study 4.1 is an example of the high-profile Chinese takeover of a British auto plant – MG Rover at Birmingham, UK.

CASE STUDY 4.1

Yuejin Motor Group Corporation (the Nanjing Automobile Group Corporation)

The history of Yuejin Motor Group Corporation (also known as Nanjing Automobile Group Corporation) dates back to 1947 when it was set up as a repair factory (previously named Nanjing Auto Works). Established in 1997, Yuejin Motor Group Corporation is one of the largest enterprise groups in China, possessing an annual production capacity of 180,000 vehicles of various models and owning three major vehicle production bases: Nanjing Yuejin, Nanjing Iveco and Nanjing Fiat. The products cover more than 400 types of models, including passenger cars, light-duty trucks, light-duty buses, cross-country vehicles, small-sized passenger/cargo transportation vehicles, special-purpose vehicles as well as various types of chasses and so on.

Yuejin Motor Group has been engaged mainly in exploring the overseas markets of automobiles and parts and components. The products are exported to many countries and regions such as Argentina, South Africa, Sudan, Ivory Coast, Namibia, Djibouti, Tanzania, Cyprus, Togo, Italy, Spain and so on. In addition, it has obtained experience in establishing abroad SKD/CKD assembly plants of trucks and minibuses. Its brand series include: YUEJIN Brand series of light-duty trucks, NANJING-IVECO series of light-duty trucks and passenger transportation vehicles, as well as NANYA-FIAT series of small-sized passenger transportation vehicles.

Yuejin Motor Group Corporation has established two Sino-foreign JV bases for manufacturing vehicles and ten Sino-foreign JVs in the field of automotive parts and components. Its international JV partners include reputable auto firms from Italy, the United States, France and Japan. The total investment of these JVs amounts to approximately US$930 million. In addition, Yuejin Motor Group Corporation has collaboration with a number of well-known international companies and institutions in the field of technology, personnel training and worldwide procurement.

Yuejin Motor Group Corporation bought the GM brand and other assets for US$97 million in 2005 after the collapse of the UK-based MG Rover Group Ltd. SAIC Motor, a General Motors Corporation ad Volkswagen AG partner, bought the design rights for two MG Rover models and for K-series engines for US$130 million. Yuejin Motor Group Corporation is now building MG TF roadster convertibles at a former MG factory in the United Kingdom. It also plans to open an R&D centre there. The Corporation believes that MG's established brand worldwide will help to promote its image and attract customers. The acquisition of the MG brand is the Corporation's attempt to use the iconic British brand as a platform for its global expansion. It plans to invest US$2 billion in the brand, including opening plants in the United Kingdom and the United States. Meanwhile, the new MG plant in Nanjing, built in under a year and employing 4500 workers, has an annual capacity of 200,000 cars, 250,000 engines and 100,000 gearboxes. It has internal roads called Birmingham Avenue and England Avenue, reflecting MG's UK roots. The huge MG logo outside the new factory is a clear evidence of how much the Chinese auto firm values the historic British brand as an asset.

Sources: compiled from *http://www.nanqi.com.cn*; Shen (10 June 2007).

Building industry cluster As discussed earlier, the Chinese auto industry is small in scale and lacks specialization. It is important for the industry to undergo restructuring and consolidation in order to develop an industry cluster that includes R&D, manufacturing, marketing and sales, maintenance, financial services, environment protection, energy and transport system (Li and Yang, 2005). In other words, Chinese auto firms should strengthen their inter-region collaboration to complement and develop each others' competitive advantage instead of competing with each in full range (Li and Yang, 2005) and on small scale. This will enable the industry to take better advantage of its domestic resources and market potential. In addition, the auto industrial-cluster base should be set up close to universities and colleges to provide R&D support and training bases. The level of collaboration between industry and research institutions and universities in China is generally low. It is equally as important for the industry to develop super-large core enterprises as the base for mass production to gain economies of scale and to develop capacities that hinge on varieties and frequent launch of new product models. This is because continuous product and production innovations and keeping cost and price down are the twin key factors in the competitiveness of car manufacturing firms, as they are in many other industries. However, these factors need to be supported by another crucial factor – human capital.

Human resource implications

Perhaps not surprisingly, the overall quality of human resources in the auto industry is relatively low. On the one hand, it is difficult for the industry to attract talent. On the other hand, many factories face the need to downsize due to automation in production and skill obsolete (H. L. Zhang, 2004). It is unclear exactly how many auto workers have lost their job as a result of enterprise downsizing and plant closure. While I have not been able to obtain up-to-date statistics on how many people are employed in the industry as a whole, partial statistics reveals that some 28 million workers were employed in the auto industry in 1998, making up 13.5 per cent of the total urban employed workers (Rui and Tao, 2004). More broadly, about a quarter of China's workers work in the manufacturing sector, which is by far the largest employing sector in the industrial economy (see Table 2.2). However, the educational level of the workforce in the manufacturing sector is relatively low (see Table 2.16) and the ratio of scientific and technical personnel to staff and workers in the sector was only 14.6 per cent, which is amongst the lowest compared with other industrial sectors (see Table 2.17). In addition, wage levels in this sector are relatively low compared with other sectors (see Table 4.5). This makes the auto industry, especially the domestic firms, uncompetitive in attracting talent.

According to Li (2004), there is a skill shortage of some 800,000 people in the auto industry – a problem shared by most industries nationwide. Over a quarter of those who are responsible for technical management in the automotive maintenance businesses have only lower senior school education qualifications or below. The percentage for the front line workers is even higher at 38.5 per cent. Only 9.3 per cent of the people have ever received management training, only 11.7 per cent have ever received technical training on the basics of maintenance. Given the rapid expansion of car use in China and the consequent need for the expansion of maintenance services, this represents a large skill gap and training need for the industry.

In the auto maintenance business, the majority of smaller maintenance garages adopt an informal apprentice system in which the master imparts basic skills and knowledge to the apprentice. However, these small operations are unable to deal with technical problems beyond the ordinary (*China Business,* 10 August 2005). The informal apprentice training system also carries its inherent disadvantages of being *ad hoc,* unsystematic and resource constraints. The technical colleges in China are not much better in providing systematic training and up-to-date knowledge to auto trainees due to resource constraints and other related problems (see Chapter 2).[5]

The aggregate pattern of skill shortage in the auto industry is that there is a worsening shortage of senior professional and technical staff in the fields of R&D, sales and marketing, maintenance, and inspection of second-hand vehicles. There is also a growing shortage of maintenance components managers and maintenance garage managers. In addition, there will be an increasing demand for talent who are multi-skilled or possessing knowledge in a number of fields, for example, technical as well as language skills, sales as well as public relations management and financial knowledge (*China Business,* 10 August 2005).

A related problem of skill shortage is the retention of skilled staff. It was reported that companies in the auto industry are poaching from each other by offering competitive salary packages and paying off any penalty clauses in the employment contracts that were supposed to shackle the poached by their

Table 4.5 Annual average wage of staff and workers by sector
(2003–5)

Sector	2003	2005
Total	14,040	18,364
Farming, forestry, animal husbandry and fishery	6,969	8,309
Mining	13,682	20,626
Manufacturing	12,496	15,757
Electricity, gas and water production and supply	18,752	25,073
Construction	11,478	14,338
Transport, storage, post and telecommunication services	15,973	21,352
Information Transmission, computer service and software	32,244	40,558
Telecommunications and other information transmission services	30,481	36,941
Computer services	41,722	52,637
Software	36,873	52,784
Wholesale and retail trade	10,939	15,241
Wholesale trade	12,295	17,953
Retail trade	9,277	12,132
Hotels and restaurants	11,083	13,857
Finance and insurance	22,457	32,228
Real estate	17,182	20,581
Leasing and business services	16,501	20,992
Scientific research, technical services and geological prospecting	20,636	27,434
Management of water conservancy, environment and public facilities	12,095	14,753
Services to households and other services	12,900	16,642
Education	14,399	18,470
Health care, social securities and social welfare	16,352	21,048
Culture, sports and entertainment	17,268	22,885
Public management and social organization	15,533	20,505

Figures in yuan
Sources: compiled from *China Statistical Yearbook* (2004, p. 162) and (2006, pp. 161–3).

previous employer (Courland Automotive Practice, 2004). While those with university degree qualifications and work experience are the most attractive recruitment targets, new graduates specializing in auto subjects are also popular with employers (*China Business*, 10 August 2005). State-owned firms are in a disadvantaged position in the war for talent. For example, a research institute in Beijing had over 300 technical staff but has been losing more than 15 per cent of them each year in recent years. The institute now has fewer than 50 employees in total. Many Chinese-owned auto enterprises are losing their most senior engineers to their foreign competitors who offer more promising employment prospects. Those who remain are seeking opportunities elsewhere (*China Business*, 10 August 2005). It is believed that the rigid and slow career progression system, the low technological level of state-owned firms and the lack of training opportunities are the main causes for talent recruitment and retention problem. The majority of graduates in auto subjects are unwilling to choose SOEs as their employer. Many graduates from top ranking universities choose to go abroad to further their education or work in other industries. While thousands of auto students are being trained each year, the industry benefits from having only a small proportion of them (*China Business*, 10 August 2005). Under these circumstances, providing skill training to the existing workforce is a major mechanism in increasing skill level and productivity of the auto workforce.

China's domestic manufacturers also suffer from poor management. Senior managers in SOEs are normally appointed by higher-level authorities. These managers thus tend to be more preoccupied with their political performance than the financial performance of their enterprises (Xing, 2002). A patronage system for recruitment and promotion is adopted by the Chinese partners in Sino-foreign auto JVs in which the Chinese partners tend to have more influence in personnel decisions (Thun, 2006).

For auto products, apart from the manufacturing workforce, the quality of marketing and sales people needs to be enhanced. For example, according to a survey conducted by Li and Yang (2005), only 10 per cent of the sales people possessed educational qualifications of university diploma or above in a major auto sales market in Guangzhou – Baiyun Auto Sales Market, 40 per cent had senior middle school qualifications, whereas the remaining 50 per cent only had lower middle school qualifications or below. To worsen the situation, the sales skills of the sales workforce tend to be low. This is a problem that needs to be addressed urgently but is one that will take a long time to overcome, given the low starting point. As Hoffe *et al.* (2003, p. 15) pointed out,

> Automakers should build their frontline sales capabilities. Some 80 per cent of Chinese buyers are in the market for the first time, and they shop around to a much greater extent than buyers in more mature car markets. Salespeople who educate consumers to make them feel comfortable with their unfamiliar purchase are more likely to build strong relationship and to promote repeat purchases.

Summary

The Chinese auto industry has grown significantly in the last two decades, stimulated by both government policies and market demand. Foreign auto giants entered the Chinese market through JVs in the 1980s, as it was the only mode of entry due to policy restriction. These foreign firms injected the much needed capital, technology and management know-how into the industry. Despite some significant developments, the auto industry of China is a large but not strong industry. It was under developed for the first 35 years under the state planned economy system. As one of the largest auto producer countries in the world, its R&D and technological capabilities are disproportionately lower than its production capacity. Whilst China has a large potential market for cars, its market expansion is heavily constrained by its associated problems, such as the rising cost of raw material, the rising price of fuel, environment pollution and road congestion. Confounded by all these problems, the Chinese auto industry has yet to become a formidable competitor in the global auto market.

In the twenty-first century, the Chinese auto industry has entered a new operating environment in which foreign auto firms are strengthening their competitive position in China not only in the manufacturing of brand-name vehicles and parts, but also in their marketing and sales, services and auto finance businesses. By contrast, indigenous auto firms have to compete in an adversarial condition in which they not only lack brand products and other organizational resources, but are also disadvantaged with weaker technology. The central government's desire to grow national champion auto firms is circumvented by technical barriers as well as inter-provincial rivalry. Increasing the level of R&D investment, developing strategic alliances and consolidation through M&As are some of the strategies that can be adopted by domestic firms to upscale themselves in both size and technological level. This will collectively lead to the enhancement of efficiency, both in energy and environmental terms, technological independence and the overall competitiveness of the industry. These strategies need to be supported by an effective product and marketing strategy, a distinctive brand position and an integrated distribution network. Finally, entering into the global market appears an inevitable developmental step in order to seek greater market beyond China. Some firms are beginning to venture forth, although limited success has been reported so far (see Chapter 9 for generic barriers to Chinese MNCs abroad).

Recommended readings

J. Child, *Management in China during the Age of Reform* (Cambridge: Cambridge University Press, 1994).

L. Gan, 'Globalisation of the Automobile Industry in China: Dynamics and Barriers in Greening of the Road Transportation', *Energy Policy*, 31 (2003): 537–51.

E. Thun, *Changing Lanes in China: Foreign Direct Investment, Local Governments, and Auto Sector Development* (Cambridge: Cambridge University Press, 2006).

M. Warner, *China's Managerial Revolution* (London: Frank Cass, 1999).

CHAPTER 5

Pharmaceutical Industry

Introduction

Like the automotive industry, the pharmaceutical industry in China is regarded as one of the 'strategic industries' by the Chinese government. Its goal is to turn the industry into 'one of the world's pharmaceutical giants' by the middle of the twenty-first century (Yeung, 2002). The pharmaceutical industry includes product development, manufacturing and commercial activities. This chapter covers all three types of activities because many of the enterprises are corporations or groups that are engaged in all aspects of product development, manufacturing and sales activities. This chapter contains six major sections. The first one outlines the size of the industry and its historical development. The second section examines the important role of the Chinese government in regulating and promoting the industry. This is followed by a brief review of the situation of foreign pharmaceutical firms in China and the likely impact of China's accession to the WTO to all pharmaceutical firms in China. The fourth section investigates problems facing the domestic medical firms that impede their growth. This is followed by a review of key elements of the business strategy adopted by leading Chinese firms. The final main section outlines the HR implications for the industry.

Background of the industry

China's pharmaceutical industry is a long-established one that was largely state-owned and state-controlled during the period of state planned economy. In the last 20 years, China's pharmaceutical market has become one of the fastest-growing pharmaceutical markets in the world that is characterized by increasing speed in production innovation and better-than-expected import and export situations. Between 1980 and 1995, the total output value of the pharmaceutical industry had tripled. In 1998, the industry had a total output value of 163 billion yuan and total commercial sales revenue of 108 billion yuan (P. Jin *et al.*, 2003).

More specifically, the industry has entered a period of rapid growth since the mid-1990s, with an average annual industrial output growth rate of 16.6

per cent (Fan and Cui, 2005). In particular, 2003 saw a huge profit rise of 25.85 per cent in the industry due to the effect of the epidemic disease SARS. However, profit levels dropped to 9.25 per cent in 2004 as the SARS effect disappeared and as a result of a series of policies enforced by the government, including the restriction of the sales of antibiotics, price reduction of drugs and GMP and GSP assurance certifications (see further discussion below) (Fan and Cui, 2005).

By the early 2000s, China had more than 6700 pharmaceutical manufacturing enterprises, over 10,000 wholesale enterprises, and over 120,000 retail enterprises in the medical industry (Rui and Tao, 2004). In particular, biological medical products are the key area for growth. It has received policy support from the government and is a fast growing branch of the industry with strong market potentials. The development of biological medical products did not start in earnest until the mid-1980s. From the late 1980s to the 1990s, the annual growth in the output of biological medicines has been maintained at about 18 per cent. Since the mid-1990s, more than 300 biological R&D companies have been established, over 200 modern biological medical enterprises have been founded and over 50 biological engineering technology development enterprises have emerged. By the early 2000s, there were over 1000 companies engaged in the R&D of biological projects, employing more than 10,000 R&D personnel (Rui and Tao, 2004). However, the development of biological medical products in China has mainly taken the form of imitation and adaptation. In addition, generic pharmaceuticals are one of the largest and fastest-growing segments in the industry and China has become increasingly prominent in the production and sales of bulk pharmaceutical chemicals in the last decade (Rajan, 1998).

In 2004, China's pharmaceutical market was ranked in the top ten worldwide. In addition to 6000 domestic pharmaceutical manufacturers (controlling roughly 70 per cent of the market by value), there were around 1700 Sino-foreign JVs, including most of the world's leading players. The value of their investment was around US$2 billion, according to IMS Health (cited in *Scrip Magazine*, 2004). According to a study in February 2003 conducted by the International Pharmaceutical Industry Association (IFPMA), the Chinese pharmaceutical market profile (excluding traditional Chinese medicine) was dominated by generic drugs, which accounted for 62 per cent of market share in 2000. Second in line were over-the-counter (OTC) products at 15 per cent, followed by branded generics at 14 per cent and patented drugs at 9 per cent. This was expected to change significantly, with the market share of patented drugs rising to 21 per cent, OTC drugs to 23 per cent, branded generics to 19 per cent and generics falling to 37 per cent by 2010. Over this period, the market share of both OTC and patented drugs will grow at double digit compound annual growth rates. It is believed that multinational pharmaceutical companies will be the main beneficiaries of this trend and experience most of the growth potential (cited in *Scrip Magazine*, 2004).

Several reasons contribute to the relatively fast growth of the medical industry. One is that health care expenditure by the government has been on the increase since 1995 (see Table 5.1). Another reason is that China has a large

Table 5.1 Expenditure on public health

Item	1995	1998	2000	2002	2003	2004
Total expenditure for public health (100 million yuan)	2,257.8	3,776.5	4,586.6	5,790.0	6,584.1	7,590.3
Government budgetary expenditure	383.1	587.2	709.5	908.5	1,116.9	1,293.6
Social expenditure	739.7	1,006.0	1,171.9	1,539.4	1,788.5	2,225.4
Resident individual expenditure	1,135.0	2,183.3	2,705.2	3,342.1	3,678.7	4,071.4

Notes: The data in this table are calculated at current prices. The data in this table are estimated (original notes).
Sources: adapted from *China Statistical Yearbook* (2002, p. 784) and (2006, p. 882).

and ageing population. According to the 2000 Census, 7 per cent of the population was over 65 years of age (cited in J. Li, 2003). Still another reason is that people are developing a stronger health care ideology as their earning increases and so is the level of wealth-related diseases such as diabetes. Consumers are also more willing to spend on health-related products that are targeted at a general improvement of health and prevention of illnesses.

Despite the rapid growth of the industry in the last two decades, the Chinese pharmaceutical industry is still very small by international standards. For example, in 2000, the total sales revenue of the 6000 or so domestic pharmaceutical enterprises in China was around 200 billion yuan – only a very small proportion of the total sales revenue of US$360 billion of the world (Wang *et al.*, 2003).

The role of the government

As well as being a major employer in the industry, the Chinese government plays an important role in regulating the industry and in promoting the growth of a small number of leading firms. Its role as an employer is perhaps less successful than its roles as a regulator and an economic manager. As Yeung (2002, p. 476) noted,

> Even in the late 1990s, China's large, old-established state plants remained quite tightly controlled by the government. These plants mainly produce relatively capital-intensive upstream intermediate pharmaceuticals, especially off-patent antibiotics, which are then processed by smaller factories, as well as producing generic, low-margin final products, for example, penicillin and aspirin. Many of these were on a downward spiral, with obsolete equipment, poor research facilities and a high debt-asset ratio.

In recent years, a number of laws and regulations have been promulgated by the Chinese government to regulate the industry. For example, the Pharmaceutical Administration Law of China was issued and came into effect in 2001 (Li, 2002).[1] Other regulations include: 'Drug Management Law' and 'Implementation Procedures for the Drug Management Law of China'. These regulations provide detailed instructions on a wide range of aspects of the industry, including the regulation of the drug market and enterprise and industrial development. In addition, the new 'Drug Science and Technology Policy' (2002) specifies the government's investment of 3 billion yuan in the next five years to support R&D. Priorities to receive the funding include the development of chemical drugs, innovations in Chinese medicines and biological drug manufacturing technology. Under the support of the national 863 Programme funded by the government (see Chapter 2), biological R&D in China received a major boost, particularly after the SARS epidemic. The introduction of these regulations is in line with the relatively heavily regulated nature of the pharmaceutical industry in the world. As Weiss and Forrester (2004, p. 17) noted, 'Pharmaceutical regulations, in China and elsewhere, affected nearly every aspect of drug manufacturing from the design and construction of manufacturing facilities to the development of procedures and the training of operations personnel performing them'.

In addition, the Chinese government has tight control over drug prices, with the basic prices of core drugs and medical services determined at central government level (*Scrip Magazine*, 2004). Since 1997, the Chinese government has enforced more than ten rounds of price reductions of medicines in order to reduce the profit level of the industry and make health care more affordable to the masses. Since 2005, over 2400 prescription drugs have been listed with regulated prices. Another 22 retail drugs had their prices reduced by 40–63 per cent, slashing profit by an estimated 4 billion yuan (Fan and Cui, 2005). Nevertheless, this is only a fraction of all the drugs that are produced in China. The vast majority of drug prices are still regulated by the market. The restriction of drug prices is part of the government's strategy to combat the epidemics of fake drugs in the market, which 'can account for 40 per cent in some regions. And, according to the Association for Asian Research, 192,000 Chinese died of fake drugs in 2001 alone' (cited in De Meyer and Garg, 2005, p. 99).

It must be noted that the Chinese government has a long-held interest in depressing drug prices because it foots a large proportion of the medical bill for its urban workers as part of the social welfare provision. The restriction of drugs price is also a remedial action in response to what many believe to be the unsuccessful reform of the medical insurance system in the last two decades, which has led to the soaring cost of health care and rendered an increasing proportion of the population unable to afford basic health care. In 1999, the State Council of China stated, as its overriding objective in the health care system reform, 'to provide relatively high-quality medical services with relatively low cost to satisfy the basic health care needs of the masses' (*China Business*, 20 September 2004). However, success remains limited so far and containing the drug prices is one way to reduce the medical bill borne by the state on the one hand and to make medical care more accessible to those who fall outside the medical insurance system on the other. In any case, it is believed that the Chinese pharmaceutical market is a mature one and that price reduction will continue to be a key feature in the competition in the foreseeable future (Fan and Cui, 2005).

According to the tenth five-year plan (2001–5) for the pharmaceutical industry, China was to grow 5–10 super-large pharmaceutical distribution corporation groups operating at national level with annual sales revenue in excess of 5 billion yuan. This was in addition to the growth of another 40 groups operating at the regional level with annual sales revenue of around 2 billion yuan. It was intended that these large and super-large groups will cover 70 per cent of the markets in the country. Meanwhile, ten retail chains that are internationally well-known were to be grown with each consisting of more than 1000 shops or retail points (W. Wang *et al.*, 2004).

To encourage the growth of large domestic companies that can compete internationally, the government has been forcing the pharmaceutical industry to consolidate through closures or M&As. In 2001, over 1000 pharmaceutical firms were displaced. Another 1000 were displaced in 2002. By the end of 2002, there were 4296 pharmaceutical firms, 929 of them were state-owned (P. Jin *et al.*, 2003). The State Food and Drug Administration (SFDA) planned to further reduce the number of manufacturers to around 2000 over a three-year period from 2004. This is to be achieved 'by attrition (poor performers will either be shut down or sold) and by requiring the remaining firms to meet the new Good Manufacturing Practices (GMP) standards' (Weiss and Forrester, 2004, p. 17). In fact, SFDA required all drug manufacturers in China, foreign or domestic owned, 'to obtain GMP certificates from SFDA by the end of June 2004 to be licensed to sell their drug products in China' (Weiss and Forrester, 2004, p. 17). By the end of 2004, 3731 of the 5071 drug manufacturing enterprises had obtained GMP certification, the remaining 1340 that had not obtained the certification were in stoppage (Fan and Cui, 2005). Drug manufacturers 'must also adopt or acquire technology standards and a knowledge base to achieve full GMP compliance' (Weiss and Forrester, 2004, p. 17). While foreign firms and Sino-foreign JVs have already possessed these and even higher standards, domestic firms had to invest heavily to import these technological standards (Weiss and Forrester, 2004).

Pressure to change for domestic medical firms in order to survive and, for some, to thrive also come from the competition of foreign firms in China as well as the impact of China's accession to the WTO.

Foreign pharmaceutical firms in China and implications of WTO

The pharmaceutical industry is one of the pioneer industries that were opened up to foreign investors in China. This has attracted a large amount of foreign investment. Foreign pharmaceutical companies see several avenues of opportunity in China (Bulcke *et al.*, 1999; Jarvis, 2005):

■ A market for their products – China is the fastest-growing pharmaceutical market globally;

■ A centre for low-cost manufacturing; and increasingly,

■ A destination for cheaper and less regulated clinical trials.

Pharmaceutical MNC giants also possess firm-specific advantages for entering and expanding in the Chinese market, including management know-how, financial resources and technological capability (Bulcke *et al.*, 1999).[2] It was reported that the Japanese MNC Otsuka was the first pharmaceutical JV established in China in 1980 (Bulcke *et al.*, 1999). By the end of 1999, there were over 1800 JVs, representing a total investment of US$1.5 billion. In fact, about 40 per cent of Chinese pharmaceutical companies have JV projects with foreign companies (Zhang, 2001b). By the early 2004, the world's Top 20 pharmaceutical MNCs had either JVs or wholly owned firms in China (see Box 5.1for example). Among the 500 largest foreign firms in China, 14 were pharmaceutical firms. Among the 50 best-selling drugs in China, 40 were made by foreign firms (*China Business*, 21 June 2004). JVs are also being piloted in the commercial wing of the industry. These new forms of investment brought to the industry new products, new technology and equipment, new operational style and new management standards and philosophy (J. Li, 2003; Yeung, 2002).

BOX 5.1

AstraZeneca China

AstraZeneca has built a business presence across China including headquarters in Shanghai, and branch offices in 15 cities across the country, a world-class manufacturing facility in Wuxi (launched in 2001) and a Clinical Research Unit in Shanghai (launched in 2002). AstraZeneca China has over 1200 employees involved in the manufacture, sales, marketing and clinical research of new products. AstraZeneca is committed to China for the long term and already manufactures over 80 per cent of the products it sells within China.

AstraZeneca's mission is to develop, supply and market innovative drugs of high quality within its prioritized therapeutic areas in China. It is determined to conduct its business responsibly, strengthen its long-term commitment to China and become a partner of choice.

Source: AstraZeneca company website: http://en.astrazeneca.com.cn, accessed on 18 April 2005.

It must be noted, however, that the large presence of foreign JVs is a result of strict restrictions on direct imports of foreign drugs into China. Imports of drugs are restricted by price considerations, strict import regulations and complex licensing procedures. Production by foreign pharmaceutical firms is only encouraged when domestic manufacturers are unable to produce the products, unable to achieve the necessary standard or unable to meet the demands (Zhang, 2001b). Promotional expenditure of foreign firms is also constrained by the Chinese government (*Scrip Magazine*, 2004). However, these restrictions are being reduced gradually and as a consequence of China's accession to the WTO (see Box 5.2).

BOX 5.2

The implications of China's WTO accession for its pharmaceutical industry

According to the WTO accord signed in November 2001, the major areas of liberalization relating to the Chinese pharmaceutical industry are as follows.

■ Import tariffs will be reduced by about 60 per cent, from an average of 9.6 per cent to 4.2 per cent, before 1 January 2003.

■ Chinese quotas and other quantitative restrictions will grow from the current trade level at 15 per cent per annum and are to be phased out no later than 2005. China will provide comprehensive trading (import and export) and distribution (wholesale, retailing, transportation and so on, including the provision of services and the goods made in China) rights to foreign-financed firms for the first time. Trading and distribution rights will be phased-in progressively over three years.

■ China will eliminate and cease enforcing contractual requirements on trade and foreign exchange balancing and local contents upon the WTO accession.

■ China will only impose and enforce laws or other provisions relating to the transfer of technology or other know-how, if they are in accordance with the WTO agreements on the protection of IPR and trade-related investment measures.

■ China will ensure that the sales and purchase of SOEs and state-invested enterprises (SIEs) are based solely on commercial considerations, such as price, quality and marketability, rather than 'government procurement'. Moreover, the SOEs and SIEs are under the WTO Agreement on Subsidies and Countervailing Measures, e.g. no export subsidies.

■ The United States will be allowed to keep its anti-dumping methodology (regarding China as a non-market economy) for 15 years after the WTO accession.

Source: Yeung (2002, pp. 481–2).

As Zhang (2001b) noted, foreign pharmaceutical firms are likely to benefit from China's WTO accession in four major ways. First, they will be able to acquire an even larger share of the Chinese market than they already have (China's State Drug Administration estimated that foreign companies will control 70 per cent of the Chinese pharmaceutical market after WTO accession). Second, they may be able to gain total control over their distribution networks instead of having to rely on the complex and costly Chinese supply network. Third, freer competition will give them a better chance of having their products included on China's provincial and municipal lists of drugs that are subject to state reimbursement. Fourth, their IPR will be better protected. In the same vein, Bulcke *et al.* (1999, p. 372) found that an increasing number of MNCs have established majority or wholly owned subsidiaries not only 'to achieve a higher return on their investment, but also to provide better technological protection, stronger management control and more intensive intra-firm linkages'.

Barriers to growth of Chinese firms

With each of the world's Top 20 pharmaceutical firms having already set up JVs in China and the impact of the WTO agreements, Chinese pharmaceutical companies not only need to compete with foreign firms in the global market, but also need to compete with MNCs in China. However, the performance of the Chinese drugs firms is constrained by several sets of inter-related problems.

Small firm size and low level of specialization A first set of problems is the industry's small firm size and low level of concentration (J. Li, 2003; Qin, 2004; Wang *et al.*, 2003). Compared with international pharmaceutical firms, the Chinese pharmaceutical firms are very small in size. For example, Guangzhou Pharmaceutical Co Ltd – one of the largest Chinese stock-listed pharmaceutical firms that had the highest sales revenue – only had sales revenue of US$0.9 billion in the year 2003, compared with US$52 billion from Merck (US), US$35 billion from Pfizer (US), and US$32 billion from GalxoSmithKline (UK) (Qin, 2004). According to *Business China*, China's 5000 or so domestic firms made up 70 per cent of the market, while the top ten firms about 20 per cent. By contrast, the top ten pharmaceutical giants in most developed countries control half of the market (cited in Weiss and Forrester, 2004). The Chinese pharmaceutical companies are also highly integrated operations that typically perform all functions from production and chemical process development, bulk active and formulation manufacturing to sales (Rajan, 1998).

Similar to drugs manufacturing, the commercial side of the pharmaceutical industry is characterized by small wholesale enterprises. By 2003, there were nearly 17,000 wholesale pharmaceutical enterprises – many of them state-owned or controlled. Only ten of them had sales revenue of over 1 billion yuan. There were 120,000 retail pharmaceutical enterprises, with the largest retail chain taking in no more than 0.5 billion yuan sales revenue (Wang *et al.*, 2004). A major difference between China's medical retailing market and that in the developed countries is that hospitals in China, most of them state-owned, are the major medicine retailers, supplying about 85 per cent of the medicines needed annually, whereas the market share for drug stores is squeezed to only 15 per cent in China (*Business Week*, 5 January 2005). There were 60,864 hospitals and health centres, 208,794 clinics, 1588 centres for disease control and prevention, 2998 maternity and child care hospitals and centres in China in 2005, in addition to medical universities and colleges. Whilst there have been talks in recent year of separating medical treatment and medicine supply as part of the nationwide health care reform, that is, separating pharmacies from the hospitals, this initiative meets with resistance from the hospitals, as drugs sales form a significant part of their revenue. Doctors also have their vested interest – some of them take commission privately from drugs suppliers to prescribe certain types of drugs.

On the retail drug stores side, again, most of them are small in business scale. There are some chain stores, but none of them really has a nationwide presence – largely a result of regional/local governments' protectionism (*Business Week*, 5 January 2005). Medical products retail chains as an operation mode started to develop in 1995. However, its pace was relatively slow until 2000. In order to combat foreign competition anticipated as a result of China's accession to the WTO, the Chinese medication administration authority decided in 2000 to encourage enterprises to grow bigger and stronger through M&As and by removing regional protection barriers. It was decided that the medical products retail market should be opened up internally first before it was opened to foreign firms in 2003. The first 41 medicine retail chain store enterprises were approved to operate across regions. This has sped up the development of the chain stores business mode in the medical products retail industry. For example, in 1999, there were about 110,000 retail medical products stores and over 200 chain stores enterprises with a total of 4600 chain stores in China. By 2001, there were 125,000 retail medical products stores, 503 chain store enterprises with a total of 18,527 chain stores, making up nearly 15 per cent of the total retail medical products shops in the country (Tian, 2003). The chain stores operation mode has the advantage of economies of scale both in product purchase prices and in management costs. Its operating cost is therefore generally lower than stand-alone shops, at least in principle. It was estimated that the profit rate of chain store enterprises is on average 3 per cent higher than that of the stand-alone shops (Tian, 2003).

However, the expansion of the chain stores operation mode is not without problems. A main barrier is local protectionism where local authority may be unwilling to approve applications for setting up chain stores by enterprises from other regions because the tax revenue will go to the home region. Delaying tactics are often deployed (also see Chapter 8). Another problem in opening cross-regional chain stores is that Chinese herbal medicine products often carry strong local characteristics. Local populations may suffer illnesses that are specific to the geographical area. People's dietary habits and healthcare mindsets may be strongly influenced by local cultural preferences. All these characteristics present further challenges to retail enterprises that originated in other localities and have established a local brand name. For example, the differences in living habits and consumption patterns between residents in the northern and southern parts of China were clearly felt by Beijing Tongrentang (see further details later) when the corporation spread its retail wing down south (Tian, 2003). These geographical and cultural differences have serious implications for the types of medical products medical firms can promote and innovate to match the demands in different regions if they are to grow into a national corporation. Equally, foreign drug firms may need to adapt their products to suit the Chinese characteristics.

Low technology level and lack of new products A second set of problems relates to the industry's low production technology, lack of product variety, lack of new products and brand-name products (Buo, 2004; J. Li, 2003; Qin, 2004; Wang *et al.*, 2003). The majority of the pharmaceutical manufacturing enterprises in China lack innovative capacity. In 2005, there were over 4000 manufacturers engaged in the mass production of low value-added products. Many of them were only operating at 40–50 per cent of their full production capacity due to the over-supply of products in the market (Fan and Cui, 2005). The low-value-added products they produce are highly polluting and resource consuming chemical products that are used as the raw material for pharmaceutical products. A relatively high proportion of these products are for export – China is the second-largest chemical product manufacturing country in the world after the United States (J. Li, 2003).

It was estimated that the total investment in the pharmaceutical industry to obtain GMP accreditation was about 150 billion yuan, about 30–40 per cent of which came from bank loans. About 20 billion yuan would become bad debts due to the over-capacity of pharmaceutical manufacturing plants. Some scholars in China believe that the enforcement of GMP has resulted in the misuse of valuable funds to expand, albeit at a high-technological level, the manufacturing capacity which was the last thing that the pharmaceutical industry needed. While the enforcement of GMP has rendered the closure of 800 pharmaceutical enterprises, it has not altered the disorderly and small-sized and low-tech state of affair of the industry (*China Business*, 9 May 2005). Until 2000, the vast majority of all new drugs approved by the authority in China were imitations (see Table 5.2).

Low level of R&D and inadequate IPR protection A third set of problems relates to the industry's low R&D capacity and inadequate protection of IPR (Grace, 2004; J. Li, 2003; Qin, 2004). According to the International Intellectual Property Alliance, in 2003, an estimated total of around US$1.9 billion

Table 5.2 New drugs approved in China

Year	Total number of new drugs	Of total, new drugs that were imitations
1990	783	763
1991–5	1,546	1,355
2000	989	966
2002	2,451	1,345

Source: Chinese State Food and Drugs Administration (SFDA), cited in Wang *et al.* (2005, p. 56).

was lost as a result of Chinese piracy, where 10–15 per cent of OTC drugs sold outside hospitals were counterfeit (cited in *Scrip Magazine*, 2004). In addition, the IPR standard of China is relatively low, as identified in Chapter 2.

The pharmaceutical business is a high-tech, high investment, high risk and high return one that benefits from a large firm size and a comprehensive industrial network to support each other's activities. As the majority of the Chinese pharmaceutical firms are very small by international standard and China as whole suffers from its low technological competence and the absence of established industrial networks, it is very difficult, if not impossible, for Chinese pharmaceutical firms to bear the high cost of R&D. This is especially the case when counterfeit products prevail in China. The R&D investment in the pharmaceutical industry in China is very limited at less than 1 per cent of its sales revenue on average. Few companies have product patents (also see Chapter 2). Even for the leading enterprises that pay attention to R&D, the investment is no more than 3 per cent. Hayiao Group Stock Ltd, for example, only has an annual fund of 30 million yuan, that is, 0.9 per cent of its sales revenue, for R&D (see below for further details about the company). Shanghai Pharmaceutical Group has an annual investment of 3.2 per cent of its sales revenue on product development (P. Jin *et al.*, 2003). Zhejiang Haizheng Pharmaceutical Ltd spent 7.8 per cent of its sales revenue in 2003 for R&D – the highest in the industry in China (Qin, 2004).

As a result, innovations in chemical, herbal and biological medical products are limited in China in general. Over 90 per cent of the chemical medical products produced in China are products under licence, with 83 per cent of the patents coming from abroad. In the herbal medicine market, foreign products are competing to occupy the Chinese market. By the end of 2000, 124 countries had set up herbal institutions. Twelve countries had registered patents in China. By contrast, innovations in herbal products in China are limited and few of them have applied for patents abroad (H. L. Zhang, 2004). This low level of innovation activities is perplexing and worrying, given China's long tradition of herbal medicine innovation and utilization. One explanation for this could be that Chinese firms are not yet familiar with the concept of IPR and have yet to develop an awareness of self-protection and the need to respect other people's inventions. Innovations in bio-medical products are equally depressing. Between 1991 and 1997, only 17 products were available in the Chinese market, the majority of them were products under licence. Between 1985 and 1999, only about 25 per cent of the patent applications came from domestic applicants (H. L. Zhang, 2004). In 2002, the Chinese IPR authority dealt with over 1800 IP applications, 90 per cent of them were for foreign firms (P. Jin *et al.*, 2003).

According to a report published by PricewaterhouseCoopers, almost 90 per cent of China's bio-engineering products are copies of foreign products and 99 per cent of the 3000 varieties of pharmaceutical medicines made in the country since the 1950s are imitations (cited in Zhang, 2001b). According to Zhang (2001b), this strategy has made economic sense for China as a developing country in its early stage of development. However, Qin's (2004) analysis of 50 stock-listed Chinese pharmaceutical companies found that new product development is a main source of enterprise competitiveness in the pharmaceutical industry. Having said that, the majority of the new products are botanical medicines and health care medicines that have relatively low technological requirement. Only a minority of the innovations are chemical or biological products. This suggests that the capacity of Chinese pharmaceutical companies for developing the latter is still weak. What is promising, though, is that China is moving towards innovation instead of imitation in its new drugs development (see Table 5.2).

Deficiency in marketing, pricing and distribution A fourth set of problems concerns the inadequacy of marketing strategy and distribution system. The majority of Chinese firms do not pay sufficient attention to marketing. By comparison, Sino-foreign JVs and a few large Chinese pharmaceutical firms which have a proactive marketing strategy to promote their products tend to have far higher levels of sales and profits than those which do not (P. Jin *et al.*, 2003). Between 2001 and 2004, the total expenditure on advertisements for drugs in China was more than 4 billion yuan. Ironically, illegal drugs advertisements made up three-quarters of the total of 40,000 illegal advertisements caught in China in the same period (*China Business*, 14 March 2005). The rampancy of fake drugs and illegal advertisements are partly a consequence of the relatively high price of authentic drugs that are beyond the affordability of a large proportion of the population, particularly those from the rural areas. A main reason for the sustained high price of drugs, despite the government's effort to contain prices, is the lack of a smooth distribution system. In the composition of drug prices, manufacturing firms take 30 per cent, wholesalers take 40 per cent and retailers take 30 per cent (*China Business*, 20 September 2004). As noted earlier, many wholesalers are state-owned or controlled and state-owned hospitals are the dominant retailers of drugs.

Generally speaking, the commercial segment of the drugs industry is experiencing a difficult time because of the low profit margins. There has been a continuous decline in profit in recent years and the net profit of the segment was only 0.59 per cent in 2004, lower than the interest rate of bank loan. Only about one-third of the retail firms were making a profit and half of the retail firms were making a loss (*Yangcheng Evening News*, 23 August 2005). For example, while the total sales revenue and gross profit of the pharmaceutical industry continued to increase at 16.4 per cent and 22.2 per cent, respectively in 2002, the overall profit had decreased by about 25 per cent, the biggest drop ever in the industry. By the end of 2002, pharmaceutical commercial firms in 15 provinces had experienced losses for the third consecutive year (P. Jin *et al.*, 2003).

Competition strategy

In spite of all the problems identified in the Chinese medical industry, leading Chinese firms have adopted a range of business strategies that have enhanced their competitiveness. These include, for example, M&As; collaborations in

R&D, for instance, partnership with foreign firms; and product branding that is also targeted at specific groups of consumers.

Mergers and acquisitions M&As have been important mechanisms for the industry to consolidate, integrate and expand. It is believed that M&As help achieve economies of scale in both production and sales, enhancing the capacity of R&D and introducing new management techniques. It is all part of China's current business trend and aspiration to be 'larger and stronger' and 'from being large to being strong' (see Chapter 3). Some well-established Chinese pharmaceutical firms realized that they could not fight against the foreign 'invasion' on their own and started to form alliances with other strong indigenous drug firms (known as 'strong-strong marriage'). In particular, firms that wish to enter the drug market in a new geographical area tend to work together with drug firms in the host area to gain their support and remove local obstacles (*China Business*, 21 June 2004). More broadly speaking, M&As in the industry take a variety of forms, for example, strong-strong marriage between state-owned companies, alliances between state-owned and private-owned companies and JVs with foreign or Hong Kong businesses (H. L. Zhang, 2004). According to Wang *et al.* (2003, p. 403), there are several motives for M&As in the Chinese drugs industry:

1. Expansion in scale to gain economies – these are M&As of enterprises with similar products and who are in direct competition.
2. Complementarity of products – these are M&As of enterprises that aim to extend their product chains and many of them are in Chinese medicines because of its geographic concentration that is constrained by the locations where the raw materials (e.g. herbs) are grown.
3. Marketing coordination – these are M&As of enterprises that aim to consolidate and enhance their distribution, marketing and sales networks. This is a low cost expansion.
4. Technological coordination – these are M&As of enterprises that aim to increase their R&D capability. They take place among larger and stronger enterprises. They also tend to acquire strong medical research institutes.

As a result, some large corporate groups are developed with new forms of operating modes, including exclusive agency and sales rights, chain stores and so on. (J. Li, 2003).

Collaboration in R&D A small but increasing number of Chinese drugs firms are developing their collaborative relationships with higher education institutions, R&D institutes and other enterprises to develop new drugs. This inter-organizational strategic partnership helps spread risk, share benefits and more importantly, build their unique resource base in order to develop competitive advantage. The biggest opportunity, however, lies in the collaboration with foreign firms. There are pull as well as push factors in this opportunity. On the one hand, conducting R&D projects for international pharmaceutical firms is likely to help China develop its own capacity to invent new drugs (Jia, 2004). On the other hand, global pharmaceutical giants are increasingly seeking partner institutions to outsource their R&D activities in developing countries, for example, China, where the regulatory and ethnical environments are less stringent in the development of drugs and their clinical trials (Jia, 2004) and the costs of human resources and clinical trials are significantly lower. There are now more than 5000 R&D institutions, including 500–1000 small- and medium sized biotech companies, in addition to 20 biotech parks in China (Agres, 2006). China has an estimated 200,000 researchers specializing in R&D, and a very competitive market for laboratory jobs with salaries being only a third to a fifth of those in the West (*Scrip Magazine*, 2004). As a result, the cost of bringing a new drug to the market in China could be as little as US$5.9 million compared to the estimated US$800 million in the West (Agres, 2006). Another advantage is China's lax attitude towards pioneering research in controversial areas. This freedom of research and governmental support has led to a number of cross-country R&D projects and centres being developed in China (*Scrip Magazine*, 2004). Recent examples include the Chinese National Human Genome Centre in Shanghai conducting joint research with Roche into diabetes and schizophrenia, and a joint project between the Shanghai Institute of Materia Medica and GlaxoSmithKline established to develop a recombinatorial chemistry laboratory (*Scrip Magazine*, 2004). Pfizer also opened a new research centre in Shanghai in 2005 and plans to 'launch another 15 drugs by 2010, including experimental drugs for cancer and smoking cessation' (Agres, 2006, p. 18).

However, there are a number of issues that the Chinese partners need to address if they are to reap the full benefits of being the outsourcing suppliers to foreign firms in the long term. These include the need to increase their market-focused research abilities, to expand their scale, to better protect their IPR (Jia, 2004) and to adopt the R&D process that is used in pharmaceutical MNCs (*Scrip Magazine*, 2004).

Product branding and targeting customer groups Product branding and targeting customer groups are two strategies deployed by some of the top-performing medical enterprises. For example, Huahong (huahong is Chinese pear-leaved crabapple, a type of medical plant) Pharmaceutical Ltd built its brand image on its high-quality and specialized products that are targeted at women of child bearing age – and there are 400 million in this customer group in China. The aim of Huahong Pharmaceutical Ltd is to be the top-brand producer of health care products for women and children in China. It is investing in product and production innovations (*Workers' Daily*, 26 September 2004). In addition, regional bases for Chinese medicines are formed to take advantage of regional resources of the individual bases. For example, Sichuan Province has become a major herbal medicine production province. Other mountainous provinces such as Yunnan, Guizhou, Qinghai, Inner Mogolia, Guangxi and Tibet are following suit (J. Li, 2003).

While not every leading medical firm in China adopts these strategies, they have been unique in matching their strategy with company characteristics. Below are examples of some of the best performers in the pharmaceutical industry in China.

Qingdao Jiante Biology Stock Ltd is a relatively new company that was floated on the stock market after asset restructuring in the early 2000s. Its main businesses are in the production, distribution and sales of health-related products. In 2002, the company relied on the sales of one particular health product – *naobaijin* ('white gold for brain') to change its fortune. *Naobaijin* made up 99.03 per cent of the total sales revenue of 2002 and rescued the firm from going bankrupt (P. Jin *et al.*, 2003). However, this over-dependence on one product is a short-term and high-risk strategy. Diversification is urgently needed for the firm to de-risk through the development of a broader range of products.

Hayiao Group Stock Ltd is one of the best performers in the stock market within the pharmaceutical industry. From 2000 to 2002, Hayiao Group Stock Ltd was at the top of the Top 100 pharmaceutical enterprises in its sales revenue. Hayiao Group Stock Ltd's main products are components for other medicines, in addition to producing its own patented brand products. However, in 2002, Hayiao Group Stock Ltd's profitability ranked third in the industry, lower than that of Qingtao Jiante Biology Stock Ltd. The main reason for that was the low-value-added and low-profit nature of medicine component production. What is needed for Hayiao Group Stock Ltd is to develop new products that are highly value-added to increase its profit margin (P. Jin *et al.*, 2003).

Guangzhou Pharmaceutical Co Ltd is one of the three largest pharmaceutical trading corporations in the industry. The corporation consists of eight medicine manufacturers and three trading companies, many of them over 100 years old. The eight manufacturers produce a broad range of Chinese medical products and apparatus and hygienic materials. Many of the medical products are household brand names and specifically target the health problems of the population in the southeast region. The trading part of the corporation trades over 4000 types of Western and Chinese medicines and medical equipment and has dominated the market in southeast China for decades. Guangzhou Pharmaceutical Co Ltd has a vast corporate customer base of over 2000 hospitals, pharmaceutical wholesalers and retailers, most of them long-term customers. Guangzhou is one of the cities in China that have the highest consumption power in pharmaceutical products with the most active retail markets. Guangzhou Pharmaceutical Co Ltd therefore possesses the advantage of geographical location and has managed to control the majority of the distribution outlets. In addition, it taps into the overseas Chinese market in Southeast Asia to take advantage of the ethnic Chinese's preference for traditional Chinese medicines (P. Jin *et al.*, 2003).

Beijing Tongrentang, with a history of over 300 years, is one of the oldest and the most prestigious Chinese medicine company in China.[3] It is the ultimate symbol of quality and reputation in the traditional Chinese medical industry. Beijing Tongrentang manufactures 24 brand-name final products, many of which are constantly in short supply in the market. In addition, it trades over 800 types of Chinese medical herbs and over 300 types of Chinese medicine/health drinks. Forty-seven of Beijing Tongrentang's products have won quality awards at the national, industrial or municipal level (P. Jin *et al.*, 2003). With ten companies, two production bases, one institute, one hospital and two centres (Information Centre and Training Centre), Beijing Tongrentang has maintained an annual growth of 20 per cent or more in recent years. Its total assets have reached 7 billion yuan, its annual turnover amounts to approximately 5.4 billion yuan. Beijing Tongrentang possesses two listed companies both in domestic and overseas stock market. It has over 400 domestic pharmacies including franchise drug retailers, branch pharmacies and shops, and 20 overseas JVs or TCM pharmacies within 13 countries and regions including Hong Kong, Malaysia, Thailand, Vietnam, Britain, Canada and Australia. Beijing Tongrentang is the trading brand name and has been registered in more than 50 countries (Beijing Tongrentang company website, accessed on 8 November 2006).

Beijing Tongrentang has developed concepts including 'Four Well-Treating', 'Four Standards' and 'Four Accelerators' as part of their corporate strategy. 'Four Well-Treating' refers to treating society, employees, business partners and investors well. 'Four Standards' refers to attracting customers with Tongrentang's culture, encouraging employees with Tongrentang's spirit, advocating standardized management and remunerating investors with great profits. 'Four Accelerators' refers to speeding up branding, quickening collaborative development, promoting talented employees development and enriching its culture (Beijing Tongrentang company website, accessed on 8 November 2006). It is not clear the extent to which these proactive and progressive concepts have been implemented and what positive impact they have demonstrated. What is clear though is that Tongrentang is adopting a stakeholder perspective in its business development with a high level of consciousness of its CSR and an astute approach to its international expansion.

It is interesting to note that although both Guangzhou Pharmaceutical Co Ltd and Beijing Tongrentang Ltd are both well-known brand-name medical companies with a long history, their competitive strategies differ. While Guangzhou Pharmaceutical Co Ltd focuses on the regional market (southeast China and Southeast Asia) and distribution/retail business, supported by its wide range of high-quality brand-name traditional Chinese medicine products, Beijing Tongrentang Ltd chooses to break into the mainstream global medicine market by modernizing traditional Chinese medicine products to suit the Western style of consumption and making the products more accessible to them by setting up overseas branches. In comparison, Guangzhou Pharmaceutical Co Ltd represents a regional success whereas Beijing Tongrentang stands for national pride and glamour with a hint of imperial superiority (P. Jin *et al.*, 2003).

It should also be noted that those firms that choose traditional Chinese medicines as their niche products to avoid competition with foreign firms may find it difficult to grow internationally. For example, Nolan (2004) noted that Sanjiu – a leading pharmaceutical company – has found it difficult to grow in the domestic market apart from its main product *Sanjiu Weitai* (a stomach medicine). The company has chosen to concentrate on traditional Chinese medicines in order to avoid direct competition with foreign MNCs. However, Sanjiu finds it difficult to expand in the international market as the 'overseas

Chinese community is not sufficiently large to provide for sustained long-term growth' (Nolan, 2004, p. 192).

Human resource implications

In many ways, the pharmaceutical industry faces similar issues in its HRM to those found in the automotive industry. A high proportion of the enterprises were state-owned as a result of the state planned economy. These enterprises have been through major organizational changes in the last two decades, including radical downsizing through several rounds of lay-offs, privatization and adoption of new management techniques.[4] This has led to the shrinking of employment in the SOEs and the growth of employment in the private sector, as well as a level of convergence in the HR practices between the state-owned and non-state-owned firms. In general, workers in the manufacturing and retail sector of the pharmaceutical industry are relatively low-paid (see Table 4.5) with relatively lower levels of educational attainment and skills (see Table 2.16). Shop assistants generally have relatively low educational qualifications with little medical knowledge. They are unable to provide medical advice to customers. While some large chain stores now have qualified pharmacists, the vast majority of the shop assistants are not qualified. This is especially the case for those working in small private businesses since many of them may be family members drawn in to help (Tian, 2003).

The industry is equally short of professional staff including marketing and sales professionals, R&D scientists and engineers and professionally trained managerial staff. For instance, over 90 per cent of the sales representatives of drug companies tend to have relatively low levels of educational qualifications in addition to a lack of sales business knowledge (*China Business*, 14 March 2005). Provision of enterprise training to develop these skills tends to be limited, especially in domestic firms.[5] By comparison, the R&D side looks more promising due to the rapid expansion of the higher education sector, the rising number of returning Chinese students who have pursued higher education qualifications abroad (see Chapter 2) and the increasing opportunities of Chinese institutions working as the outsourcing providers for Western firms and universities in R&D projects. These are important mechanisms to train up R&D scientists and engineers and accumulate innovative capacity for the industry.

Summary

China's pharmaceutical industry shares many similar problems with its automotive industry. It is an old industry that is highly fragmented, small in scale, low in manufacturing standard and has a low level of human capital, R&D investment and product innovation. These are all intertwined factors that constrain the development of the industry. While rich opportunities exist for growth, at least in the domestic market, the potential for domestic firms to grow into national ones is circumvented by cultural (e.g. different nature of local illnesses and consumer preferences) and political (e.g. local government protectionism) barriers. Meanwhile, the industry has been facing a growing level of competition from foreign MNCs – a major source of pressure that is likely to intensify as the effect of the WTO agreements deepens. Although still unable to compete with foreign pharmaceutical giants, whose entry to the Chinese market has benefited domestic firms in many ways, the Chinese pharmaceutical industry has undergone significant changes in the last two decades. The pressure to reform has come from the government as well as from market forces. These changes are set to continue as China is determined to close its gap with the Western world.

Recommended readings

D. Bulcke, H. Zhang and X. Li, 'Interaction between the Business Environment and the Corporate Strategic Positioning of Firms in the Pharmaceutical Industry: A Study of the Entry and Expansion Path of MNEs into China', *Management International Review*, 39, 4 (1999): 353–77.

C. Grace, *The Effect of Changing Intellectual Property on Pharmaceutical Industry Prospects in India and China: Considerations for Access to Medicines* (London: DIFD Health Systems Resource Centre, June 2004).

P. Nolan, *Transforming China: Globalisation, Transition and Development* (London: Anthem Press, 2004).

G. Yeung, 'The Implications of WTO Accession on the Pharmaceutical Industry in China', *Journal of Contemporary China*, 11, 32 (2002): 473–93.

CHAPTER 6

Information Technology Industry

Introduction

The information technology (IT) industry is a showcase high-tech industry for the Chinese government. According to its tenth five-year plan (the Ministry of Information Industry, 2001), the information industry is 'a pillar industry in the national economy', 'a strategic industry fundamental to national security' and 'a driving force for innovation and the growth in other industries'.

The IT industry is a broad one that is linked to a number of related industries, including the computer (both hardware and software) industry, the telecommunication industry and the electronics industry. In fact, it is very difficult to provide a clear cut boundary between these industries, as IT forms a core part of the technology in them. While this chapter focuses on the computer sector which is the key sector of the IT industry, it touches upon the electronics and the telecommunication industry since it is difficult to talk about the computer sector without relating to the other two in terms of the IT development. Due to space constraints, this chapter will not go into detail of the historical development and industrial structure of the electronics and the telecommunication industry. It is worth noting, however, that the telecommunication industry is another industry that is listed as a 'strategic industry' by the Chinese government. While sharing similar features of government protectionism and monopoly with the computer industry, the telecommunication industry has a much longer history than the computer industry. Much of the industry is state-owned and heavily protected by the government from foreign and private competition. In recent years, the government has restructured the industry by creating four main players and two second-tier players to work across different sectors of the industry (e.g. mobile, broadband, fixed lines etc.), bringing in private capital and introducing a moderate level of competition while still keeping the industry under the control of the central government (Roseman, 2005).[1]

This chapter contains six main sections. The first two sections outline the development of the computer industry and the growth of industrial clusters. These are followed by a discussion of the important role of the Chinese government in shaping the industry through a series of industrial policies. The fourth section explores the opportunities for as well as challenges to the growth of the industry. The fifth section contemplates the HR issues facing the industry. The final main section examines the competitive strategy of the industry at the national, industrial and enterprise level. While the IT industry faces similar opportunities for growth and HR problems as the automotive and pharmaceutical industry, the IT industry has benefited from a higher level of government support in its development. The role of the government is therefore evident in the discussion of the thematic sections.

The development of the computer industry

The Chinese computer industry is a young one which did not take off seriously until the mid-1980s.[2] Rui and Tao (2004) divided the growth of the industry into three stages. The first stage (1956–72) was the birth period when developing the computer technology was listed as one of the six key projects in the 'Twelve-Year Plan for Science and Technology Development' in 1956. The first computer was produced in 1958. The focus in this period was on R&D and scientific projects in national defence. The second stage (1973–85) was the formative period of the computer industry during which batch production of computers started to take off in the mid-1970s. It was also during the mid-1970s when the development of the micro-computer began which led to the production of the first micro-computer in China in 1977. The third stage (1986 to the present time) saw the development period of the computing industry when computing technology became increasingly accessible to the masses. Over 4 million personal computers (PCs) were sold in 1998, 72 per cent of them were made by Chinese firms. In 2002, the size of the computer market in China was nearly 236 billion yuan, selling more than 9 million PCs and attracting a total export value of US$218 billion (Rui and Tao, 2004).

Rui and Tao (2004) further divided the development of the software wing of the Chinese computer industry into three periods. The first (1989–91) was the birth period when the concept of software development started to catch the interest of academics, policy makers, enterprises and IT professionals. During this period, individual software developers played a significant role in adapting Western software into a Chinese context, including developing the Chinese word processing system. The second period (1991–94) was the early growth period when professional software developing companies started to emerge in China. Due to the constraints of funding and technical competence, the main developing activities in this period were related to adapting Western software into the Chinese context and the development of basic software packages. The third period (from 1994 onwards) is the prosperous period when a widening range of Chinese software packages for education, business and entertainment have been developed against strong competition from imported foreign software packages (Rui and Tao, 2004). Despite this rapid growth, the development of software in China only makes up a very small proportion of world production output compared with that of the United States and western Europe. For example, in 2002, China's software development only made up 2 per cent of the world's total whereas the United States and western Europe made up 40 per cent and 31 per cent, respectively. In addition, the United States self-supplied 97 per cent of its market demand for software products while China could only satisfy about one-third of its market demand (Rui and Tao, 2004).

Driven by the burgeoning market, the Chinese computer industry as a whole has developed rapidly from being manufacturing and application oriented to being a fully fledged and multi-functioned industry that consists of manufacturing, software developing, sales, after-sales services and consulting and information services (Rui and Tao, 2004). By the end of the 1990s, there were over 18,000 companies in this industry, employing 0.5 million workers (see Table 6.1) (Rui and Tao, 2004).

In recent years, the industry has been developing at an accelerating rate. Since the late 1990s, its annual growth rate has been over 40 per cent and has become one of the fastest-growing markets in the world. In 1990, the sales revenue was 5.6 billion yuan. In 2002, it was over 235.8 billion yuan. Over 67 per cent of the sales were hardware while the remaining were software and information services. However, the growth rate of software and information services is faster than the overall growth rate of the industry (see Table 6.2) (Rui and Tao, 2004). By the end of 2002, there were a total of 4700 software development, maintenance and service companies of above designated size (i.e. with annual sales revenue of over 5 million yuan) in China, employing some 590,000 people. Nearly a quarter of the companies had annual sales revenue of more than 10 million yuan (Rui and Tao, 2004).

Table 6.1 The structure of the Chinese computer industry

Structure of the industry	No. of companies	No. of employees (1000 persons)
Manufacturing	1,000	165
Software development	1,000	115
Information services	16,000	215
R&D	50	5
Total	18,050	500

Source: Rui and Tao (2004, p. 88).

Table 6.2 Comparison of the Chinese IT market in 2001 and 2002

Market structure	2001		2002	
	Sales value (billion yuan)	Growth rate (%)	Sales value (billion yuan)	Growth rate (%)
Hardware	142.6	14.0	158.4	11.1
Software	28.5	23.9	34.5	21.0
Information services	32.3	24.4	42.9	32.9
Market total	203.4	16.8	235.8	16.0

Source: Rui and Tao (2004, p. 89).

It was reported by the Deputy Minister of the Ministry of Commerce in January 2005 that China's software industry had developed rapidly in recent years with an average annual growth of 30 per cent on sales and seven times growth on software export over the past five years. It has become a strategic industry for the national economy and social development (cited in the China Software Industry Association, 2005). According to the statistics from the China Software Industry Association (2005), the sales revenue of the Chinese software industry had increased from 59.3 billion yuan in 2000 to 160 billion yuan in 2003, with software exports increasing from US$0.25 billion to US$2 billion in the same period. By the early 2000s, China had become one of the top three world exporters of information communication technology (ICT) products, capable of manufacturing high-tech intermediate goods (Amighini, 2005).

The growth of the Chinese computer industry benefits considerably from the earlier development (e.g. experience and production capacity) of the electronics industry, particularly in the household electronics products (e.g. TVs) which accounted for half of the total electronics production in 1990 (Kraemer and Dedrick, 2001). When the demand for household electronics products started to slow down in the early 1990s (see Table 1.2),[3] Chinese firms were utilizing only 50 per cent of their production capacity. As most of these firms were SOEs, the government subsidized the restructuring of these inefficient firms and moved them into the computer sector where growth opportunity existed (Chung, 1999, cited in Kraemer and Dedrick, 2001). 'By 2000, computer hardware accounted for 32 per cent of total electronics output, while consumer electronics had dropped to 25 per cent' (Kraemer and Dedrick, 2001, p. 4). More specifically, the output of integrated circuits shot up to 5.5 billion units in 1995 from 0.48 billion units in 1994. This was followed by a reduction of output in the next four years until 2000. In 2004, over 21 billion integrated circuit units were produced (see Table 1.2). According to Kambil and Lee (2004), China's share of the global integrated circuit market is expected to increase from 13.7 per cent in 2003 to 23.5 per cent in 2008. For PCs, only 75,000 units were produced in 1989. In 1994, 245,700 units were produced, followed by a huge increase to 835,700 units in 1995. From then on, the annual output of PCs grew dramatically. In 2005, over 80.8 million units were produced (see Table 1.2).

The Chinese firms' growing production capacity of PCs enabled them to reduce the prices to make PCs affordable to Chinese families, thus stimulating more demands and sales. In 1999, a price war ignited which led to a series of price reductions at the lower-end of the market. The Chinese PC manufacturers' aggressive price slashing strategy, whose prices were lower than those of foreign brand-name products (e.g. IBM, Compaq and HP) anyway, has resulted in a shrinking market share for the foreign products (R. Chen, 2004). For example, Compaq Computer was the leader in 1994 with a 21 per cent share of China's PC business. By 1999, it only possessed 9 per cent, while Legend Computer (now Lenovo) based in Beijing had become the country's most successful PC maker with a 17 per cent market share (Sesser, 1999) (see further discussion of Lenovo later).

The growth of China's computer industry is parallel to and symbiotic with the growth of the wider electronics and IT industry, including, for example, DVDs, mobile phones and the Internet markets.[4] China is the world's leading manufacturer of DVD players, with 60 per cent market share. It is also the world's largest cellular mobile market with an output of 303.54 million mobile phones in 2005 (see Table 1.2) and over 377 million subscribers at the end of September 2005 (*People's Daily Online*, 26 October 2005). The total number of mobile phone subscribers was expected to reach 440 million by the end of 2006 (*ChinaToday.com*, 18 November 2006). China's domestic market for electronic information products grew from US$20.2 billion in 1999 to US$77.1 billion in 2002 (Kambil and Lee, 2004).

The explosive growth of China's electronics and IT industry is necessarily a result of its catching-up with the technology through technological adaptation and innovation in the last decade or so (e.g. Fan, 2006; Lu, 2000). For example, Fan's (2006, pp. 361–2) study found that China's telecom-equipment market 'is one of the most competitive ones in the world' and that 'innovation capability and self-developed technologies have been the key to their catching-up with the MNCs and to determine who the domestic industrial leaders are'. In some areas, Chinese firms are now amongst the world technology leaders. The most successful of them is perhaps *Huawei* (see more details later) which has established itself as a strong global competitor, through heavy investment in the development of the third generation (3G) mobile communication systems and the global system for mobile communications (GSM).[5] As Kambil and Lee (2004, p. 1) observed,

> Everyone recognizes China as a low-cost manufacturer and a huge potential market. But most do not realize China is emerging as a key player in shaping technology standards – standards that could define the nature of global competition in the technology, media and telecommunications sector for years to come. From operating systems and software applications to storage media, wireless communications and satellite positioning, Chinese Government agencies and companies are looking to break the hold of developed economies on standards and working to shape new technology standards for economic advantage.

IT industrial clusters

The competitiveness of a particular industry depends upon the existence of internationally competitive supplier industries or related industries (Porter, 1990). In addition, developing industrial clusters to exploit the locational advantages (e.g. human, economic, natural and industrial resources and government policy) is important in enhancing the competitiveness of a national industry and firms in that industry. The development of the Chinese IT industry has benefited significantly from the development of several major IT industrial clusters located in or close to premium cities in the eastern part of the country. Beijing (Zhongguancun), Shanghai, Kunshan, Shenzhen and Dongguan clusters are among the best known examples (Lai *et al.*, 2005). In particular, Zhongguancun is the cradle of China's IT industry, where the pioneer indigenous IT firms were incubated, including Legend (now Lenovo). More specifically, Zhongguancun Electronics Avenue has become Beijing's 'Silicon Valley', with 80 per cent of the business being in the field of electronics. There are more than 50 institutions of higher learning in the neighbourhood, including the Chinese Academy of Sciences. There are 138 research centres in the area, employing over 80,000 technicians, most of them university graduates. So far, the Chinese government has invested over 10 billion yuan in this area. High-tech firms in this area fall within three broad categories: state – or collectively owned organizations set up by state organizations, scientific academies or institutions of higher learning; collectively owned companies managed and operated by holding basis; and collective corporations organized by technicians and individuals (China.org.cn, 2006).

Lai *et al.*'s (2005)[6] comparative study of the innovative capacity of China's IT industrial clusters reveals that each of the Shanghai, Kunshan, Shenzhen and Dongguan clusters has its unique characteristics. The Shanghai IT Industrial cluster is located in the Pudong New Area of Shanghai and is now, according to the authors, China's foremost IT industrial cluster, surrounded by several national R&D institutes and premier universities. It also benefits from the existence of other industrial clusters including biotechnology, for example. The Kunshan IT industrial cluster is located in the Shanghai economic zone between Shanghai City and Suzhou City. A booming industrial cluster focusing mainly on manufacturing and processing for export, its growth is said to be entirely local government oriented. Taiwanese investment features prominently in this industrial cluster. By the early 2000s, there were more than 300 IT firms with a total investment exceeding US$3 billion. The Kunshan IT industrial cluster takes advantage of its proximity to Shanghai. The Shenzhen IT industrial cluster is situated in the southeast coastal region of Guangdong Province. Shenzhen contains one of the earliest special economic zones in China that were set up in the early years of China's open door policy. It has become one of the largest bases for IT industrialization as well as a powerhouse for high-tech manufacturing, processing, financial securities, insurance, information services and transportation.

Unlike Shanghai and Kunshan, Shenzhen City does not have its own prestigious universities; however, several top Chinese universities, including Beijing University and Tsinghua University, have set up research institutes in Shenzhen which play an important part in the cluster. The Dongguan IT industrial cluster is situated in Dongguan city in the mid-south of Guangdong Province. There were some 227 IT firms in this cluster by the end of 2001. It has benefited from the shift of IT manufacturing from Taiwan to southern China. As one of the largest manufacturing sites in the world, Dongguan-made computer and peripheral products have a large share of the international market, as do other products it produces such as shoes and garments. Compared with the other three industrial clusters, Dongguan has the competitive advantage of supporting and related industries and the presence of clusters instead of isolated industries. For example, most computer components can be obtained within one and a half hours in this area and 70–90 per cent of the accessories are available locally. Similar to Shenzhen, Dongguan does not have its own prestigious universities, but has benefited from the research institutes set up here by several famous universities from mainland China (e.g. Shanghai Jiaotong University) and Hong Kong (Hong Kong Polytechnic University). Both the Shenzhen and Dongguan industrial clusters have the advantage of being close to Hong Kong – a financial, economic, technological and service centre of the world. However, they are both disadvantaged from not having their own advanced educational institutions and have to reach out to major cities nearby, for example, Guangzhou and Hong Kong and even further for their human resources (Lai *et al.*, 2005).

These IT industrial clusters, together with those not mentioned here, have contributed to the dramatic development of China's IT industry. They help attract foreign suppliers to transfer the earlier stages of the production process to China (Chen and Wei, 2003). In other words, China will gradually be transformed into a base for the main production of the IT products and not just as a base where product components are assembled.

The role of the government

As the IT industry is regarded as a 'strategic industry' by the Chinese government, it has a close involvement in ensuring the rapid development of the industry. The government's intervention include: ownership control, R&D investment, restrictive policy on foreign investment and HR development (see discussion later for this point). In terms of ownership control, the government facilitates the growth of SOEs on the one hand, and restricts the expansion of foreign firms in China on the other, to ensure the growth of the former. The ownership structure of the leading Chinese computer firms are typical examples of the Chinese socialist market economy (Kraemer and Dedrick, 2001) because of the unique way they are connected to the state on the one hand, but enjoy an unusual level of autonomy to operate as an SOE on the other. For example, market leader Legend is closely affiliated with the Chinese Academy of Science and China Great Wall Computer is a spin-off of the Ministry of Electronics Industry (Lu, 2000). 'In spite of their status as state-owned or COEs, each is clearly managed in an entrepreneurial, market-oriented manner, and the Chinese PC market is highly competitive' (Kraemer and Dedrick, 2001, p. 6). Lu (2000) argued that state-ownership (in various forms) of the four major computer enterprises (Stone, Legend, Founder and China Great Wall Computer) during the early period of development of China's computer industry helped to ensure that the intellectual productive resources developed in the state sector were developed fully into commercial products and they 'contributed the most to the rise of a viable Chinese domestic computer industry' (p. 189).

According to the tenth five-year plan of the Chinese government (the Ministry of Information Industry, 2001), the organization of SOEs in the electronic industry was to be restructured strategically in the following ways:

■ Encourage M&As, support the development of internationally competitive enterprises, further assist the small- and medium-sized enterprises (SMEs) to develop towards specialization, excellence and innovation. Accelerate the development of new products and innovations, achieve economies of scale, encourage or reform applied R&D institutions into business operations.

■ Enable large enterprises to have the capabilities to innovate, perform scale production, system integration, consolidate services and develop new markets with supporting policies and capital. Also aim to increase technological innovations and exports in order to earn foreign exchange. Support the development of brand-name products.

■ Adjust the strategies for the development of the state-owned IT manufacturing sector, encourage other economic sectors to participate in the asset restructuring of SOEs and acquire SMEs.

■ Support major R&D projects launched by SOEs through funding and tax relief and subsidize basic research and technological innovation by SOEs (Internet source: http://www.trp.hku.hk/infofile/2002/10-5-yr-plan.pdf).

The Chinese government also introduced other procedural and policy barriers aimed at slowing down the speed of development of foreign IT firms in China to allow time for domestic firms to establish themselves. For example, the role of foreign firms in telecoms, datacoms and Internet services are restricted. Foreign computer makers are invited to enter China to help develop its IT industry. But they are required to transfer technology and form alliances with domestic companies in return for production licenses and market access. Moreover, foreign MNCs' production for the domestic market was restricted to a certain percentage of their export production (Kraemer and Dedrick, 2001). By contrast, domestic firms are supported with favourable treatment in government procurement of computer ware and 'access to technologies developed in the state R&D institutions' (Kraemer and Dedrick, 2001, p. 17). In order 'to encourage exports, the government also created "export processing zones" where imported materials used in production would be free from duties and taxes when they were directly exported' (Kraemer and Dedrick, 2001, p. 6). Despite all these obstacles, the potential size and growth of China's computer market made it a business opportunity that many foreign firms felt they could not ignore (see further discussion later). Many leading PC companies have entered the Chinese market (Kraemer and Dedrick, 2001). For example, Hewlett-Packard, Toshiba and Compaq formed JVs with local companies in order to market their own products and gain access to local distribution channels. IBM entered a JV with Great Wall in 1994 that provided IBM with local distribution channels and gave Great Wall access to IBM technology and manufacturing know-how (Kraemer and Dedrick, 2001; Lu, 2000).

Compared with other industries, the IT industry benefits from more funding opportunities created by the government to develop its technology capacity. According to the Ministry of Information Industry (MII), China was to spend one trillion yuan (about US$120 billion) to spur its information industry during the tenth five-year plan (2001–5). A total of 500 billion of which was to be spent on telecommunications, 50 billion on post service and 400 billion on electronic IT. Funds were to be raised from domestic and international capital markets. It was planned that by 2005, the information industry would become a major pillar industry of the country. The Chinese government would make great efforts to push forward and give priority to the application of IT as a way of boosting economic and social development. The government also provided more channels for the investment and especially encouraged direct investment from private and foreign funds.

Detailed information is not available on the extent to which the tenth five-year plan has been fulfilled. But judging from the rapid growth of the production outputs of PCs and mobile phones and the number of Internet users and mobile subscribers, we can reasonably assume that the fulfilment of the plan was on track. Developing China's IT capacity continues to be high on the government's agenda. According to the eleventh five-year plan (2006–10), several major high-tech projects are to be carried out during this period. A significant proportion of these projects are IT related, including:

- Integrated circuits and software: establishing integrated circuit R&D centres, industrializing the technology for 90-nanometer and smaller integrated circuits and developing basic software, middleware, large key applied software and integrated systems;
- New-generation network: building next generation Internet demonstration projects, a nationwide digital TV network and mobile communication demonstration networks with independent property rights;
- Advanced computing: making breakthrough in technology for petaflop computer systems, building grid-based advanced computing platforms and commercializing the production of teraflop computers (Xinhua News Agency, 6 March 2006).

In addition to policy direction and administrative intervention, the government directly participates in the R&D activities. Box 6.1 below is an example of the R&D partnership between the Chinese government and leading international firms.

BOX 6.1

The MII–Thomson innovation initiative

The creation of the MII–Thomson Joint Lab for Intellectual Property Development means that China is now empowered with the most innovative and comprehensive knowledge tools from Thomson. At a meeting held on 1 December 2005 in Beijing, the agreement was hailed as a significant step forward in China's pursuit to discover new and better ways to develop technology.

The joint lab was to be located in the MII–China Silicon Intellectual Property Public Service Platform (CSIP) building, and will equip Chinese researchers with the most complete and accurate resources for scientific innovation, including the most advanced and powerful scientific and knowledge tools for patent and literature search and analysis.

The mission of the lab is:

■ To promote the rapid development of intellectual property within the IT industry;

■ To educate researchers throughout China about efficient and effective ways to conduct research using world-class intellectual property research and analysis tools;

■ To work together to accelerate the awareness and capabilities of (self-made innovation) Chinese companies.

MII–CSIP is a public service organization that guides industry development with the provision of resources and technical services to Chinese software and information communication (IC) enterprises. It is funded by MII Electronic Cooperating with Microsoft Corp and Hewlett-Packard Corp (HP), CSIP set up two software development labs (Windows/.net with Microsoft Corp. and Linux with HP) and one embedded system lab (Windows CE with Microsoft). Microsoft was to invest about US$10 million over a two-year period in software development lab and 80 million yuan in Windows CE embedded system lab; HP would invest about US$23 million over a three-year period to establish a lab for the development, testing and certification of Linux software.

Source: adapted from Thomson (2005).

Opportunities and challenges to growth

The rapid expansion of the Chinese IT industry is influenced by the technology push factor, that is, technological innovations and the entry of foreign firms that have brought technology, as well as the market pull factor. Since the twenty-first century, the Chinese government's determination to speed up the IT process in government administration and public sector services as part of its tenth five-year plan provided timely opportunities for the IT industry to grow. Local governments are encouraged by the central government to adopt the e-government initiative as an integral part of the development of an information system for government administration. For example, in the first six months of 2002, a total of 15.5 billion yuan was spent on purchasing products for e-government administration. Electronic information systems were being adopted in public services areas such as social welfare insurance, governmental organizations, banking, tax and custom and excise. A preliminary system was established in data collection, processing, storage and utilization. Towards the end of 2002, 187 departments had intranet or national information systems (Chen and Wei, 2003). The majority of the large and medium-sized enterprises are also engaged in the modernization of their management systems through the investment in information management systems in production, logistics, finance and services. The falling prices in household electronic products and other consumers' electronic products stimulated the demand for newer and more varieties of these products which in turn promoted the rapid development of software for those products.

More importantly, the increasing number of people using the Internet in their work, study and life has been a major factor in the development of the IT industry. According to China Internet Network Information Centre (CNNIC),[7] by the end of June 2002, the number of Internet users in China had reached 45.8 million, an increase of 19.3 million or 72.8 per cent over the same period in 2001. This has made China the third largest Internet user in the world, after the United States and Japan (*People's Daily Online*, 22 July 2002). By the end of 2004, there were 94 million Internet users in China. Over 35 per cent of them were aged between 18 and 24, and 61 per cent of all users were male users. Over 98 per cent of them reported using the Internet as the main tool for obtaining information, with 74 per cent and 45 per cent of users getting news and entertainment from the Internet, respectively (CNNIC, 2005). In 2005, the total number of Internet users reached 111 million (*China Statistical Yearbook*, 2006).

These parallel developments in the public and private domain are the major driving forces in the growth of the Chinese IT industry, particularly in the development of software packages. However, this new industry faces a number of serious challenges. Competition is fierce amongst the many domestic and foreign firms, although this competitive pressure also serves as a driving force for firms in the industry to collaborate in the sharing of software development as well as hardware manufacturing. The provision of after-sales services including maintenance services and upgrading services is limited, lacking both in customer service ethos and a taskforce that is capable of delivering the services (Rui and Tao, 2004). According to the China Software Industry Association (2005), increasing standards and innovation capability, developing marketing channels, deploying capital operation and resource consolidation are the key issues in the development of the Chinese IT industry. More specifically, capital operation is not about simple financing modes but about the process of generating handsome profit by modes of investment, penetration, merger, stock holding and so on with its own capital. The Association argues that modern enterprise competition has been transformed from that between single enterprises to competition between enterprise networks, which makes enterprise resource consolidation even more important (China Software Industry Association, 2005).

More broadly, the major challenges facing the industry are summarized by the Ministry of Information Industry (2001) (see Box 6.2).

BOX 6.2

Challenges facing China's IT industry

- The use of information resources is still lagging behind the development in communication network infrastructure.

- Existing regulations are inadequate in facilitating the development of the industry and that there is a need to establish a comprehensive legal and regulating system.

- Structure and the organization of the industry needs to be improved. The construction of telecommunication supporting networks lagged behind the development in communication ability. The development of telecommunications manufacturing industry was slower than network construction. In general, the industry lacked planned and organized development.

- Gaps exist in productivity and operation efficiency between local organizations and other global organizations.

- The management standard and operation efficiency was comparatively low.

- The key technologies still need to rely on other countries. The industry's profit ratio was far below the standard in developed countries.

- There are insufficient channels in financing the industry and there is a lack of R&D funds.

- There is a lack of innovation and mechanisms for R&D in enterprises and a shortage of human resources. Among the electronic information products, there are a small number of products that have their own brand names or property rights. Commercialization of scientific research results has been limited. A creative system that integrates the production, learning, research and exploitation does not yet exist in most of the enterprises. There is an imbalance in the HR structure. There is a surplus in general labour supply on the one hand, and a shortage in managerial talent, technological specialists and high level system integrating experts on the other.

- Software, integrated circuit and components industries are the bottleneck that curbed the development of the IT manufacturing industries.

Source: adapted from the Ministry of Information Industry (2001), cited in http://www.trp.hku.hk/infofile/2002/10-5-yr-plan.pdf.

Human resource implications

The abundant supply of relatively cheap labour in China has been a major force that drives the growth of the computer manufacturing business, particularly in component production and assembling. However, the size of IT companies is relatively small in general. According to Rui and Tao (2004), over 90 per cent of the 18,000 IT-related companies were sales agency firms. The average size of the hardware and software manufacturing firms was just over 100 employees. Most of them were production workers and sales personnel. Relatively few of them were IT engineers or technicians. According to Jiang and Wang (2004), by the end of 2002, a total of 3.23 million workers were employed in the electronics and IT industry. About 60 per cent of them were shopfloor workers. There was a significant shortage of technical and engineering staff and managerial staff. The shortage of software development engineers was particularly severe. There were only 3000 integrated circuit design engineers and 150,000 software specialists in the early 2000s in China. By contrast there were 230,000 software specialists in India, 1 million in Japan and 2 million in the United States (Rui and Tao, 2004).

The Chinese software development enterprises are generally small in size and lack both human resources and core technology. In 2002, there were only 157,000 software development engineers in the 4700 software development companies of designated size or above, employing a total of 592,000 employees. Only 7 per cent of the 592,000 employees had postgraduate qualifications and one-third had graduate qualifications. Two-thirds of the companies employed fewer than 50 people and a quarter employed between 50 and 200 people. By contrast, in 2001, India had about 6000 software development companies, employing over 400,000 people. Over 100 of the companies employed more than 1000 employees. During the early 2000s, China trained 33,000 IT engineers each year (15,000 of them on software) whereas India trained 55,000 software engineers each year (Rui and Tao, 2004). According to a survey jointly conducted by various ministries of China, there will be an annual demand from various sectors for 1 million computing specialist workers (cited in Jiang and Wang, 2004). Senior IT specialists, including software engineers, test engineers, advanced programmers and product project managers, was one of the six categories of professionals who were most sought after in 2005 (*China Business*, 8 August 2005). It must also be noted that the IT training market is a lucrative one, with total sales revenue of 2.44 billion yuan in 2004 – an increase of 22.1 per cent from 2003 (*Workers' Daily*, 14 September 2005).

Since a major ingredient for software R&D is that of human capital, both in terms of human capital for market intelligence and human capital for programme design, the shortage of software and system design engineers and competent marketing personnel has been a bottleneck for the development of the Chinese IT industry. To worsen the situation, the shortage of human capital has led to a war for talent in the industry. There has been a serious brain drain from the privately owned and state-owned enterprises to foreign firms in China and abroad, which offer more attractive employment packages and career opportunities. According to Jiang and Wang (2004), the turnover rate of R&D staff in the IT industry in Beijing and Shanghai was about 20 per cent on average, with the privately owned IT enterprises suffering a much higher turnover rate (28 per cent) than their state-owned and collectively owned counterparts (10.6 per cent) (Jiang and Wang, 2004). To combat the problem, some Chinese firms are beginning to address the retention problems through HR initiatives. For example, Lenovo (see Case Study 6.1) was the first Chinese IT firm to adopt the employee stock options and enterprise culture management initiatives to motivate and retain its workforce (Rui and Tao, 2004).

At the national level, the Chinese government is acutely aware of the importance of developing human resources for the IT industry. In particular, the tenth five-year plan of the Chinese government (the Ministry of Information Industry, 2001) emphasized the following objectives:

■ Overall planning of HR development according to the development of the industry;

■ Promote cooperation between business enterprises and universities in developing professionals, provide for on-the-job training to improve the quality of human resources;

■ Train up or bring into the country technical and managerial professionals, attract professionals who have both technical expertise as well as managerial and marketing capabilities; and

■ Encourage the inclusion of capital and technologies in the rationing of revenue, introduce bonus and share options to the remuneration of company directors, provide an attractive environment to attract human resources (the Ministry of Information Industry, 2001, cited in http://www.trp.hku.hk/infofile/2002/10-5-yr-plan.pdf).

There are a number of sources from which IT skills are being trained and pooled to combat the skill shortage problem. One is that universities and technical colleges have rapidly expanded their enrolment of students on IT-related courses. For example, in 2002, only 197,310 IT students graduated from vocational and technical colleges in China. In 2005, this figure rose to 908,377 (*China Statistical Yearbook*, 2003 and 2006). Another source is that a small but growing number of overseas Chinese who have become successful in high-tech places such as Silicon Valley in the United States, have been returning home to take advantage of China's booming technology market and the Chinese government's favourable policy to attract them back home. This is in addition to a rising number of graduates returning to China after receiving their further education abroad.

In spite of the shortage of R&D engineers, an increasing number of MNCs are setting up their R&D centres in China to take advantage of China's low-cost human resources as well as to exploit the market (see Box 6.3 for example). According to the China Software Industry Association (2005), China has become the largest overseas software outsourcing manufacturing base for Japan. China exported US$150 million to Japan in 2004 and the trade value is expected to increase by 50 per cent per year. Analysts forecast that in 2005, China would need some 3750 more Japanese language software engineers and the number is expected to increase by 150 per cent per year. As the outsourcing market for IT software business and other business processes grows intensively in India, India is going to face skill shortages. In fact,

---

BOX 6.3

Motorola's R&D centre in China

In March 2006, Motorola announced the launch of its Hangzhou R&D Centre – the Company's 17th R&D facility in China. The new R&D centre is designed to provide Chinese operators with local access to Motorola's comprehensive network technologies as well as develop local talent while driving network innovation and the growth of China's wireless communications industry.

The new R&D centre will support both Motorola Network's technologies and products, helping to develop, test and launch software and hardware for final integration into commercialized product offerings for customers. It will also provide extensive R&D services for next generation technologies.

With the establishment of the new Hangzhou R&D centre, Motorola is taking another step towards addressing the specific needs of operators in the China market by developing seamless mobility strategies that will generate new sources of revenue and differentiated service offerings.

With the close participation and support from the Hangzhou government, Motorola's new global R&D centre will further help transform Hangzhou into a global telecommunications development and innovation hub.

Motorola's first R&D centre in China was established in 1993. The Motorola China R&D Institute was founded in 1999. Motorola is known around the world for innovation and leadership in wireless and broadband communications. A Fortune 100 company with global presence and impact, Motorola had sales of US$36.8 billion in 2005.

Source: Motorola Inc. (2006), 'Motorola opens R&D Centre in Hangzhou, China', Internet source: http://www.webwire.com/ViewPressRel.asp?SESSIONID=&aId=11583, accessed on 6 April 2006.

---

it is turning to China not only to fill some of the skill gaps but also to develop new markets in China and other countries in eastern Asia including Japan. For example, India's second-largest software export company Infosys planned to recruit 6000 programmers from China. It had over 290 programmers in China by the end of 2005 where wage cost was only 40 per cent of that in India for the same type of jobs. Three of the four largest Indian software developer firms have established business operations in Beijing and set up collaborative relationships with Chinese and foreign firms there (*Development and Management of Human Resources*, 2005).

Competition strategy of the Chinese IT industry

The rising competitiveness of the Chinese IT industry in the world market is attributed to a number of related factors at national, industrial and enterprise level. One is the national protectionism operated by the Chinese government,

as mentioned earlier, in order to facilitate the growth of national firms. Consequently, unlike the automotive industry which is dominated by foreign brand
products, national brand-name products tend to occupy the main share of
the market in the IT industry. At a deeper level, however, this protectionism is
related to the Chinese government's desire to catch up technologically through
learning from outsiders 'without surrendering technological or economic control' (Kraemer and Dedrick, 2001, p. 17). Compared with other industries
which are also open to foreign competition, policies for the IT industry are more
centralized and controlled. According to Kraemer and Dedrick (2001, p. 17),

> China's desire to develop strong domestic computer makers with indigenous
> technological capabilities is similar to that of Japan, Korea and to some
> extent Taiwan. Each provided financial and technical resources to domestic
> companies, and in some cases protected them from foreign competition.
> China's strategy of extracting concessions from foreign MNCs in return
> for market access is most similar to Japan, which likewise had a large and
> attractive market.

Another factor is that the investment of foreign MNCs in the IT industry
in China has sharpened the competitive edge of the Chinese-owned IT firms
through technology transfer and spill-over, introduction of advanced management techniques and skill training. Foreign firms' entry into China is an integral
part of their global competition strategy because of the vast development
potential of the Chinese market. The Chinese IT industry has been attracting
an increasing amount of foreign investment since the late 1990s. For example,
in 2004, a total number of 1622 projects were signed, with a total contract
value of US$2.02 billion and an actual utilized value of 906 million through
FDI in the information transmission, computer services and software sector
(see Table 2.5). The increase of FDI has led to the growth of various forms of
R&D centres set up by foreign investors in China (see Boxes 6.1 and 6.3). Furthermore, there is clear evidence that the products produced by foreign-owned
enterprises are moving up the value chain (Chen and Wei, 2003).

Meanwhile, foreign investors are beginning to integrate their businesses
in China and expand them through M&As. An increasing number of foreign
investment projects are in the form of wholly foreign-owned businesses and
an increasing number of existing JVs are shifting towards wholly foreign-owned
or foreign-controlled. This strategic move is likely to pose serious challenges to
China's policy that aims to push Chinese-owned IT firms up the quality chain
through JVs with foreign businesses (Chen and Wei, 2003). There is a danger
that the loosening grip of the 'market for technology' policy adopted by the
Chinese government, in part as a result of the WTO agreements, may enable
foreign firms to control both the market and the technology of IT products in
China.

At the enterprise level, the IT product market and manufacturers in China
can be divided into two strategic groupings of leading enterprises, according to
Rui and Tao (2004). One consists of leading indigenous Chinese IT firms (e.g.
Lenovo) and the other consists of leading foreign firms. The former exploits

its indigenous advantage to develop localized products and occupies the market with prices lower than that of foreign firms. By contrast, the latter targets the commercial market with pioneering technology, international brand-name products and excellent customer services as their unique selling point to justify their high prices. By comparison, Chinese firms have a much better understanding of the needs of the Chinese customers and market segmentation, and are advantaged from the co-location (within the same country) of marketing people and R&D staff. They are able to compete with top-brand foreign firms whose products are globally oriented instead of tailored for the Chinese market. In addition, Chinese firms design their promotion methods to be more suitable to the Chinese customers. For example, Dell takes less than 1 per cent of the Chinese PC market in part because its sales technique (e-commerce and telephone sales) and direct customer services approach (without sales agency or counter) is not yet suitable for the Chinese IT market, because the Chinese consumers are still relatively inexperienced as IT product consumers and are not familiar with these methods. Similarly, the distribution channels and payment methods are not yet established in China to accommodate Dell's operational style (Rui and Tao, 2004).

Below are mini case studies of two leading Chinese IT firms – Lenovo and Huawei (Case Studies 6.1 and 6.2; also see Lu, 2000 and Fan, 2006 respectively for more details of these two firms).

CASE STUDY 6.1

Lenovo

Company profile

Established in 1988, Lenovo Group Limited (formerly known as 'Legend Group Limited') is the largest IT enterprise in China. For the year ended 31 March 2004, Lenovo reported a turnover of HK$23.2 billion and net profit of HK$1.05 billion. As of September 2004, with a market capitalization of about HK$19.6 billion, Lenovo employed about 9200 staff.

In 1984, with an initial capital of RMB 200,000 funded by the Chinese Academy of Sciences, 11 researchers formed the parent company of Lenovo. It was the first company to introduce the concept of home computer in China. Lenovo was listed on The Stock Exchange of Hong Kong Limited in 1994 (Stock code: 992) and is currently a constituent stock of the Hang Seng Index (HIS) and Hang Seng China-Affiliated Corporations Index (HKCCI). Lenovo's American Depositary Receipts (stock code: LNVGY) are also being traded in the United States.

Currently, Lenovo engages primarily in the sale and manufacturing of desktop computers, notebook computers, mobile handsets, servers, printers and so on in China. Lenovo brand PCs have been the best seller in China for the last few years, commanding a 30 per cent share of the Chinese PC market and selling more than 1.47 million PCs in 2000. Lenovo PCs also ranked number one in the Asia Pacific (excluding Japan) with a share of 12.6 per cent in 2003.

Headquartered in Beijing, Lenovo runs PC assembly lines in Beijing, Shanghai and Huiyang (Guangdong province) with a total annual production capacity of about 5 million. Lenovo has divided the China market into 18 sales sub-regions with more than 4000 retails shops serving customers across the country. Dedicated to providing comprehensive services to its customers, Lenovo offers 24-hour customer hotline services and an extensive network of maintenance centres in China. Lenovo is committed to continuously enhancing its R&D capabilities. As of June 2004, it has secured an accumulative total of 787 patent rights from the State Intellectual Property Office of China. One of the most significant technological achievements by the Group was the successful development of the 'Deepcomp 6800' supercomputer in 2003. With actual computing speed of 4183 GFLOPS, 'Deepcomp 6800' ranked 14th among the world's top 500 supercomputers as of November 2003.

In April 2003, the Group adopted a new logo and the English brand name 'Lenovo', replacing the original English brand name 'Legend' in order to appeal to the international market. The English company name was also officially changed to 'Lenovo Group Limited' a year later. In March 2004, on joining the International Olympic Committee's global sponsorship programme, The Olympic Partner (TOP) Programme, Lenovo injected new passion and energy into its brand. This was the first time a Chinese enterprise joined the IOC's top level worldwide marketing programme. Over the next five years, Lenovo will provide computing technology equipment, funding as well as technological support to the 2006 Turin Olympic Winter Games, the 2008 Beijing Olympic Games and over 200 national Olympic committees around the world.

Lenovo ranked 2nd on the Asia's Leading Companies list published by the Far Eastern Economic Review in December 2003, and ranked 13th among Fortune's list of China's 100 largest Companies published in August 2003. The Lenovo brand is the 4th most valuable brands in China and its brand value was estimated at Rmb26.8 billion in 2003. In the 11th Best Managed Companies Poll by Asiamoney in 2003, Lenovo was the 4th 'Best Managed Company', 2nd in 'Best Financial Management' and 1st in 'Best Corporate Governance' and 'Best Investor Relations'.

In December 2004, Lenovo spent US$1.25 billion to acquire IBM PC business. This was the largest cross-border acquisition in China's IT industry (*China Business*, 13 December 2004). The marriage of IBM and Lenovo created one of the world's largest PC powerhouses, with a combined annual PC revenue of US$12 billion and volume of 11.9 million units, based on the results of 2003. IBM possessed strong competitive advantage in the higher end of the customer market in its distribution channel, high-quality customer resources which complemented that of Lenovo. The two companies will maintain long-term strategic ties. Lenovo will have access to IBM's technology, sale force, PartnerWorld, and to IBM Global Finance and IBM Credit.

For more than a decade, Lenovo has devoted itself to 'making things easier for customers' and persisted in providing leading-edge technology products to Chinese users. In the future, Lenovo will continue to satisfy the needs of various types of customers by offering customer-oriented computer products and services, so as to realize its aspiration of becoming 'a technology driven, service oriented, and international Lenovo'.

Fourfold mission:

For customers

To streamline our customers' living and working conditions by providing them with the latest and best in IT products and services;

For shareholders

To maximize our shareholders' long-term benefits;

For staff

To provide a stimulating and challenging working environment in which employees can find multiple opportunities for personal and professional advancement;

For the community

To contribute responsibility to the development of the wider community.

Corporate Culture:

Four core values

1) **Serving customers**
   Serving customers defines value enhancement; this principle is a DNA that imprints in every Lenovo employee's genes.

2) **Accuracy and truth seeking**
   Conclusion is based on facts and scientific analysis; the respect for rules and guidelines; having discipline and courage to face up to reality and take responsibility.

3) **Trustworthy and integrity**
   Trustworthy and integrity is Lenovo's 'Golden marquee', a vital business philosophy.

4) **Innovative and can do spirit**
   Ownership mentality, being proactive and humble, with strong sense of urgency and can do; change ready.

Source: adapted from Lenovo company website, http://www.lenovogrp.com/cgi-bin, accessed on 14 June 2005 and *China Business* (13 December 2004).

CASE STUDY 6.2

Huawei Technologies Co Ltd

Huawei is an employee-owned company that was established in 1988 by Zhengfei Ren, a former army officer. It is a high-tech enterprise which specializes in R&D, production and marketing of communication equipment, and providing customized network solutions for telecom carriers in different areas. Huawei became China's largest telecom and networking equipment maker by the mid-1990s and soon made plans to go global. It started by supplying developing countries with technology good enough for local needs. In 2000 it made its first significant international sale to a Russian telecom carrier. That was quickly followed by sales to Advanced Info Service, Thailand's largest mobile phone carrier, and Brazil's fixed-line carrier Tele Norte Leste Participacoes. More recently Huawei has won deals with a Dutch mobile operator, Telfort, and the second-largest Internet service provider in France – Free.

Huawei's products can be divided into the following categories: fixed network, mobile network, data communications, optical network, software and services and terminals. Huawei's contracted sales in 2005 reached US$8.2 billion, an increase of 47 per cent year on year, among which 60 per cent of sales came from international sales. Huawei's customers include China Telecom, China Mobile, China Netcom, China Unicom as well as BT, NEUF, AIS, Telefonia, Telfort, Telkom Kenya, SingTel, Hutchison Global Crossing, PCCWHKT, SUNDAY, Etisalat (UAE), Telemar (Brazil), Rostelecom (Russia), Magyar Telekom (Hungary) and CANTV Movilnet (Venezuela). Currently Huawei provides telecom products and solutions for over 270 operators worldwide and 22 of the world's top 50 operators are using Huawei's products and solutions. Huawei's products are deployed in over 70 countries.

In order to support its global operations, Huawei has set up 55 branch offices worldwide. Eight regional headquarters and a host of customer support and training centres have been established. Several research institutes including Dallas, Texas (USA), Silicon Valley (USA), Bangalore (India), Stockholm (Sweden), Moscow (Russia), Beijing and Shanghai have been set up.

The Huawei threat comes not from low-cost manufacturing – which is now a given throughout the industry – but from low-cost engineering. Each year, Huawei invests no less than 10 per cent of its sales revenue into R&D. Among Huawei's 34,000 employees (around 3400 foreign staff), 48 per cent are engaged in R&D. Many of whom have Masters or PhD degrees and whose salaries are one-third to one-fifth those of their Silicon Valley counterparts. This engineering workforce enables the company 'to tailor-make innovative solutions for big customers that are looking to reduce their capital expenditures', according to Huawei's Vice President of Marketing.

Huawei is now moving upstream with more sophisticated products. For example, Huawei is emerging as a leading player in 3G mobile phone equipment, which brings broadband Internet access and videoconferencing to mobile phone handsets. The company is supplying 3G systems to carriers in Europe, Africa and the Middle East, even before China settles on a 3G standard.

To ensure steady and sustainable growth and to sharpen the core competitive edge, Huawei seeks strategic partnership with leading global players in the industry on both product development and marketing.

Source: adapted from http://en.wikipedia.org/wiki/Huawei and http://www.naukri.com/gpw/huawei, accessed on 1 April 2006.

It is obvious that strong leadership with strategic foresight, heavy R&D investment, a strong innovation culture, product branding, a customer-oriented business culture, good HR policies (e.g. incentive-related reward schemes and career development opportunities), strategic alliances with foreign MNCs, and importantly, the support of the government are all important factors that have led to Lenovo's success. However, it is worth noting that, like other firms, Lenovo's development is not without problems, both technical and organizational. It is also worth noting that while Lenovo represents one of the best Chinese companies, with a growing global presence and confidence, it seems to share a similar feature with the majority of Chinese firms. That is, it pays much more attention to its customers' needs and customer relationship management than it does to the notion of CSR (see Chapter 9). CSR features only very briefly in its mission statement and company websites. The actual CSR activities carried out are mainly in the form of charity donations to support poor children's education (*China Business*, 18 September 2006). The absence of the public statements somehow makes one wonder if the notion of CSR, something that western MNCs are increasingly paying strategic attention to at least in rhetoric if not in reality, has caught sufficient attention of its senior management. In fact, the senior management of Lenovo publicly admitted that the Corporation has not yet developed a comprehensive strategic plan for CSR and pledged that this issue is going to become one of the top priorities of Lenovo (*China Business*, 18 September 2006). Whether this pledge is going to translate into real action remains to be seen.

Huawei's success seems to share much in common with that of Lenovo, that is, strong leadership with strategic foresight, heavy R&D investment, a strong innovation culture and strategic alliances with foreign MNCs to acquire technology as well as overseas market. What is more unique of Huawei is its aggressive but strategic move to occupy the international market in different areas of the world, tailoring its technology and service provisions to local needs (see Chapter 9 for further discussion of Huawei).

Summary

China has 'seized the opportunity created by the microelectronics revolution and developed a viable indigenous computer electronics industry' (Lu, 2000, p. 189). The industry started to grow in the late 1980s with product redesign (adaptation of foreign products) and product design, which has benefited from the S&T capabilities that China had accumulated during its central-planned economy period (Lu, 2000). It was partially opened to foreign firms in order to attract investment and technology, and to promote exports by joining the global production networks of the MNCs. The Chinese government and MNCs have been the two major sources of investment in the Chinese IT industry. Government protectionism and R&D support, the entry of foreign MNCs and the entrepreneurship of domestic firms have played an important role in shaping China's IT industry and facilitated the rapid growth of indigenous firms. The unique institutional and organizational arrangements of the major

Chinese computer firms, that is, state-owned/affiliated and privately managed (Lu, 2000), has contributed to the early success of these firms. Moreover, the rapid growth of the IT industry has been fuelled by Chinese consumers' growing appetite and increasingly sophisticated demand for faster, more novel and stylish telecommunication and household electronic products.

After over a decade's catching-up race, the Chinese IT industry is now emerging into the global arena with growing competence and confidence. The main factors of competitive advantage in the IT industry are the speed of innovation, human resources and market. China is rapidly developing its innovation capability and possesses an enormous market with growing demands. The cost of software development engineers is relatively low. These are the comparative advantages of China in the development of its software industry. However, there is a severe shortage of skill supply, and compared with other industries, the poaching problem is more prominent in the IT industry. Nevertheless, given the increasing trend of outsourcing from MNCs to developing countries, providing outsourcing services for software development should be the key business areas of Chinese IT firms, in addition to hardware manufacturing. More generally, domestic IT enterprises need to sharpen up their competitiveness by enhancing their product innovation capability, strengthening enterprise core-tech R&D. They also need to explore more effective marketing channels and improve enterprise capital operation capability and resource consolidation capability in light of the intensifying global competition (China Software Industry Association, 2005).

Recommended readings

A. Amighini, 'China in the International Fragmentation of Production: Evidence from the ICT Industry', *The European Journal of Comparative Economics*, 2, 2 (2005): 203–19.

M. Katsuno, 'Status and Overview of Official ICT Indicators for China', *OECD Science, Technology and Industry Working Papers* 2005/4 (Paris: OECD Publishing, 2005).

H. Lai, Y. Chiu and H. Leu, 'Innovation Capacity Comparison of China's Information Technology Industrial Clusters: The Case of Shanghai, Kunshan, Shenzhen and Dongguan', *Technology Analysis and Strategic Management*, 17, 3 (2005): 293–315.

Q. Lu, *China's Leap into the Information Age: Innovation and Organization in the Computer Industry* (Oxford: Oxford University Press, 2000).

CHAPTER 7
Retail and Exhibition Industry

Introduction

We have explored two of the oldest manufacturing-based industries in China – the automotive and pharmaceutical industries in Chapters 4 and 5. We then investigated how the Chinese IT industry has taken off rapidly as a new industry. In this chapter, we are going to look at two industries in the service sector – the retail industry and the exhibition industry. The former is an old industry whilst the latter is a new one. Both carry strong traces of state involvement during the planned economy period.

This chapter is divided into two main parts. The first one concentrates on the retail industry and the second on the exhibition industry. Retail industry contains three main sections. The first one provides a brief summary of the background of the retail industry. This is followed by a discussion of the competition pressure in the industry and strategies adopted by both foreign and Chinese retail enterprises operating in China. The third section analyses the profile of human resources in this industry. The discussion of the retail industry in this chapter will focus on the commodities sector of the industry. The retail sector of other industries may be touched upon in the chapters that deal with those particular industries (e.g. the pharmaceutical industry in Chapter 4). The second part of this chapter consists of three main sections. The first one outlines the stages of development of the exhibition industry. In the second section, a number of problems in the development of the industry are identified. Not surprisingly, many of these problems echo those manifested in other industries in China. The third section describes some of the strategic responses that are emerging in the industry in its effort to establish a more market-oriented industry. Institutional barriers to do so remain strong and investment in exhibitions will prove highly risky for some time to come.

Retail industry

Background of the industry

The Chinese retail industry is a long-established one that was primarily state-owned or collectively owned until the 1980s. The state planned economy system carried a number of weaknesses in the development of the commercial business. One of the major weaknesses was the neglect of the development of distribution business, believing that it was a low-capital and low-technology aspect of the business. This has led to an under-investment of capital, technology and skills in the distribution system. A related misconception was that

Table 7.1 Total retail value of
commodities in China in selected years

Year	Total retail value of com- modities (billion yuan)
1978	155.9
1980	214.0
1985	430.5
1990	830.0
1995	2,062.0
1996	2,477.4
1997	2,729.9
1998	2,915.3
1999	3,113.5
2000	3,415.3
2001	3,759.5
2002	4,091.1
2003	4,584.2

Source: adapted from H. L. Zhang (2004, p. 379).

wholesale business was seen as an additional layer of the commercial business that would lead to increased transactional cost. This has resulted in the
under-development of the wholesale business (Song and Li, 2004).

Since the late 1970s, the retail industry has experienced steady growth.
According to H. L. Zhang (2004), in 1978, the total retail value of
commodities was 155.9 billion yuan. This had increased to 4584.2 billion yuan by 2003 (also see Tables 7.1 and 7.4). By 2003, the annual
sales volume of consumer goods had reached 4.58 trillion yuan. It is
believed that the industry will continue to grow by about 10 per cent
each year, reaching an expected 20 trillion yuan by 2020 (http://www.wal-
martchina.com/english/news/20041102.htm). According to a study conducted by PricewaterhouseCoopers on 14 countries in the Asia Pacific area in
2002, China is the world's largest single potential market for consumer goods,
with its maturing consumption patterns and increasing disposable incomes
(PricewaterhouseCoopers, 2003). Compared with developed countries such
as the United States, France, Australia and Japan, the Chinese retail industry
makes up a relatively large proportion of the tertiary sector in terms of added
value (see Table 7.2). This is in spite of the fact that it makes up only 12.56
per cent of China's GDP, a proportion that is considerably smaller than that
of other countries (see Table 7.3).

There are several problems with the Chinese retail industry. One is its small
size and scale with a relatively low level of concentration, particularly of the
Chinese-owned retail enterprises. In the United States, annual sales by Wal-
Mart alone account for 8 per cent of the country's total retail sales, whereas in
China, total sales by all the chain stores account for less than 6 per cent of the

Table 7.2   The added value of the
wholesale and retail industry and the
goods transportation industry as
percentage of the tertiary sector of
selected countries in the year 2000*

Country	Proportion
China	37.79
India	39.78
Indonesia	40.46
Iran	45.12
Japan	30.49
South Korea	33.03
Philippines	36.05
Singapore	45.89
Thailand	47.00
Mexico	93.10
USA	29.96
France	27.40
Italy	34.32
Australia	25.90

*The authors calculated the figures based on the statistics in the *International Statistical Yearbook* (2002) (original note).
Figures in %
Source: Song and Li (2004, p. 86).

country's overall retail sales (*Economic Information and Agency*, 24 February 2003). This makes it very difficult for the Chinese-owned retail enterprises to compete against foreign retail giants. Another problem is the lack of distinctive style and competitive advantages of the Chinese-owned retail enterprises in general. Since the mid-1990s, the retail market in China has gradually shifted from being a supplier's market to a buyer's market. In the first half of 2002, 86 per cent of commodities were over-supplied and the remaining 14 per cent were in supply and demand balance (Wang *et al.*, 2003). This was a result of the opening up of the economy and the entry of foreign retail operators who offered shoppers a new shopping experience with new fashions and commercial products. Sales revenue and profits of traditional department stores have been in sharp decline for a number of years. Those traditional department stores that have managed to make the transition and became supermarkets and chain stores were evidently performing better than those that did not. Those with financial problems included some of the once big-name national department stores with decades of history, such as Beijing Wangfujing Department Store that was the first department store in China established in 1955. Until the 1990s, visiting this 'First Shop of the New China' was a must-trip for visitors to Beijing as

Table 7.3 The added value of the wholesale and retail industry and the goods transportation industry as percentage of the GDP of selected countries in the year 2000*

Country	Proportion
China	12.56
Bangladesh	21.26
India	21.30
Indonesia	20.19
Iran	26.59
Japan	21.15
South Korea	18.43
Philippines	20.26
Singapore	30.88
Thailand	25.60
Mexico	30.25
USA	22.72
France	20.33
Italy	24.87

*The authors calculated the figures based on the statistics in the *International Statistical Yearbook* (2002) (original note).
Figures in %
Source: Song and Li (2004, p. 86).

part of their experience of touring the Capital city. The decline of well-known shops that were associated with specific locality reflects the fact that locality-associated brands may be a barrier to developing national and international chain stores on the one hand, and that brand names are a valuable resource that the enterprises should take advantage of in their business re-engineering on the other. One example of a successful business transformation is Beijing Tongrentang (see Chapter 5).

Competition and strategy

According to W. Wang *et al.* (2004), there are a number of characteristics in the retail industry in China. One is the sustained high growth rate of retail chains, fuelled by the accession to the WTO. According to W. Wang *et al.* (2004), the total sales revenue of the Top 100 retail chains was 246.5 billion yuan in 2002, an increase of 52 per cent from that of the previous year (162 billion yuan). The total number of stores had also grown by 29 per cent from 13,177 in 2001 to 16,986 in 2002. While shopping space had grown by 59 per cent, the number of employees had increased by 24 per cent from 416,400 in 2001 to 519,700 employees in 2002. A second characteristic is that M&As have become the main mechanism for expansion for domestic retail chains in order to increase their size to compete with foreign retail giants. Some of them have expanded from a regional to a national base. Some of the mergers of retail corporate groups may involve a large number of stores, several stock-listed subsidiaries and international JVs (W. Wang *et al.*, 2004). A third characteristic is that foreign retail chains are becoming increasingly dominant in the Chinese retail industry (W. Wang *et al.*, 2004).

From 2002 onwards, MNC and Chinese retailers have accelerated their speed of competition. In 2002 alone, a total of 678 new retail shops were approved by the Chinese authorities, including three large department stores, 68 large supermarkets, 350 convenience stores and the rest mainly medium-sized supermarkets. Among the 678 shops, 14 were new branch shops from MNC retailers already operating in China, 19 were from MNC retailers entering China for the first time. Only one of the 19 new MNC retailers entering the Chinese market was a single-store operator, all the others were chain-store corporations (P. Jin *et al.*, 2003). The strategies adopted by foreign retail giants and domestic-funded retail enterprises are analysed below.

Western retail giants' strategy in China

Since China's accession to the WTO, the retail industry has been the first to be fully opened up to FDI. By the end of 2004, China had lifted all barriers to foreign retail firms operating in China. This fuelled a new wave of competition and the retail industry has become a major site of M&As among Chinese-owned firms as well as by foreign retail giants (see W. Wang *et al.*, 2004). This industry has relatively low entry barriers with plenty of well-established domestic retail enterprises that provide a ready platform for acquisitions. With the Chinese retail industry currently undergoing a period of re-structuring, acquisition is a major route for international retail firms entering the Chinese commodities retail market. An increasing number of MNC retail giants are setting up branches in major cities in China in order to gain a share of the Chinese retail market. It was estimated that 70 per cent of the Top 50 large retailers in the world have already set up JVs in China (Xu, 2003). In 2005, the Ministry of Commerce approved the applications of 1027 foreign-invested commercial enterprises with 1660 stores that were worth a total of 1.82 billion yuan. This was a significant growth compared with the total of 314 stores approved in the previous 12 years (*China Business*, 20 February 2006). By the end of 2005, the world's largest eleven retail corporations had all entered the Chinese market (*China Business*, 20 February 2006). The world's top three retail giants – Wal-Mart, Carrefour and Metro are all engaged in their strategic expansion in China to occupy new markets (Tian, 2003). By the end of 2005, foreign-funded retail enterprises made up 2.1 per cent of all the 73,774 retail enterprises that were above designated size, employing 5.1 per cent of the 2.95 million employees in these enterprises (*China Statistical Yearbook*, 2006). These may look like small proportions, but they were significant increases from the figures in 2002, which were 1.67 per cent of all the 28,751 enterprises of above designated size and 3.5 per cent of the 2.25 million employees (*China*

Statistical Yearbook, 2003). Chain stores appear to be the main mode of growth (see Table 7.4).

Most of the foreign firms entering China deploy supermarkets as their main business mode which includes both comprehensive supermarkets and warehouse supermarkets, they are all aiming at long-term strategic development in China and are therefore real investors (P. Jin *et al.*, 2003). They tend to start with the biggest cities, for example, Beijing, Shanghai and Guangzhou, where

Table 7.4   General information of retail chain store enterprises of above designated size* by status of ownership

Status of ownership	No. of stores (units)		Operational area(10,000 sq.m)		Employed person 10,000) persons)	
	2003	2004	2003	2004	2003	2004
Total	46,517	54,891	2,780.2	3,517.1	92.4	105.6
Domestic funded enterprises	43,256	51,110	2,379.5	3,021.4	78.3	89.2
State-owned enterprises	6,571	6,999	435.8	534.2	8.1	8.1
Enterprises with funds from Hong Kong, Macao and Taiwan	1,237	1,396	185.5	242.8	5.6	6.4
Foreign funded enterprises	2,024	2,385	213.3	250.5	8.4	9.8

Status of ownership	Total sales (100 million yuan)		Retail (100 million yuan)		Total profits (100 million yuan)	
	2003	2004	2003	2004	2003	2004
Total	4,258.6	5,580.7	3,464.1	4,509.9	57.3	78.7
Domestic funded enterprises	3,527.5	4,636.6	2,818.0	3,686.9	51.7	67.9
State-owned enterprises	375.0	504.5	228.9	304.5	16.1	23.1
Enterprises with funds from Hong Kong, Macao and Taiwan	265.0	339.5	250.3	318.4	1.0	0.2
Foreign funded enterprises	462.4	600.4	392.2	500.4	4.6	10.5

Table 7.4   (Continued)

	Total assets (100 million yuan)		Total liabilities (100 million yuan)	
	2003	2004	2003	2004
Total	1,450.7	1,800.6	1,063.8	1,309.4
Domestic funded enterprises	1,185.8	1,491.3	859.7	1,081.8
State-owned enterprises	118.4	152.3	65.3	101.1
Enterprises with funds from Hong Kong, Macao and Taiwan	108.5	116.0	87.5	91.3
Foreign funded enterprises	154.6	189.0	115.1	132.6

* 'Above designated size': see Table 3.1 for definition.
Source: adapted from *China Statistical Yearbook* (2005, pp. 603–5).

the physical infrastructure is much more developed and where living standards are much higher in comparison with that in other areas. They then permeate into the mid-ranking cities and venture into the western region where the competition is far less fierce but the potential for market development is more attractive. International retailing giants such as Carrefour, Auchan and Wal-Mart are amongst those that are venturing west.

Carrefour is perhaps the most aggressive foreign retail giant in China in terms of its expansion strategy. Carrefour first entered China in 1995 and established stores in a number of major cities including Shanghai, Shenzhen, Beijing, Tianjin, Wuhan and Chongqing relatively quickly with a rising brand name reputation. By the end of 2000, Carrefour had 27 stores in China, five of them opened in 2000, yielding total sales revenue of 8 billion yuan (Tian, 2003). Metro's expansion plan in China is equally as ambitious. By the end of 2000, it had opened ten stores in China. It was reported that Metro's ambition is to open a total of 100 stores in China (Tian, 2003).

By comparison, US retail giant Wal-Mart's expansion strategy was relatively low key in the first few years since opening its first store in China in 1996. However, in a bid to catch up with Carrefour of France, it started its offensive strategy at the end of 2000 by opening three new giant supermarkets in three major cities – Shenzhen, Fuzhou and Shantou. In 2001, the State Council of China approved Wal-Mart's expansion plan of developing 60 supermarkets in 20 major cities in China, with a sales revenue target of 18 billion yuan (Tian, 2003). By March 2005, Wal-Mart had 44 stores with over 23,000 employees in China. It will open another 15 new stores in China by the end of 2005. Wal-Mart has opened more than 30 stores with the same partner, Shenzhen International Trust & Investment Corp, which holds a 39 per cent stake in Shenzhen Wal-Mart River Department Store Co Ltd (http://www.accessasia.co.uk).

Establishing business operations in China is not without institutional and cultural barriers for Western retail chain giants. Protectionism and bureaucracy of some local governments (also see Chapter 8) and regional variations in the business environment make it difficult to implement a pan-China operations strategy through standardization and integrated process management. While possessing sophisticated supply chain and distribution systems is an important and integral part of foreign retail giants' success, the underdevelopment of these systems in China presents a major barrier to their successful operations in China. In terms of location, the majority of Chinese people do not have private transport but like their food fresh and tend to do their food shopping on a daily basis. Most of the commercial and business activities therefore take place in the town centre for the convenience of commuting. However, premium space requires premium rent, thus constraining foreign retailers' typical business mode of having super-large supermarkets to gain economies of scale. Moreover, established local retail enterprises have already occupied most of the premium spots in town. Discount stores may not do well in China because most retailers offer periodic discounts as a marketing and sales strategy to attract customers. Competition in China's retail industry is still one that is largely based on price which tends to be kept low by retail operators, further squeezing the margins of discount stores. In addition, despite the Chinese consumers' open-mindedness and enthusiasm in embracing foreign products and concepts, cultural adaptation proves necessary to suit local characteristics. For example, Chinese do not have a do-it-yourself (DIY) culture, for example, assembling furniture or household equipment themselves; retail enterprises that sell household goods, such as IKEA (see Case Study 7.1 for more detail), may need to have a large customer service section to help assemble and home delivery as part of the purchase deal (Miller, 2004).

CASE STUDY 7.1

IKEA China

IKEA Group, a franchisee of Inter IKEA Systems BV, entered China in 1998 when it opened its first store in Shanghai. A new, redesigned Shanghai store opened in 2003, replacing the original outlet. IKEA expects to have ten large stores up and running in China by 2010. IKEA's mission is to provide smart solutions for homes by implementing three criteria: good design, functionality and low price. IKEA offers a range of 8000–10,000 products depending on each store's size. But the company adapts the layout of the store, presentation of the goods, home solutions offered and prices according to national economic and cultural conditions. In China, the store layouts reflect the layout of many Chinese apartments, and since many Chinese apartments have balconies, the stores even include a balcony section.

When IKEA first entered China, the store was considered too expensive for its target consumers – young, professional couples – and the company lowered its prices. The store's prices are now considered mid-range in Shanghai. Most of IKEA China's customers are 20–35 years old, but the stores now attract an increasing number of customers closer to the age of 45, most likely a result of the store's market repositioning.

IKEA plans further expansion in China. IKEA's two stores in Beijing and Shanghai continue to be successful: up to August 2004 sales in China are estimated at US$121.2 million (1 billion yuan), an increase by 50 per cent over 2003. Although this represents still a small portion of its total global sales of US$13.6 billion, the rise in disposable household income and the desire to show affluence promises further business potential. To meet this trend most products follow Scandinavian design trends, except for traditional Chinese utensils. However, in the home furnishing market, the competition has become more intense since local stores have improved design and quality – a challenge for IKEA. IKEA announced plans for a further expansion in China by opening 10 new stores within the next 6–8 years in cities with a population of over 4 million people. On a global scale, IKEA expects to source approximately 23 per cent of its worldwide purchasing from China this year – an ideal combination of Scandinavian design and low manufacturing cost.

Sources: adapted from Miller (2004) and Fiducia Management Consultants (2004c), http://www.fiducia-china.com/News/2004/73-1840.html, accessed on 10 December 2004.

In general, Western retail giants have played an important role in the recent development of the retail industry in China by shaping the competition and upgrading the operation mode of the industry. They have fundamentally altered China's single retail business model of traditional department stores by introducing a variety of retail business models, including hypermarkets, supermarkets, cash & carry, hard discount, warehouse clubs and home improvement superstores. They brought to China new products, new ways of shopping, new customer relations management, new concepts, new logistic management including supply chain management, and importantly, new R&D centres (see Box 7.1).

BOX 7.1

Wal-Mart's donation to set up a China retail research centre

In November 2004, Wal-Mart China announced a US$1 million commitment to establish the China Retail Research Centre at the School of Economics and Management of Tsinghua University. This is the first academic institution in China dedicated to the research of China's fast growing retail industry. China's rapidly

growing economy continues to create unprecedented opportunities for retail corporations like Wal-Mart. The US$1 million donation for establishing the China Retail
Research Centre is an example of Wal-Mart's long-term commitment to China.

It is believed that Wal-Mart's support for the Centre will facilitate China's participation and cooperation in the international retail field and drive the healthy
development of the country's retail sector. It is hoped that the China Retail
Research Centre would develop into a world-class research institution and boost
the theoretical research and management of China's retail industry.

Source: adapted from http://www.wal-martchina.com/english/news/20041102.htm, accessed on
15 April 2005.

However, the negative impact of foreign retail giants' expansion in China on its
indigenous retail businesses should not be ignored. It was reported that within one
month of the opening of the second Carrefour store in Shanghai, the sales revenue
of the 32 department stores and supermarkets of small- and medium-size in its five
kilometre radius had dropped by 50 per cent. On average, the opening of each
foreign retail store will close down three large and another 30 small- and medium-
sized Chinese retail stores (*China Business*, 14 March 2005). To exacerbate the
situation, some local governments offer more favourable conditions to foreign
retail giants than they do to local retailers as incentives to attract top-performing
enterprises to their region (*China Business*, 20 February 2006). This makes local
retailers' business environment even more adversarial.

To a large extent, retail giants' marginalization of smaller and independent
stores is a common problem faced by smaller retail businesses in other countries.
However, when the Chinese indigenous corporations are small and unable to
compete, then there is a real danger that the Chinese retail industry will be
wiped out. It was estimated by McKinsey that within five years, 60 per cent
of China's retail business will be controlled by three to five world-class foreign
retail giants, 30 per cent will be controlled by domestic national giants and
the remaining 10 per cent will be shared by regional retail enterprises (cited
in *China Business*, 14 March 2005). The closure of Chinese retail enterprises,
including some of the strongest Chinese retailers such as Beijing City Light
(*China Business*, 20 February 2006), also has a serious knock-on effect on their
suppliers, especially those smaller ones. It has been reported that it is difficult
enough as it is for small suppliers to receive payment from the retail enterprises
under normal circumstances. The closure of the stores will lead to a direct
financial loss for the suppliers (*China Business*, 26 December 2005). Threatened
by the aggressive expansion strategy of foreign retail giants, surviving Chinese
retail enterprises have responded with their own strategy.

Strategies of Chinese retail enterprises
Compared with foreign retail chain groups, the Chinese retailers generally operate on a small scale and a basic mode, paying little attention to the whole value
chain involving the supply, distribution, transportation and storage processes.

They lack management skills and technical know-how to develop these processes to improve the efficiency of distribution and add value to their business. Against the strong head-on competition from foreign retail giants, the Chinese retail enterprises are accelerating the pace of their business restructuring and transformation by adopting advanced operation models and becoming more strategic in their business planning. Developing Western-style chain stores and brand names is a twin strategy adopted by retail enterprises to enhance their competitiveness.

Indeed, the large Western-style chain-store supermarket has been the dominant model in the development of China's retail industry since the late 1990s (see Table 7.4 for its growth rate). It has been growing at the rate of 50 per cent annually, especially in major cities such as Beijing, Shanghai, Wuhan and Guangzhou. This model is considered to have a quick and high return rate of investment (P. Jin *et al.*, 2003). However, the most important sector of the retail industry – the commercial sector – did not develop its chain-store mode of operation until 2000 (P. Jin *et al.*, 2003). In 2002, the total sales revenue of the Top 100 retail chain-store enterprises in China was 246.5 billion yuan, making up 6 per cent of the total commodity sales revenue of the country. Most of the Chinese chain-store operators had no more than 10–30 stores across the whole country (P. Jin *et al.*, 2003). According to P. Jin *et al.*'s (2003) survey finding on the popularity and branding of 307 enterprises in China, Chinese consumers have a far better knowledge of foreign-invested supermarkets in China, such as Carrefour and Wal-Mart, than top-ranking Chinese retail enterprises. This indicates that Chinese-owned retail enterprises have not yet become national enterprises.

Hualian Supermarket Group (Beijing), one of the largest Chinese-owned retailers, was one of the first movers among the Chinese retail enterprises to develop large chain-store supermarkets. It has invested in the establishment of seven large supermarkets, acquired six large supermarkets from another retail enterprise and sub-contracted the management of at least ten large supermarkets (P. Jin *et al.*, 2003). Its business strategy is to develop a wide variety of stores, including large and standard sized supermarkets and convenience stores and to compete, using lower cost than its competitors. Its motto is 'for the convenience of people, benefit people and serve people' (P. Jin *et al.*, 2003, p. 264). In early 2006, Hualian poached over twenty senior managers from Carrefour to help its development (*China Business*, 13 March 2006).

The development of retail chain operations is in line with the Chinese government's agenda. According to the 'National Retail Chain Operations Plan' which was issued by the National Economy and Trade Committee as part of the tenth five-year plan (2001–5) of China, by the end of 2005, there were to be a total of 100,000 chain stores in the whole country with sales revenue of 700 billion yuan. This would mean an annual growth rate of approximately 35 per cent (cited in W. Wang *et al.*, 2004). There were to be 20 retail chain corporations that would have annual sales revenue of above 5 billion yuan, in addition to 40 retail chain corporations that would have annual sales revenue of between 2–5 billion yuan. Above all, it was intended to grow five to ten nationwide large retail chain corporation groups that possess distinctive core competences with early signs of international competitiveness (W. Wang *et al.*, 2004). It is not clear whether this plan has been achieved at the time when the manuscript of this book was finalized in December 2006.

In conjunction with the development of retail chains, M&As have been the main engine for growth of the industry. According to W. Wang *et al.* (2004), there are four driving forces for this:

1. Government policy, mainly as a result of China's accession to the WTO and the tenth five-year plan that specifies the direction of the growth of the industry (see above);
2. M&As have become an indispensable part of the business strategy of global retail enterprises;
3. Consolidation and integration are a necessary stage of development of the Chinese retail industry; and
4. M&As are seen as a quick way to gain resources and expand.

In addition to undertaking M&As to become 'bigger and stronger', smaller indigenous retail operators have started to join forces by sharing supply and distribution resources, for example, in order to fight off the threat posed by foreign retail giants. Others attempt to diversify their business, but with limited success (see Case Study 7.2 for example).

CASE STUDY 7.2

Business strategies of Chinese retail enterprises

Hanshang Group began as a district shop in Wuhan city. In the first two years following its stock market floatation in 1996, the company developed relatively quickly due to its focus on the commercial retail business. However, the company's fortunate changed once it started to diversify into other businesses from 1998. First, the company took on the construction of a multi-storeyed car park and shopping centre which ended up as a single-storey car park due to relocation disputes. It then attempted to develop a tourist division as its second 'pillar business', which never took off. In 1999, the company jumped on the supermarket band wagon and planned to build 28 convenience supermarkets in two years with financial support (an interest-free loan) from the Wuhan Municipal Government. A year later, only two supermarkets had been opened by Hanshang. By contrast, its competitor Wuhan Zhongbai overtook Hanshang, opening many shops along the way. The Wuhan Municipal Government later switched its financial support to Zhongbai. In 2000, Hanshang dabbled with the exhibition business but then diverted into the housing decoration business aiming to model 'the American advanced operation mode with a 25% return rate'. Six months later, the company returned to the exhibition business by investing 120 million yuan in the stock of Wuhan International Exhibition Centre. After six months' trading, the Exhibition Centre was 600 million yuan in debt. After three years of chopping and changing its business orienta-tion, Hanshang has lost its lead as one of the top five commercial enterprises in Wuhan city and became the worst performer amongst its stock-listed commercial retail competitors in Wuhan. By contrast, Wuhan Zhongbai focused firmly on the commercial retail business as its core business and has developed a comprehensive chain-store network in Wuhan.

Source: adapted from P. Jin *et al.* (2003).

Despite the rapid growth of large chain-store supermarkets and shopping cen-tres in recent years, the Chinese retail industry is in the early stage of its transformation. It will be some time before cross-sector and cross-ownership national retail corporations are established. This requires management compe-tence and the support of a sophisticated management information system in the development and integration of marketing and market intelligence, supply and distribution networks, capital and goods flow control and customer rela-tionships management. As retail MNCs possess far more resources and operate in a standardized mode through chain stores in China to gain economies of scale, it is very difficult for the Chinese-owned retail enterprises to compete with MNCs deploying the same operational mode. Instead, developing niche markets based on the Chinese culture and creating their own core competitive advantage may be the way forward.

Human resource implications

The retail industry is a relatively large employer compared with other industries in China (see Table 7.2), although it is relatively small compared with that of other countries (see Table 7.5).

According to Zhou and Li's (2005) calculation from the China statistical yearbooks, by the end of 2003, the retail industry had a total of 2.68 million employees, 51.3 per cent of them being female. About 0.94 million were employed by SOEs, 0.68 million by COEs and the remainder by other forms of ownership, including Chinese-owned private firms and foreign-owned MNCs. The total number employed in the retail industry has been in steady decline since 1995 when over 7.6 million people were employed (see Figure 7.1). This was partly a result of successive rounds of downsizing and privatization of the SOEs. In addition, the retail industry was affected by the Asia Economic Crisis in 1998. This has led to a significant drop in the workforce from over 7.2 million by the end of 1997 to 5.1 million by the end of 1998 (Zhou and Li, 2005).

It needs to be pointed out here that the continuing downsizing in SOEs and COEs has taken place in parallel with the steady growth of the number of employed in the retailed businesses of other forms of ownership which had seen its employment figure from 0.41 million employees at the end of 1995 to 1.06 million at the end of 2003 (see Figure 7.2). By 2003, they had become

Table 7.5 Employment in the wholesale and retail industry and the goods transportation industry as percentage of the total employment of selected countries in the year 2000*

Country	Proportion
China	9.32
Indonesia	23.61
Japan	29.29
South Korea	33.21
Philippines	23.80
Singapore	28.59
Thailand	17.43
Canada	31.42
Mexico	30.26
USA	26.72
Germany	22.99
Italy	25.35
Australia	31.39
New Zealand	28.11

*The authors calculated the figures based on the statistics in the *International Statistical Yearbook* (2002) (original note).
Figures in %
Source: Song and Li (2004, p. 87).

the largest employer in the Chinese retail industry (see Figure 7.3) (Zhou and Li, 2005).

The overall education and skill levels of the workforce in the retail industry are low compared with that in other industries. The majority of the employees only have junior or senior school qualifications, less than 5 per cent of them possess college or university qualifications (see Table 2.16). Compared with other industries, the retail industry has a smaller proportion of scientific and technical personnel in its urban workforce (see Table 2.17). Not surprisingly, human resources are unevenly distributed in the retail industry. Whereas foreign retail giants are able to attract technical and managerial talent and well qualified sales assistants, SOEs and other Chinese-owned retail employers are losing their well-qualified staff to their foreign competitors. It was reported that in some large cities, such as Beijing, Shanghai and Tianjin, staff turnover rate in Chinese-owned retail enterprises was as high as 35 per cent. Most of them were at the managerial level (Zhou and Li, 2005). Hualian's (Chinese-owned) poaching of Carrefour's (French-owned) managerial talent as mentioned above remains the exception rather than the norm. Like many other industries, the retail industry is far more developed in the eastern coastal areas than the inland and western areas. This

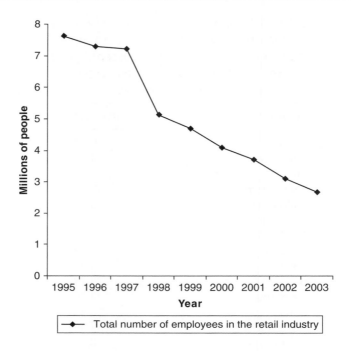

Figure 7.1 Number of employees in the retail industry (end-of-year figures)

Sources: Zhou and Li (2005, p. 99).

imbalance means that there is less retail talent in the latter which will in turn serve as a bottleneck for its growth, leading to further waves of war for talent.

In addition to the brain drain of talent to foreign firms in China, the retail industry suffers from insufficient training and a low level of technological innovation in general. The level of training and development activities is low compared with that in the manufacturing industry (Cooke, 2005a). It is traditionally believed that the retail industry is an unskilled and labour-intensive industry, primarily staffed by female employees working behind the counter. Skill requirement is low and so is the wage level (see below).

Like other industries in China, there is a serious skill gap that is constraining the growth of the retail industry. Areas of skill shortages include, for example, senior managers who are strategic and familiar with global competition, technical and professional expertise from a range of areas such as supply chain management, IT systems, international trade, business law, super-large shopping centre management and HRM. Even foreign retail enterprises in China are encountering skill shortages. For example, Carrefour planned to open 100 chain stores in China by the end of 2007. Some 3500 senior and middle ranking managers need to be recruited to manage these businesses. However, Carrefour was taken aback by the extent of the skill shortage. In addition,

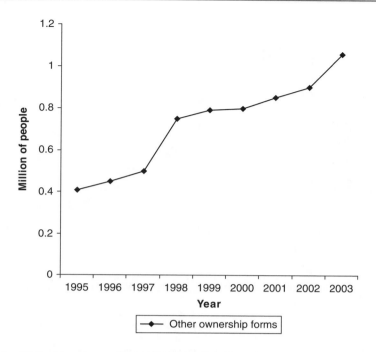

Figure 7.2 Number of employees employed in retail enterprises of
other ownership forms
Sources: Zhou and Li (2005, p. 99).

skill shortages in related/supporting industries, such as the transport and distribution industry, are likely to have a negative impact on the retail industry.
According to statistics revealed by the Chinese Transport and Distribution
Association, there is a shortage of 6 million professional specialists in the distribution industry in China (cited in Zhou and Li, 2005). A positive sign is that
the industry is starting to realize the importance of human resources and is
beginning to invest in training, particularly the larger operators. For example,
in 2005, Carrefour launched a training programme in Tianjin City called the
'Second Tier Training Plan' in which 16 university graduates would receive
intensive training for an 18-week period. Other foreign retail giants also set up
their own training centres in China to develop their managerial staff in-house.
   Generally speaking, the wage level of the retail industry has been increasing
steadily from 3826 yuan in 1995 to 9277 yuan in 2003 (Zhou and Li, 2005).
While this growth is in line with the general wage increase trend in the country,
there appear to be significant wage differentials across different ownership forms
in the retail industry (see Figure 7.4). For example, the annual average wage
was 8786 yuan in SOEs, 6045 yuan in COEs and 11,856 yuan in other forms
of ownership in 2003 (Zhou and Li, 2005). This wage disparity, together with
the employment trends in this industry, is a strong indicator of the different

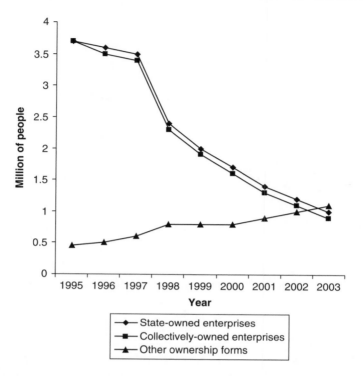

Figure 7.3 Number of employees employed in retail enterprises by ownership forms

Sources: Zhou and Li (2005, p. 102).

financial situations and business performance across the three categories of ownership forms. A major reason for the significantly higher wage level in the other forms of ownership compared with that in SOEs and COEs is the rapid expansion of foreign retail giants in China, which generally operate at the upper end of the market and pay higher wages. As discussed above, foreign-invested retail businesses are more competitive than the domestic retail enterprises, forcing a number of the local enterprises into bankruptcy and the majority of the remainders making a loss or a reduced profit. The wage differentials between the SOEs/COEs and the other ownership forms makes the former even less able to attract talent and compete with the latter.

It also needs to be pointed out that the wage level in the retail industry is generally low and significantly lower than that in other industries (see Table 4.5). For example, it was reported that the monthly wage of the general manager of Guangzhou Department Store Corporation was around 15,000–20,000 yuan. Some 20 per cent of the wage would be deducted if the annual sales target was not met. A store manager of the Corporation earned 4500–5000 yuan per month, whereas a deputy manager and department manager earned 2000–4000 yuan per month. An average employee in the headquarters

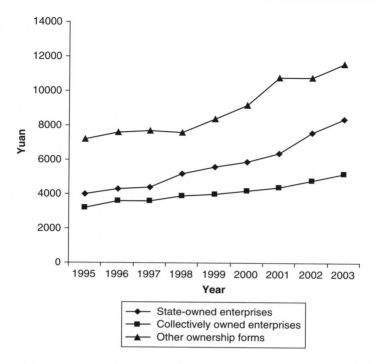

Figure 7.4 Annual average wage of employees in retail enterprises of different ownership forms

Sources: Zhou and Li (2005, p. 103).

of the Corporation earned 1100–1200 per month, whereas sales assistants in the stores earned 800 yuan per month (Zhou and Li, 2005). Those who work outside premium cities like Guangzhou are likely to be earning much less. For example, my study of the commercial retail sector in a medium-sized city in southern China found that shop assistants typically earned about 500–600 yuan per month whereas managers earned no more than 1500 per month (Cooke, 2005a). It is quite common that a relatively large proportion of the wage income of the retail employees is linked to the sales performance of the individuals and the groups, adding further financial insecurity to the employees.

Summary

In summary, the Chinese retail industry is in its growth period with great market potential. Its rapid expansion is accompanied by intensifying competition concentrated primarily at the upper end of the market where foreign-invested enterprises have the clear competitive advantages. Chinese-owned retail enterprises mainly expand at the lower end of the market which will eventually shrink as the upper and middle end of the market becomes more established and the

Chinese consumers become more affluent and sophisticated in their shopping behaviour. The entry of foreign retail firms has transformed the nature and structure of ownership and competition in the industry. They have brought with them advanced concepts, technologies and techniques. Traditional Chinese department stores as the main mode of the commodity retail industry have been experiencing an inevitable decline since the mid-1990s. Newly emerged chain-store supermarkets have overtaken some of the traditional well-known shops that were once regarded as the national pride and ultimate shopping experience. More broadly, the retail industry in China is developing itself through the emergence of a variety of operational modes, including supermarkets, convenience shops and warehouse-style supermarkets. The trend of large one-stop shops is likely to be accompanied by the development of theme shops and specialty shops that are tailored for the new middle-class consumers in large municipal areas. As the IT systems and credit systems become more established in China, e-commerce will enter the arena as one of the shopping forms.

In addition, the intensifying competition within the retail industry has transformed the market from a sellers' market to a consumers' market, resulting in changes of the relative bargaining power among suppliers, retailers and consumers. As competition further intensifies, market positioning and targeting customers become an important part of the competition strategy. The ability to capture in time the new market trends and opportunities and the ability to learn from Western retailers' advanced management techniques are decisive factors in enhancing the competitiveness of the Chinese-owned enterprise. This requires strategic management foresight as well as human capital at the operational level – a pool of skills and competence that the industry has yet to develop.

In some ways, the relatively unregulated nature of the retail industry, its disorderly market competition, and skill shortages partly triggered by new modes of operations are similar to that in another service industry – the exhibition industry. It is to this industry that we now turn.

Exhibition industry

Background of the industry

The Chinese exhibition industry existed mainly as a series of government-sponsored and organized events and was managed through a top-down control mode during the state planned economy period. Perennial trade fairs and exhibitions have been held since the advent of the open door economy policy in the late 1970s, mostly sponsored and organized by the state-owned import–export trading corporations. The industry was treated as the major mechanism for promoting trades, science and cultural activities instead of an independent industry that could be grown through strategic planning and management (Wang and Feng, 2005). In recent years, however, fairs and exhibitions have become increasingly popular in China as a method of obtaining information, promoting market presence and increasing economic exchange and cooperation.

According to China Information News (27 December 2001, cited in *China Online*, 7 January 2002), China's exhibition industry has undergone two stages of development. The first stage was from the 1950s to the 1980s. The international exhibitions sector of the industry only started to develop in the early 1980s when China was opening up. Exhibition themes covered the major industries in China, including automotive, telecommunication, textiles, engineering machinery and medical equipment. Most of the exhibitions were held in a small number of large cities, such as Beijing, Shanghai and Guangzhou. The majority of participants in the exhibitions were from overseas and the exhibition organizers were primarily from Hong Kong supported by mainland Chinese companies. Government influence was strong and the main objectives of the exhibitions were trading and participation. As trade fairs and exhibitions were limited with virtually no duplicates, competition was non-existent. The Chinese organizers were hardly aware of the fact that organizing exhibitions could be a lucrative business (27 December 2001, cited in *China Online*, 7 January 2002).

The second stage was the development stage from the mid-1980s till the early 2000s. There was a dramatic development in exhibitions in terms of quantity, size and themes during this period. The number of Chinese exhibition organizers has also grown, gradually moving from a facilitating to a leading role, whereas the role of Hong Kong organizers has declined significantly. Domestic enterprises started to realize the importance of exhibitions and an increasing number of overseas companies also participated in the exhibitions, many in collaboration with their Chinese JV partner firms. The objectives of exhibitions have expanded from trading to brand promotion, ordering of goods and discussion of setting up JVs and other forms of cooperation. Disorderly competition and duplicate exhibitions became major problems, with local authorities under financial and political pressure to give the green light to exhibition applications (27 December 2001, cited in *China Online*, 7 January 2002).

It can be said that China's exhibition industry has now entered the third stage of development – the mature stage, during which the number of exhibitions will decline whereas the overall scale will increase. Exhibitions will become more international, with JVs of domestic and foreign exhibition organizers emerging as the main mode of business operation to exploit their complementary advantages. For example, the cities of Germany Hanover, Dusseldorf and Munich have established JVs in Shanghai to build exhibition halls and have obtained the rights to operate and organize exhibitions, each having their own themes. The industry will become more orderly through market competition and improved management competence (27 December 2001, cited in *China Online*, 7 January 2002).

The Chinese exhibition industry is small compared with that of developed countries. For example, in 2001, the industry had a total output value of 4 billion yuan, approximately 0.05 per cent of China's GDP of the same year. This is a very small proportion in comparison with that of advanced countries such as Germany, the United States and Singapore, whose total output value is about 0.2 per cent of their GDP (Wang and Feng, 2005). However, like many other industries in China, the relatively small exhibition industry is a fast growing one. It is estimated that it is going to grow at an annual rate of 15–20 per cent in the next few years (*China Business*, 9 August 2004). In 2003, over 3000 large exhibitions were held in the country, generating a direct income of over 10 billion yuan (*China Business*, 9 August 2004). In major exhibition cities such as Shanghai, Guangzhou, Shenzhen and Dongguan, the annual growth of the industry was over 20 per cent. It was reported that the total revenue of the exhibition industry in Guangdong Province (where Guangzhou, Shenzhen and Dongguan cities are located) was 3.2 billion yuan in 2004 (*China Business*, 8 August 2005). In 2004, Shanghai alone held an average of 5.5 exhibitions per week (Song, 2005). According to the Shanghai Convention and Exhibition Industries Association, in 2005, Shanghai held 276 international conventions and exhibitions with a total coverage of 3.76 million square metres – an annual increase of 23 per cent (*SinoCast China Business Daily News*, 2006). In addition, there were over 3000 registered exhibition organizers by the end of 2004. A large proportion of them were SMEs with little experience or capacity to host large events (Liu and Jiang, 2005).

Problems in the development of the industry

There are a number of intertwined problems in the development of the exhibition industry in China. These are discussed below.

Lack of industrial planning, regulation and integration A fundamental problem in the development of the exhibition industry in China is the lack of planning, regulation and integration within the industry and between the industry and the rest of the regional economy. All too often, municipal governments develop a passion for building exhibition halls and holding exhibition fairs without taking into consideration whether the exhibition themes match and promote the economic structure of the region (Wang and Feng, 2005). The motive is often opportunistic and profit driven. As the industry is still highly unregulated and uncoordinated, the industry is controlled through various administrative systems (Wang and Feng, 2005). That is, exhibitions are controlled, from the administrative point of view, through the dual-structure of the industry they feature (e.g. steel industry for steel exhibition) and through the level of administrative government at which they are located (e.g. municipal and provincial level). Exhibition applications can be approved by different organizations in different cities (e.g. industrial body or local government) (Song, 2005). This dual-control system invariably causes bureaucracy, leaves gaps and creates conflicts of interest between parochial controlling parties and leads to other problems in the industry.

Overcapacity of exhibition space There was an over-expansion in the construction of the exhibition halls since the late 1990s (Ni *et al.*, 2004; Song, 2005; Wang and Feng, 2005). By the end of 2004, there were more than 120 exhibition centres in China. The total exhibition space had reached over 5 million square metres, surpassing Germany – the leading country of exhibition (2.5 million square metres) – and became the second-largest in the world

(Song, 2005). However, less than 30 per cent of the exhibition capacity is being utilized (Wang and Feng, 2005) and more exhibition centres are planned. By contrast, there is an insufficient number of high-quality exhibition halls (Ni *et al.*, 2004). According to Song (2005), most exhibition centres in China share the following problems:

- Lack of market research with ambiguous targets (unclear objective, whether it is built for exhibitions, conferences or balls);
- Impractical location (with associated problems in transportation, logistics and reserved space for future development);
- Impractical construction (impressive layout, but problematic internal facilities);
- Incomplete supporting facilities (lack of accommodation, transportation, communication and restaurants); and
- Imbalanced geographic distribution of exhibition centres (surplus exhibition centres in small- and medium-sized cities, but insufficient in large cities like Beijing and Shanghai).

Lack of economies of scale, quality and branding of exhibitions Another major problem is the repetition of exhibitions on similar themes and the lack of high-quality exhibitions (Ni *et al.*, 2004; Wang and Feng, 2005). As a whole, China holds hundreds of exhibitions each year, few of them have international competitiveness. For example, by the end of 2003, only 17 of the exhibitions had gained the recognition of the Global Association of the Exhibition Industry (UFI) (Wang and Feng, 2005). Most of the exhibitions are small in scale and lack branding and professionalism (Wang and Feng, 2005). The over-supply of exhibitions creates destructive competition amongst exhibition organizers and causes immense confusion to both exhibitors and visitors (Song, 2005). In spite of the organizers' lavish advertising, some exhibitions attract few visitors who are often disappointed with the quality of the display. Other exhibitions only focus on the short-term profit instead of treating the business as a long-term development (Ni *et al.*, 2004). By contrast, there were only around 300 fairs in 2003 in Germany. As a country highly celebrated for its exhibitions, Germany holds around two-thirds of the world's most prestigious international exhibitions (Song, 2005).

Government intervention Exhibitions industry is one of the remaining industries in China that still have a relatively heavy involvement from the government. As part of the legacy of the state planned economy, local governments in China continue to play a major role in organizing and financing exhibitions (Wang and Feng, 2005). There are many reasons for holding an exhibition. An important one is to raise the profile of the city and to attract investments and businesses. For this purpose, the involvement of local governments has been substantial and crucial, even though there has been a long-standing call for the disengagement of government with the exhibition industry. However, when government involvement is withdrawn, grievances may arise. For instance, the 'Shenzhen International Exhibition for the Art and Culture Industry' was held on 18 November 2004. Unlike other large exhibitions in Shenzhen that were heavily sponsored by the Shenzhen Municipal Government, the exhibition co-organizer Shenzhen Broadcast and TV Group decided not to take any funding from the municipal government with the aim of creating a bigger corporate impact and attracting more corporate advertising. Although the central government had decreed that all arts and culture type of exhibitions must succeed for political reasons, the municipal government-supported Shenzhen Broadcast and TV Group's decision, seeing this exhibition as the first step towards the marketization of Shenzhen's exhibition industry. This decision not only upset its co-organizer the Shenzhen Newspaper Group, but also antagonized some would-be exhibitors because of the withdrawal of government subsidies and other forms of government network support. This example suggests that there is some way to go before the exhibition industry is really marketed (*China Business*, 7 June 2004). It must be noted, however, that the exhibition was deemed a success in that it had attracted 655 exhibition companies, 102 of them from overseas, and over 50,000 visitors on the first day. The exhibition raised its international profile and the organizers did not make a loss. It must also be noted that although Shenzhen Municipal Government did not provide direct funding to the organizers, it did fund the refurbishment of the village where the exhibition was held (*China Business*, 29 November 2004).

Opportunistic behaviour As the industry expands and moves towards marketization, opportunistic behaviour emerges. For example, some companies secured exhibition spaces and then sold them on the black market to those which failed to secure spaces (*China Business*, 14 March 2005). More seriously, due to the lack of IPR protection, various aspects of exhibitions may be copied, for example, logo, product, plan and other exhibition content. Some large successful exhibitions have been 'cloned'. This has led to the duplication of exhibitions, albeit on a smaller scale. For example, the first International Advertisement Four-New (new media, technology, equipment and material) Exhibition (referred to as 'Beijing Four New Exhibition' from here onwards) was jointly created by China Electronics International Exhibition Advertisement Ltd and the China Foreign Economy and Trade Advertisement Association in Beijing in 1994. By the end of 2004, there were at least 40 similar exhibitions in China. Many exhibitions at provincial and municipal level adopted the phrase 'Four New' in their title (*China Business*, 22 November 2004). When the 11th Beijing Four New Exhibition was held during August 2004, it focused on the theme 'Visual Transmission' in part to avoid the, by now, much abused phrase 'Four New' (*China Business*, 16 August, 2004).

Lack of industrial cluster The success of the exhibition industry is highly dependent upon a number of supporting industries as well as related organizations, as Figure 7.5 shows. However, these industrial networks have not been established and related organizations have yet to develop their expertise in the exhibition business. For instance, security to counter theft and insurance against losses (e.g. safety of exhibition hall, theft, injury and death) is an issue. There is currently no insurance regulation specific to the exhibition industry. Few insurance companies in China have the expertise to provide insurance services to exhibitions. This is particularly the case in jewellery exhibitions. For

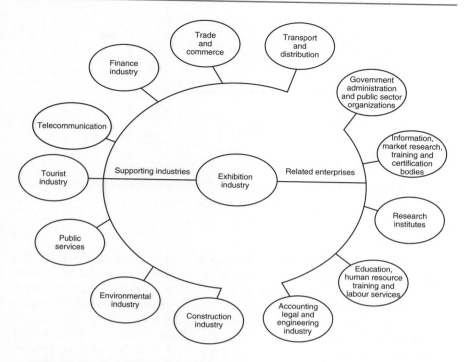

Figure 7.5 A diagram of the compositional structure of the exhibition industry

Sources: Ni *et al*. (2004, p. 308).

example, there was a total of 1 billion yuan worth of jewellery in the Beijing Jewellery Exhibition held in November 2004. The exhibition was heavily guarded by security personnel but was uninsured because it could not find an insurance company (*China Business*, 15 November 2004). Even if there were an insurance service, the insurance fee would be so high that many exhibitors would not be able to afford it. It is estimated that it may cost 50 million yuan to ensure an exhibition with jewellery that is worth a total of 1 billion yuan (*China Business*, 14 March 2005). The biggest jewellery theft case in 2003 occurred during the Fourth Shanghai International Jewellery Exhibition where diamond worth of US$690,000 was stolen (*China Business*, 30 August 2004). Not long after that, some 20 exhibitors were burgled in the Fifth National Toys and Children's Products Exhibition held in the China International Trade Centre (*China Business*, 30 August 2004). More generally, there is a serious shortage of expertise in exhibition risk management (see next point for further discussion).

Whilst many cities see exhibitions as a good opportunity to make a profit, to raise the profile of the city and to attract investment, not all cities have the supporting facilities needed to ensure the success of a large exhibition. These include the development of the transport industry, the tourist industry and

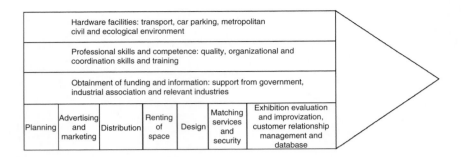

Figure 7.6 Industrial chain of the exhibition industry

Sources: Ni *et al.* (2004, p. 309).

the hotel and catering industry, as well as an attractive city environment (see Figure 7.6). To some extent, the absence of an efficient industrial network for the exhibition industry has been part of the reason for the local governments' continuing involvement as a safety net to ensure the success of exhibitions.

Lack of human resources The exhibition industry is an industry that requires inter-disciplinary knowledge and skills. These include, for example, project management and language translation skills, as well as skills specific to different aspects and stages of an exhibition (see Figure 7.6). These are the skills in which the industry faces serious shortage. For example, in 2004, there were no more than 50 senior project managers, and 100 professionals with all-round knowledge of the exhibition industry in Shanghai. Each large international exhibition requires at least 80–90 specialists in the field (*China Business*, 6 June 2005). Another example is that interpreters not only require good language translation skills, but also specialist knowledge of the exhibits. In the sixth 'China Western Region International Exhibition' held in Chengdu in 2005, some enterprise exhibitors could not find qualified interpreters and had to use their own staff to act as such. Their English was not up to the professional standard needed for the exhibition. Worse still, some of them could not even speak mandarin (the official language of China) properly and had difficulty in communicating with visitors from other parts of the country (*China Business*, 6 June 2005). The exhibition was meant to be the premium show of the western region, because it was the region's first national show after the exhibition had been upgraded to a national level with the approval of the central government (*China Business*, 6 June 2005).

On the whole, there is a 65–70 per cent skill shortage in major exhibition host cities like Shanghai, Beijing and Guangzhou. It was reported that 90 per cent of the people working in the exhibition industry have not been trained in the field (*China Business*, 9 August 2004). The majority of people working in the industry adopt a learning-by-doing approach or adapt foreign practices in a simplistic way instead of taking their own initiative to produce innovative ideas and to conduct market research to explore market needs systematically (Ni *et al.*, 2004). It needs to be pointed out that the quality standard of the frontline staff who provide services to visitors and exhibitors is equally important, because the quality of services is an important kite mark of the standard of the exhibition industry (Ni *et al.*, 2004).

The development of education and training for human resources in exhibitions is lagging behind, as is commonly the case for human resources in other industries in China. There are few universities that have courses tailored for the exhibition industry. It was not until April 2004 that the Ministry of Education approved the specialist courses on exhibition economy and management that were to be piloted by Shanghai Normal University and Shanghai Institute of Foreign Business and Trade (Wang and Feng, 2005). The same year saw the first batch of students who specialized in exhibitions and advertising subjects graduating from vocational technical college (Zhejiang Economics and Trade Vocational Technical College) (*China Business*, 27 December 2004). However, the danger is that there will be a drastic and irrational expansion in exhibition education and training in China. For example, until 2004, there were no more than 30 higher education institutions that offered courses related to the exhibition subject. In 2005, there were some 20 institutions that offered this kind of course in Zhejiang Province alone, in addition to a growing number of vocational and technical training colleges entering the training business. Many of these courses had not been approved by the Ministry of Education, which means that students graduating from the courses may not have their qualifications officially recognized (*China Business*, 15 August 2005). This is an example of China's irrational manner of development. Once a business opportunity is spotted, a gold rush is triggered.

The landmark of the Chinese exhibition industry is undoubtedly Shanghai's winning of the World Exposition 2010 bid in 2002. It will be a commercial, technological and cultural Olympics of global significance. With the date of the event approaching, Shanghai World Expo 2010 is facing a huge shortage of human resources in a number of areas, as Case Study 7.3 reveals.

Case Study 7.3
Shanghai World Expo 2010

Shanghai World Expo 2010 will be the first registered world exposition held in a developing country. It will attract governments and people from across the world, focusing on the theme 'Better City, Better Life'. For the duration of its 184 days' exposition, participants will display urban civilization to the full extent, exchange their experiences of urban development, disseminate advanced notions on cities and explore new approaches to human habitat, life style and working conditions in the new century. They will learn how to create an eco-friendly society and maintain the sustainable development of human beings. The exposition will centre on innovation and interaction. Innovation is the soul and cultural interaction is an important mission of world expositions. The Shanghai World Expo 2010 organizer is hoping to attract 200 nations and international organizations to take part in the exhibition as well as 70 million visitors from home and abroad.

A major challenge to Shanghai World Expo 2010 is the severe shortage of human resources in both quantity and quality. In particular, expertise in the areas of food safety inspection, exhibition and tourism is in the shortest supply. The first cohort of food safety specialists are being trained in Shanghai in 2007. Trainees will sit in a national examination on completion of their course. Those who pass the test will be issued a qualification by the national food industry association authority. Obtaining such a qualification is a pre-requisite for being employed by the Shanghai World Expo 2010 organization as a food safety inspection specialist.

Similarly, tourist guides conversant with a foreign language, particularly languages that are not commonly used, are in great demand. Many luxury hotels and travel agencies are already at wars for talent. In the first tourist guides recruitment fair in 2007, more than 80 luxury hotels, tourist restaurants and travel agencies participated, offering nearly 4000 posts. Many more fairs will be held and posts offered as the event draws closer.

According to a survey conducted by the Shanghai World Expo 2010 organizer, exhibition operational managers, project managers, public relations and language specialists are most needed but in short supply. Emergency training is being provided jointly by the Municipal exhibition industry association, vocational qualification examination college and the expo organizer. The first batch of 31 senior exhibitionists and 19 exhibitionists were accredited in 2006.

Sources: compiled from http://www.expo2010china.com/expo/expoenglish/oe/es/userobject1ai 35588.html; http://www.expo2010china.com/expo/shexpo/sbrc/rcxx/userobject1ai41859.html.

Competition strategy

Although the exhibition industry in China is still in its early growth period and is constrained by several major problems, a number of business strategies are emerging that should be adopted more broadly in the industry (Ni *et al.*, 2004; Wang and Feng, 2005).

Formation of large corporate groups In line with other industries, the exhibition industry is undergoing some regrouping process to form larger corporate groups. This takes the form of vertical and horizontal integration of business undertakings as well as through international expansion (Wang and Feng, 2005).

Internationalization Compared with other industries, the exhibition industry has relatively low entry barriers. While the entry of foreign firms into China's exhibition business may bring competition and challenges to domestic Chinese firms, they also bring with them technology and management know-how that will be highly beneficial to the development of Chinese firms (Wang and Feng, 2005), as has proved the case in other industries. In spite of the many problems in the exhibition industry, there are signs that professional exhibition companies from developed countries have begun collaboration with Chinese governmental departments and exhibition organizing bodies. Attracted by China's market potential, internationally prestigious exhibition companies, such as Messe Frankfurt, Messe Hannover, Messe Munich and Reed Expo, have already entered the Chinese market. Likewise, organizers from Italy and the United Kingdom have embarked on their journey of seeking partnerships in China (Song, 2005). By collaborating with these international firms, the Chinese exhibition industry can learn fast and raise its competitiveness in the international market.

Diversification There is a growing variety of exhibitions to promote an increasing range of products and to market them in different ways. This is in addition to an expanding range of functions and services associated with the exhibition, such as business negotiation, sight seeing and other entertainment activities (Wang and Feng, 2005). In other words, organizers are turning the exhibition experience into a combined holiday experience to attract visitors and stimulate expenditure. This is when the support of related industries becomes crucial to the success of the exhibition.

Branding of exhibitions Whilst it is true that there are few branded exhibitions in China, it is worth noting that a small number of exhibitions in major cities in China, such as Beijing, Shanghai, Dalian, Guangzhou and Shenzhen, are beginning to establish their brand image at an international level (Wang and Feng, 2005). These include, for example, Beijing's automobile show, Dalian's fashion show and Guangzhou's International Trade Fair.

Specialization and professionalization Exhibitions in China have tended to focus on comprehensive exhibitions in the hope of capturing a wide range of businesses and audience. In recent years, exhibition organizers have begun to realize the importance of specialization in attracting high-quality exhibitors and visitors. The marketing, design and organization of the exhibition activities are also becoming more professional (Wang and Feng, 2005). Through specialization of each stage and aspects of the exhibition, the provision will become more professional and comprehensive (Ni *et al.*, 2004).

Innovations and informatization More promisingly, exhibitions are gradually moving from imitation and adaptation towards innovation. These include innovations in exhibition concept, exhibition product, exhibition operation and service (Wang and Feng, 2005). These innovations are facilitated by informatization in gaining access to the most up-to-date global information related to the industry and in utilizing IT in the exhibition business to enhance its performance (Wang and Feng, 2005).

Environmental and ecological orientation There is a growing awareness in the Chinese exhibition business of the need to be environmentally friendly, from the choice of exhibition sites and construction materials to the internal function of the exhibition hall and waste recycling (Wang and Feng, 2005). Given the worsening shortage of natural resources and pollution in China, treating environmental issues as an important part of the strategic planning is a necessary way forward.

Summary

The Chinese exhibition industry is an emerging industry from what could be seen as a collection of former government-sponsored and organized exhibition events. Hosting exhibitions can be a lucrative business that may help to enhance the reputation and competitiveness of a country and city. It is a particularly valuable route to create jobs for countries that face employment pressure (Ni *et al.*, 2004), although the ability of countries to do so is highly dependent on a number of contextual factors such as the availability of human resources and technology. These are precisely some of the major problems encountered by the exhibition industry in China. Other problems exhibited in the industry include the lack of regulation by administrative policies and industrial norms, parochialism of local governments, sectional interest and the lack of industrial cluster to support the growth of the industry. Deficiency in strategic planning and control at the macro level is the main cause for many of the problems manifested in the industry.

In spite of all these problems, there are positive signs that the industry is progressing towards the direction of building a stronger, more competitive and socially acceptable industry. The deepening marketization of the industry will lead to an increasing level of foreign investment and competition. A clearer business strategy and a greater level of professionalism from the Chinese exhibition companies, as well as their ability to attract talent, are some key factors to enable them to become competitive. In order to combat the bottleneck of skill shortages, investment and support from the government is needed to build and expand university capacity in training for exhibition skills and in research on the industry as a long-term development. In the short term, experts from overseas can be brought in to provide short training courses in addition to sending people abroad for training.

Recommended readings

J. Gamble, 'The Rhetoric of the Consumer and Customer Control in China', *Work, Employment and Society*, 21, 1 (2007): 7–25.

M. Korczynski, *Human Resource Management in Service Work* (New York: Palgrave, 2002).

Y. Luo, *China's Service Sector: A New Battlefield for International Corporations* (Copenhagen: Copenhagen Business School Press, 2001).

P. Stearns, *Consumerism in World History: The Global Transformation of Desire* (London: Routledge, 2001).

PART III

FDI Into and Out of China: Motives, Barriers and Management Implications

Acquisitions of Chinese State-Owned Enterprises by Foreign MNCs: Driving Forces, Barriers and Implications for HRM

Introduction

China has been one of the two largest FDI recipient countries in the world in recent years (*International Statistical Yearbook*, 2004). This is largely due to two factors: investment incentives offered by the Chinese government, and the country's abundant availability of cheap labour. It has been argued that the strong emphasis on foreign investment and foreign trade has been one of the key factors, if not *the* key factor, in the unprecedented growth of the Chinese economy in recent years. Attracting FDI has been an important part of China's 'open door' economic policy since 1979 and this proactive policy has led to the rapid increase of FDI in China in the last 25 years (see Tables 8.1 and 8.2).

It needs to be noted, however, that China's FDI figures have been questioned by some. It was suggested that China has overstated its FDI figures by one-quarter to one-third, amounting to US$12–16 billion less a year. This is believed to be a result of 'round tripping', where capital originating from China goes through another country, often an offshore tax haven, before reentering China as 'foreign' investment (*China Daily Online*, 22 June 2004; *FDI Magazine*, 2 April 2003). It was reported (*China Daily Online*, 22 June 2004) that Hong Kong and three British island offshore tax havens accounted for US$23.5 billion in FDI from China during 2003. Much of that fund may have been directed back to China, which means the fund would appear to have been coming from outside China and contributed to an inaccurate total for the year.

Table 8.1 Utilization of foreign capital between 1979–2005 (end-of-year figures)

Year	Total		Foreign loans		FDIs		Other foreign investments
Total amount of contracted foreign capital	No. of projects	Value	No. of projects	Value	No. of projects	Value	
1979–84	3,365	287.69	117	169.78	3,248	103.93	13.98
1985	3,145	98.67	72	35.34	3,073	59.31	4.02
1989	5,909	114.79	130	51.85	5,779	56.00	6.94
1990	7,371	120.86	98	50.99	7,273	56.96	3.91
1995	37,184	1,032.05	173	121.88	37,011	912.82	6.35
1996	24,673	816.10	117	79.62	24,556	732.77	3.71
1997	21,138	610.58	137	58.72	21,001	510.04	41.82
1998	19,850	632.01	51	83.85	19,799	521.02	27.14
1999	17,022	520.09	104	83.60	16,918	412.23	24.26
2000	22,347	711.30	–	–	22,347	463.80	87.50
2001	26,140	719.76	–	–	26,140	691.95	27.81
2002	34,171	847.51	–	–	34,171	827.68	19.82
2003	41,081	1,169.01	–	–	41,081	1,150.70	18.32
2004	43,664	1,565.88	–	–	43,664	1,534.79	31.09
2005	44,001	1,925.93	–	–	44,001	1,890.65	35.28
1979–2005	554,625	14,634.06	1,638	1,385.38	552,942	12,856.74	391.91

Total amount of foreign capital actually utilized				
1979–84	171.43	130.41	30.60	10.42
1985	44.62	25.06	16.58	2.98
1989	100.59	62.86	33.92	3.81
1990	102.89	65.34	34.87	2.68
1995	481.33	103.27	375.21	2.85
1996	548.04	126.69	417.25	4.10
1997	644.08	120.21	452.57	71.30
1998	585.57	110.00	454.63	20.94
1999	526.59	102.12	403.19	21.28
2000	593.56	100.00	407.15	86.41
2001	496.72	–	468.78	27.94
2002	550.11	–	527.43	22.68
2003	561.40	–	535.05	26.35
2004	640.72	–	606.30	34.42
2005	638.05	–	603.25	34.80
1979–2005	8,091.50	1,471.57	6,224.29	395.64

Value figures in 100 million US dollars
Source: adapted from *China Statistical Yearbook* (2006, p. 752).

Table 8.2 Examples of utilization of foreign capital and foreign investment (end-of-year figures)

Item	2000			2002			2004		
	No. of projects	Contract value	Actually used value	No. of projects	Contract value	Actually used value	No. of projects	Contract value	Actually used value
Total	22,347	711.30	593.56	34,171	847.51	550.11	44,001	1,925.93	638.05
Foreign direct investment	22,347	623.80	407.15	34,171	827.68	527.43	44,001	1,890.65	603.25
Joint ventures enterprises	8,378	196.48	143.43	10,380	185.02	149.92	10,480	324.42	146.14
Cooperative operation enterprises	1,757	81.17	65.96	1,595	62.17	50.58	1,166	86.91	18.31
Foreign investment enterprises	12,196	343.09	192.64	22,173	572.55	317.25	32,308	1,459.09	429.61
Foreign investment share enterprises	8	1.94	1.30	19	7.39	6.97	47	20.22	9.18
Cooperative development enterprises	8	1.12	3.82	4	0.55	2.72	–	–	–
Others	–	–	–	–	–	–	–	–	–
Other foreign investment	–	87.51	86.41	–	19.82	22.68	–	35.28	34.80
Sale share	–	69.31	69.31	–	–	–	–	0.05	1.60
International lease	–	0.24	0.34	–	1.30	1.31	–	1.08	1.08
Compensation trade	–	0.12	0.11	–	–	0.04	–	–	0.16
Processing and assembly	–	17.84	16.66	–	18.52	21.33	–	34.15	31.96

Value figures in 100 million US dollars
Sources: adapted from *China Statistical Yearbook* (2002, p. 629); (2003, p. 671); and (2006, p. 752).

During the 1980s, the main route of FDI entering the Chinese economy was through JV with Chinese SOEs. Into the twenty-first century, cross-border acquisition remains the main investment mechanism for foreign investment entering the Chinese market with an increasing level of freedom. This trend is being accelerated by China's accession to the WTO and the introduction of a number of laws and guidelines by the Chinese government in 2003 that are aimed to promote M&A activities from foreign investment. It was reported that 16 per cent of the M&A fund (about US$3.84 billion) in first three quarters of 2003 in China came from FDI (Jin and Nie, 2004) and that M&A activities in China have been increasing by 20 per cent annually in recent years (*China Business*, 7 March 2005). This new development is in line with the international trend in the last two decades in which, it is noted, the level of M&A activities has increased considerably (Evans *et al.*, 2002; Hubbard, 1999) in response to a range of political, economic, social and technological pressures and opportunities, with cross-border M&As particularly noticeable (Boxall and Purcell, 2003). It must be pointed out at the outset of this chapter that acquisitions, instead of mergers, remain the main pattern of Sino-foreign alliances and therefore the discussion of this chapter will focus mainly on acquisition, although M&As will be referred to where appropriate.

Generally speaking, acquisitions of Chinese firms by foreign firms mainly concentrate in the manufacturing sector, which has long been the target for FDI in China. It is characterized by relatively high capital investment and technological content. The industry also has the comparative advantage of cheap labour cost. Foreign-invested firms are now well-established in this sector with garment, footwear, toys, drinks, automobile, chemical and petroleum and engineering as the popular industries for investment. By the late 1990s, ten of the 50 largest and strongest Chinese tyre factories were acquired by MNCs (Chen, 1999). China's pharmaceutical industry and the medical market is another entry point for MNCs through M&As. By the late 1990s, over 45 per cent of the key Chinese pharmaceutical companies had been acquired by MNCs (Chen, 1999; also see Chapter 5). In addition, China's accession to the WTO and the subsequent full-opening of its retail industry to FDI has attracted the majority of the world's leading retail giants to set up operations in China (see Chapter 7). More recently, M&A focus has been turning to the finance and banking, telecommunication, energy and insurance industry. M&A is now an important channel for the Chinese enterprises to expand, consolidate and compete in the international market. According to the stock market statistics, by the early 2003, over 400 foreign banks had either entered or were preparing to enter China's banking industry following the opening up of the industry. More than 200 of them were already in operation in China (Wang, 2003).

Despite the growing significance of international acquisitions in China's economy, there have been insufficient studies into the driving forces for, barriers to and patterns of cross-border acquisitions in China, their post-acquisition strategies and operating policies and the implications of these for the governance structure of the firm and its HRM. This is perhaps in part due to the fact that research on M&As is sensitive because of the often-required confidentiality and speed of change (Walter, 1985, cited in Salama *et al.*, 2003) and the consequent difficulty in gaining access to organizations to carry out the study (Salama *et al.*, 2003). However, these issues are especially important for the SOEs where international acquisition practices through JVs have existed for nearly two decades as a government strategy to rescue the poor-performing state industry. Although a considerable amount of academic research has been carried out since the late 1980s on international JVs in China (e.g. Björkman and Fan, 2002; Björkman and Lu, 2001; Child, 1994; Child and Faulkner, 1998; Cooke, 2002; Ding *et al.*, 1997; Luo, 2000a), these works focus mainly on the management practices of the JVs rather than the acquisition process prior to the establishment of the JV. Equally, although Luo (2000b,c has written extensively on how foreign businesses may enter China, these works focus primarily on the pre-acquisition process rather than the HR implications of acquisition for the workforce.

In practice, confusion, conflicts and barriers widely exist that restrict the level of international acquisition activities in China (see Luo, 2000b,c for more details). This is particularly the case in the acquisition of SOEs. This is reflected in the fact that when implementing the strategy and policy, the Chinese authorities have swung between advance and retreat, between loosening up and holding back, ambivalence between benefits and problems, gains and losses. Another problem is that there is a lack of transparency and participation from M&A experts when governmental departments formulate rules and policies that govern M&As. As a result, M&A administrators (including other authorities involved in the process) often find it difficult to interpret and implement the regulations. In addition to regulatory loopholes, the impact of acquisition on local employment is another important factor that influences the attitude of government officials and workers towards the acquisition. Post-acquisition changes in the management of human resources are also very sensitive issues as the cultural differences between the Chinese ex-SOEs and the acquiring foreign firm may be at their starkest, especially given the fact that HR issues often pose the greatest difficulties and are of crucial importance in M&As and post-M&A integration (Schuler, 2001; Schuler *et al.*, 2003; Stahl *et al.*, 2004). Given the Chinese government's determination to continue the privatization or partial privatization of SOEs through domestic and international acquisitions, it is important that issues related to international M&As of Chinese SOEs are discussed in detail.

The chapter is divided into four main sections in addition to this introduction section. The first main section reviews the driving forces for international acquisitions of SOEs in China by contemplating the objectives from both the Chinese and the FDI's point of view. It also outlines the patterns of acquisition of Chinese firms by foreign investment in terms of the industries they target. The second section questions the level of objectives alignment between the Chinese side and the foreign investors when entering international JVs. Issues related to the Chinese managerial skills and behaviour in acquisition negotiation are discussed as well as the multiple role of local governments. The third section then analyses the barriers to acquisitions for foreign investors in the context of the above issues. This is followed by the fourth section which discusses the implications of cross-border acquisitions for HRM, including its major aspects such as job security, training and development, pay and performance management, industrial relations, adoption of Western management techniques, managerial skills and post-acquisition integration. FDI's expansion in China has been part of the discussion of competition and strategy of specific industries in the previous chapters. The primary objective of this chapter is to provide a more focused analysis on the problems and likely effects of cross-border acquisitions of Chinese state-owned firms.

International acquisitions in China: driving forces and patterns of acquisitions

The development of foreign investment in China has been through three overlapping stages since the early 1980s. The first stage began in the early 1980s when the majority of foreign investment came from Hong Kong, Macao, Taiwan, Japan, Korea and other countries in Southeast Asia. Many of the investors were overseas Chinese. The second stage began in the early 1990s when MNCs from Western countries started to use China as a long-term development base by setting up their production plants in China. The third stage began after China's accession to the WTO. One emerging feature of FDI is the acquisition of SOEs, often through the stock market by offshore foreign investors or by MNCs in China.

Driving forces for FDI acquisitions of Chinese SOEs

There are a number of driving forces for the acquisition of Chinese SOEs (Dong and Hu, 1995). First, the Chinese government was forced to reform the ailing SOEs in the 1980s. The plan involved three steps: reducing the intervention of the state in these enterprises by redefining the role of the state as a shareholder with limited liabilities; revitalizing large and some medium-sized SOEs by further devolving decision rights to management and continuing economic reform towards a fair and competitive market; and privatization and leasing of the small- and medium-sized SOEs. As SOEs are controlled by the state through the local government, the performance of SOEs is a strong indication of the administrative performance of local governmental officials. For their own interest, officials want to maximize the profit level of the SOEs. The profit level of SOEs also has a direct impact on the tax income and consequently the building of the infrastructure of the region. Therefore, local officials are keen to improve the performance of SOEs through M&As when it becomes apparent that an SOE cannot survive on its own. During the early and mid-1990s, a popular way to pay off liabilities and create working capital for SOEs was to convert them into JVs with foreign investors (Child, 2001). Other important reasons for the Chinese side entering into a JV agreement include the desire to acquire knowledge, latest technology and management skills, and the desire to generate export income (see Brunner *et al.*, 1992; Child, 1994; Child and Faulkner, 1998; Gu, 1997; Luo, 2000b for more details). The reform of SOEs has been pushed to new heights since 1997 (Gu, 2003; L. Li, 2003; Zhang *et al.*, 2002) when large-scale downsizing, privatization and M&As involving SOEs, COEs, domestic private enterprises and foreign investment took place (Cooke, 2005a; Garnaut and Huang, 2001; Nolan, 2004; Parris, 1999; Saich, 2001). The idea behind the M&As is to let the SOEs be voluntarily acquired by or merged with better managed firms. Such an approach is believed to have combined ownership transfer with management adjustments, technology upgrading and capital injections (Dong and Hu, 1995).

A second motive is to exert control over foreign firms in China. In the early stage of the 'open door' policy, the Chinese government decided that in order to control the operations of foreign companies in China, FDI would be confined to JVs with local (state) partners. Numerous restrictions were also imposed on the JVs in their operations, including the management of human resources. In addition, there was strong pressure on JVs not to lay off workers. However, the level of control and influence from the local authorities has begun to ease off since the early 1990s (Pomfret, 1991) and foreign companies now have considerably more latitude in their business operations in China, including decisions in HR policies. The Chinese government now permits 100 per cent foreign ownership in most industries and the number of new wholly owned foreign subsidiaries surpassed that of equity JVs for the first time in 1998 (Björkman and Lu, 2001).

A third driving force comes from the growing needs of profitable Chinese enterprises as part of their development strategies. MNCs can bring the much needed capital, advanced technology and managerial techniques to China through acquisitions (C. X. Jin *et al.*, 2003). It is true that most of the technologies introduced to China by MNCs may not be the state-of-the-art technologies. Nonetheless, they are still better than what most enterprises in China have. The introduction of these technologies into China will have a spill-over effect and promote the upgrading of technology by other enterprises in the same industry in China (Liu, 2000). A fourth motive for SOEs to be acquired by foreign firms is to attract foreign capital and to develop international markets by association with prestigious international brand names.

In short, as Nolan (2004) summarized, larger SOEs have been through major changes. They have:

- Grown rapidly in terms of value of sales;
- Absorbed a great deal of modern technology, learned how to compete in the marketplace;
- Substantially upgraded the technical level of their employees;
- Learned wide-ranging new managerial skills, gained substantial understanding of international financial markets;
- Become sought-after partners for multinational companies (Nolan, 2004, p. 188).

The driving forces for international acquisitions from the Chinese government and industries, the policy change and the resultant investment environment have to some extent shaped the patterns of acquisitions by foreign investments.

Patterns of international acquisitions in China

According to C. X. Jin *et al.* (2003), there are three major characteristics of acquisitions of SOEs by foreign investments. A first characteristic is that foreign investors are increasing their level of investment and stock control of the acquired SOEs, some even become solely foreign-owned. A second feature is that foreign investment has been shifting away steady from traditional industries towards the new, high-tech and high value-added industries. There is also a growing interest in investing in light industries and commercial industries. A third feature is that while foreign investment prior to the 1990s had mainly come from Hong Kong, Taiwan, Macao and other countries in the Asian Pacific rim, with relatively low level of technology and in relatively small scale and simple operation mode, investors since the 1990s have been large MNCs, with larger investment projects and strategic operations. These operations also develop a sophisticated business chain, from product development and manufacturing to marketing, sales and after-sale services. Establishments/offices are set up in different geographical locations in China for strategic purposes. Some MNCs have also set up R&D centres and regional headquarters in China to complete their China business strategy (C. X. Jin *et al.*, 2003).

In the 1990s, foreign firms mainly acquired smaller SOEs that might be average performers. Into the twenty-first century, MNCs' M&A activities in China were becoming more strategic. They began to target larger and profit-making SOEs and from targeting individual enterprises to targeting the whole industry, as the Chinese government began to open up its industries to FDI. For example, in the 1990s, MNCs acquired and gradually dominated the drinks industry, cosmetics industry, detergents industry and films industry. Since the 2000s, MNCs have been expanding proactively into China's rubber, pharmaceutical and household electrical appliance industry. The acquisition pattern also changed from *ad hoc* acquisitions to concentration acquisitions, purposefully targeting key companies in the same industry or all SOEs in the same geographical locations. In the 1980s, MNCs entered the Chinese market with capital and technology assets. In the 1990s, they entered with their own brand-name products that replaced the Chinese brands or acquired the Chinese brands and then replaced them with their own. This has typically been the case in the car industry, with most of the Chinese brands replaced by foreign ones through international JVs (Liu *et al.*, 2001). As legal restrictions are gradually relaxed, international JVs as a common corporate mode is being replaced by wholly foreign-owned enterprises. Currently the attractiveness for foreign investment is in M&A deals especially in the manufacturing industry, most notably in semiconductors and microelectronics, home appliances, electronic medical equipment, machinery and services (e.g. retail and hotel).

In general, MNCs embark on M&A activities in China to develop product market, to consolidate their international competitive position, to take advantage of its cheap production cost and to streamline the chain of supply, production, marketing and sale in the same location (C. X. Jin *et al.*, 2003). There are two main reasons for MNCs acquiring SOEs. One is that they foresee the upsurge of China's economy and the enormous market potential, therefore enter their target industry and product market through acquisitions. They intend to defeat their competitors to monopolize the market and gain economies of scale (e.g. Koda). This is the investment type of acquisitions. The other reason is that they consider the price of the SOEs on sale to be pitched too low, therefore intend to buy it and then make a profit by selling it. This is the opportunistic type of acquisition (C. X. Jin *et al.*, 2003), although the former seems to be more dominant than the latter.

MNCs' acquisition of SOEs – a win-win solution?

Despite the push and pull factors that fuel the international acquisition activities in China in recent years, cross-border acquisitions may not yield the desired benefits for the Chinese for a number of reasons. These include the likely mis-alignment between the objectives of the SOEs/Chinese government and that of the foreign investors, the skill gaps and opportunistic behaviour of the Chinese managers in acquisition activities and the undue intervention from local governments. For the MNCs, there are also a range of barriers in the whole process of acquisition, from pre-acquisition negotiation, acquisition to post-acquisition management, that prevent their anticipated benefits from being achieved.

Objectives alignment?

While Chinese SOEs wish to join forces with MNCs for survival, product and technological development, system innovation and human capital development, MNCs may only be interested in picking the well-performing SOEs for acquisition rather than helping troubled SOEs to survive (Xu, 2003). By the 1990s, MNCs targeted mainly the well-performing large SOEs for acquisition. They were keen to be the controlling party by becoming the sole owner of the acquired enterprise or controlling at least 50 per cent of its stocks (Chen, 1999). They tend to leave the debt to the Chinese side and may also sell their stocks suddenly to make a quick profit. Profits may be transferred out of China instead of being re-invested for development. It has been reported (Chen, 1999) that MNCs imported out-of-date or second-hand equipment into China as being new, or quoting a higher than actual price. It has also been noted (Chen and Wang, 2003) that in the acquisition negotiation process, the proportion of share holdings between the two parties is often the focus of disagreement. There tend to be major differences between the strategic objectives of large SOEs and that of the acquiring MNCs. Meanwhile, some SOEs are the flag ship companies of their industry and represent the Chinese state-of-the-art in the international arena. Surrendering ownership and control to MNCs may have a negative strategic consequence to the Chinese industry. This is especially the case in industries of strategic importance such as automobile, chemical and petroleum, electronics, metallic and aviation where large SOEs concentrate.

Even when the Chinese side owns the majority of the shares, the MNC partner makes the decision of what technology to introduce to China. On many occasions, only old technology is introduced to China. For example, the

US government strictly forbids the export of advanced technology to other countries. Therefore, most of the R&D activities for product development are carried out in the United States. This makes it difficult to fulfil the wish of the Chinese-acquired enterprise to upgrade their technology through acquisition by an American firm (Zhan, 2003). As a result, the enterprise in China only serves as a cheap site for the MNC to manufacture and assemble low value-added components with the intensive use of semi-skilled workers who have little opportunities to upgrade their skills, a situation similar to that in other Asia Pacific developing countries such as Malaysia (Frenkel and Peetz, 1998; Wilkinson *et al.*, 2001). In addition, the incentive for firms to innovate or for MNCs to introduce state-of-the-art technology into China may be reduced when technology spill-over and unintentional leakage of technical know-how enables the Chinese to imitate the product and technology.

International M&As have brought relatively limited R&D activities to China, a situation worsened by the fact that some MNCs abolished the original Chinese R&D departments after the acquisition and rely on the MNC's own R&D centre abroad for technical support.[1] This reduces China's development capacity. This is especially the case in industries which have a high proportion of MNC investments and product market share. The dominance of MNCs in an industry quashes the opportunity for survival and development of domestic enterprises (Wang and Liu, 2002). A case in point is that of the film manufacturing industry. Koda and Fuji's price war in China has pushed the rest of the (Chinese-owned) photographic film manufacturers close to bankruptcy. Koda and Fuji have now monopolized the film market in China and if one of them withdrew from China or retreated from the price war, it would undoubtedly lead to a price increase. This is in addition to the financial and social burdens that are transferred to the state by MNCs through redundancy of surplus workers.

At a macro level, the monopoly of a given industry by MNCs may tip the balance of the industrial sectors in China. It will also suppress the growth of indigenous enterprises. Once the industry is open to foreign investment, the government will have little power to influence the business strategy of the MNCs operating in that industry, thus reducing the government's capacity to oversee the strategic balance of that industry in relation to the whole economic structure of the country. At the corporate level, the MNC establishment in China may become more dependent upon the rest of the MNC in its new international labour division in terms of product development, marketing and sale, and concentrating solely on manufacturing (Liu, 2000). This is reflected in the fact that many MNCs control the most senior positions in China in order to implement their global strategy and force the Chinese managers into lower positions, although many MNCs have started to localize their professional and managerial staff.

Managerial skills and behaviour

The low effectiveness of acquisitions of SOEs has been a focus of academic debate in China. However, one fundamental problem has often been neglected, that is, the role of senior managers in SOEs in M&A activities. A number of problems may occur during the decision-making and negotiation period of the acquisition that may have a negative effect on the target enterprise. One relates to the competency, and another to the behaviour of the managers. Chinese managers have often been criticized for their lack of managerial skills and opportunistic behaviour in general (e.g. Child, 1994; Cooke, 2005a; Ralston *et al.*, 1997; Tsang, 2001). Similar problems appear to exhibit themselves in acquisition pricing, negotiation and post-acquisition integration.

Entrepreneurs use M&As as a business strategy to advance their own interest instead of that of the enterprise. These include financial benefits (e.g. salary, bonuses and stocks) and non-financial benefits such as power to control, personal prestige and reputation. The absence of an independent asset evaluation system provides an opportunity for senior managers to use their position to reduce the SOE asset value for acquisition to bargain for their new position and terms and conditions in the new organization (Cai and Shen, 2002). This is evidenced by a research report published by the Shanghai Stock Exchange Institution. The report revealed that many restructured enterprises involving the transfer of ownership tended to make a profit in the first year but made a loss from the second year. This indicates that short-term profit-making may be the top priority of senior managers instead of long-term development of the enterprise (cited in Cai and Shen, 2002).

The lack of a sophisticated asset evaluation system and the absence of an open and competitive tendering for the targeted SOEs may also lead to a heavy loss of state assets. While tangible assets may be valued at too low a price, intangible assets, including tacit knowledge, special skills, brand name, reputation, image and technical know-how, are often left out in the evaluation. The Chinese have yet to learn how to protect their IPR through patent rights, as noted in Chapter 3. Other loss of intangible asset includes the loss of famous domestic brand names in recent years following the acquisition by MNCs. A strategy adopted by some foreign firms to extend their market share is to purchase already well-known Chinese brands in order to tap into their distribution networks and subsequently replace the Chinese brands with their own brands. For example, in late 2003, L'Oreal acquired the Chinese brand Mini-nurse, which allowed the company to sell its products through the 280,000 sales outlets established by Mini-nurse across China. One month later, it took over another famous Chinese brand (*China Daily Online*, 7 June 2005) (C. X. Jin *et al.*, 2003).

Efficiency in negotiations is also low from the Chinese side, often involving many people and numerous meetings. The government officials I have interviewed (see Cooke, 2006) described the negotiation process of one of the acquisitions they were involved in as a Marathon. In addition to the initial intentional discussions before the acquisition negotiation formally started, the Chinese negotiation team held over ten internal meetings, each meeting involving at least half a dozen of people. More than 170 head counts from the Chinese team were involved in the actual negotiation meetings with the MNC representatives. By contrast, the MNC sent only two representatives throughout the negotiations, with the senior executive showing his face only on a couple of the most important occasions. The two MNC representatives had a clear idea of what the company wanted and were able to stick to their agenda throughout the negotiation in spite of the repeated attempts from the Chinese representatives to soften those demands. In the end, the two parties signed the deal with plenty of concessions from the Chinese side with the MNC basically getting what they wanted. In addition, all the logistic costs (e.g. chauffeured transport, banquets and gifts) of these negotiation meetings were borne by the Chinese SOE, as part of the Chinese hospitality and face gaining exercise. According to the government officials interviewed, this is just a typical example of negotiations with foreign investors. The reason why so many people were involved from the Chinese side was that nobody wanted to take responsibility of the decision in case it went wrong and yet everybody (especially those from the local government) wanted to be involved and have a say in it.

Intervention from local governments

A unique feature in the (international) M&As of Chinese SOEs is that local governments tend to have a close and direct involvement in the decision-making and negotiation process. In principle, SOE assets belong to all people and the state; local governments are entrusted to look after these assets from an administrative point of view. Enterprise managers are employed to manage the assets from an operations' point of view. Therefore, enterprise managers cannot make decisions in the transfer of asset ownership without authorization. Because of this complex ownership and governance structure of SOEs, local governments tend to have heavy involvement in SOE M&A activities. Local governments have vested interest in the asset of the SOEs and are reluctant to give enterprise managers full autonomy to handle the M&A activities. In the absence of a well-developed capital market and M&A agency bodies, the M&A of SOEs will be difficult to complete smoothly without the support and participation of the local government. Many methods commonly used in M&As in developed countries are not applicable in China. In addition, an M&A agency system centred by investment banks is not yet established. Investment banks have not been able to provide financial consultancy services to the enterprises involved. Under those circumstances, local governments have to step in to broker the deal. The positive role of local governments in M&A activities therefore includes that of an agency, monitoring and harmonization role. Moreover, the administration of SOEs in China is segmented by regional administration and industrial administration. Cross-region and cross-industry M&As will disrupt the status quo and require a new balance of interests. The involvement of local governments will help oversee the flow of assets and the rebalance of the interests of different administrative regions and industries.

However, the direct and often parochial interest of local governments in SOEs also creates problems that compromise the interest of the enterprise concerned. For example, local governments may be keen to get rid of the burden of poor-performing SOEs and quote a low price for acquisitions. Some local governmental officials may be eager to establish their own performance record and therefore cut corners to make it easy for the MNCs to acquire their targeted SOEs. Tax regulations are sometimes interpreted generously by the local tax authorities in order to attract FDI. A minority of government officials are also involved in corruption and benefit from the low pricing of SOEs (Liu, 2000).[2] As Kracht (2002) points out, two more forces – government and *guanxi* – need to be added to Porter's five-forces system of analysing the different market forces concerning competitors, customers, suppliers, substitutes and new potential competitors as key factors determining success.

Barriers to foreign investors' acquisition of Chinese SOEs

While the intervention of the local governments and the opportunistic behaviour of some managers may be to the advantage of MNCs, there are a number of barriers that make their acquisition activities a difficult task which may dampen enthusiasm for acquisitions from FDI.

First, the existing administrative system, as discussed above, poses a range of related administrative problems and makes it very difficult to carry out cross-region and/or cross-industry acquisitions. These problems include, for example, taxation problems (based on same region, same industry and same fiscal level)[3] and banking problems (bank loan based on region). These problems mainly affect those MNCs that are already in China and wishing to acquire SOEs in another region rather than MNCs wishing to enter China through acquisitions.

Secondly, foreign investors may encounter difficulties in selecting SOEs for acquisition due to the lack of information in the market and the lack of good SOEs in the stock market because the majority of SOEs have not yet reached the minimum standard requirements for being listed in the stock market (Wang and Liu, 2002). These problems are in part caused by the fact that the stock market of China is not well-established and there is insufficient transparency and information flow.

Thirdly, there is generally a lack of clear regulatory guideline related to M&As, although this situation is being addressed by the Chinese government. For example, the State Restructuring Regulations, enacted in January 2003, set out the requirements and procedures for the approval of the restructuring of SOEs into foreign-invested enterprises. This is followed by the promulgation of the M&A Regulations in March 2003 that set out a framework for foreign investors' acquisitions of all types of domestic enterprises and the restructuring of such enterprises upon acquisition, including SOEs. Thus, the M&A Regulations will also apply to the acquisition of SOEs, although conflicts may arise between the two new regulations (*China Legal News*, November 2003). In the light of the absence of a clear set of legal or administrative procedures for M&A approval, M&A parties often have to rely heavily on administrative approval involving the authorization of different administrative departments (C. X. Jin *et al.*, 2003). This practice carries an inherent bureaucratic low efficiency (Cooke, 2003). In addition, the enforcement of business and employment laws in China is not without problems due to variations in

the interpretation of the laws and the often lax approach of officials in enforcing the laws (Cooke, 2002; Dicks, 1989; Lubman, 1995; Taylor et al., 2003;
Warner, 1996).

Fourthly, as was discussed earlier, an independent system consisting of
financial and legal agency bodies is yet to be developed in China to provide
professional services for M&A activities. While large MNCs can tap into their
global corporate base of expertise to overcome this deficiency, small foreign
businesses wishing to expand their operations in China will find it difficult, if
not impossible, to find their own way in this jungle.

The growth of international acquisition activities in China creates a new set
of requirements for and problems in HRM. For example, there is a lack of
managerial talent in acquisition deals; there is also a deficit in professional
staff familiar with acquisition businesses in the existing legal and banking
industries to enable these institutions to develop M&A businesses. Similarly,
post-acquisition integration will trigger further challenges to the management
that are specific to the Chinese institutional environment. It is to these issues
that we now turn.

Implications of acquisitions for HRM in China

Western literature on the implications of M&As for HRM has highlighted
the 'human'- related challenges to post-M&A integration (e.g. Cartwright and
Cooper, 1993; Hubbard and Purcell, 2001; Marks and Mirvis, 1982; Morrison
and Robinson, 1997; Nikandrou et al., 2000; Robinson and Rousseau, 1994;
Schraeder and Self, 2003; Schuler and Jackson, 2001; Schuler et al., 2003;
Stahl et al., 2004; Weber, 1996). They often point to issues such as cultural
differences, communication problems, workforce morale, trust, management
style and organizational politics as barriers to integration which may contribute
to M&A failures. They point out that financial benefits anticipated from M&As
are often unrealized because of conflicts of organizational cultures and that
cultural integration remains a major managerial challenge (Cartwright and
Cooper, 1993). Marks and Mirvis (1982) showed that HR issues accounted
for a third to a half of all merger failures, and 'there is no indication that things
have improved in the last two decades' (Boxall and Purcell, 2003, p. 220).

While these Western lessons may have generic implications for M&As in
China, cross-border acquisitions in China exhibit their own characteristics of
HRM that are unique to the Chinese context. As we can see from Tables 8.2
and 8.3, MNCs and JVs are making up an increasingly large proportion of
businesses and employment in China whose employment policy and practice
have a strong bearing in reshaping the pool of human resources and the experience of work for a significant proportion of workers. Cross-border acquisitions
in China therefore have both positive and negative impacts on HRM in SOEs
specifically and in HRM in China more generally. These HR implications stem
from changes required as a direct result of the acquisition itself and as a longer-
term HR strategy that evolves after the acquisition under the influence of the
MNC.

Table 8.3 Information on enterprises of selected ownership forms in China (end of 2003 figures)

Item	No. of enterprises*	Gross industrial output value (billion yuan)**	Value-added of industry (billion yuan)	Total assets (billion yuan)	Sale revenue (billion yuan)	Sales profit (billion yuan)	Value-added tax payable (billion yuan)	Employment (in million persons)	Average annual wage (yuan)
National total	196,222	14,227	4,199	16,881	14,317	834	549	57.5	14,040
State-owned and state-holding enterprises	34,280	5,341	1,884	9,452	5,803	384	303	21.6	14,577
Enterprises with funds from Hong Kong, Macao and Taiwan	21,152	1,743	468	1,622	1,675	93	45	7	14,691
Foreign funded enterprises	17,429	2,693	692	2,304	2,685	185	74	5.6	19,366

* Figures refer to industrial enterprises above designated size, i.e. enterprises with an annual sales income of over 5 million yuan.
** The gross industrial output value is calculated at current prices (original notes from *China Statistical Yearbook*, 2004, p. 513).
Source: adapted from *China Statistical Yearbook* (2004, pp. 176–7, 513–21).

Job security

One immediate concern after the acquisition is that of job security. The majority of SOEs are overstaffed and downsizing has been a major initiative in the restructuring of SOEs in the last decade. Issues related to redundancy are often the focus of debate in acquisition negotiations. While the MNC aims to retain only a minimum number of employees selected on the basis of competency, the SOE concerned and the local government would like the MNC to retain as many employees as possible and offer a generous redundancy package in order to reduce the burden of the state and to minimize the negative social impact (C. X. Jin *et al.*, 2003). In some cases, it is not the most competent employees who are retained, but those who are considered 'most suitable' by managers. This suitability may be interpreted in a number of ways depending on the criteria used by those who are in charge, including perceived morality and loyalty of the candidate and his/her guanxi (relationship) with the decision maker. The same was true for selecting managers and candidates for key posts.

Job security level in MNCs and JVs is generally lower than that in SOEs, especially for the older workers, with fixed-term employment contracts being the norm. The aggressive competitive strategy adopted by some MNCs also causes on-going job losses. For example, it was reported that in 1997, Koda launched a price war with Fuji in China. This had led to the redundancy of 20,000 employees in 1997, followed by another 3400 in 1999 and 3000 in 2001 (Zhan, 2003).

Training and development

Acquisition creates immediate needs for training, especially for employees who are most affected by the acquisition and those who have direct dealings with customers and suppliers, such as marketing and sales personnel. These employees need to communicate to the suppliers and customers on why the acquisition has taken place and what the company's new business strategy and policy would be and so forth. Training may also be given to the employees in order to create a new corporate identity and organizational culture and to establish new ways of working. The employees are then expected to communicate their new corporate image to the external stakeholders. In addition, acquisition may lead to the introduction of new technology as a result of the need for post-acquisition system integration. This will bring new training opportunities for employees.

More generally, MNCs and JVs in China provide a higher level and variety of health and safety and skill training opportunities to their employees than most other forms of ownership (Cooke, 2005a). Many blue chip MNCs and JVs also pride themselves on employee training and development. However, it should not be taken for granted that all MNCs and JVs in China will provide the level of skill training that is anticipated of acquisitions. As was noted earlier, the majority of FDI is mainly in the manufacturing industries relying on intensive labour rather than advanced technology. The lack of R&D investment and activities may also reduce the need and opportunity for the Chinese technical staff. Another negative impact is that the entrance of MNCs into China increases the employment cost of Chinese professional and managerial staff in the light of the wage war to compete for the rare supply of local talent. This in turn reduces the workforce stability and organizational competence of domestic Chinese firms.

Pay, performance management and work intensification

A tangible benefit for employees of those SOEs that have been acquired by foreign firms is that there is generally an increase in their wage income after the acquisition. This reflects the fact that wage levels are the highest in foreign-funded enterprises in China (see Table 8.3). This is in part because foreign-funded businesses are required by regulations to pay wage at a level no lower than the average wage of the same industry in the local area. However, wage increases are commonly accompanied by longer working hours and much tighter performance control that is more closely related to individual and collective productivity. The seniority-oriented (i.e. the length one works for the company) pay structure of SOEs is often replaced with performance-related pay.

Employment regulations and labour disputes

There are a number of employment-related regulations that MNCs need to follow, at least in principle, during and after the acquisition. These include, for example, the State Restructuring Regulations, the Labour Law of China (1995) and the Trade Union Law (amended in 2001). The State Restructuring Regulations require the SOE being reorganized to first seek the opinions of the staff and Workers Congress of the SOE. In addition, the Labour Law provides a general framework of labour protection in terms of recruitment and dismissal, pay, working time, training, social security and health and safety protection and so on which applies to all employing organizations in China. However, in contrast to their relatively higher level of pay and training provision than SOEs, MNCs and JVs tend to be more pragmatic in their observation of the employment regulations with frequent violations of certain aspects of the regulations, notably in working hours and social insurance (Chan, 2001; Cooke, 2004; Gallagher, 2005; Ngai, 2005; Thireau and Hua, 2003).

There is a much lower level of union recognition and a higher level of labour disputes in MNCs and JVs that are also more collectively involved compared with the state sector (Cooke, 2008). The trade union officials also reported that foreign-invested firms were the most difficult ones to tackle in terms of persuading them to recognize the trade union and to establish a collective negotiation system. When trade union officials visit the MNCs and JVs to negotiate union recognition, managers typically do not say 'No' directly, but deploy a delaying tactic to deny union recognition and any union activities that may be seen as a threat to management authority. Where trade unions were established during their SOE years, they may be retained after the acquisition by foreign investors and became JVs or wholly foreign-owned. However, trade unions generally play little role in the acquisition negotiation and subsequently play a less active (welfare) role after the acquisition, as if there had been a *de facto* trade union de-recognition. This is not necessarily a result of the foreign partners' unsympathetic/hostile attitude towards unionism. Rather, it may reflect the limited role of the trade unions in major decision-making of the enterprises, even though this is their right as specified in the Labour Law, and the ensuing ambiguity of organizational identity felt by the workforce.

Adoption of Western management techniques and workforce resistance

MNCs are often regarded as a potential source of convergence in international HRM in that they are expected to use their international perspective to promote the diffusion of 'best practice' HR techniques (Evans *et al.*, 2002; Rubery and Grimshaw, 2003). This appears to be the case in China, but only started to happen recently (Björkman and Lu, 2001; Lasserre and Ching, 1997) after they had been granted more autonomy to operate in China. One of the most important consequences of foreign involvement in Sino-foreign JVs has been the introduction of a more systematic management approach in that the systems were defined in writing, standardized and operated on a regular basis (Child, 1994). Braun and Warner (2002) found that a majority of MNCs in their sample have placed a high strategic importance to the HRM function and have attempted to introduce internally consistent high-performance HRM practices. Björkman and Fan (2002) further observed that the MNCs in their sample had HR practices that tended to be more closely in line with the 'high-performance HRM system' as defined by Western HRM scholars than with the personnel practices found in local Chinese companies. This is in spite of the fact that these HR 'best practices' were mainly Western practices transferred and adapted to suit the Chinese environment.

However, the HR policies of MNCs and JVs are not necessarily embraced by their Chinese employees with enthusiasm. For example, an earlier study by Child (1994) found that, in the 30 JVs studied, there had been various attempts to introduce Western HR tools with varying, but never significant, degrees of success. A common complaint amongst Western managers was that Chinese staff were reluctant to accept personal responsibility (Child, 1994). Another earlier study (Ilari and Grange, 1999) on a Sino-Italian JV motor company in southern China also revealed that the Italian partner found it difficult to transfer its firm-specific advantages to the Chinese ground because of the cultural differences in the two employment systems. Legewie's (2002) study on issues related to the control and coordination of Japanese subsidiaries in China further highlights the problems of an expatriate-based management system in transferring a typical Japanese firm's strength, namely socialization and networking, abroad and in building up an efficient transnational network of global operations. Nonetheless, there is evidence to suggest that effort is made by MNC managers to reconcile the twin pressures for control and adaptation rather than satisfying one at the expense of the other (Child and Heavens, 1999). A discernible trend is that Western HR policies are gradually being accepted and internalized by the younger generation of the Chinese workforce who can no longer seek job security in the state sector. This is reflected in the fact that MNCs and JVs are often perceived to be the 'most popular employers' (*Beijing Youth Newspaper*, 15 November 2002).

Western management techniques are commonly implemented after the acquisitions, notably that of performance-related pay, ISO 9000 quality series recognition, team-working, problem-solving and plant care (Cooke, 2002, 2006; Evans *et al.*, 2002). However, these initiatives are reported to have received only moderate enthusiasm from the shopfloor workers who displayed compliance rather than commitment to them. What they seemed to resent most was the performance-related pay system and the secrecy of bonus distributions. This is one of the areas where the cultural difference between the West and the East is most distinct. Differences in organizational cultures have often been cited as one of the most insurmountable barriers to post-acquisition integration. MNCs acquiring Chinese SOEs are likely to encounter even more difficulties in the integration because of the differences of national as well as organizational culture.

Post-acquisition integration and harmonization of terms and conditions

Unlike Western firms that may face fierce market competition and hostile bids, there is a relatively lower level of competition in China which allows organizations more time for post-M&A adjustment. While M&A failure rate tends to be relatively high in Western countries, China may have a lower M&A fatality rate in part because MNCs are considered to be desirable employers and in part because of the high unemployment rate which may suppress any workforce discontent for fear of job losses. In any case, the SOE concerned may be in a very bad shape in the first place and any change may inject new life, or at least hope, into the organization. However, the extent to which anticipated improvements have been made for those that were profit-making prior to the acquisition is unknown.

What tends to be a problem is the discontent caused by the gaps in terms and conditions between expatriate and Chinese managers. As more and more Chinese managers and professionals have acquired management know-how and technical competencies that were once held by expatriate managers and professionals when foreign firms first entered China, this closing gap of knowledge increases the bargaining power of local managers and professionals. They are beginning to feel a sense of distributional injustice arising from the differentials between expatriates and local Chinese (Leung *et al.*, 2001) and demand terms and conditions similar to those enjoyed by expatriates. For example, Tsang's (2001) study revealed that a third of the Chinese managers studied considered that the pay gap between the Chinese managers and the expatriate managers were unfair since their skills and efforts were similar. Expatriate managers also saw the pay gap as a barrier to their integration with their Chinese colleagues who resent pay differentials. This barrier may be further compounded by the perceived social distance between expatriate and local managers due to their language and cultural differences (Tsang, 2001). Integration between the expatriates and the Chinese and harmonization of the terms and conditions between the two groups is therefore an important issue in post-acquisition management.

Conclusions

This chapter has provided an overview of the driving forces for the acquisition of Chinese SOEs by foreign investors. These forces come from both political and economic needs from the Chinese side as well as the foreign investors' strategic intent. While cross-border acquisition activities have been increasing and spreading into more and more industries, there are a number of pitfalls in the process that may prevent the anticipated benefits from being realized for both sides involved and for China at a macro level. These pitfalls may also be a source that discourages potential foreign investors from acquiring Chinese firms. Importantly, cross-border acquisitions trigger a range of implications for HRM that are unique to the Chinese context.

There are a number of lessons to be learned for both the foreign investors and the Chinese. For foreign investors, the infrastructure for M&A deals in China is not yet fully developed and they should rely on their own professional support for advice. Nevertheless, the entry of foreign banks in the Chinese finance and banking industry will undoubtedly facilitate the development of an independent and professional finance agency system to provide services for M&A activities. There are also complicated and potentially conflicting laws in China that need to be followed when operating in China, in spite of the fact that the interpretation and observation of them tend to be lax. Interventions from the local governments also tend to be relatively frequent which can be a source of support as well as undue interference, causing non-market behaviour. Care should be taken in implementing HR strategies in order to minimize cultural clashes and inter-group disputes.

For the Chinese side, the primary motive for foreign investors to acquire Chinese enterprises is to expand their business and gain competitive advantages rather than the economic and social well-being of China and its people, although this may be a co-incidental outcome. There is an urgent need for the Chinese to acquire managerial skills in handling acquisition negotiation and post-acquisition management. The Chinese government also has the dilemma between the need to control the way MNCs should carry out their acquisitions in China so that they are not harmful to the balance of the macro economy of the country on the one hand, and the need to attract FDI to create employment and stimulate economic growth on the other. With China gradually improving its policies, regulations, taxation and credit mechanism, the level of international acquisition is likely to grow, supported by international capital back-up and the growth of healthy Chinese enterprises. Many of the challenges and pitfalls identified here in the cross-border acquisition of Chinese SOEs share common characteristics with that when Chinese MNCs venture abroad – a topic that we are going to turn to in the next chapter.

Recommended readings

D. Guthrie, *Dragon in a Three-Piece Suit: The Emergence of Capitalism in China* (Princeton, NJ: Princeton University Press, 1999).

J. Hassard, J. Sheehan, M. Zhou, J. Terpstra-Tong and J. Morris, *China's State Enterprise Reform: from Marx to the Market* (London: Routledge, 2007).

Y. Luo, *Partnering with Chinese Firms: Lessons for International Managers* (Aldershot: Ashgate Publishing Ltd, 2000c).

M. Warner, *China's Managerial Revolution* (London: Frank Cass, 1999).

CHAPTER 9

Chinese MNCs Abroad: Internationalization Strategies and Implications for HRM

Introduction

An important phenomenon in the rapid globalization of the world economy has been the steady increase of outward FDI from the developing countries (see Table 9.1). Driven by its growing economic power, China is increasingly seeking overseas investment opportunities. It must be noted, however, that despite the fact that FDI outflows from mainland China extended to more than 160 countries and regions around the world by the end of 1998 (Li, 2000), China is still in its early stage of development as an international investor, making up only a very small proportion of the world's outward FDI. Nevertheless, China is emerging as one of the top FDI exporters among developing countries (*Asian Pacific Bulletins*, 2004). While much attention has been attracted to the fact that China is one of the largest (the largest since 2002) FDI recipient countries in the world, little attention has been drawn to the other side of the coin – the growth of China's outward FDI. According to UNCTAD's *World Investment Report 2002*, the Top 12 Chinese transnationals, mainly SOEs, controlled over US$30 billion in foreign assets with over 20,000 foreign employees and US$33 billion in foreign sales. The Chinese corporations' international expansion aspirations are backed by both the Chinese government and the host country government. As such the growth of Chinese FDI may have significant implications for global competition and the management of MNCs that cannot be ignored.

This chapter is divided into five main sections. The first one provides a brief overview of the growth of Chinese outward FDI. The second section analyses the driving forces for Chinese firms to invest overseas. This is followed by a review of their internationalization strategies through choices of host countries. The section explores further why Chinese firms invest in developed countries where they apparently do not have competitive advantages of a higher pecking order over their Western competitors. It looks at what investment strategies

Table 9.1 Chinese FDI overview in selected years

FDI flows	1994–99 (Annual average)	2000	2001	2002	2003	2004	2005
China							
Inward	40.7	40.7	46.9	52.7	53.5	60.6	72.4
Outward	2.2	0.9	6.9	2.5	−0.2	1.8	11.3
United States							
Inward	124.9	314.0	159.5	74.5	53.1	122.4	99.4
Outward	114.3	142.6	124.9	134.9	129.4	222.4	−12.7
East Asia							
Inward	58.5	116.3	78.8	67.4	72.2	105.1	118.2
Outward	32.3	72.0	26.1	27.6	14.4	59.2	54.2
Asia and Oceania							
Inward	92.9	148.3	112.2	96.2	110.5	157.3	200.0
Outward	43.5	82.2	47.2	34.7	19.0	83.4	83.6
Developing economies							
Inward	166.4	266.8	221.4	163.6	175.1	275.0	334.3
Outward	64.9	143.8	76.7	49.7	35.6	112.8	117.5
World							
Inward	548.1	1,409.6	832.2	617.7	557.9	710.8	916.3
Outward	553.1	1,244.5	764.2	539.5	561.1	813.1	778.7

Figures in millions of US dollars
Source: United Nations Conference on Trade and Development, *World Investment Report 2006*; www.unctad.org/fdistatistics.

Chinese MNCs adopt to overcome the liability of foreignness with the added disadvantage of being from a downstream country. The fourth section identifies a range of challenges that Chinese firms may encounter in their overseas' investment drive. These four main sections provide a context for the discussion of the fifth section, which contemplates different implications of HRM for Chinese MNCs in developed and developing countries. Given the fact that China has been suffering from an increasing shortage of management talent, especially with expertise in managing international operations, and given the fact that an increasing amount of Chinese outward FDI is achieved through cross-border acquisitions (Table 9.2), these are particularly important issues to be explored.

It needs to be noted here that there are already a number of excellent textbooks on international HRM (e.g. Briscoe and Schuler, 2004; Harzing and Ruysseveldt, 2004; Sparrow *et al.*, 2004) which provide detailed and comprehensive guidelines for HRM in cross-border M&As and MNCs. This chapter will therefore not be engaged in the general discussion of HRM in MNCs.

Table 9.2   Cross-border merger and acquisition overview, 1995–2003

	1995	1996	1997	1998	1999	2000	2001	2002	2003
China									
Sales	403	1,906	1,856	798	2,395	2,247	2,325	2,072	3,820
Purchases	249	451	799	1,276	101	470	452	1,047	1,647
South, East and South-east Asia									
Sales	6,278	9,745	18,586	15,842	28,431	21,105	33,114	16,807	20,167
Purchases	6,608	17,547	17,893	6,001	11,335	21,139	24,844	10,778	16,978
Developing economies									
Sales	16,493	35,727	66,999	82,668	74,030	70,610	85,813	44,532	42,130
Purchases	13,372	29,646	35,210	21,717	63,406	48,496	55,719	27,585	31,234
World									
Sales	186,593	227,023	304,848	531,648	766,044	1,143,816	593,960	369,789	296,988
Purchases	186,593	227,023	304,848	531,648	766,044	1,143,816	593,960	369,789	296,988

Figures in millions of US dollars
Source: UNCTAD, *World Investment Report 2004*; www.unctad.org/fdistatistics.

Instead, it will draw attention to HRM issues that are relevant to Chinese MNCs, particularly the different cultural and institutional characteristics in developed and developing countries that may have a major impact on HR practices.

Growth of Chinese outward investment

Prior to 1978 when China adopted its open door policy, the amount of Chinese outward FDI was minimal, mainly in the form of small branch offices of banking and overseas trade services. In 1979, the Chinese outward FDI was 0.8 million yuan (about US$0.5 million of the value at the time) (Cai, 1999). The Chinese outward FDI has progressed through three main stages (see Cai, 1999; Wu and Chen, 2001; Zhang and Van Ben Bulcke, 1996 for a brief historic overview of the development of Chinese outward FDI). The first stage began in the late 1970s until the mid-1980s. During this period, only state-owned import–export corporations and enterprises seeking foreign economic and technological cooperation under the auspices of the Foreign Trade Commission had permission to invest abroad. Between 1979 and 1985, 185 non-trading enterprises were established in more than 45 countries (primarily developing countries) mainly in the catering, engineering, finance and insurance industries (Cai, 1999). The second stage ran from 1985 to 1990 when Chinese outward FDI experienced a significant growth in line with China's economic growth. In 1985, the Chinese FDI reached US$628 million (almost five times that of the previous year), and by 1990, this figure had increased to US$830 million (Cai, 1999). During this period, many Foreign Trade Corporations of the national and provincial governments, which had lost their former monopolies in the 1980s, restructured themselves and launched new corporate strategies including internationalization. Similarly, another major category of Chinese FDI firms – banks and financial enterprises – also underwent restructuring with internationalization as part of their corporate strategies (this is with the exception of the Bank of China which already had branches in over 20 countries before 1950) (Young *et al.*, 1998). It was during this stage that the first batch of Chinese-owned MNCs emerged. The third stage started from the early 1990s during which both inward and outward FDI increased dramatically (see Table 9.1).

As we can see from Tables 9.1 and 9.2, China's outward FDI performance is completely over-shadowed by its profile as the world largest recipient country of FDI. Despite the fact that FDI outflows from mainland China extended to more than 160 countries or regions around the world by the end of 1998 (Li, 2000), China is still in its early stage of development as an international investor, making up only a very small proportion of the world's outward FDI. By 1998, trade-oriented investment accounted for 6.1 per cent, natural resource-oriented investment accounted for 19.4 per cent and manufacturing investment accounted for only 11.5 per cent. Over 90 per cent of the FDI projects were below US$1 million in scale, and the average investment in each project was US$1.12 million. In comparison, the FDI by developed countries average US$6 million per project and that by developing countries was above US$4.5 million per project. In addition, 58 per cent FDI outflows from mainland China went to Hong Kong and Macao, they were not FDI outflows in the real sense (Li, 2000). There was a preference for earlier Chinese FDI to form JVs in order to reduce investment risk, often relying heavily on ethnic and cultural links. 'These measures to reduce risk and psychic distance are an attempt to compensate for an unfamiliarity with local business conditions and a shortage of qualified staff who possess appropriate language skills and international business experience' (Child, 2001, p. 687). Nevertheless, China is emerging as one of the top FDI exporters among developing countries (*Asian Pacific Bulletins*, 2004).

By the early 2000s, the Chinese outward investment had spread across many sectors, with the greatest focus on ICT, computer service and software (33 per cent). The bulk of the remainder is in trading (20 per cent) and mining companies (18 per cent). Almost half of new investment in 2003 went into the mining sector, mainly in oil and gas exploration in order to meet the rising demand for energy resource in China (*Asian Pacific Bulletins*, 2004). According to Li (2000), China's FDI outflow investment shares two similar characteristics with that of Japan: a relatively large proportion oriented to natural resources and the dominance of trade-oriented investment over manufacturing-oriented investments. Not surprisingly, the large SOEs are the major players of outward FDI, holding 43 per cent of the total outward investment stock, followed by public corporation (33 per cent) and private companies (10 per cent) (*Asian Pacific Bulletins*, 2004). The majority of the overseas plants were established by large-scale enterprises in manufacturing, labour-intensive industries or companies with core technology making good quality products (*The Standard*, 2004).

From 2004 onwards, there has been a surge of interest in overseas acquisitions among Chinese enterprises. Among China's brand-name companies that have invested abroad successfully are the world's largest TV and DVD players manufacturer Shenzhen-listed TCL Corp, based in Huizhou; Shanghai-listed Haier, a major home appliance maker based in Qingdao, Shandong province; and Galanz, the world's largest microwave oven manufacturer based in Shunde, Guangdong. In particular, TCL has invested more than US$100 million in Vietnam, where annual production has reached about 500,000 TVs and 300,000 digital cameras. TCL also acquired the French-owned Thomson. Haier has set up at least 13 factories overseas as well as industrial parks in the United States and Pakistan.[1] Galanz has invested US$20 million in a R&D centre in Seattle (*The Standard*, 2004).

Some commentators believe that this is an important indication that Chinese entrepreneurs have now learned to understand the value chain in the global economy and that China now possesses sufficient resource power, manufacturing capacity and R&D capability to compete with its foreign competitors. Some Chinese enterprise leaders also feel that now is the opportunity for China to expand through cross-border acquisition. For example, the CEO of TCL reportedly said, 'Our objective is very clear. It is to complete our global business framework. If we move too slowly, the chance would be gone. However, we cannot rush, otherwise we may fall' (*China Business*, 7 March 2005).

Driving forces for Chinese outward investment

According to Dunning and Narula (2004), there are four major motives for FDI: marketing-seeking, resource-seeking, asset-seeking and efficiency-seeking. Exactly where firms can fulfil these motives are often location-specific. Recent studies (e.g. Dunning, 1995; Frost, 2001; Makino *et al.*, 2002) suggest that firms engage in FDI 'not only to transfer their resources to a host country' (asset exploitation), 'but also to learn, or gain access to, the necessary strategic assets available in the host country' (asset-seeking) (Makino *et al.*, 2002, p. 405). Strategic assets include, for example, technology, marketing and management expertise. Makino *et al.* (2002, p. 404) therefore argue that firms in newly industrialized economies engaged in FDI in developed countries not only to exploit their existing advantage but also to seek technology-based resources and skills 'that are superior or not available in their home countries in a particular product market domain'. Dunning (1993) also suggested that firms seek market expansion opportunities through FDI for various reasons, such as:

- to expand the existing domestic buyer–supplier relationships in host countries;
- to either pre-empt or to avoid being pre-empted by rival's entry into particular host country;
- to produce products close to local markets;
- to lower transportation costs; and
- to benefit from investment incentives (cited in Makino *et al.*, 2002, p. 411).

A number of factors are at play in pushing China's outward investment agenda, with the Chinese government playing a central role in it (see Table 9.3). Some of these motives correspond to those categorized by Dunning above.

Push strategy by the Chinese government China's outward investment is very much government-backed. As Cai (1999, p. 870) notes, 'in any analysis of Chinese outward FDI, it is important to point out that political considerations always play an important role'. The Chinese government began encouraging Chinese companies to invest overseas in 1999, initially as part of its strategy to deal with the extra competition to domestic industry which would follow its accession to the WTO. Since early 2000, the Chinese central government and regional governments have been actively encouraging Chinese enterprises to 'Go Global' under an increasingly broader set of strategic intents (see Chapter 3 and below). A number of incentives have been deployed, including tax incentives, subsidies, national bank loans with preferential terms and better access to the domestic market for goods produced by Chinese overseas affiliates (Child, 2001). In the government-sponsored 8th China International Fair for Investment and Trade (the sole national event focusing on FDI) in September 2004, equal emphasis was placed on attracting foreign FDI and encouraging Chinese outward FDI (*Asian Pacific Bulletins*, 2004). In particular, state-owned natural-resource companies are under orders from the central government to secure reserves abroad (e.g. oil, gas and mining activities in resource-rich countries) in order to meet the country's booming demand for fuel and other raw materials. In addition, Chinese firms are also encouraged to expand overseas to transfer matured technologies in which Chinese firms have a comparative advantage (e.g. electronics, textile and garment processing industries). Not only are large enterprises with relatively strong capacities urged to 'Go Global', but also SMEs are supported by the government to expand in international markets. The Chinese government's push strategy coincides with the pull strategy by foreign governments, many of which from developed countries, to attract Chinese investment.

Pull strategy by foreign governments In recent years, governments from developed countries (e.g. Britain, Canada, Demark, Germany and Japan) have been keen to attract Chinese investment to their countries to help, for example, revitalize their regional economy and rescue ailing plants. This is evidenced by favourable investment policies, government-led development agencies lobbying and delegate visits to China led by senior government ministers. For example, the First Minister Rhodri Morgan led a 20-strong team from Wales to China in September 2004 to help boost Welsh trade and investment with the Far East (*BBC News*, 11 August 2004). During German Chancellor Gerhard Schroeder's visit to Beijing in December 2004, his sixth trip to China since 1998, more than 38 German business leaders accompanied Schroeder on his trip, and 11 agreements on bilateral cooperation were signed (Zhou, 2005). Recognizing the role of China as an emerging home country of MNCs and the potential for further growth of China's outward FDI, many investment promotion agencies have set up offices in China to court Chinese firms that are potential outward investors (UNCTAD, 2003). The Japanese External Trade Organization (JETRO) is one of the key government agencies tasked to

Table 9.3 Reasons for and patterns of Chinese firms investing overseas

Process and outcome	Ownership	
	SOEs	Private firms
Strategic intent*	Monopoly (e.g. trading firms with import and export monopoly)	Long-term strategic objectives
	Relations with corresponding foreign firms (e.g. banks)	Ambition to be an international player
	Expansion	Expansion of production capacity
	Mission of internationalization, industrialization and diversification	Market penetration through access to distribution channels
	Promoting industry adjustment	Acquisition of technical know-how to raise technical competence
	Acquisition of technical know-how to raise technical competence	Access to management experience
	Access to management experience	Acquisition of brand names to enhance company profile to raise its competitive order
	Resource seeking (e.g. petroleum)	Making use of overseas funding
	Long-term strategic objectives	Generating foreign exchange
	Ambition to be an international player	Utilization of global trading centres
	Generating foreign exchange	Bypassing import tax tariff set by foreign countries (e.g. the United States)
	Utilization of global trading centres	
Patterns of internationalization	Branch office, acquisition, joint venture	Branch office, acquisition, joint venture, new factories
Types of countries and industries to invest in	Oil, gas, and mining industries in resource rich countries	Manufacturing plants and R&D centres in developed and developing countries
Demonstration effects	Internationalization experience of other countries and regions in Asia, particularly Japanese and Korean firms	

* The number of inter-related factors summarized in Table 9.3 are for illustrative purposes rather than an exhaustive summary.
Sources: adapted and expanded from (Young *et al.*, 1998); (UNCTAD, 2003); and (Wu and Chen, 2001).

attract and assist Chinese firms to invest in Japan to help its economy recovery. JETRO's efforts are part of a global five-year plan in which the Japanese government hopes to double FDI 2001 level, raising it to a target US$119.3 billion by 2006 (Curtin, 2004). The Chinese companies have responded positively to the incentives offered by foreign governments and other location-specific advantages. For example, a number of Chinese companies are reported to have chosen the United Kingdom to take advantage of investment grants (UNCTAD, 2003).

Financial factors There are a number of financial factors that motivate Chinese firms to invest overseas. One is that, with growing financial strength, Chinese companies have reportedly been lured into a buying spree abroad to acquire assets whose price may have been negatively affected by the current international economic downturn. For instance, TCL bought the bankrupt Schneider Electronics (Germany) in 2002 for US$8 million, and Huayi Group of Shanghai bought the bankrupt Moltech Power Systems (United States) for an estimated US$20 million (UNCTAD, 2003). Global expansion also enables Chinese firms to make use of overseas funding to finance the expansion on the one hand, and secure foreign exchange for China through profit-making on the other. It was estimated that one-third of China's overseas investment was in the form of cash investment, with only 10 per cent of this amount actually remitted out of China (Wu and Chen, 2001). It was also estimated that 55 per cent of China's overseas investment enterprises were making a profit, 17 per cent were making a loss, whilst the remaining 28 per cent were breaking even in the mid-1990s (Shi, 1998). Profit-making companies contribute to the inflow of foreign exchange. An additional financial reason for Chinese firms investing abroad is to avoid trade quotas for exports to developed countries. For example, some Chinese textile companies invested in Cambodia to take advantage of quota-free access for exporting to the United States and the European Union. Other Chinese textile companies have also invested in Africa to utilize advantages of host countries. Shanghai Huayuan Group Corporation's investment in Nigeria is a case in point (UNCTAD, 2003).

On a more veiled side, since equity markets remain relatively small in size, and are subject to discretionary administrative intervention in China, offshore investments can offer protection against domestic inflation and exchange rate depreciation. 'China's enterprises have the incentive to set up subsidiaries overseas to achieve a more balanced portfolio, and to evade foreign exchange and other restrictions with which they are saddled at home' (Wu and Chen, 2001, p. 1251). This is the phenomenon generally referred to as capital flight. It is believed that a relatively large amount of SOE assets have been lost as a result of capital flight in the name of overseas development, although the actual amount is unknown or cannot be precisely calculated.

Knowledge and know-how seeking It has been recognized that host country-specific knowledge is a driving force behind international expansion because such knowledge cannot be easily acquired (Inkpen and Beamish, 1997). This is undoubtedly the case for Chinese firms, which have demonstrated a growing appetite in acquiring technological and management expertise through international JVs and M&As. For example, in 2002, eight Chinese companies formed technological alliances with or acquired Danish firms, mostly for accessing technology (UNCTAD, 2003, also see Box 9.1).

BOX 9.1

International acquisition for technology know-how

Shenzhen-based China International Marine Container (CIMC) Group is the biggest manufacturer of marine container in the world. CIMC holds 40 per cent market share in the world market. It provides various marine containers to main logistic systems in North America, Europe and Asia. CIMC has recently acquired 60 per cent share of a Leamington Spa-based marine/folder container design company and its flat rack container patents – Clive-Smith Cowley Ltd. The total deal was worth US$700,000. The Vice President of CIMC believed that the acquisition was worthwhile because it helped CIMC to acquire DOMINO, a special technology for folder container design which is crucial for CIMC's product development.

Source: adapted from http://www.invest.uktradeinvest.gov.uk/asiapacific/site_chi, accessed on 14 April 2005.

Accessing foreign technology also takes the form of establishing R&D centres in developed or developing countries that have these competitive advantages such as India. For example, Huawei Technologies and ZTE Corporation have each established an R&D centre in Sweden; Guangdong Galanz Group Co an R&D centre in Seattle; Konka (an electronics company) an R&D facility in Silicon Valley; Haier an R&D centre in Germany and a design centre in Boston, United States; and Kelon a design centre in Japan (UNCTAD, 2003).

Brand-name product building and market access The need to develop brand-name products and access to markets to enhance their competitiveness are two related motives for Chinese firms to form strategic alliance with well-known Western firms, often through M&As. For instance, the merger of TCL's television and DVD operations with Thomson (France) has given the former the brand name of Thomson in Europe and RCA in the United States. Other examples include Lenovo with Microsoft, and Huawei Technologies' JV agreements with Siemens, NEC, Matshishita and Infineon. The resource and effort involved with brand-building and the stereotypical image of Chinese firms and products as being inferior in expertise and quality are important factors that encourage Chinese firms to opt for buying-in these intangible assets from reputable corporations (see Box 9.2 for example). Acquiring brands and selling branded products give Chinese manufacturers a greater control over their profit margin and raise their corporate profile. Partnership with reputable Western firms also provides access to mature distributors for each product, with developed marketing channels. These distributors are familiar with local marketing practices and environment, and face no language and cultural barriers. They also have the credibility and brand image among customers as reputable distributors.

BOX 9.2

Huawei builds its brand name overseas through joint ventures

Huawei has a branding problem in the enterprise networking market. When US and European companies buy switches, routers and phone systems that use voice over internet protocol (VoIP), Huawei is not the first name that comes to mind. In addition, Huawei has lacked the distribution connections to sell enterprise network equipment in the United States and Europe.

Huawei has tried to address these problems by working with 3Com, a US networking company that has been struggling since the Internet bubble burst. In November 2003, the two companies launched a JV to develop and market enterprise networking equipment. 3Com put up $160 million in cash and contributed intellectual property, its business operations in China and Japan and several dozen managers. Huawei threw in its enterprise networking business, plus the majority of the JV's 2000 employees. The JV's headquarters are in Hong Kong but it has new R&D and production facilities in Hangzhou, China. 3Com sells the Huawei–3Com products under its own brand throughout the world excepting China and Japan, where Huawei sells its own and 3Com's products.

Source: adapted from Normile (2005).

Aspiration to be international players The success of China in attracting FDI has provided Chinese firms with valuable exposure to international business. Inflow FDI has encouraged Chinese outward investment through demonstration and spill-over effects on domestic firms. As a result, some large Chinese firms have gained confidence and become ambitious to be key international players as part of their corporate strategy. For example, Shanghai-listed Shanghai Automotive Industry Corporation (SAIC) wants to become one of the top six global automaker by 2010. The aspiration of the CEO of Haier, Ruimin Zhang, to compete globally and become one of the Global 500 has played a fundamental role in Haier's active pursuit of internationalization. Zhang believed that Haier must go overseas and develop Haier's design, manufacturing and marketing networks internationally, particularly in the United States, to build up Haier's international brand reputation (Liu and Li, 2002).

Increased competition Since the late 1990s, sluggish domestic demand, intensifying competition from foreign firms in China, and excess industrial production capacity in certain industries, especially in machinery and electronic appliances, have encouraged Chinese firms to look for growth opportunities abroad. This is often achieved by acquiring a portfolio of locational assets and transferring matured industries to low-income developing countries, for example, bicycle production to Ghana and video players to Southeast Asia (UNCTAD, 2003).

Expansion and support of export While the majority of the earlier Chinese FDI was in the form of small overseas branch office set up by trading companies to support their export activities, this trend is continuing at an accelerated rate and on a wider scale. Chinese firms are increasingly investing abroad to support their exports, to service their markets or to expand their market presence (see Box 9.3). In markets with which China has considerable trade surplus (e.g. the United States), FDI subsidiaries provide an alternative vehicle to supply those markets. Establishing plants overseas also bypasses the technical and other non-tariff barriers imposed by developed countries to restrict imports from developing countries. As part of such a strategy, Chinese firms are also buying local distribution networks (UNCTAD, 2003).

BOX 9.3

International joint venture to get closer to the market

ZTE, China's largest listed telecommunications equipment manufacturer, is forming a JV with its British Partner, Redcomm, a North-East-based Chinese business development company. The JV, ZTE UK Ltd, will have 51 per cent owned by ZTE and 49 per cent by Redcomm and will commence a major marketing push for ZTE products in the United Kingdom. The new company will be based in Newcastle and initially employ 15 staff to provide customer and engineering support. According to the Chairman of ZTE Corporation, this move will help the company to focus on the European market, with the United Kingdom being the natural gateway.

Source: adapted from http://www.invest.uktradeinvest.gov.uk/asiapacific/site_chi, accessed on 14 April 2005.

The above interrelated driving forces that fuel Chinese investment overseas suggest that Chinese firms are becoming more sophisticated in their strategic intent to venturing abroad, being selective in locations and types of business and firms they invest in. In addition to investing in other developing countries where they have clear competitive advantages, as conventional wisdom on FDI from developing countries suggests, Chinese firms are also buying in competitive advantages of a higher order, for example, technological competence, brand name and recognized distribution channels, through strategic alliances with reputable firms in developed countries where these intangible assets are more likely to exist. The next section provides further analysis on Chinese MNCs' internationalization strategy, particularly in their choice of locations, as issues of why and where to invest have direct implications for HRM.

Internationalization strategy and choice of host countries

Somewhat similar to Dunning and Narula's (2004) four typologies of FDI motives as mentioned earlier, Bartlett and Ghoshal (2000) identify three different strategic objectives for multinational firms. The first objective is global efficiency to exploit national differences and economies of scale and scope. A second objective is multinational flexibility to manage the risks and to exploit the opportunities that arise from the diversity and volatility of the global environment. Sources of diversity and volatility include macro-economic factors, national government policies, responses of competitors in the host market and resources (e.g. natural, financial and human resources). A third strategic objective of MNCs is worldwide learning through the exposure to diverse national environments that create opportunities for resource and capacity development. This learning process will enhance MNCs' ability to innovate and exploit these innovations in different parts of the world. The Chinese MNCs' internationalization strategies seem to fall within all these three categories (see Table 9.4).

Broadly speaking, there are three main types of target countries for Chinese FDI: countries with abundant natural resource endowments; countries with technological leadership; and countries with potential markets. More specifically, Chinese firms seem to have a preference to Germany and Japan for their infrastructure, good engineering base and skilled workforce. By contrast, America attracts Chinese MNCs for its markets and brand name – a high-profile example of this is the white good manufacturer Haier – whereas Britain has more appeal for its tax relief, and other developing countries for cheap production cost and untapped market. As a result, Chinese FDI in developed countries is rising, occasionally charted by high-profile deals that take the world by surprise. Ernst & Young European Investment Monitor (EYEIM) recorded 70 FDI projects into Europe from mainland China between 1997 and 2004, generating estimated employment for 4800 people. Among these projects, manufacturing took the main share by Chinese manufacturers who are seeking access to the European market, followed by sales and marketing (Greater London Authority, 2004).

The preference of Chinese firms for German and Japanese firms is particularly interesting and deserves further discussion here.

The case of Chinese FDI in Germany

In spite of the fact that Germany has an unemployment figure of over 5 million, a costly social welfare system and some powerful trade unions which Chinese managers are not familiar in dealing with (see further discussion later),

Table 9.4   Investment strategy of Chinese MNCs and choice of host countries

Investment strategic objectives		Examples of choice of host countries	State of economic development of host countries
Asset-seeking oriented	Natural resource seeking	Canada, Russia, Iran and Sudan	Developed and developing countries
	Technological leadership, skill base and management competence, brand image/reputation and distribution channel (also in line with Bartlett and Ghoshal's worldwide learning strategic objective)	United States, Germany, Japan, United Kingdom, France, Sweden and India (for R&D)	Developed and developing countries
Asset exploitation oriented	Market exploitation (also in line with Bartlett and Ghoshal's global efficiency and multinational flexibility strategic objectives)	United States, Germany, Sweden, Thailand, Indonesia and Pakistan	Developed and developing countries
	Low cost labour, tax tariff exemption (also in line with Bartlett and Ghoshal's global efficiency strategic objective)	Cambodia, Thailand, Ghana, Pakistan and Vietnam	Developing countries

some Chinese manufacturers see benefits in being situated within the European market and closer to customers that increasingly demand quick service (Fletcher, 2005). This is in addition to the engineering and skill base offered by German firms. In just two years, China has overtaken France, Britain, and Italy to become the second-largest buyer of German machinery, after the United States. Chinese companies are interested in acquiring German patents and engineering expertise. China's Shengyang Machine Tool Group is a case in point. It recently bought Schiess, a 140-year-old maker of heavy-duty lathes and boring machines based on the East German town of Aschersleben. With

120 employees, Schiess typifies the Mittelstand machine-tool makers that are the backbone of the German economy. However, the wage cost in Germany is far higher than that in China. Schiess has therefore transferred the production of smaller machinery, Shengyang's specialty, to China, while retaining Schiess' core business in heavy-duty machines, where transport costs are a major factor. Schiess will market Shenyang's smaller machines to Europe, and Shenyang will be able to draw on Schiess' expertise to produce large equipment for the Asia market (Fletcher, 2005). In other words, Germany, a technological power-house, and China, the largest emerging Asian market, are benefiting from their pragmatic cooperation (Zhou, 2005). This suggests that the commonly held perception of a low-cost, low-regulated Chinese manufacturing sector ripe for foreign investment and an expensive and inefficient German sector may need to be revised (Fletcher, 2005).

In fact, Germany and China have enjoyed a sound business relationship for over two decades. Germany has been one of the largest investor countries in China and tops all European countries in technology transfer to China. As of July 2003, China has signed 6768 technology transfer contracts with Germany, with a total worth of US$26.14 billion (Zhou, 2005). China's investment in Germany has also increased in recent years. As of June 2003, China had established 159 non-financial business organizations in Germany, with investment totalling US$74.77 million (Zhou, 2005). A new study by the management consultancy Bain & Company predicts that between 2004 and 2015, Chinese firms will invest some 2 billion annually in Germany (cited in *Invest in Germany: Newsletter*, 2004). Based on surveys of 50 Chinese companies that have already invested in Europe or are planning to do so, the Bain report identifies two key features that make Germany eminently attractive: market access and skilled management. No other EU country offers a bigger market (82 million consumers) or a better strategic location for tapping other European markets. Indeed, the Bain study – China Goes West – describes customer proximity and market size as Germany's trump cards within Europe. While Germany's market characteristics attract investors from all over the world, its management acumen is particularly appealing to developing countries. Growing companies in China know that if they buy into a German firm they reap the benefits of first-rate managerial expertise. German managers also tend to be multilingual, making it that much easier to pursue a global strategy (*Invest in Germany: Newsletter*, 2004).

The case of Chinese FDI in Japan

Similarly, since the beginning of the twenty-first century, Chinese enterprises have been acquiring a wide variety of Japanese companies, not least those in financial trouble. Many of them were brand-name firms. For example, in October 2001, low profitability forced Sanyo Electric Co, a major Osaka-based home appliance maker, to sell its entire microwave-oven division to China's Guangdong Midea-Holding Co, the second-largest household electrical appliance maker in China. In most acquisition cases, the Chinese acquirer was able to turn around an ailing Japanese business by restructuring the business and relocating some production to China, where labour costs are cheaper (Curtin, 2004, see Box 9.4 for example).

BOX 9.4

Chinese SEC acquires brand name Japanese manufacturer

In 2002, the Shanghai Electric Group Corp (SEC), a heavy electronics and industrial equipment manufacturer purchased the troubled Akiyama Printing Machinery Manufacturing Corp, a globally renowned manufacturer of high-tech printers. The new Chinese-owned entity was renamed Akiyama International Co Ltd (AIC). It immediately hired back many of the Japanese company's former employees. SEC decided to keep its factories in Japan as it was able to trim production costs through renegotiating contracts with suppliers. This rapidly made the new venture profitable. SEC then overhauled the entire management system, cutting benefits for senior staff, instituting a merit-based pay system and encouraging all employees to take initiative. The Japanese staff adjusted relatively well to the changes, although many found it difficult to come to terms with being taken over by a Chinese company.

Source: adapted from Curtin (2004).

Geographic and cultural proximity is an additional factor that encourages Chinese firms to acquire Japanese firms. After more than 25 years of imports of Japanese products, especially in household electrical appliances, automobile and commercial goods, the Chinese consumers are familiar with and prefer Japanese products for their quality and agile design. With a relatively large number of Japanese firms operating in China, often in the form of JVs with Chinese firms, Chinese managers are also relatively familiar with the Japanese management style and business culture.

More broadly, geographic closeness and cultural similarity has been a key factor for Chinese FDI in Southeast Asian countries. China's direct investment in this region can enjoy convenient communications and transportation with them. The relative similarity in economic development level between China and these countries to some extent restrains the negative effect of international transaction efficiency for goods on the expansion of FDI. In addition, this region has over 21 million overseas Chinese, the largest concentration of overseas Chinese in the world, which enjoys considerable economic power and business networks (Yang, 2003). The common cultural and linguistic roots shared by mainland Chinese and overseas Chinese further reduce barriers often experienced by FDI in a foreign environment. All these factors have been influential in the growth of China's outward FDI in these countries.

As cross-border acquisition experience grows, Chinese multinationals are becoming increasingly confident and strategic in deploying acquisition as a vehicle to fulfil their international business plan that goes well beyond Asia. For example, TCL's business strategy is to focus on their core competence – production of TV and DVD players and establish a global network to facilitate its production and sales. With this strategic plan in mind, TCL goes for the same type of manufacturers – TV and DVD players in different countries, developing markets in the developing countries (e.g. Vietnam) while acquiring brand names, market, technical know-how and skilled workforce from developed countries (e.g. Germany and France) to create a truly international corporation. As a result, TCL's deal with Thomson (France) to produce TVs and DVD players would create the world's top television-set maker with expected annual revenues of more than US$3.78 billion. The new firm brought together TCL's factories in China, Vietnam and Germany and Thomson's factories in Thailand (Vatikiotis, 2004).

Chinese MNCs differ in their strategic choice of how and where they develop their global presence. For example, the strategic intent of the Haier Group, a key player in the Chinese drive for globalization and diversification, is to build a brand reputation of its own overseas. Long dominant in China as one of the top five makers of white goods and one of the first truly national brands, Haier aggressively pursues a globalization strategy on several international fronts, now selling its products in 160 countries and owning 13 factories outside China. It chose to enter the United States while seemingly it had neither techno-logical nor cost advantage and was further disadvantaged by having no brand reputation in the market. Its strategic intent was to gain locational advantage by setting up plants overseas to avoid tariffs and reduce transportation cost. Internationalization advantage has been attained through controlling services and marketing/distribution, and ownership advantage has been achieved by developing design and R&D capabilities through utilizing high-quality local human resources (Liu and Li, 2002). Haier's strategy also differs in its pref-erence to be successful in big and developed markets, such as the United States and Europe, before tackling what are considered the easier-to-penetrate developing markets such as Southeast Asia. Haier's success in the US market supports its investment and operations in other countries through the spin-off of technology and reputation/image (Liu and Li, 2002).

By contrast, a different, and perhaps more cautious, strategy is taken by the leading Chinese PC maker, Legend Group Ltd (now Lenovo), which also decided on a future based on new products and conquering overseas markets. Legend decided to target the Asian markets first before the US and European markets were targeted. Unlike Haier (which had made inroad into brand recognition abroad), it accepted that it had a dominant home brand which no one overseas had heard of. Re-branding – such as the 'Lenovo' English brand – would play a part in the strategy (*Strategic Direction*, 2005).

Chinese companies are also developing R&D centres in various strategic locations abroad as part of their global corporate network and help them upgrade their technical competence by tapping into locational advantages (see Box 9.5).

BOX 9.5

Examples of Chinese R&D centres abroad

Huawei Technologies set up its Indian R&D centre in Bangalore in February 2001. This centre is the company's largest software development centre outside China. It is engaged in research in telecommunications and networking solutions, especially 3G systems. It has invested over US$8 million in the centre so far and employs over 250 software engineers. Huawei Technologies' customers include China Telecom, China Mobile, China Unicom, China Netcom as well as Thai AIS, South Korea Telecom, Sing Tel, Hutchison Global Crossing, PCCW and Telemar (Brazil). In addition to its India R&D centre, Huawei Technologies has research institutes in Dallas (USA), Stockholm (Sweden), Moscow (Russia), Beijing and Shanghai (adapted from Lyengar, 2003).

Guangdong Midea Group, the second-largest household electrical appliances manufacturer after Haier in China that has business in industrial design, logistics, IT and real estate, has established seven overseas offices in Germany, the United States, Japan and so on. Its UK office, set up in November 2003, serves as the company's first overseas product design centre and will also become its European HQ for small home appliance products. One of Midea's major achievements in the United Kingdom has been the signing of the 'Strategic Purchase Frame Agreement' worth US$75 million between Midea and Kingfisher Group/BP (source: adapted from http://www.invest.uktradeinvest.gov.uk/asiapacific/site_chi, accessed on 14 April 2005).

The first China-UK Innovation Park was opened in Cambridge in September 2003. The Innovation Park will act as a base for Chinese S&T companies looking to set up their business in the United Kingdom and/or Europe. It could also potentially serve the existing Chinese student base in the United Kingdom who might wish to set up enterprises in the United Kingdom post graduation (source: adapted from http://www.invest.uktradeinvest.gov.uk/asiapacific/site_chi, accessed on 14 April 2005).

The bourgeoning outward investment activities of Chinese firms since the twenty-first century are achieved within a number of institutional and organizational constraints, although paradoxically some of these constraints are also the very reasons for Chinese firms to seek alliances abroad. These are discussed in the next section.

Challenges to Chinese outflow investment

There are several major challenges that affect Chinese firms' ability to implement their FDI strategy successfully.

System inefficiency As Chinese outward FDI only began to take off in earnest in the twenty-first century, the development of a legal framework and administrative policies are lagging behind. Bureaucracy, government intervention and management behaviour, a remnant of the state planned economy, is still playing a part in the process in ways similar to that in the inflow FDI (see Chapter 8). This is particularly the case when SOEs play a major role in the development of Chinese outward FDI (Li, 2000). Successful implementation of China's FDI strategy, therefore, depends on systematic cost-benefit analysis of SOE FDI proposals and on the sound development of outward FDI from the private sector.

Technical challenges Insufficient technical advantage is perhaps the biggest challenge facing Chinese firms generally in their outward investment move. While China is making a serious effort in catching-up with technological development, more can be done, especially for SOEs, in absorbing, improvizing and localizing imported technologies to turn them into their competitive advantages. As the development of technical competence takes time, lack of technical advantages is likely to remain a long-term factor restricting China's development of MNCs (Li, 2000).

Capital constraints Most Chinese FDI tends to come from large and state-owned enterprises which have the advantage of state support in financing their FDI. Smaller private enterprises, however, are less likely to benefit from the financial support in China's underdeveloped capital markets. China's banks were once dominated by state-owned banks and have suffered from high levels of bad debts incurred from years of loans given to poorly run SOEs that were often made on non-commercial grounds. For this reason, China's financial system is unable to play an active role in developing China's FDI (Li, 2000).

Image problems (both technical and social) In spite of an increasing level of recognition from the West of the growing competitiveness of Chinese firms, they generally suffer image problems in the Western world as being low-cost and low-quality producers. While some firms choose to invest heavily in building their own brands overseas (e.g. Haier), others choose to buy in established foreign brands. For example, D'Long Strategic Investments concentrates on buying well-known but ailing foreign brands. It retains their marketing, distribution and R&D operations, but transfers the bulk of the manufacturing to China to cut costs (*The Economist*, 2003). Box 9.1 is another example of how Huawei, one of China's best performers and FDI pioneers, tried to overcome its branding and distribution network problems overseas. How Chinese firms transform their image to be high-quality and value-added manufacturers producing products with the latest in-built technology remains a serious and expensive challenge to many of them.

Chinese firms also tend to suffer a social image problem in the Western world in their perceived undesirable attitude towards business ethics and social responsibility, most notably in their approaches to IPR (see Chapters 2 and 3) and labour standards. Chinese product pirates are often the main offenders of copying new products and technologies invented by foreign firms. Hill & Knowlton's Annual Survey of Senior Executive Opinions on Corporate Reputation Management (2004) reveals that Western CEOs' views demonstrate a much broader and more complex approach to managing corporate reputation than the Chinese CEOs (see Chapter 3). A wider view of stakeholders, a more sensitive awareness of the need for risk management and an appreciation of the business and institutional environment of the host countries are needed from the Chinese CEOs if their firms were to expand globally with some success.

Management autonomy and competence in strategic decisions Management autonomy and management competence are two related dimensions that are often notably absent in Chinese SOEs. Since SOEs make up a large proportion of the Chinese FDI, these deficiencies may have serious implications for the performance of Chinese FDI. It is reported that Chinese managers have no obvious expertise to help them make sensible investment decisions abroad (*The Economist*, 2003). Many Chinese companies reach their decisions on overseas investment without a clear idea about why they are investing overseas, where they should locate their subsidiaries, and how they can develop overseas markets. In particular, the government's policy of developing various medium-size and large SOEs into business groups and its insistence that the groups should establish themselves to be amongst the world's largest enterprises within a specified period of time has led some companies to rush into overseas investment (Li and Li, 2000).

While government pressure has a coercive isomorphic effect in forcing Chinese firms venturing abroad, cash-rich Chinese senior executives may go on a buying spree that is fanned by national pride and personal ambition and get burnt by the high prices of declining Western brand-name firms. The often defective corporate governance function of Chinese enterprises does not help rectify any likely distortions of management objectives. Either way, any overseas investment decision that is devoid of strategic management foresight may be a costly exercise for the firm in the long term. As Zhang *et al.* (2006, p. 142) observed, 'the huge differences between national business systems and international development stages constrain the competencies of many Chinese MNCs'.

The shortage of skills among the Chinese management in handling M&A negotiation and post-M&A integration in China has been noted in Chapter 8. Embarking on overseas acquisition, post-acquisition integration and managing overseas subsidiaries present greater difficulties for Chinese managers because of their lack of knowledge of the business environment of the host countries and international standards. While external consultants may be able to provide advice on certain specific issues, they are unlikely to be able to contemplate the overall strategic plan for the company.

Many Chinese firms investing abroad lack a sound understanding of host country environments or knowledge of how to assess the credibility of local partners (Child, 2001; Li, 2000). While Chinese firms have the clear advantage of low-cost and some large enterprises have sufficient financial resource to carry out acquisition, these two conditions are not sufficient to ensure a successful acquisition process. There are considerable differences between China and the host country in terms of business regulation, labour law and organizational culture. These are important factors that may influence the success or otherwise of the acquisition. However, some Chinese companies only focused on price alone and neglected other important factors. Others lack negotiation skills in the international business arena. Despite some big moves of overseas acquisitions by large Chinese SOEs in recent years, the acquisition process has not on the whole been very smooth, with some negotiations ending in failure and others entangled in a negotiation marathon (*China Business*, 7 March 2005).

How to select the new CEO after the M&A process is another issue of concern. On the one hand, Chinese managers lack exposure and experience of international operation and are not the ideal candidates to take over the senior posts of the newly acquired firms. On the other hand, the Chinese side may not be keen to deploy senior managers from the foreign-acquired firm due to concerns of trust and loyalty. Even when the original senior executives were appointed to lead the new firm, they may not wish to stay. TCL's Thomson deal is an example. Thomson had agreed that the new CEO of the new JV would be the original CEO of Thomson. His resignation on the first day of the founding of the new firm took the Chinese side by surprise. TCL's senior management admitted that they had been going forward too quickly, had been too optimistic about the post-acquisition integration and had learned a painful lesson from the acquisition (*China Business*, 24 October 2005). Moreover, Liu and Li's (2002) Haier study revealed that managers from the Chinese and American sides in Haier's US plant both reported difficulties in communications, in part due to language barriers. In particular, it is difficult to carry out 'brain storming' exercise in which innovative ideas can be generated and good practices shared. Yet to date, 'language and culture is deemed to be the least important factor when Chinese leading companies are considering where to expand' (Roland Berger Strategy Consultants, 2003, p. 1). Earlier studies on Chinese overseas enterprises employing mainly Chinese staff (e.g. Cai, 1999; Child, 2001; Li, 2000; Young *et al.*, 1998) also revealed that they have a relatively low level of managerial competence.

Stock market confidence Even when investment decision is based on management foresight, share holders may not always respond to major business decisions positively. This is especially the case in China's volatile stock market that is still in its infancy. The Lenovo and IBM deal is a case in point. To keep growing, Lenovo needed to reach markets beyond the highly competitive domestic electronics sector, and buying IBM's PC unit gives the company control of one of America's most respected brands. But Lenovo's share price in Hong Kong has fallen 21 per cent since the deal was announced in December 2004. Investors are questioning the prudence of acquiring a unit that has lost nearly US$1billion in the three-and-a-half years prior to 30 June 2004 (Forney, 2005). Similarly, when TCL bought the French company Thomson's television operations in 2004, TCL's profits later dropped 69 per cent in the third quarter (Forney, 2005). It is worth noting that in spite of the significant negative impact on the company's stock market performance following high-profile deals such as Lenovo and TCL, the Chinese government continues to encourage more companies to invest abroad to make China a stronger country.

In some sense, having a lower-than-anticipated profit return from FDI and upsetting stock market confidence with M&A moves are not necessarily problems specifically associated with management [in]competence or with Chinese firms alone. Rather, they are generic risks that many well-established foreign MNC giants have encountered. As was noted by Meschi and Hubler

(2003), empirical studies that focus on analysing the stock market impact of JV announcements have obtained inconclusive results. While some studies identify a positive effect of JV announcements, others reveal either a non-positive or a significant negative valuation effect. Numerous studies also point to the difficulties experienced by JVs in their medium and long-term value creation process, with some previously prosperous JVs achieving only modest profits (Meschi and Hubler, 2003). While a significant proportion of foreign-funded MNCs have been reporting a low profit return in China and are rolling back their scale of the operation, Chinese MNCs abroad will experience a much deeper learning process than their Western counterparts coming to China, especially in terms of management know-how and organizational image.

More importantly, managing the internationalization process presents significant challenges to Chinese MNCs' HRM. The next section discusses these issues by comparing and contrasting the institutional and socio-cultural environments for HRM in developed and developing countries.

Implications of HRM for Chinese MNCs in host countries

Harzing (2004, p. 59) noted, 'One of the central questions in MNC literature is the extent to which subsidiaries adapt their practices to local circumstances and behave as local firms (local isomorphism) versus the extent to which their practices resemble those of their parent company (internal consistency)'. More specifically, the extent of transfer is contingent to 'the restrictiveness of employment regulations in the host environment, the level of cultural and institutional differences between home and host country and the role and function of individual subsidiaries' (Harzing, 2004, p. 61).

Other authors (e.g. Budhwar and Debrah, 2001; Clark and Mallory, 1996) on international HRM have highlighted a number of institutional, cultural and industrial/sectoral factors that may influence the configuration of HR practices (also see Figure 1.1). It has been argued (e.g. Acuff, 1984, cited in Paauwe and Dewe, 1995) that HRM of MNCs is exposed to a higher level of external influences, particularly the type of government and the state of the economy, the role of unions, consumer organizations and other interest groups. While these external groups also exist in the home country, MNCs may be less familiar with the influence of these bodies in the host country. These bodies may also exert more pressure on foreign firms than they do on local firms (Paauwe and Dewe, 1995) to conform to the host country's norm.

This section explores opportunities and challenges that Chinese MNCs may experience in HRM in their subsidiaries in developed and developing countries, using Figure 1.1 as a framework to guide the discussion. It needs to be pointed out here that the discussion below targets primarily at the 'true' MNC subsidiaries, that is, larger Chinese MNC subsidiaries that employ mainly local workforce. Small overseas branch offices of trading businesses that employ primarily Chinese expatriates or overseas Chinese are not the main concern here.

HRM of Chinese MNC subsidiaries in developed countries – challenges due to institutional and cultural differences

It has been noted (e.g. Budhwar, 2004; Budhwar and Debrah, 2001; Elvira and Davila, 2005) that approaches to HRM in developing countries are less sophisticated compared with that in developed countries and are still largely in the mode of traditional personnel management. For example, Zhu and Warner (2004) found that whilst the term HRM is more readily used in the more prominent Sino-foreign JVs, managers in these firms still seem to be more inward-looking, focusing on operational rather than strategic issues. Zhu's study (2002) of Vietnamese enterprises reveals similar role of the HR function.

Table 9.5 summarizes some major differences in the key HR aspects between developed and developing countries in which Chinese MNCs may have operations. This summary is based on findings of existing literature and my research experience. It must be noted that these differences are in relative terms and exhibited at a national level as a broad picture.

The implications of these differences may be more prominent when Chinese MNCs invest in developed countries for asset-seeking (learning) purposes and developing countries for asset-exploiting (efficiency) purposes. These differences are elaborated in the text that follows.

Labour/employment law A major difference between the HRM environment of developed and developing countries is the provision of employment legislation and its enforcement. It is likely that employment legislation of the former is more comprehensive (e.g. working time directives, minimum wage regulations and equal opportunities acts) and more actively monitored. By contrast, labour rights are less comprehensively legislated and even less effectively enforced in developing countries. Relatively low labour cost associated with poor labour standard is commonly the main competitive advantage of developing countries. Issues related to employment rights and labour standards in developing countries are often the focus of criticism by media and NGOs.

For Chinese MNCs, one of the most difficult aspects of HRM in an international context is the necessity to manage a diverse workforce, at least as a legal obligation, if not as an effective HRM approach to enhance organizational performance. The majority of domestic Chinese organizations have a relatively homogenous workforce in terms of ethnic origin. Despite the fact that there is a relatively comprehensive set of legislation and administrative policy on gender equality to protect women's employment interests, gender discrimination is a common practice in China in both state-owned and private firms (Cooke, 2005a). Chinese managers tend to have a weak level of awareness of and a lax approach to labour standards, and the enforcement of employment regulations in China is far from being stringent. A workplace-related disability act has yet to be fully developed in China, as are other employment-related acts. Ageism is widely practiced in China where most women above 40 years of age and men above 50 may be forced to take early retirement or made redundant as part of a downsizing movement in state-owned and collectively owned firms. These HR practices specific to the Chinese institutional context are clearly not appropriate in the Western context where the need for cultural diversity is growing and

Table 9.5 A comparison of the key characteristics of the HRM environment encountered by Chinese MNCs in developed and developing countries

Aspects of HRM	Characteristics in developed countries	Characteristics in developing countries
Labour/employment law	More comprehensive and closely monitored (e.g. working time directives, minimum wage regulations, equal opportunity legislation)	Less comprehensively legislated and less effective enforcement
Recruitment	More sophisticated selection techniques	Traditional and basic recruitment methods, nepotism, local government intervention
Performance management and reward system	Collective bargaining, greater variety in pay schemes, individual performance-related incentives, above market rate to attract and retain talent Financial reward as well as intrinsic reward (e.g. career development and progression opportunities)	Pay level primarily determined by the state and employer, market rate, egalitarian approach to wage and bonus distribution to maintain social harmony More focus on monetary rewards
Training and development	Relatively high level of training and development investment and provision, more variety of delivery mechanisms	Relatively low level of investment, training focusing on immediate needs, less focus on career development and HR planning
Employee participation and involvement, knowledge management	More familiar concepts to management and workforce, relatively higher level of activities	Less familiar concepts to management and workforce, relatively low level of interest and participation, may be more confined to elite employee groups
Employee welfare/well-being schemes	Well-being focused, psychological	Welfare focused, material and physical
Relationship with trade unions	Partnership approach, cannot afford to be seen as uncooperative	Management prerogative due to unemployment pressure and weak trade union influence
Corporate social responsibility (CSR)	Broader notion of CSR, for example, environmental issues, employer branding, identification of national and local culture, community projects	Narrower notion of CSR, donation and charity as the main CSR activities, emphasis on the influence in local community

the employment legislation framework is far more comprehensive and effective compared with that of China.

Recruitment Firms in Western developed countries may deploy more sophisticated selection methods for recruitment as a result of the development of advanced HR techniques and tools. There may be a much higher level of transparency in the recruitment process and greater fairness in the outcome due to the relatively more democratic atmosphere in Western societies supported by more stringent regulatory procedures and monitoring processes. Moreover, since Chinese MNC subsidiaries in Western developed countries are more likely to be engaged in knowledge-intensive businesses as a result of the asset-seeking strategy of investment, Chinese MNCs may need to adopt a more sophisticated recruitment selection approach to recruit knowledge workers with specialist skills. While some firms in China are beginning to adopt Western methods of recruitment, the majority of Chinese firms are still using traditional and basic recruitment methods with traces of nepotism. In addition, local government intervention may be more common, especially in the staffing issue of foreign-invested firms, in order to reduce unemployment pressure (Ahlstrom *et al.*, 2005). Since a major motive of Chinese MNCs investing in other developing countries is to exploit the host country's cheaper labour cost and market, mass production by employing relatively low-skilled and lowly paid workers are likely to be the dominant production mode, hence less sophisticated recruitment methods are required, especially where there is a large pool of labour supply in the market.

Performance management and reward system Performance management is another aspect of HRM where considerable differences may exist between the Chinese approach and that practiced in Western countries. Performance appraisal criteria in China typically focus on one's morality, political attitudes, seniority and the maintenance of harmonious relations with colleagues as much as, if not more than, one's productivity-related performance. By contrast, the performance management system for knowledge workers adopted in Western countries may be relatively more 'objective' and measurable. Performance appraisal is used not just for financial reward but also for intrinsic reward purposes, such as career development and progression opportunities. Shen's (2005) study of Chinese subsidiaries in the United Kingdom reveals that performance appraisals on the Chinese expatriates were more straightforward in these subsidiaries with little emphasis on morality and seniority, but the main purpose of appraisal was on remuneration rather than for personal or organizational development. Such a narrow approach to performance management is unlikely to be effective to attract, retain and motivate a Western skilled workforce.

Similarly, pay systems for knowledge workers in Western countries may demonstrate a greater level of complexity, involving collective bargaining, variable pay schemes, individual performance-related incentives and the need to pay above the market rate to attract and retain talent. By contrast, pay level may be determined primarily by the state and employers in some sectors in China. Market rate may be the norm for a pool of undifferentiated and less-skilled workers. This is especially the case when social welfare provision is limited, thus forcing people to remain employed and accept low wages. An egalitarian approach to wage and bonus distributions may also prevail in order to maintain social harmony (Cooke, 2005a). Where unemployment and inflation rates are relatively high, job security and immediate financial reward may be the main concern of workers instead of longer-term career development as potential reward.

Training and development In general, firms in developed countries invest more in training their workforce than developing countries, and the Western workforce is generally more highly skilled and engaged in more knowledge-intensive production activities than their counterparts in developing countries. It can therefore be argued that Chinese MNCs in developed countries may need a relatively high level of training and development investment and provision, with more varieties of delivery mechanisms. By contrast, the level of training investment in developing countries tends to be relatively low. Training provision often focuses on immediate skill needs rather than on individual career development and HR planning.

Employee participation and involvement, knowledge management Employee participation and involvement and knowledge management may be HR concepts more familiar to both management and workforce in developed countries. These initiatives are also more widely adopted in the workplaces in developed countries, although the motive for and the effectiveness of implementing these schemes have been widely debated elsewhere (Marchington and Wilkinson, 2005). As the majority of Chinese MNC subsidiaries in developed countries are likely to be engaged in knowledge-intensive businesses, the adoption of these schemes may be more common and necessary to elicit employees' commitment and harness their innovativeness. Even though there are manufacturing subsidiaries that are engaged in mass production in developed countries, workers in these plants may be more receptive to the Western notions of HRM than their counterparts in developing countries.

By contrast, management and workforce in developing countries are less familiar with the concepts of employee participation and involvement and knowledge management. Even when they have been familiarized with the concepts, enthusiasm in participating in these schemes may be more confined to the elite employee group. For example, Cooke's (2004) study of a foreign-owned toy manufacturing plant in China reveals that shopfloor employees showed little interest in the employee involvement schemes as they saw little benefit for themselves. Similarly, Hermawan's (2005) empirical study of manufacturing plants (including Japanese-owned and Chinese-owned) in Indonesia shows that shopfloor workers were not familiar with the concepts of employee involvement and empowerment. Nor were they interested in participating in the schemes, believing that these were managerial responsibilities and not theirs. Likewise, supervisory employees saw these 'Western' HR techniques irrelevant to their work environment and were not keen to implement the schemes in part to avoid doing more work. More broadly, employees in manufacturing plants in developing countries are reported (e.g. Ahlstrom *et al.*, 2005; Budhwar and Debrah, 2001; Elvira and Davila, 2005) to be more used to having specific task instructions, less keen to take their own initiatives in order to avoid risks and maintain a high social distance between themselves and their firm/manager.

Employee welfare/well-being schemes In Western developed countries, attention is increasingly paid to employees' psychological well-being, at least in principle. For example, more and more firms have adopted some form of employee counselling and stress management schemes. Issues related to work–life balance are becoming prominent, often driven by European Union directives and national government responses (Bamber *et al.*, 2004). By contrast, the HR function of local firms in developing countries may still focus on the material and physical well-being of employees. For example, a major function of the Chinese trade union at workplace level is to carry out the welfare role, including organizing social and sports events, organizing tourist trips and visiting employees on sick leave. In developing countries where unemployment rate is high and decent jobs are scarce, workers are considered to be lucky to have a job, leaving their work-related psychological well-being far less attended to.

Relationship with trade unions In developing countries where job opportunities are scarce and social welfare provision is limited, labour–management relationship may be characterized by management prerogative with weak, if any, trade union influence, particularly in the private sector. It has been widely noted (e.g. Chan, 2000; Ding *et al.*, 2002; Howell, 1998; Levine, 1997; Ng and Warner, 1998; Sheehan, 1999) that the trade union in China[2] lacks independence and power, plays primarily a welfare role at workplaces and has proved highly ineffective in protecting labour interests in the emerging market economy of China. By comparison, trade union organizations in Western developed countries possess far more bargaining power and political networking skills. While trade unions' strengths and functions tend to differ across Western developed countries, such as Britain, Germany and the United States (Bamber *et al.*, 2004), they generally play a much more influential role than their Chinese counterpart in the labour–management relationships. In addition, their approaches to management–union negotiations may differ. For example, some trade unions may take on a more adversarial stance in certain industries and countries whereas others may be more supportive and take on a more genuine social partnership approach. This requires the Chinese MNCs to adopt a very different approach to managing their relationships with the trade unions in Western countries. The ability to understand trade union agreements and trade union-related laws and the ability to work with the trade unions effectively are skills that Chinese managers need to develop. Where trade unions are recognized at the workplace, a partnership approach may need to be adopted because Chinese MNCs cannot afford to be seen as uncooperative if they are to manage a skilled workforce effectively to win their trust and commitment, and more broadly, social acceptance (see below for further discussion).

The above analysis of differences in the employment environments and approaches to HRM between developed and developing countries suggests that there may be little opportunity for Chinese MNCs to transfer their home country HRM practices to their subsidiaries in developed countries due to the significant differences in institutional environments, national and organizational culture and level of sophistication of management techniques. It also suggests that, as cross-border acquisition has been a main mode of international expansion of Chinese MNCs in developed countries, Chinese MNCs are likely to encounter image problem among their newly acquired workforce as being a company from a less developed country. This problem may reduce the level of identification from these employees with their new employer.

Organizational image and identity To some extent, establishing employees' identification with the new employer/organization is a major but generic challenge in post-M&A integration due to cultural differences and incompatible corporate identities (Bartels *et al.*, 2006; Cartwright and Cooper, 1993). However, the severity of this problem could be exacerbated for Chinese MNCs in developed countries as employees may see it as a downward adjustment, given the relatively poor organizational image of Chinese firms and products in the West. Therefore, being sensitive to local cultures and employees' perspectives is particularly important for Chinese MNCs that are engaged in JVs and post-acquisition integration in developed countries.

There have been plenty of studies on how HR practices introduced by foreign managers of MNCs in China have encountered resistance from the Chinese workforce in part due to the cultural differences (e.g. Cooke, 2002; Legewie, 2002). The same issues are likely to occur to Chinese managers abroad. Shanghai Electric Group Corp (SEC)'s acquisition of the financially troubled Akiyama Printing Machinery Manufacturing Corp in 2002 is a case in point (Curtin, 2004). What SEC did to revitalize the Japanese operation was in many ways similar to what the Japanese and Western MNCs have adopted in enhancing the performance of the Chinese subsidiaries. That is, trimming production costs through renegotiating contracts with suppliers, overhauling the entire management system, cutting benefits for senior staff, instituting a merit-based pay system and encouraging all employees to take initiatives. The Japanese staff adjusted relatively well to the changes, although many found it difficult to come to terms with being taken over by a Chinese company (Curtin, 2004). Indeed, how to make employees from a developed country feel proud of working for a Chinese firm is a sensitive and challenging issue for Chinese managers. While most individuals in China see it as a privilege to work for prestigious foreign MNCs, Chinese MNCs abroad may not be in this league yet. This may lead to recruitment and retention problems as well as other HR problems. One possible solution is to employ local managers, adopt local HR practices, maximize employment security and carry out a thorough review before radical changes are made. This will help to gain social recognition in the host countries.

Existing studies of HR practices of Chinese MNCs in Western countries show that local practices tend to be adopted by Chinese subsidiaries. For example, Zhang's (2003) study found that Chinese managers in their UK subsidiaries adopt British HR practices for various reasons. Some adopted the British practices in order to comply with the British labour regulations while others did so in order to compete for talent. Only a small minority of managers saw learning modern techniques from the host country on how to manage people as integral to the success of their overseas branches. Nevertheless, there are notable exceptions where Chinese MNCs have made a conscientious effort to align their corporate culture with local practices to develop a corporate culture and identity that is acceptable to local employees and customers. Haier US is an example (Liu and Li, 2002).

HRM of Chinese MNC subsidiaries in developing countries – greater opportunities for transfer

By contrast, Chinese MNCs in other developing countries are more likely to adopt HRM practices that are similar to that in China due to their similar level of economic development and institutional, geographical and cultural proximity. For instance, manufacturing industry, often in mass production mode providing low-pay and low-skill jobs, plays a major role in the economic growth of developing countries. The workforce tend to be relatively young, but with relatively low levels of education and job skills and limited awareness of labour rights and health and safety issues. As noted earlier, employment legislation is less comprehensive and loosely enforced. The level of administrative bureaucracy and corruptions may be higher in developing countries due to less transparent government functions and less efficient, if exists, legislative monitoring mechanism. Trade unions possess far less power and resources than their counterparts in developed countries for a number of reasons. While trade unions in some sectors in developing countries remain relatively powerful, they are largely operating in the state-owned sector where trade unions have long been established and supported by the state. As foreign MNCs are more likely to invest in the private sector of developing countries, trade unions' influence in management practices is likely to be minimal. A consequence of weak trade unionism and the absence of alternative collective representation mechanism means that workers are largely exposed to management prerogatives and market forces. Living standards of the mass population are still relatively low, therefore direct and immediate financial reward may be the main concern of employees instead of intrinsic rewards. In spite of the fact that developing countries tend to share a more collectivist culture, the co-existence of a power distance culture means that it may be difficult to implement HR initiatives that are associated with the soft approach to HRM, such as employee involvement and empowerment schemes.

Indeed, a review of studies on HRM in developing countries points to some common characteristics that are influenced by similar societal cultural norms, even though they are continents apart (e.g. Budhwar, 2004; Budhwar and Debrah, 2001; Elvira and Davila, 2005; Hermawan, 2005). In particular, the value of power distance, benevolent paternalism, masculinity, collectivism, harmony and egalitarianism is evident in workplace relationships. Authority and hierarchical positions are respected on the one hand but superiors have personal obligation to look after their subordinates on the other. Nepotism and special treatment of 'elite' class (e.g. based on a person's social, economic, religious or job class) is acceptable and sometimes expected. Open confrontation with superiors or colleagues is avoided. Rewards are often focused on financial aspects and distributions are often group-based with minimal differentials among members to maintain social harmony. For example, Zhu's (2002) study of Vietnamese enterprises reveals that while work relations in these Vietnamese enterprises are becoming more flexible, their HR practices are still heavily influenced by its cultural and institutional traditions, such as adherence to rules and norms. Collectivist values and the notion of harmony are reflected in many of the team/group-based HR practices. Since Vietnam is emerging as a preferred country for Chinese-owned manufacturing plants, as are other developing countries in Asia such as Indonesia and Thailand, these shared values may facilitate the convergence of HR practices between subsidiaries and parent companies.

In short, given the fact that a primary motive for Chinese MNCs entering developed countries is to acquire technological and managerial know-how, and to learn from their Western partners, it is reasonable to predict that there is a stronger chance for the transfer of HR practices from the subsidiary to the parent company in China than the other way round (see Figure 9.1). By contrast, since a major motive for Chinese MNCs to invest in other developing countries (which are more likely to be less developed than China) is asset exploitation, the Chinese MNC parent company may be in a stronger bargaining position than its subsidiaries. Therefore, there may be more scope for the parent company's HR practices to be transferred to its subsidiaries (see Figure 9.1).

However, it is not to suggest here that a convergent approach to HRM should or can easily be adopted by Chinese MNC subsidiaries in developing countries. Nor is it to suggest that the common features of employment environment and HR practices shared by firms in developing countries are beneficial to the workforce. Rather, it is argued that there may be more opportunities for the home country's approach to HRM to be transferred to the host countries, since they share relatively more similar institutional and cultural environments than they do with developed countries. However, despite the proximities, total transfer of HR practices is highly unlikely due to the enduring national

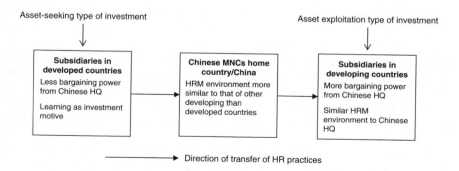

Figure 9.1 Transfer of HR practices between Chinese MNC home country and host countries

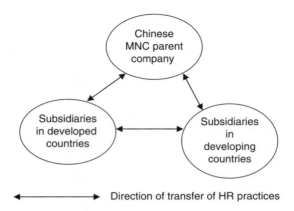

Direction of transfer of HR practices

Figure 9.2 Transfer of HR practices between Chinese MNC home country and host countries in knowledge-intensive businesses

institutional and cultural influences and the nature of local management adaptation (Edwards, 2004; Ferner and Quintanilla, 1998; Rosenzweig and Nohria, 1994).

HRM for subsidiaries in knowledge-intensive businesses – greater opportunity for convergence across subsidiaries in developed and developing countries

So far, the analysis in this main section has been focusing on the institutional and cultural differences between developed and developing countries and how these variations may influence the HR practices of asset-seeking Chinese MNC subsidiaries in developed countries differently in comparison with those in developing countries for asset exploitation. However, caution needs to be taken not to over-generalize these differences, because there are Chinese MNC subsidiaries in developing countries, albeit only a small proportion for the time being, that are engaged in knowledge-intensive business operations. As has been well argued by HR theorists (e.g. Drucker, 1989; Ulrich, 1998), a soft approach to HRM needs to be adopted to manage knowledge workers in order to elicit their commitment and innovativeness for the competitive advantage of the firm, it is reasonable to assume that there is greater potential for the convergence of HRM practices within Chinese MNCs that have knowledge-intensive business operations in both developed and developing countries (also see Figure 9.2).

For example, Lin's (2006) study of high-tech firms in Taiwan observes that firms, foreign-owned and Taiwanese-owned alike, adopt similar HR practices that are associated with the soft HRM model in managing their knowledge workers. These practices include more sophisticated recruitment methods, higher pay and more training and career development opportunities. Since worldwide learning is a major motive for Chinese MNCs in knowledge-intensive business operations (e.g. R&D centres), there may be added incentives for these Chinese MNC subsidiaries to share information and knowledge with each other and adopt similar business processes, including some HR practices. Managers in developing countries may also be eager to learn 'advanced' Western management techniques to be seen as effective and modern (Cooke, 2004). This will lead to a level of convergence of HR practices within the MNC through the transfer of HR practices across subsidiaries (Figure 9.2). However, it is important to point out that a transnational set of HR practices is unlikely to be adopted due to national differences, as argued above. For example, Hempel and Chang (2002) found that the characteristics of HRM in high-tech firms in Taiwan contain strong influence of Chinese-specific culture.

In addition, while generic challenges to integrating the HR system for MNCs have been noted (e.g. Schuler *et al.*, 2003; Sparrow *et al.*, 2004), Chinese MNC HR headquarters may face specific challenges in their attempt to integrate, even if only partially, the HR system. For example, the interpretation of HR concepts may vary across subsidiaries and the process of HR administration may differ. One example is that there is an increasing trend for the adoption of HR information system and HR outsourcing in Western countries – these practices are less common in Asian countries (Cooke and Prouska, 2006).

Conclusions

This chapter has analysed major reasons for the growth of Chinese FDI in recent years. It revealed that the emergence of China's overseas investment is associated with a broad range of political, financial, technological, environmental and business motives. Leading Chinese firms invest overseas for a combination of reasons rather than just one reason and are becoming increasingly strategic and adventurous in how and where they invest, notably in their desire to gain more direct access to technology and other strategic assets such as human resources, brand names, as well as access to markets in developed countries. In addition to going abroad to exploit and consolidate their existing core competences, they are eager to acquire and develop core competences and competitive advantages rapidly through strategic alliances.

The venturing abroad by Chinese firms has a number of management implications, particularly in the management of human resources. In general, Chinese managers still lacks foreign market knowledge, experience and international expertise. They also have insufficient understanding of host countries' employment legislation and characteristics of labour relations, particularly the different attitudes towards trade unionism. Chinese firms further suffer from an image stereotyping in developed countries where they may be seen as inferior. To succeed in exploiting local opportunities, Chinese MNCs need to create a favourable image perceived by stakeholders in the host country, to tap into well-established marketing and distribution networks, to gain familiarity with the legal environment and socio-cultural-specific business practices, and to develop greater ability to reduce operational uncertainties and financial risks. These are generic lessons for MNCs, as noted by authors on experience and performance of MNCs in China (e.g. Child and Faulkner, 1998; Luo, 1997; Luo and Peng, 1999; Shenkar, 1990). And the Chinese managers have the advantage of learning from their Western counterparts' experience.

More broadly, the strategy of localizing human resources, capital and culture to build a world famous brand requires a high level of management competence. Having HR talent at the headquarters of Chinese MNCs who are capable of designing and implementing corporate HR strategy that forms an integral part of their corporate business strategy therefore has a strategic implication for the success of Chinese MNCs. Such a corporate HR strategy needs to be informed by the legal environment, labour market characteristics and cultural norms of the host country. In many senses, managing HRM in a global context is a generic challenge encountered by MNCs, although each may face a unique institutional and cultural environment that shapes management practices of each specific host country.

This chapter hypothesises that there is a greater opportunity for the Chinese HR practices to be transferred to their subsidiaries in developing countries than that to developed countries due to different characteristics in the institutional and socio-cultural environment between the developed and developing countries. Nevertheless, there could be greater opportunity for a level of convergence of HR practices across subsidiaries in knowledge-intensive businesses in both developed and developing countries. However, it must be noted that the main objective for MNCs investing in host countries is to exploit their own advantage and to take advantage of host countries' resources. The need to transfer best practices is not necessarily their primary concern, although transfer may take place through the deliberate effort of the MNC when perceived beneficial or through unintended spill-over effect (Rubery and Grimshaw, 2003). Further studies that compare HR practices of Chinese MNCs in both developed and developing countries are needed. While an increasing number of studies have been carried out on Chinese MNCs abroad, these are not specific to Chinese MNCs that span across both developed and developing countries. It may be the case that research findings will reveal similar patterns and logics to that of Western MNCs, but unless these empirical studies are carried out, we cannot be certain that Chinese MNCs follow the same pattern as Western MNCs in developed and developing countries.

Recommended readings

C. Bartlett and S. Ghoshal, *Managing Across Borders: The Transnational Solution* (Boston, MA: Harvard Business School Press, 2000).

J. Child and D. Faulkner, *Strategies of Co-operation: Managing Alliances, Networks and Joint Ventures* (Oxford: Oxford University Press, 1998).

J. Dunning and R. Narula, *Multinationals and Industrial Competitiveness: A New Agenda* (Cheltenham: Edward Elgar, 2004).

R. Schuler, S. Jackson and Y. Luo, *Managing Human Resources in Cross-Border Alliances* (London: Routledge, 2003).

CHAPTER 10
Conclusions

Introduction

This book has explored the nature of competition and firms' strategy in China. The dual force of the globalization of competition and the decentralization of state control has had significant impact on the Chinese firms' competitive position against their foreign competitors. It has helped shape the mode of competition and business strategy of both Chinese and foreign firms across many industries in China. However, the structure of the Chinese industries remains highly fragmented in general and populated by small firms. There is a damaging absence of industry-specific rules for competition and collaboration across firms that forms part of the value chain. Instead, firms are engaged in a comprehensive range of small-scale production activities. Although there is growing evidence that market institutions are becoming more dominant in China's transition economy, this has not transformed the nature of the competition. Brand-name products are difficult to develop and maintain due to limited protection of IPR, market norms are difficult to establish and laws and regulations are tentative and equally difficult to enforce (Li and Wong, 2003).

For the last two and a half decades, the competitive advantages of China have been widely considered to be its relatively cheap cost of labour, raw materials and rent. This has attracted a large amount of FDI into China, making it one of the largest FDI recipient countries in the world. However, the majority of the FDI is in the manufacturing sector, engaging in mass production of low-quality and low value-added products for export. The Chinese producers only receive a small share of the profit for producing the products, whereas the majority of the profit is retained by the foreign partners in the value chain. Although FDI brought China the much needed investment for its economic development and created timely employment opportunities to absorb the vast surplus of rural labour, it has had limited impact on upgrading the level of human resources and technological capability of China. In terms of FDI outflow, while it is true that the majority of Chinese firms remain uncompetitive, evidence suggests that they are learning fast from their international counterparts to preserve their home market in the face of foreign competition whilst at the same time moving towards the centre in the global economy.

This concluding chapter provides a summary of the key themes and issues discussed in the previous chapters and points to a number of research avenues for readers who are interested in exploring further these issues and others that have not been discussed in this book. The chapter consists of five main sections.

The first discusses the effectiveness of the role of the Chinese government in directing the economy of the country, especially its industrial policies. The second section summarizes the key challenges present in a number of Chinese industries and the key elements of strategic response adopted by the indigenous firms. The managerial implications for firms, particularly leadership skills, are then discussed in the third section. This is followed by a comparison of the key resources and constraints between foreign-invested and Chinese-owned firms. Whilst foreign firms possess more organizational resources, this competitive advantage may be offset by the disadvantage associated with being a foreign player in the Chinese market. The chapter concludes with a list of broad research questions that are aimed to prompt researchers to formulate their agenda.

The role of the Chinese government and the effectiveness of its industrial policies

It is evident that the government has played a central role in reshaping the path of China's economic development since the late 1970s. Whilst the role of the government as an employer has been shrinking, its role as an economic manager and a regulator remains dominant and necessary in the restructuring and development of key industries such as the automotive, IT and pharmaceutical industry. In particular, the government has been selective in the key industries it wishes to support through its differential industrial policies. For example, the Chinese government's 'techno-nationalism' – 'the desire to demonstrate or acquire the status of being a technologically advanced country' (Goldstein, 2005, p. 25) has led to its heavy investment in building up the IT industry. The difference in the government's policy stance between the IT industry and the retail industry has had a pronounced impact on the development of the two industries. In addition, the government's role in the internationalization of Chinese firms has been pivotal, initially by fostering JVs with foreign firms in China and more recently by encouraging Chinese firms to 'go global'.

However, the central government's determination to liberalize the Chinese economy is not necessarily fully shared by regional and local governments who wrestle to remain autonomous and pursue their parochial interests. As a result, the ability of the central government to enforce its industrial and economic development policies at regional level is circumvented by inter-regional power politics and the capability of local governments to bypass those policies or to interpret them in ways to suit their local agenda. Here, the automotive industry is a typical example. Despite criteria set by the central government to control entry of new firms, the number of firms have actually grown rather than decreased. Existing firms also fail to re-organize capacity through M&As, product specialization and ultimately rationalization of the industry. Regional and local institutional environment plays a more crucial role than the national policy in shaping the nature of the competition, patterns of innovation and types of business growth.

The ability of the central government to implement a national industrial policy is further constrained by international regulations, especially following China's accession to the WTO. International trade regulations mean that the Chinese government is unlikely to be able to direct the development of its industries in ways similar to those pioneered by the Japanese and Korean governments during the period from the 1950s to 1970s (Perkins, 2001). Nevertheless, a level of national protectionism remains, as is commonly found in other nation states. It is believed that even as China reduces tariffs and allows wholly foreign-owned firms to operate in various sectors, Chinese governments at all levels enact policies that favour domestic producers over their foreign counterparts and impose constraints for the latter in accessing the Chinese market. This may be so, but some local governments are criticized for offering preferential treatment to foreign firms in their blind attempts to secure foreign investment at the risk of the survival of local firms. The retail industry is a case in point.

The extent of the positive impact of industrial policy is equally questionable. It is evident that changes in the automotive and pharmaceutical industries are driven by market forces as much as, if not more so, by industrial policies. In the automotive industry, it is the growth of private enterprises and the intensifying competition that force auto firms to slash prices and produce with new designs that appeal to the Chinese car consumers. Here, price reduction can be seen as an indicator of the strengthened role of the market. In the pharmaceutical industry, the imposition of GMP accreditation has forced small firms to invest in size rather than in the much needed advanced technology. According to Nolan (2002), China's industrial policies of the 1980s and 1990s were both a success in supporting large firms and a failure in most key respects as evidenced in micro and macro data. It is a success because:

- large state-owned enterprises avoided the collapse that took place in the state sector in the former USSR;
- industrial output grew at around 13 per cent per annum from the early 1980s to the late 1990s, with sustained rapid growth for large firms;
- major changes took place in the operational mechanism of large, state-owned enterprises: they absorbed a great deal of modern technology; learned how to compete in the market place; substantially upgraded the technical level of their employees; learned wide-ranging new managerial skills; and gained substantial understanding of international financial markets;
- China's large firms became sought-after partners for multinational companies. China attracted huge amounts of foreign direct investment. Increasingly, global corporations viewed China as a central element in their long-term strategy;
- a group of large mainland firms were listed successfully on international stock markets;
- by the year 2001, China had 11 firms listed in the Fortune 500 (Nolan, 2002, pp. 121–2).

It is a failure because:

- At the start of the twenty-first century, not one of China's leading enterprises had become a globally competitive giant corporation, with a global market, a global brand, and a global procurement system.
- The Chinese companies included in the Fortune 500 all faced huge problems of downsizing. China had no less than five of the top ten companies in the Fortune 500 in terms of number of employees.
- China had just two companies in the FT 500 which ranks firms by market capitalisation (*Financial Times*, 11 May 2001). These were China Mobile and China Unicom, both of which operate in a totally protected domestic environment. The vast bulk of their IT hardware equipment was purchased from the global giants.
- China did not have one company in the world's *Top 300 companies by R&D* expenditure (DTI, 2000).
- China did not have any representatives in *Morgan Stanley Dean Witter's* list of the world's Top 250 'competitive edge' companies.
- China did not have a single company in *Business Week's* list of the world's Top 100 brands (Nolan, 2002, pp. 130–1, original emphases).

These facts suggest that, 'after two decades of reform, the competitive capability of China's large firms is still extremely weak in relation to the global giants' (Nolan, 2002, p. 131).

Challenges facing Chinese businesses and their strategic response

As we can see from previous chapters (also see Table 10.1 for summary), each Chinese industry faces a unique set of competitive pressure, industry legacy (or the absence of it) and a government–business relationship which facilitates or hinders the speed of development of the industry as a whole as well as certain segments of the industry. For example, the IT industry took off much more successfully than the exhibition industry although both are relatively new industries. There are significant differences in the level of government support and market demand, the scope for participation from individual entrepreneurs and the level of resources needed. Similarly, in the pharmaceutical industry, small businesses can take part and fake drugs are an endemic problem, whereas in the automotive industry, entry barriers are high for small and micro private firms due to the amount of resources needed to set up viable operations. But in general, the Chinese government is increasingly aware of the importance of market forces in achieving and sustaining a healthy economy. Where possible, a degree of competition is introduced and the level of direct involvement of the government is rolled back. However, tension remains between the desired efficiency and flexibility associated with decentralization and privatization on the one hand, and the perceived need for the government's

Table 10.1 Competitive pressure and strategic response of selected industries in China

Industry	Key challenges and competitive pressure	Role of the Government	Strategic response from domestic firms
Automobile	Technological innovation	Encouraging industrial re-organization through M&As to achieve economies of scale	Opening up and collaboration through joint ventures with foreign brand name manufacturers
	Efficiency	Protecting domestic firms from foreign competition through importation barriers and restricting ways through which foreign manufacturers operate in China	Mergers and acquisitions to consolidate business
	Intensive competition from foreign brand-name products		Developing models tailored for segments of domestic market
	Lack of overseas market		Exploration of overseas markets
Pharmaceutical	Efficiency	Closing down small and unprofitable enterprises to help the industry improve efficiency and achieve economies of scale	Product and enterprise branding
	Low technological capacity	Introducing GMP to raise the production standard of the industry	New product development
	Lack of R&D investment	Investment and policy encouragement in R&D	New markets – from regional to national
	Lack of innovation	Clamping down on fake drugs operations	New market segments – identifying new segments of customers
	Low value-added product leading to low profit margin		Internationalization

Table 10.1 (Continued)

Industry	Key challenges and competitive pressure	Role of the Government	Strategic response from domestic firms
IT	Technological innovation	Proactively promoting the rapid growth of the industry by strategically directing the growth of the industry and funding R&D	Strategic alliances with foreign brand-name firms to encompass the technology and to raise the company profile in the global market in order to increase sales revenue and to upgrade the firm in the competition order
	Efficiency	Restricting the way foreign firms enter and operate in the Chinese market	Creating demand in domestic market with affordable prices for the masses
	Prices	Listing the IT industry as a strategic industry and a future pillar industry	Intensive technological innovation in order to be the key player in the future generations of the technology
	First mover advantage and technological sophistication of foreign brand-name firms		
Retail	Lack of economies of scale	Least government intervention	Transformation from traditional stand-alone department stores to supermarket chains and shopping centres and malls
	Massive competition from brand-name foreign retail and super-market chain operators	Favourable policy of local governments to attract foreign retail giants to the disadvantage of local retail firms	Revitalizing the brand value of long-established household name shops
	Backward logistic and distribution management systems		

Exhibition	Lack of industrial regulations Lack of rules of the game due to its relatively new presence as an industry Resource demanding but severe skill shortages in all related fields Inter-industry collaboration needed but absence of established industrial clusters	Lack of policy intervention from the government Participation of local governments as sponsors and organizers of exhibitions	Joint ventures with foreign firms
Drinks (soft and alcoholic)	Low entry barriers Intensive competition on price and varieties of products	Introduction of tax regulations and production standard regulations to force closure of shoddy firms	Economies of scale Profitability Market positioning through product branding

continuing intervention to direct, regulate, subsidize and invest on the other. While many old Chinese state-owned firms have been undergoing a reforming process to simply survive, new Chinese privately owned firms are experiencing a period of growth.

Despite the unique environment under which a specific industry operates, Chinese firms across industrial sectors appear to share a number of common characteristics. One is that they are all facing shortages of natural and human resources and a worsening ecological environment. Ineffective law enforcement, weak commercial and IPR protection, relatively low levels of R&D investment and activities and skill shortages at the macro level are some of the institutional deficiencies under which they have to operate. How to acquire scarce resources and bypass institutional deficiencies therefore becomes a strategically important issue for firms seeking to gain competitive advantage. And some firms are better able to do so than others.

A second characteristic is that Chinese firms are generally small in terms of firm size. They lack economies of scale and suffer from a low capacity for technology and innovation. According to the national statistics, 99 per cent of the enterprises in China are SMEs and the vast majority of SMEs are privately owned. SMEs contribute 55.6 per cent of China's GDP, 74.7 per cent of industrial new added value, 58.9 per cent of total sales revenue, 46.2 per cent of tax and 62.3 per cent of total export value. In addition, SMEs provide over 75 per cent of the employment and hold 65 per cent of the patents. Over 75 per cent of technological innovations are conceived by SMEs and over 80 per cent of new products are developed by SMEs (*China National Conditions and Strength*, 2004). The majority of Chinese firms still carry out most of their business activities in-house with a low level of specialization and division of production in the industry. This is a phenomenon that is called *xiao er quan* (small but full-range) in China. In spite of this, there are now signs that Chinese firms are growing in size and forming strategic alliances, encouraged by the Chinese government's 'bigger and stronger' agenda in order to compete internationally.

A third feature is that the majority of Chinese firms compete on price instead of product differentiation and lack brand value for their products. For example, China has already become the world's largest ceramic-producing country, exporting daily pottery to 166 countries and regions (*Asiainfo Daily China News*, 2002). However, lacking internationally recognized brand names, most products can only enter the foreign lower-middle range market carrying very low prices. A large number of high-quality products can only enter the top market bearing foreign brand names. In the first half of 2002, China exported a total of 3.6 billion pieces of ceramic products worth US$712 million. The average price for each piece was only US 20 cents (*Asiainfo Daily China News*, 2002). Within the domestic market, the majority of Chinese firms operate at local and regional level and encounter difficulties in establishing a national market and distribution network. Firms typically face geographical segmentation as well as consumer group segmentation. Local government's interventions remain strong and regional variance is high with regard to stages of economic development, level of income and cultural preference.

A fourth feature is that globalization and global competition now presents a key challenge that many Chinese businesses are encountering as a consequence of China's accession to the WTO. Whilst Chinese firms are developing collaborative relationships with firms within and outside China in order to gain entry and competitive power, there is still a long way to go in forging strategic groups.[1] It has been noted that during the 1980s and 1990s, JVs with foreign MNCs (e.g. in the automotive industry) have left many Chinese firms 'in a position of dependent subcontractors' for the foreign MNCs (Nolan, 2004, p. 171). Many Chinese managers lack international exposure and experience. This shortage of talent capable of managing international operations has become an ever more pressing problem. And the cost of learning to compete in the global market has been high for leading Chinese firms.

Firms respond differently to these key challenges. However, business diversification, product and service innovation, strategic marketing through product and corporate branding and internationalization appear to be the key elements of strategic response from successful Chinese firms. In fact, both foreign MNCs in China and Chinese firms wishing to expand abroad have realized the importance of being close to the market and customers and are building R&D centres and distribution networks locally. There are signs which indicate that the Chinese firms are beginning to adopt a broader notion of innovation to include not only technological innovations, but also product, marketing, services and management innovations. The majority of innovations, however, have been in the mode of imitation and adaptation of Western models. With some exceptions such as firms in the IT and biotechnology industries, Chinese firms in general have not assumed the central role in technological innovation through collaboration with research institutes and strategic partnership with other firms. In terms of internationalization, a small but increasing number of Chinese firms are emerging as global investors. As Zeng and Williamson noted:

> four groups of Chinese companies are simultaneously tackling the global market. China's national champions are using their advantages as domestic leaders to build global brands. The country's dedicated exporters are attempting to enter foreign markets on the strength of their economies of scale. China's competitive networks have taken on world markets by bringing together small, specialized companies that operate in close proximity. And the technology upstarts are using innovations developed by China's government-owned research institutes to enter emerging sectors such as biotechnology. Each group, starting from a strong base of cost competitiveness, has found a way to make its presence felt outside China's borders.
>
> (2003, p. 95)

The motives of Chinese firms venturing abroad are manifold. It is a resource- and market-seeking strategy to compensate for the depleting reserves of natural resources at home and the saturated domestic market for some products. It is also a strategy to overcome trade barriers such as export quotas imposed by Western countries to protect their own markets. But above all, it is an ambitious strategy by national champions, such as Haier, to build their global brands.

Managerial implications for Chinese firms

The competition strategy adopted by leading Chinese firms in response to competitive pressures has a number of implications for the development of their organizational competence in a number of functional areas, as outlined in Table 10.2. Many of these issues have been discussed in previous chapters and touched upon earlier in this chapter. It is worthwhile to summarize them again here. These required organizational competences and managerial skills are not unique to Chinese firms that wish to succeed, but are to some extent, universally applicable to firms in other nation economies that wish to pursue similar strategies.

A number of aspects warrant further discussion here. One is the need for enterprise leaders to develop and manage their network relationships. As we have already discussed in Chapter 3, transition economies generally suffer from an incomplete institutional support system external to the firm. Organizational leaders need to develop political and social ties through their own personal networks 'to at least partially overcome the infrastructure deficiencies by facilitating

Table 10.2 Competition strategy and implications for Chinese firms

Competition strategy	Business competence*	Leadership and HR implications*
Diversification	Industry knowledge	Strategic vision
Marketing and branding	Competitor understanding	Strategic planning and decision-making skills
Product and business innovation	Market intelligence	Value shaping
Internationalization	R&D capacity	Creating a learning culture and managing learning and knowledge transfer across organizational boundary
	Skilled and motivated workforce	Network building
	Financial understanding	Managing cultural diversity
	Global perspective/knowledge	
	Strategic analysis	
	Strategic alliance	
	Multiple stakeholder sensitivity	
	Wider approach to CSR	

* adapted and expanded from Schuler et al. (2001, p. 128).

economic exchanges among members' (Peng, 2001, p. 99). This network relationship is particularly important for smaller private firms in China where state
intervention and law enforcement is at its weakest and local officials have considerable autonomy to interpret and enforce laws and regulations contingent
to the circumstances.

Another aspect is the need for Chinese firms to take a broader approach to
innovation. Innovation entails not only technological breakthrough in products
and production processes in manufacturing firms, but also the development of
merchandising concepts, store designs, customer and supplier relationship management, product specifications and branding. The phrase 'concept product'
has entered Chinese consumers' language and is increasingly influencing their
choice of products, especially in the purchase of luxury goods such as cars. However, the Chinese market is not a single market but a highly segmented one.
On the one hand, affluent Chinese consumers are pursuing a concept and an
image of modernity when purchasing luxury products and services. On the other
hand, the majority of consumers are still relatively poor and price remains a key
consideration in their purchasing decision. Chinese firms need to tailor their
products and services to the different needs of the consumers and position themselves in the market accordingly. To gain long-term competitiveness and to be
able to compete globally, they must have their own products and a competitive
business strategy. A promising sign is that Chinese business organizations are
becoming more competitive and efficiency-driven, as well as seeking to maintain
growth by entering new markets and diversifying their product ranges.

A third issue is that Chinese firms need to build a corporate reputation that is
based on quality, trustworthiness, willingness to innovate, being environmentally responsible and being a good employer. Enhanced economic freedom
granted to the Chinese firms by the government necessarily brings a higher
level of corporate responsibility. The Chinese government is now calling for
enterprises to 'serve an expanded role in society' (*People's Daily Overseas Edition*, 16 March 2006). Without such a virtuous corporate reputation, foreign
companies will continue to be reluctant to share their technological know-how
with their Chinese partners. Whilst prosperity reaches a relative few, pollution
affects all, and firms have both the legal and moral obligation to carry out their
production activities in an environmentally responsible way. Equally, differential employment policies adopted by firms on different groups of workers may
contribute to the rising inequalities in income and opportunity between the
economic elite and other social groups including the laid-off SOE workers and
the rural migrant workers. These inequalities are likely to lead to rising social
discontent from the poor on the one hand, and protectionism from the elite to
maintain their privileged position on the other. These competing demands may
undermine the social cohesion crucial as the foundation for China's continuous transformation and growth (Hofman, 2005). In fact, threats of pollution
and polarization of the poor and the wealthy are amongst the key issues of
concern recognized by the government. Humanity-oriented reform, common
prosperity and growth that is less resource-intensive and more knowledge and
innovation-driven are now listed as the key objectives of China's eleventh five-
year plan (2006–10) (China.org.cn, accessed 18 November 2006). It appears

that the Chinese government is becoming aware that the economic and social well-being of the nation is a vital factor in determining the competitiveness and comparative advantage of China. This policy orientation is likely to have an impact on the way firms are allowed to operate and require them to adopt a socially more responsible approach to business development.

A fourth aspect is how Chinese firms should manage their human resources strategically to match their business strategy.[2] As we can see from the discussion in previous chapters, firms in China are generally facing a shortage of talent. Whilst well-performing Chinese firms appear to have become more strategic in a number of their business functions, they seem to be much less so in their HRM by comparison. Moreover, the majority of Chinese managers, including those in both foreign-invested and Chinese-owned firms, need to develop their leadership skills and think more strategically and internationally. According to a survey conducted by Development Dimensions International (Bernthal et al., 2006) on the HR professionals and 394 leaders from 43 organizations in China, only 20 per cent of the leaders demonstrated strengths in the skills which they believed to be most critical for success in their roles. These skills include: the ability to motivate others, building trust, retaining talent and leading high-performance teams. In addition, more than half of Chinese leaders are believed to be inadequately prepared for their roles in the new business environment. What is more revealing is that the survey found that three out of ten new employees recruited are not good hiring decisions and nearly half of Chinese leaders only have 'poor' or 'fair' interview skills. Given the importance of effective HRM in enhancing organizational competitiveness, Chinese firms have much to catch up with in developing a strategic approach to managing and developing their human resources.

Foreign firms versus domestic firms in China

A general finding from the industry-specific chapters has been that foreign MNCs in China are in a relatively better competitive position than the majority of Chinese firms. They are able to offer differentiated products that are marked by high-quality, innovative design and high brand value. They are also more likely to be able to attract talent because of their prestigious corporate image and better employment prospects. However, the competitive advantage of foreign firms in China over domestic firms is by no means absolute. As we can see from Table 10.3, there are a number of key differences in their operating environment and organizational resources. It must be pointed out here that this summary of relative strengths and weaknesses of foreign-invested and Chinese-owned firms is meant for comparative purpose instead of being a categorical generalization.

According to a survey conducted in 1999 by AT Kearney and the Economist Intelligence Unit (EIU) on 70 MNCs operating in China, 52 per cent of the MNCs had failed to reach their profitability goals, 45 per cent were profitable, 25 per cent broke-even and 25 per cent were unprofitable. Factors cited by respondents for disappointing results included: overestimated market demand;

Table 10.3 Key resources and constraints of foreign firms versus Chinese firms

Business environment and organizational resource	Foreign firms	Chinese firms
Level of support from the Chinese government (including provincial and local governments)	Relatively more restriction from the Chinese government in their business operations	Relatively more support from the Chinese central and local governments, especially state-owned and flagship enterprises
Social capital	Less familiar with the local culture, more difficult to break into the social network to obtain business resources	Familiar with the local culture, better able to mobilize social networks, including that with government bodies, to obtain business resources and bypass legal constraints
	More difficult to develop networking relationship with local governments, and where developed, may be subject to international pressure groups' scrutiny for corruption	
Product market	Higher end of the product market, ability to demand premium price due to perceived higher quality and novelty of products and brand prestige	Lower end of the product market, lack of brand-name products, competing on low price, but gradually moving towards higher quality and better services
	Generic products appealing mainly to affluent consumers	More familiar with consumer needs and offering tailored products
	Focused mainly on larger cities, barriers to expand into less affluent areas	More able to expand into less developed cities and rural areas

Table 10.3 (Continued)

Business environment and organizational resource	Foreign firms	Chinese firms
Innovation and technological competence	Relatively high level of R&D investment and technological competence, but more prone to be copied by local firms	Low level of R&D investment and technological competence, limited product innovation, adapter of foreign firm's technology and innovation
Human capital	Skill shortages but better able to attract and retain best candidates in the labour market because of organizational prestige, better employment packages and career prospects	Severe skill shortages which serves as a bottleneck for growth and a constraint to organizational competitiveness Competitive pressure from other developing countries in the region with even cheaper labour cost
Organizational resource back-up	Able to draw on global corporate resources (e.g. finance, technology, business process model, management expertise) and business solutions through organizational learning May be constrained by the need to conform to corporate global strategy	Limited organizational resources as back-up due to relatively small firm size and absence of industrial cluster/network More flexible in making organizational decisions and able to respond more quickly to local changes

intensive local competition; poor productivity; inability to develop local management skills; and industry over-capacity (cited in *FDI Magazine*, 4 August 2003). Nevertheless, a more recent survey conducted by the World Bank on 12,400 enterprises in 120 cities in China (28 per cent of the enterprises surveyed were foreign firms) reveals that the return of investment of foreign enterprises in China was at a high average of 22 per cent (cited in *People's Daily Overseas Edition*, 13 November 2006).

Foreign firms usually seek to establish themselves in the major cities in China first and then attempt to expand to the second or even third tier cities. However, consumer tastes and behavioural patterns in premium cities are not necessarily good guides for the rest of the country where level of affordability is still generally low and basic needs remain the main reasons for consumption. Foreign MNCs have to 'contend with a minefield of competing local interests, overloaded infrastructure, difficulties in retaining skilled people, tortuous supply chains, unfamiliar local HR practices and communication barriers', as well as 'the emergence of tough competition from local Chinese players' (Williamson and Zeng, 2004, p. 85).

In addition, the cost of maintaining a strong global brand is high and may not be fully recouped in the Chinese market. According to Lasserre and Schütte (2006), many foreign firms do not adapt their products sufficiently to tailor for the Chinese markets. Instead, they transplant their products and programmes which are attractive and affordable to only a small number of Chinese affluent consumers. Box 10.1 is a good example that highlights the need for sensitivity to price and cultural adaptation in the Chinese market in order to compete successfully. As Melewar *et al.* (2004) observed, local culture is one of the

---

BOX 10.1

Promoting foreign beers in China

A large portion of the Chinese beer market was made up of low-cost, low-quality beer that was cheaper than bottled water. The foreign brands spent heavily on advertising to justify their higher prices but were still too expensive. Some dropped their prices, but when Australian brewer Foster's decided it could not make money at this level and raised the cost of a bottle by US$0.4, their hard-won market share – involving massive losses to build – evaporated overnight. Other beer brands found themselves unable to connect with local consumers. Bass promoted its highly successful Scottish lager with bagpipes to much bemusement and few sales. Soon Foster's wrote off their substantial investment and went home. Ireland's Guinness, Denmark's Carlsberg and New Zealand's Lion Nathan all followed suit in short order.

Source: French (2003).

most important influences on marketing efforts and the strong Chinese culture is unlikely to be changed by an innovative Western idea or product if it is perceived impractical. These factors have contributed to the limited success of many foreign firms, with a much less market share and lower profit margin than anticipated.

By comparison, Chinese-owned firms are advantaged in China in that the price of their products is generally lower. They have a better understanding of their local customers' needs and preference, and they may be better connected with local governments. As Luo (1995) noted, Chinese people are *guanxi* oriented and have acquired sophisticated skills to develop interpersonal relationships.

Leading foreign firms are nevertheless learning their lessons in China and have adapted their strategy more proactively to win market share. For example, global retail giants such as IKEA and Tesco are now more proactive in tailoring their products and store layouts to suit the Chinese consumers' tastes. They are also aiming to retain customers by offering high-quality products at highly competitive price. Francis *et al.*'s (2002) comparative study of English and Chinese brand names of Fortune 500 companies also found that many of these firms operating in China have deployed an adaptation and localization strategy in translating their brand name into the Chinese language to reflect the significant linguistic, social and cultural differences across societies. They argue that such a strategy enables firms to 'capitalize on the localization of their brand names that are more meaningful, reflect more positive connotations, reflect more product benefits or characteristics, and possess more desirable linguistic characteristics than the original names' (Francis *et al.*, 2002, p. 114).[3]

Moreover, leading foreign MNCs in China are beginning to recognize the need to take a more responsive approach to managing their corporate relationship with the Chinese government and its associated political bodies. For example, Wal-Mart had been resisting for years China's request to establish a trade union for its workforce, claiming that it was its global corporate HR policy to have a non-unionized workforce (see Chapter 7 for more details about Wal-Mart in China). Wal-Mart was publicly criticized by the All-China Federation of Trade Unions (ACFTU) in the early 2000s for its refusal to recognize the trade union. In 2006, Wal-Mart softened its tone by stating that if its employees in China had the desire to become unionized, Wal-Mart (China) would respect their wish. This resulted in the establishment of the first union on one of its new sites in a small city on 29 July 2006 (*China Business*, 7 August 2006). Within a month, another 18 Wal-Mart sites in China had established a trade union organization on site. Wal-Mart further stated that it would help ACFTU set up branches in all its 60 Chinese outlets employing over 23,000 people and perform its employer's duty in accordance to the Trade Union Law of China. It stated that its hope was to establish a good relationship with the ACFTU and its local branches that would benefit both Wal-Mart's employees and its business development (*People's Daily Online*, 13 August 2006), although the effect of this unionization remains to be assessed.

In the broader domain of CSR, it has been observed (*CorpWatch*, 2005) that more attention has been given by foreign MNCs in China to integrating their

CSR practices into business objectives and, above all, redefining the role of their company in the society and its environment (see Box 10.2 for examples).

BOX 10.2

Examples of CSR activities of MNCs in China

■ HSBC implements comprehensive anti-money laundering standards across its entire business line. The firm uses careful identification procedures for opening accounts, close monitoring of transactions and a worldwide network of control officers for tracking and reporting. In addition, the company conducts money laundering awareness programmes for every new member of staff and refresher training courses where relevant.

■ Boeing China provided support to more than 1020 Chinese teenagers to develop their entrepreneurial skills through the Junior Achievement business plan programme. Mentored by volunteer consultants from the business community, these young entrepreneurs developed their business ideas and organized and operated actual business ventures. They also had a chance to participate in programmes that cultivated leadership, team spirit and interpersonal skills.

■ In 1999, Microsoft China provided nearly 4.5 million yuan to support computer skills training projects for laid-off and migrant workers in several major cities in China, including Liaoning, Sichuan, Guangdong and Shanghai.

Source: adapted from *CorpWatch* (2005).

Research implications

In this textbook, we have touched upon many topics although unfortunately few have been discussed in depth. The intention has been to provide an introduction to the topics and point to further studies from which interested readers can develop a deeper understanding of the issues concerned. In this concluding section, I would like to offer a set of research questions which researchers may wish to explore further as part of their endeavour to deepen their understanding of China. Again, this list serves as pointers only and is not meant to be an exhaustive guide.

1. Given the importance of innovation to firms' competitiveness on the one hand, and the high cost of R&D and difficulties in protecting intellectual property in China to reap the benefit on the other, should Chinese firms pursue an innovation-driven strategy or a follower's strategy for their long-term growth? What will be the main forms of competition in China in the coming years? What types of organizational resources will these forms of competition require? In a critique to Porter's (1990)

argument on competitive advantage of nations, Davies and Ellis (2000, p. 1209) argue that a nation 'does not need to reach the innovation-driven stage in order to achieve sustained prosperity'; that industries 'which are internationally competitive do not generally have strong diamonds'; and that 'international success does not always need to be based upon "up-grading" through innovation, product differentiation and branding'. To what extent, if at all, are these arguments applicable to the Chinese situation? What implications do these arguments, if held true for China, have for Chinese firms' competitive strategy?

2. How will the strategic intent and industrial policy guidance of the eleventh five-year plan (2006–10) affect the development of Chinese industries differently? What changes do firms have to make, if any, to follow this policy guidance? What new opportunities may arise under this new five-year plan and how can firms take advantage of these opportunities?

3. It is now evident that privately owned enterprises play a more significant role than their SOE counterparts in innovation in China despite the fact that the latter are endowed with stronger government support. What are the main success factors for the private firms? What strategic gaps do these firms have and how can these be overcome to help them become even stronger? What lessons can SOEs learn from them?

4. What are the most urgent sets of skills that Chinese organizational leaders need to develop? How can these skills be best developed? To what extent are the Western models of leadership theories applicable to the Chinese operations? How can the essence of Western theories and practices on leadership be assimilated by firms in China and adapted to suit the Chinese business environment?

5. Given the generally low level of sophistication in logistics and supply chain management as well as in marketing of Chinese businesses, how can these functions be improved in order to enhance their organizational performance? What implications do these improvement methods have for their business network? In particular, what management techniques can the Chinese retail enterprises learn from their foreign counterparts in these functional areas to enhance their competitiveness?

6. In light of the worsening skill shortages in many technical and professional areas on the one hand, and the increasing difficulties of university graduates to find employment on the other, what changes need to be made to the Chinese higher education system and the vocational training system to alleviate these problems? What roles should the stakeholders (e.g. the state, the higher education institutions, vocational training providers, employers, trade unions and individuals) play in implementing these changes? Since skill shortages and unemployment of university graduates are also a dual problem encountered by other countries such as the United Kingdom, what lessons and good practices can be drawn from these countries to help China solve these problems? What are the policy implications for the Chinese government?

7. There have been a growing number of international acquisitions in China in recent years. What impact may these cross-border acquisitions have on China in terms of its HR development, R&D and technological advancement? It is believed that a significant proportion of M&As in the Western economies do not deliver the anticipated results, with some considered as failures. Are cross-border M&As in China a facing similar fate? What may be the major differences between cross-border M&As and M&As among domestic firms in China in terms of their motives, processes and implications for post-M&A integration? What is the likely impact of M&As on HRM in the Chinese context? For example, how may M&As affect employees' loyalty, identity, trust, commitment and motivation at work? How are these psychological feelings managed and to what effect, and what are the implications for managerial skills? As existing analyses of the M&A phenomena in the Western economies may not provide an adequate analytical tool to make sense of what takes place in China, what theoretical models can be advanced that can help us come up with more informative analysis of patterns and outcomes of M&As in China?

8. A large number of studies, both qualitatively and more so quantitatively, have now emerged on the management of MNCs in China. However, there have been limited attempts so far to differentiate the typologies of foreign MNCs in China, for example, along the lines of Bartlett and Ghoshal's (1989) four categories.[4] What typologies of foreign MNCs do we have in China, and which type appears to be more dominant? What are their major differences in ownership structure, nature of corporate governance, product market, business strategy, labour market position and HRM in China? Consequently, what may be the implications of each type for the development of China's competitive advantage as a nation? And how may these implications be further complicated by the evolution of the types of MNCs themselves as part of their business life-cycle and the development of their international profiles? Given the resource constraints and worsening environmental problems in China, what types of FDI should it then attract to ensure its sustainable economic and social development?

9. The Chinese government encourages firms to invest overseas, especially in developed countries in order to raise the profile of China and Chinese businesses. But should Chinese firms go international by establishing high-profile overseas operations, often involving high-profile and high-cost acquisitions and even higher-cost post-acquisition management? Can the true cost of this political motive be calculated and who pays for it? Despite being small in number and limited in success, do the recent activities of international acquisitions by Chinese firms abroad nevertheless signal the beginning of a fundamental change in the current balance of power and image of China as a global political and economic power? What impact will the growing competitive advantages of Chinese enterprises have on the developed economies and other developing economies? How will the global automotive and IT industries be affected by the rise of Chinese producers? It is unlikely that previous global governance policies will remain

appropriate, if so, how may these be revised? Given the complex motives and patterns of Chinese outflow FDI, can they be fully explained by existing FDI theories that are mainly derived from observations of Western practices?

10. What may be the similarities and major differences in the HRM practices of Chinese MNC subsidiaries in developed and developing countries, particularly in those HR elements that are not constrained by national and local employment regulations? To what extent are HR practices transferred across national and organizational boundaries, and what mechanisms are in place for the transfer? What is the role of management in the host and home countries in promoting these transfers? To what extent do country-specific practices persist and what are the major reasons that can explain these enduring differences? How do Chinese expatriate managers work together with managers from the host country and third country? What may be the major cross-cultural and interpersonal issues, how are they manifested and how are these issues managed?

Recommended readings

B. Krug and H. Hendrischke (eds), *China in the 21st Century: Economic and Business Behaviour* (Cheltenham: Edward Elgar, 2007).

C. K. Lee, *Working in China: Ethnographies of Labor and Workplace Transformation* (London: Routledge, 2007).

M. Peng, *Business Strategies in Transition Economies* (Thousand Oaks: Sage Publications, 2000).

M. Porter, *Competitive Strategy* (US: Free Press, 1980).

Notes

1 Introduction

1. See Miles and Snow (1978), Mintzberg *et al*. (1998), Freeman (1995), Whittington (1993), Johnson and Scholes (2002) for comprehensive discussions of typologies of strategy, corporate strategy and competitive strategy.
2. See Budhwar and Debrah (2001), Budhwar (2004), Elvira and Davila (2005) for more detailed discussions of HRM in developing countries in Asia, Africa and Latin America; Cooke (2005a), Warner (2005) for HRM in China.

2 Business Environment in China

1. The term 'industrial policy' here refers to the policy that is initiated by the central government with the intent of promoting a specific industry and the Government's capability to manipulate intra-industry policy, especially industrial organization policy (Eun and Lee, 2002, p. 2).
2. Please see Huang *et al*. (2004) for a detailed analysis of the institutional stakeholders involved in the design innovation policy framework.
3. See Cooke (2004) for a more detailed analysis of the history of and problems in the vocational and enterprise training in China.

3 Competition Strategy of Leading Chinese (Private) Firms

1. Employer branding is 'the image of the organization as seen through the eyes of *external* stakeholders' and 'represents an extension of brand management and is another development whereby HR thinking has been influenced by that of the marketing function' (Sparrow *et al*., 2004, p. 115).
2. See Davies *et al*. (2003) and Kotler *et al*. (2005) for more detailed discussions on brands, product and corporate branding and strategic brand management.
3. Also see Zuo (2004, article in Chinese) for a more detailed account of Wuliangye's competitive strength that has arisen from the company's long history (established in 1909) of rice wine making, unique recipe, technological advancement, well-honed crafts skills, product innovations and a strong branding and marketing strategy.
4. This view is akin to the altruistic approach to CSR.
5. Chinese-owned firms have attracted wide criticism for their poor structure of corporate governance, which is seen as a major cause of the poor performance of many indigenous firms, particularly SOEs. Corporate governance reform has been identified by the Chinese government as an important issue in its market-oriented economic reform. See J. Chen (2004), Clarke (2003), Shi and Weisert (2002), and Tenev *et al*. (2002) for more detailed discussions of the history, problems and reforms of corporate governance in China.

4   Automotive Industry

1. Gan (2003) offers a useful overview of the state of the automobile industry and urban road transport management in China.
2. Also see Eun and Lee (2002) for a brief account of the history of the Chinese auto industry and an in-depth analysis of what they believe to be the failure of the Chinese government's industrial policy to promote the industry by rationalizing it due to vested interest and power of local governments.
3. See Thun (2006) for a more detailed study of the major auto manufacturers in China, including the role of FDI, relationships between the foreign and Chinese auto partners, barriers to grow large indigenous auto firms and a comparison of policy differences between Beijing, Shanghai and Guangzhou municipal governments in the development of their provincial auto industry.
4. Also see Francois and Spinanger (2004) for more detailed analysis of the interaction of regulated efficiency and the likely impact of China's WTO accession on its automotive industry.
5. Also see Cooke (2005a, Chapter 5) for more details regarding problems of vocational training and enterprise skill training in China.

5   Pharmaceutical Industry

1. See Li (2002) for a more extensive review of the new developments in China's pharmaceutical regulatory framework regarding various aspects of the industry from manufacturing and R&D to sales and import of drug.
2. See Bulcke *et al.* (1999) for detailed analysis of the entry and expansion paths of foreign pharmaceutical enterprises into China, changes in the entry conditions of the Chinese pharmaceutical market and their impact on the strategic choices of pharmaceutical MNCs during the period of 1980–96.
3. Tongrentang has a very good company website that gives detailed information on the history of the firm, how it has renovated itself to maintain competitive during different economic periods and historic turning points, http://www.tongrentong.com/en/organization.php.
4. See Cooke (2005a, Chapter 3) for further discussion on state sector reform.
5. See Cooke (2005a, Chapter 5) for further discussion on enterprise training.

6   Information Technology Industry

1. See Roseman (2005) for more detailed discussion of the telecommunication industry.
2. See Lu (2000) for a detailed account of the growth of the Chinese computer industry in the 1980s and 1990s through in-depth case studies of the then four leading Chinese-owned computer enterprises: Stone, Legend, Founder and China Great Wall Computer and an analysis of the growth of the Chinese computer market and changing patterns of market dominance. Also see Lazonick (2004) for a brief analysis of the historical and innovation profile of these four leading Chinese IT firms.
3. For example, between 1985 and 1989, the output of TVs was doubled, whereas the output of 1993 was only 40 per cent higher than that of 1990 (see Table 1.2).
4. See Linden (2004) for a more detailed account of the development of the VCD, DVD and EVD technology and market in the electronics industry in China.
5. See Fan (2006) for a more detailed analysis of the development of innovation capability of China's telecom-equipment industry.
6. See Lai *et al.* (2005) for more details of the characteristics of the four IT industrial clusters and different factors influencing their innovative capacities.
7. CNNIC was founded on 3 June 1997. It is a non-profit-making organization of administration and service (*People's Daily Online*, 22 July 2002). CNNIC had been

entrusted by the Ministry of Information Industry of China to conduct bi-annual surveys regularly on the use of the Internet in China since 1997 (see http://www.chinese-search-engine.com/china-internet-resource/china-internet-marketing.htm for more reports).

8 Acquisitions of Chinese State-Owned Enterprises by Foreign MNCs: Driving Forces, Barriers and Implications for HRM

1. It must be noted that in the last few years, there are a growing number of foreign-funded R&D activities and centres in China as an increasing number of MNCs are looking to outsource their business activities to developing countries to take advantage of their low cost and other favourable conditions (see Chapter 2).
2. Also see Luo (2004, 2006) for more detailed analyses of patterns of political behaviour and organizational corruption activities and how organizations can resist corruptions.
3. See Gordon and Li (2005) for more detail.

9 Chinese MNCs Abroad: Internationalization Strategies and Implications for HRM

1. See Liu and Li (2002) and Lin (2005) for detailed case studies of Haier's business strategy and management.
2. Only one trade union – the All-China Trade Union Federation – is recognized by the Chinese government.

10 Conclusions

1. 'Strategic groups are organizations within an industry with similar strategic character-istics, following similar strategies or competing on similar bases' (Johnson and Scholes, 2002, p. 122).
2. See Schuler et al. (2001) for detailed guides on how to plan and implement HRM to match the chosen business strategy.
3. See Francis et al. (2002) and Melewar et al. (2004) for more detailed discussion on marketing foreign brands in China.
4. Bartlett and Ghoshal (1989) classify MNCs into four categories: multi-domestic com-panies that are organized on a decentralized basis; international organizations that are organized to exploit the parent company's know-how and knowledge, with 'core competence' centralized and others decentralized (Leong and Tan, 1993); global cor-porations that treat the world market as an integrated whole and operate a tightly centralized management system with limited delegation to local subsidiaries; and transnational corporations that combine aspects of each of the first three types in order to be sensitive to local conditions, to develop competitive strategies at a global level and to generate and share knowledge throughout the corporation (Rubery and Grimshaw, 2003).

References

References in English

Accenture, 'The Innovator's Advantage – Using Innovation and Technology to Improve Business Performance: China', Accenture, Internet source: http://www.accenture.com/xdoc/en/ideas/pca/innovators/regions_china.pdf (2003).

T. Agres, 'Foundations for Chinese Pharma', *Drug Discovery & Development*, 9, 2 (2006): 16–18.

D. Ahlstrom, S. Foley, M. Young and E. Chan, 'Human Resource Strategies for Competitive Advantage in Post-WTO China', *Thunderbird International Business Review*, 47, 3 (2005): 263–85.

A. Amighini, 'China in the International Fragmentation of Production: Evidence from the ICT Industry', *The European Journal of Comparative Economics*, 2, 2 (2005): 203–19.

H. Ansoff, *Corporate Strategy: An Analytic Approach to Business Policy for Growth and Expansion* (New York: McGraw-Hill, 1965).

Asiainfo Daily China News, 'Chinese Ceramics Faces Brand Crisis', 6 August (2002), Internet source: http://proquests.umi.com, accessed on 25 January 2006.

Asian Pacific Bulletins, 10 September (2004).

AstraZeneca company website, http://en.astrazeneca.com.cn, accessed on 18 April 2005.

X. Bai and L. Bennington, 'Performance Appraisal in the Chinese State-owned Coal Industry', *International Journal of Business Performance Management*, 7, 3 (2005): 275–87.

G. Bamber, R. Lansbury and N. Wailes (eds), *International and Comparative Employment Relations: Globalisation and the Developed Market Economies* (4th edition) (London: Sage, 2004).

D. Baron, 'Private Politics, Corporate Social Responsibility, and Integrated Strategy', *Journal of Economics and Management Strategy*, 10, 1 (2001): 7–45.

J. Bartels, R. Douwes, M. de Jong and A. Pruyn, 'Organizational Identification During a Merger: Determinants of Employees' Expected Identification with the New Organization', *British Journal of Management*, 17 (2006): S49–67.

C. Bartlett and S. Ghoshal, *Managing Across Borders: The Transnational Solution* (Boston, MA: Harvard Business School Press, 1989).

C. Bartlett and S. Ghoshal, *Managing Across Borders: The Transnational Solution* (Boston, MA: Harvard Business School Press, 2000).

BBC News, 11 August (2004).

G. Becker, *Human Capital: A Theoretical and Empirical Analysis, with Special Reference to Education* (Chicago: University of Chicago Press, 1964).

Beijing Tongrentang company website, http://www.tongrentong.com/en/organization.php, accessed on 8 November 2006.

J. Benson and Y. Zhu, 'Markets, Firms and Workers in Chinese State-owned Enterprises', *Human Resource Management Journal*, 9, 4 (1999): 58–73.

P. Bernthal, J. Bondra and W. Wang, *Leadership in China: Keeping Pace with a Growing Economy* (Development Dimensions International, 2006), Internet source: http://www.ddiworld.com/pdf/ddi_leadershipinchina_rr.pdf, accessed on 25 January 2007.

I. Björkman and X. C. Fan, 'Human Resource Management and the Performance of Western Firms in China', *International Journal of Human Resource Management*, 6 (2002): 853–64.

I. Björkman and Y. Lu, 'Institutionalisation and Bargaining Power Explanations of Human Resource Management in International Joint Ventures: The Case of Chinese-Western Joint Ventures', *Organization Studies*, 22 (2001): 491–512.

M. Boisot and J. Child, 'From Fiefs to Clans and Network Capitalism: Explaining China's Merging Economic Order', *Administrative Science Quarterly*, 41 (1996): 600–28.

P. Boxall and J. Purcell, *Strategy and Human Resource Management* (Basingstoke: Palgrave Macmillan, 2003).

J. Boyarski, R. Fishman, J. Lawrence, J. Linn and T. Young, 'International Developments', *Intellectual Property & Technology Law Journal*, 13, 11 (2001): 28.

M. Branine, 'Observations on Training and Management Development in the People's Republic of China', *Personnel Review*, 25, 1 (1996): 25–39.

W. Braun and W. Warner, 'Strategic Human Resource Management in Western Multinationals in China: The Differentiation of Practices across Different Ownership Forms', *Personnel Review*, 5 (2002): 553–79.

D. Briscoe and R. Schuler, *International Human Resource Management: Policy and Practice for the Global Enterprise* (2nd edition) (London: Routledge, 2004).

G. Brown, Speech given by The Chancellor of Exchequer Gordon Brown at the Academy of Social Science, Beijing, China, 21 February (2005), Internet source: http://www.hm-treasury.gov.uk/newsroom_and_speeches/press/2005/press, accessed on 16 April 2005.

J. Brunner, A. Koh and X. G. Lou, 'Chinese Perceptions of Issues and Obstacles Confronting Joint Ventures', *Journal of Global Marketing*, 1/2 (1992): 97–127.

P. Budhwar (ed.), *Managing Human Resources in Asia-Pacific* (London: Routledge, 2004).

P. Budhwar and Y. Debrah (eds), *HRM in Developing Countries* (London: Routledge, 2001).

D. Bulcke, H. Zhang and X. Li, 'Interaction between the Business Environment and the Corporate Strategic Positioning of Firms in the Pharmaceutical Industry: A Study of the Entry and Expansion Path of MNEs into China', *Management International Review*, 39, 4 (1999): 353–77.

Business Week, 'Foreign Medicine Retailers Keep Watch', 5 January (2005), Internet source: http://www.chinadaily.com.cn/english/doc/2005-01/05/content_406179.htm, accessed on 12 April 2005.

K. Cai, 'Outward Foreign Direct Investment: A Novel Dimension of China's Integration into the Regional and Global Economy', *China Quarterly*, 160 (1999): 856–80.

S. Cartwright and C. Cooper, 'The Role of Culture Compatibility in Successful Organizational Marriage', *The Academy of Management Executive*, 2 (1993): 57–69.

M. Castells, *The Rise of the Network Society* (Oxford: Blackwell, 1996).

A. Chan, 'Globalisation, China's Free (Read Bonded) Labour Market, and the Chinese Trade Unions', in C. Rowley and J. Benson (eds), *Globalisation and Labour in the Asia Pacific Region* (London: Frank Cass, 2000, pp. 260–81).

A. Chan, *China's Workers Under Assault: The Exploitation of Labour in a Globalising Economy* (New York: M. E. Sharpe, 2001).

A. Chandler, *Strategy and Structure* (Cambridge, MA: MIT Press, 1962).

B. Chen, 'Studying Abroad', *China Scholars Abroad*, 9 (2005): 12–13.

J. Chen, *Corporate Governance in China* (London: Routledge, 2004).

R. Chen, 'Corporate Reputation: Pricing and Competing in Chinese Markets – Strategies for Multinationals', *The Journal of Business Strategy*, 25, 6 (2004): 45–50.

J. Child, 'Organizational Structure, Environment and Performance: The Role of Strategic Choice', *Sociology*, 6, 3 (1972): 1–22.

J. Child, *Management in China during the Age of Reform* (Cambridge: Cambridge University Press, 1994).

J. Child (ed.), 'China and International Business', *Oxford Handbook of International Business*, Oxford Scholarship Online, 1, 29 (2001): 681–716.

J. Child and D. Faulkner, *Strategies of Co-operation: Managing Alliances, Networks and Joint Ventures* (Oxford: Oxford University Press, 1998).

J. Child and S. Heavens, 'Managing Corporate Networks from America to China', in M. Warner (ed.), *China's Managerial Revolution* (London: Frank Cass, 1999, pp. 147–80).

J. Child and D. Tse, 'China's Transition and Its Implications for International Business', *Journal of International Business Studies*, 32, 1 (2001): 5–21.

China.org.cn, Internet source: http://www.china.org.cn/english/features/beijing/30837.htm, accessed on 18 November 2006.

China Daily Online, 31 August (2002), Internet source: http://www.china.org.cn/english/scitech/41026.htm, accessed on 1 April 2006.

China Daily Online (2004a), 'Vulnerability behind Auto Boom', Internet source: http://www.chinadaily.com.cn/english/doc/2004-06/01/content_335573.htm, accessed on 23 May 2005.

China Daily Online (2004b), 'China Close to World Level in Auto-part', Internet source: http://www.chinadaily.com.cn/english/doc/2004-06/01/content_335575.htm, accessed on 23 May 2005.

China Daily Online (2004c), 'New Auto Industry Rules State JV Guidelines', Internet source: http://www.chinadaily.com.cn/english/doc/2004-06/02/content_335759.htm, accessed on 23 May 2005.

China Daily Online, 22 June (2004), Internet source: http://www.chinadaily.com.cn/english/doc/2004-06/22, accessed on 17 June 2005.

China Daily Online, 1 March (2005), Internet source: http://www.chinadaily.com.cn/english/doc/2005-03/01, accessed on 1 April 2006.

China Daily Online, 7 June (2005), Internet source: http://www.beijingportal.com.cn/7838/2005/06/07/1820@2666683.htm, accessed on 19 June 2005.

China Economic Net, 13 September (2004), 'Well-known Brands in China are Pre-emptively Registered Abroad', Internet source: http://en-1.ce.cn/main/insight/200409/13/t20040913_1804619.shtml, accessed on 19 June 2005.

China Economic Net, 18 May (2005), 'China Could Forge its Own Auto Brands Through International Cooperation, SAIC President', Internet source: http://en-1.ce.cn/Industries/Auto/200505/18/t20050518_3864051.shtml, accessed on 19 June 2005.

China Internet Network Information Centre (CNNIC) (2005), 'The 15th Statistical Survey Report on the Internet Development in China', Internet source: http://www.chinese-search-engine.com/china-Internet-resource/china-Internet-marketing.htm, accessed on 31 March 2006.

China Legal News, November (2003), pp. 15–19, Internet source: http://www.tk-diplom.de/header_defaultmasterborder.html, accessed on 2 April 2004.

China Online, 'Overseas Exhibition Firms Intensify Competition', 7 January (2002): 1–2.

China Software Industry Association, 'Industry News' (2005), Internet source: http://www.csia.org.cn/chinese_en/index/index.htm, accessed on 25 March 2006.

ChinaToday.com, 18 November (2006), Internet source: http://www.chinatoday.com/, accessed on 18 November 2006.

T. Clark and G. Mallory, 'The Cultural Relativity of Human Resource Management: Is There a Universal Model?' in T. Clark (ed.), *European Human Resource Management* (Oxford: Blackwell, 1996, pp. 1–33).

D. Clarke, 'Corporate Governance in China: An Overview', *China Economic Review*, 14, 4 (2003): 494–507.

F. L. Cooke, 'Ownership Change and the Reshaping of Employment Relations in China: A Study of Two Manufacturing Companies', *Journal of Industrial Relations*, 1 (2002): 19–39.

F. L. Cooke, 'Seven Reforms in Five Decades: Civil Service Reform and Its Human Resource Implications in China', *Journal of Asia Pacific Economy*, 3 (2003): 381–405.

F. L. Cooke, 'Foreign Firms in China: Modelling HRM in a Toy Manufacturing Corporation', *Human Resource Management Journal*, 14, 3 (2004): 31–52.

F. L. Cooke, *HRM, Work and Employment in China* (London: Routledge, 2005a).

F. L. Cooke, 'Employment Relations in Small Commercial Businesses in China', *Industrial Relations Journal*, 36, 1 (2005b): 19–37.

F. L. Cooke, 'Acquisitions of Chinese State-owned Enterprises by MNCs: Driving Forces, Barriers and Implications for HRM', *British Journal of Management*, 17, 1 (2006): S105–21.

F. L. Cooke, 'Competition and Strategy of Chinese Firms: An Analysis of Top Performing Chinese Private Enterprises', *Competitiveness Review*, 18, 1 & 2 (2008).

F. L. Cooke, 'The Dynamics of Employment Relations in China: An Evaluation of the Rising Level of Labour Disputes', *Journal of Industrial Relations*, 50, 1 (2008).

F. L. Cooke and R. Prouska, 'HR Outsourcing and Challenges to the HR profession', *The Human Factor*, May–July (2006): 19–25.

CorpWatch, 'China: Corporate Social Responsibility' (2005), Internet source: http://www. corpowatch.org/article.php?id=12317, accessed on 1 April 2006.

Council for the Promotion of International Trade, *China: Supply and Demand Survey on Automotive Components*, South-South Trade Promotion Programme (Beijing, 2002).

Courland Automotive Practice, 'The Industry Turns the Corner', *Automotive Matters*, 7 (2004), Internet source: http://www.courland.com/news/cap_am07.pdf, accessed on 20 April 2005.

S. Curtin, 'The Dragon Invests in Japan' (2004), Internet source: *Asia Times Online* http://www.atimes.com/atimes/South_Asia, accessed on 15 March 2005.

G. Davies, R. Chun, R. V. da Silva and S. Roper, *Corporate Reputation and Competitiveness* (London: Routledge, 2003).

H. Davies and P. Ellis, 'Porters' Competitive Advantage of Nations: Time for the Final Judgement?' *Journal of Management Studies*, 37, 8 (2000): 1189–213.

A. De Meyer and S. Garg, *Inspire to Innovate: Management and Innovation in Asia* (Basingstoke: Palgrave Macmillan, 2005).

Deloitte, 'More Chinese Companies Embracing New Business Strategies to Build Competitive Strength in Post-WTO China', Deloitte Touch Tohmatsu shanghai, CPA Ltd – (China) (2004), Internet source: http://www.deloitte.com/dtt/press_release, accessed on 15 March 2005.

A. Dicks, 'The Chinese Legal System: Reforms in the Balance', *The China Quarterly*, 119 (1989): 541–76.

D. Ding, D. Fields and S. Akhtar, 'An Empirical Study of Human Resource Management Policies and Practices in Foreign-invested Enterprises in China: The Case of Shenzhen Special Economic Zone', *International Journal of Human Resource Management*, 8, 5 (1997): 595–613.

D. Ding, K. Goodall and M. Warner, 'The Impact of Economic Reform on the Role of Trade Unions in Chinese Enterprises', *International Journal of Human Resource Management*, 13, 3 (2002): 431–49.

J. L. Dong and J. Hu, 'Mergers and Acquisitions in China', *Economic Review – Federal Reserve Bank of Atlanta*, Nov/Dec, 6 (1995): 15–29.

P. Drucker, 'The Coming of the New Organization', *Harvard Business Review*, January–February (1988): 45–53.

P. Drucker, *The New Realities* (Oxford: Heinemann, 1989).

J. Dunning, 'Internationalising Porter's Diamond', *Management International Review*, 2 (1993): 7–15.

J. Dunning, 'Re-appraising the Eclectic Paradigm in an Age of Alliance Capitalism', *Journal of International Business Studies*, 26, 3 (1995): 461–91.

J. Dunning and R. Narula, *Multinationals and Industrial Competitiveness: A New Agenda* (Cheltenham: Edward Elgar, 2004).

Economic Information and Agency, 24 February (2003), Internet source: http://www. tdctrade.com/report/mkt/mkt_030202.htm, accessed on 2 April 2004.

T. Edwards, 'The Transfer of Employment Practices across Borders in Multinational Companies', in A. Harzing and J. Ruysseveldt (eds), *International Human Resource Management* (London: Sage, 2004, pp. 389–410).

T. Edwards and C. Rees, 'The Internationalisation of the Firms', in T. Edwards and C. Rees (eds), *International Human Resource Management: Globalisation, National Systems and Multinational Companies* (London: Prentice Hall Financial Times, 2006, pp. 45–65).

M. Elvira and A. Davila, *Managing Human Resources in Latin America* (London: Routledge, 2005).

J. Eun and K. Lee, 'Is an Industrial Policy Possible in China?: The Case of the Automotive Industry', *Journal of International and Area Studies*, 9, 2 (2002): 1–21.

P. Evans, V. Pucik and J-L. Barsoux, *The Global Challenges: Frameworks for International Human Resource Management* (New York: McGraw-Hill, 2002).

P. Fan, 'Catching up through Developing Innovation Capability: Evidence from China's Telecom-Equipment Industry', *Technovation*, 26 (2006): 359–68.

Y. Fan, 'Made in China', *Brand Strategy*, April (2005): 30–1.

FDI Magazine, 'China's FDI merry-go-round', 2 April (2003), Internet source: http://www.fdimagazine.com/news, accessed on 14 April 2005.

FDI Magazine, 'Show Me the Money', 4 August (2003), Internet source: http://www.fdimagazine.com/news, accessed on 14 April 2005.

A. Ferner and J. Quintanilla, 'Multinationals, National Business Systems and HRM: The Enduring Influence of National Identity or a Process of "Anglo-Saxonization"', *International Journal of Human Resource Management*, 9, 4 (1998): 710–31.

Fiducia Management Consultants, 'Research & Development Trends in China', Internet source: http://www.fiducia-china.com/Information/Newsletter/2311-1600.html (2004a), accessed on 10 December 2004.

Fiducia Management Consultants, 'Local Famous Brands in China', Internet source: http://www.fiducia-china.com/Information/Newsletter/2311-1602.html (2004b), accessed on 10 December 2004.

Fiducia Management Consultants, 'International Companies Continue to Enlarge Their China's Operation' (2004c), Internet source: http://www.fiducia-china.com/News/2004/73-1840.html, accessed on 10 December 2004.

A. Fletcher, 'Chinese Firms Tapping into Potential of EU Market', 17 February (2005), Internet source: http://www.foodanddrinkeurope.com/news, accessed on 20 March 2005.

M. Forney, 'China's going-Out Party', *Time Asia* (2005), Internet source: http://www.time.com/time/asia/magazine, accessed on 20 March 2005.

J. Francis, J. Lam and J. Walls, 'The Impact of Linguistic Differences on International Brand Name Standardisation: A Comparison of English and Chinese Brand Names of *Fortune*-500 Companies', *Journal of International Marketing*, 10, 1 (2002): 98–116.

J. Francois and D. Spinanger, 'Regulated Efficiency, World Trade Organization Accession, and the Motor Vehicle Sector in China', *The World Bank Economic Review*, 18, 1 (2004): 85–104.

J. Freeman, 'Business Strategy from the Population Level', in C. Mantgomery (ed.), *Resource-Based and Evolutionary Theories of the Firm: Towards a synthesis* (Boston, MA: Kluwer, 1995, pp. 219–50).

R. Freeman, *Strategic Management: A Stakeholder Approach* (Boston: Pitman, 1984).

P. French, 'Making a Mark: The Challenge of Branding in China', *EuroBiz Magazine*, September (2003), Internet source: http://www.sinomedia.net/eurobiz/v200309/story0309.html, accessed on 19 June 2005.

S. Frenkel and D. Peetz, 'Regional Studies of Comparative International Industrial Relations, Globalisation and Industrial relations in East Asia: A Three-Country Comparison', *Industrial Relations*, 3 (1998): 282–310.

M. Friedman, 'The Social Responsibility of Business Is to Increase Its profits', reprint of 1973 article in G. Chryssides and J. Kaler (eds), *An Introduction to Business Ethics* (London: Chapman and Hall, 1993, pp. 249–54).

T. Frost, 'The Geographic Sources of Foreign Subsidiaries' Innovations', *Strategic Management Journal*, 22, 2 (2001): 101–23.

H. Fuchs, 'Fareast Goes West – New Opportunities for Asian Brands in Europe', *Asia Pacific Journal of Marketing and Logistics*, 15, 3 (2003): 20–33.

M. Gallagher, *Contagious Capitalism: Globalisation and the Politics of Labour in China* (Princeton: Princeton University Press, 2005).

J. Gamble, 'The Rhetoric of the Consumer and Customer Control in China', *Work, Employment and Society*, 21, 1 (2007): 7–25.

L. Gan, 'Globalisation of the Automobile Industry in China: Dynamics and Barriers in Greening of the Road Transportation', *Energy Policy*, 31 (2003): 537–51.

R. Garnaut and Y. P. Huang, *Growth without Miracles – Readings on the Chinese Economy in the Era of Reform* (Oxford: Oxford University Press, 2001).

A. Goldstein, 'The Political Economy of Industrial Policy in China: The Case of Aircraft Manufacturing', *The William Davidson Institute Working Paper* No. 779 (2005).

R. Gordon and W. Li, 'Taxation and Economic Growth in China', in Y. Kwan and E. Yu (eds), *Critical Issues in China's Growth and Development* (Aldershot: Ashgate, 2005, pp. 22–40).

C. Grace, *The Effect of Changing Intellectual Property on Pharmaceutical Industry Prospects in India and China: Considerations for Access to Medicines* (London: DIFD Health Systems Resource Centre, June 2004).

R. Grant, *Contemporary Strategy Analysis* (6th edition) (Malden, MA: Blackwell Publishing, 2008).

Greater London Authority, *Enter the Dragon: An Analysis of Chinese FDI into London* (London: London Development Agency, 2004).

E. Gu, 'Foreign Direct Investment and the Restructuring of Chinese State-Owned Enterprises (1992–1995): A New Institutionalist Perspective', *China Information*, 3 (1997): 46–71.

D. Guthrie, *Dragon in a Three-Piece Suit: The Emergence of Capitalism in China* (Princeton, NJ: Princeton University Press, 1999).

G. Hamel and C. Prahalad, 'Strategy as Stretch and Leverage', *Harvard Business Review*, 71, 2 (1993): 75–84.

A. Harzing, 'Strategy and Structure of Multinational Companies', in A. Harzing and J. Ruysseveldt (eds), *International Human Resource Management* (London: Sage, 2004, pp. 33–64).

A. Harzing and J. Ruysseveldt (eds), *International Human Resource Management* (London: Sage, 2004).

J. Hassard, J. Sheehan, M. Zhou, J. Terpstra-Tong and J. Morris, *China's State Enterprise Reform: from Marx to the Market* (London: Routledge, 2007).

P. Hempel and C. Chang, 'Reconciling Traditional Chinese Management with High-tech Taiwan', *Human Resource Management*, 12, 1 (2002): 77–95.

A. Hermawan, *Analysing Variations in Employee Empowerment in Indonesia*, Unpublished PhD thesis (University of Manchester, UK, 2005).

Hill and Knowlton, *China Corporate Reputation Watch Survey* (2004), Internet source: http://hillandknowlton.com/crw, accessed on 2 August 2005.

A. Hillman and G. Keim, 'Shareholder Value, Stakeholder Management, and Social Issues: What's the Bottom Line?' *Strategic Management Journal*, 22, 2 (2001): 125–39.

D. Ho, 'Can China's Heritage Brands Be Saved?' Brandchannel.com (2005), Internet source: http://www.brandchannel.com/print_page.asp?ar_id=109&section=brandspeak, accessed on 19 June 2005.

J. Hoffe, K. Lane and V. Nam, 'Branding Cars in China', *McKinsey Quarterly*, 4 (2003): 14–7.

B. Hofman, 'Issues for China's Eleventh Five-Year Plan', Stanford Center for International Development Conference on: China's Policy Reforms: Progress and Challenges (2005), Internet source: http://scid.stanford.edu/events/china2005/hofman.pdf, accessed on 23 March 2006.

R. Hoskisson and M. Hitt, 'Antecedents and Performance Outcomes of Diversification: A Review and Critique of Theoretical Perspectives', *Journal of Management*, 16 (1990): 461–509.

R. Hoskisson, L. Eden, C. Lau and M. Wright, 'Strategy in Emerging Economies', *Academy of Management Journal*, 43, 3 (2000): 249–67.

J. Howell, 'Trade Unions in China: The Challenge of Foreign Capital', in G. O'Leary (ed.), *Adjusting to Capitalism: Chinese Workers and the State* (New York: M. E. Sharpe, 1998, pp. 150–72).

http://en.wikipedia.org/wiki/Huawei, 'Huawei', accessed on 1 April 2006.

http://www.accessasia.co.uk, accessed on 10 March 2006.

http://www.edu.cn/20011102/3007992.shtml, 'Hi-tech Industry Most Vigorous, a Strategic Task for China: Official', accessed on 14 April 2005.

http://www.expo2010china.com/expo/expoenglish/oe/es/userobject1ai35588.html, accessed on 23 June 2007.

http://www.expo2010china.com/expo/shexpo/sbrc/rcxx/userobject1ai41859.html, accessed on 23 June 2007.

http://www.invest.uktradeinvest.gov.uk/asiapacific/site_chi, accessed on 14 April 2005.

http://www.nanqi.com.cn, Nanjing Automobile (Group) Corporation website, accessed on 23 June 2007.

http://www.naukri.com/gpw/huawei, 'About Huawei', accessed on 1 April 2006.

http://www.trp.hku.hk/infofile/2002/10-5-yr-plan.pdf, 'China: Summary of the Tenth Five-Year Plan (2001–2005) – Information Industry', accessed on 23 March 2006.

http://www.wal-martchina.com/english/news/20041102.htm, 'Wal-Mart Donating US$1 Million to Establish Tsinghua University China Retail Research Centre', accessed on 15 April 2005.

C. Huang, C. Amorim, M. Spinoglio, B. Gouveia and A. Medina, 'Organization, Programme and Structure: An Analysis of the Chinese Innovation Policy Framework', *R&D Management*, 34, 4 (2004): 367–87.

N. Hubbard, *Acquisition Strategy and Implementation* (Basingstoke: Palgrave Macmillan, 1999).

N. Hubbard and J. Purcell, 'Managing Employee Expectations during Acquisitions', *Human Resource Management Journal*, 2 (2001): 17–33.

S. Ilari and A. Grange, 'Transferring Ownership-Specific Advantages to a Joint Venture in China', in M. Warner (ed.), *China's Managerial Revolution* (London: Frank Cass, 1999, pp. 119–46).

A. Inkpen and P. Beamish, 'Knowledge, Bargaining Power, and the Instability of International Joint Ventures', *Academy of Management Review*, 22 (1997): 177–202.

Invest in Germany: Newsletter, 'FDI Special: Why do the Chinese Invest Abroad?' 15 March (2004), Internet source: http://www.invest-in-germany.de/en/news/newsletter, accessed on 15 March 2005.

L. Jarvis, 'Pharma Mulls Strategy in China', *Chemical Market Reporter*, 18 December (2005): 32–3.

H. P. Jia, 'Pharmaceutical Giants Outsourcing R&D', *Business Week*, 24 September (2004), Internet source: http://chinadaily.com.cn/english/doc/2004-09/28/content_378977.htm, accessed on 1 April 2006.

G. Johnson and K. Scholes, *Exploring Corporate Strategy: Text and Cases* (6th edition) (Harlow: Pearson Education Ltd, 2002).

A. Kambil and P. Lee, 'United Kingdom: Changing China – Will China's Technology Standards Reshape Your Industry?' Deloitte (2004), Internet source: http://www.mondaq.com, accessed 15 March 2005.

R. Kanter, 'The New Managerial Work', *Harvard Business Review*, November–December (1989): 85–92.

M. Katsuno, 'Status and Overview of Official ICT Indicators for China', *OECD Science, Technology and Industry Working Papers* 2005/4 (Paris: OECD Publishing, 2005).

T. Khanna and K. Palepu, 'Why Focused Strategies May Be Wrong for Emerging Markets', *Harvard Business Review*, July–August (1997): 41–51.

M. Korczynski, *Human Resource Management in Service Work* (New York: Palgrave, 2002).

P. Kotler, V. Wong, J. Saunders and G. Armstrong, *Principles of Marketing* (4th European Edition) (London: Prentice Hall, 2005).

J. Kracht, 'Mergers and Acquisition in China: A New Generation of Investment Opportunities', *China*, July–August GC.comm (2002): 15–17.

K. Kraemer and J. Dedrick, 'Creating Computer Industry Giant: China's Industrial Policies and Outcomes in the 1990s', China PC paper for web-june-01.doc., Center for Research on Information Technology and Organizations, University of California, USA (2001).

B. Krug and H. Hendrischke (eds), *China in the 21st Century: Economic and Business Behaviour* (Cheltenham: Edward Elgar, 2007).

H. Lai, Y. Chiu and H. Leu, 'Innovation Capacity Comparison of China's Information Technology Industrial Clusters: The Case of Shanghai, Kunshan, Shenzhen and Dongguan', *Technology Analysis and Strategic Management*, 17, 3 (2005): 293–315.

P. Lasserre and P. S. Ching, 'Human Resource Management in China and the Localisation Challenge', *Journal of Asian Business*, 13 (1997): 85–99.

P. Lasserre and H. Schütte, *Strategies for Asia Pacific: Meeting New Challenges* (3rd edition) (Basingstoke: Palgrave Macmillan, 2006).

C. Lau, H. Ngo and C. Chow, 'Private Businesses in China: Emerging Environment and Managerial Behaviour', in L. Kelley and Y. Luo (eds), *China 2000: Emerging Business Issues* (London: Sage Publications, 1999, pp. 25–47).

W. Lazonick, 'Indigenous Innovation and Economic Development: Lessons from China's Leap into the Information Age', *Industry and Innovation*, 11, 4 (2004): 273–97.

C. K. Lee, *Working in China: Ethnographies of Labor and Workplace Transformation* (London: Routledge, 2007).

J. Legewie, 'Control and Co-ordination of Japanese Subsidiaries in China: Problems of an Expatriate-Based Management System', *International Journal of Human Resource Management*, 6 (2002): 901–19.

Lenovo company website, http://www.lenovogrp.com/cgi-bin, accessed on 14 June 2005.

D. Leonard-Barton, *Wellsprings of Knowledge: Building and Sustaining Sources of Innovation* (Boston, MA: Harvard University Press, 1995).

S. Leong and C. Tan, 'Managing across Borders: An Empirical Test of the Bartlett and Ghoshall (1989) Organizational Typology', *Journal of International Business Studies*, 24 (1993): 449–64.

K. Leung, Z. Wang and P. Smith, 'Job Attitudes and Organizational Justice in Joint Venture Hotels in China: The Role of Expatriate Managers', *International Journal of Human Resource Management*, 6 (2001): 926–45.

M. Levine, *Worker Rights and Labour Standards in Asia's Four New Tigers: A Comparative Perspective* (New York: Plenum Press, 1997).

C. L. Li, 'New Developments in China's Pharmaceutical Regulatory Regime', *Journal of Commercial Biotechnology*, 8, 3 (2002): 241–8.

D. Li, J. Davis and L. Wang, 'Industrialization and the Sustainability of China's Agriculture', *Economics and Planning*, 31 (1998): 213–30.

M. Li and Y. Wong, 'Diversification and Economic Performance: An Empirical Assessment of Chinese Firms', *Asia Pacific Journal of Management*, 20, 2 (2003): 243–65.

M. Li and H. Zhou, 'Knowing the Business Environment: The Use of Non-Market-Based Strategies in Chinese Local Firms', *Ivey Business Journal*, Nov/Dec (2005): 1–5.

P. Y. Li, 'Importance of Foreign Direct Investment by Developing Countries' (2000), Internet source: http://www.tcf.or.jp/data/20000512_Peiyu_Li.pdf, accessed on 15 March 2005.

S. F. Lin, *Management of Knowledge Workers in the High-Tech Industry in Taiwan*: Unpublished PhD thesis (Cardiff University, UK, 2006).

G. Linden, 'China Standard Time: A Study in Strategic Industrial Policy', *Business and Politics*, 6, 3 (2004): 1–26, electronic version produced by The Berkeley Electronic Press (2005), Internet source: http://www.bepress.com/bap/vol6/iss3/art4.

N. Lindholm, 'Performance Management in MNC Subsidiaries in China: A Study of Host-Country Managers and Professionals', *Asia Pacific Journal of Human Resources*, 37, 3 (1999): 18–35.

H. Liu and K. Li, 'Strategic Implications of Emerging Chinese Multinationals: The Haier Case Study', *European Management Journal*, 20, 6 (2002): 699–706.

J. Liu and W. Jiang, 'Exhibition Sector on Right Track', *China Daily* (North American Edition), 11 January (2005), Internet source: http://proquest.umi.com/pqdweb?did=776939651&sid=7&Fmt=3&clientld=44986&RQT=309&VName=PQD, accessed on 17 April 2006.

Q. Lu, *China's Leap into the Information Age: Innovation and Organization in the Computer Industry* (Oxford: Oxford University Press, 2000).

S. Lubman, 'Introduction: The Future of Chinese Law', *The China Quarterly*, 141 (1995): 1–21.

R. Lucas, 'On the Mechanics of Economic Development', *Journal of Monetary Economics*, 32 (1988): 3–42.

Y. Luo, 'Business Strategy, Market Structure, and Performance of International Joint Ventures: The Case of Joint Ventures in China', *Management International Review*, 35, 3 (1995): 241–45.

Y. Luo, 'Partner Selection and Venturing Success: The Case of Joint Ventures with Firms in the People's Republic of China', *Organization Science*, 8 (1997): 648–62.

Y. Luo, *Multinational Corporations in China: Benefiting from Structural Transformation* (Copenhagen: Copenhagen Business School Press, 2000a).

Y. Luo, *How to Enter China: Choices and Lessons* (Ann Arbor, MI: University of Michigan Press, 2000b).

Y. Luo, *Partnering with Chinese Firms: Lessons for International Managers* (Aldershot: Ashgate Publishing Ltd, 2000c).

Y. Luo, *China's Service Sector: A New Battlefield for International Corporations* (Copenhagen: Copenhagen Business School Press, 2001).

Y. Luo, *Multinational Enterprises in Emerging Markets* (Copenhagen: Copenhagen Business School Press, 2002).

Y. Luo, 'An Organizational Perspective of Corruption', *Management and Organization Review*, 1, 1 (2004): 119–54.

Y. Luo, 'Political Behaviour, Social Responsibility, and Perceived Corruption: A structuration Perspective', *Journal of International Business Studies*, 37, 6 (2006): 747–66.

Y. Luo and M. Peng, 'Learning to Compete in a Transition Economy: Experience, Environment, and Performance', *Journal of International Business Studies*, 30, 2 (1999): 269–96.

J. Lyengar, 'India Pulls Welcome Mat from Chinese Investors', *Asia Times Online* (2003), Internet source: http://www.atimes.com/atimes/South_Asia, accessed on 15 March 2005.

S. Makino, C. Lau and R. Yeh, 'Asset-Exploitation Versus Asset-seeking: Implications for Location Choice of Foreign Direct Investment from Newly Industrialised Economies', *Journal of International Business Studies*, 33, 3 (2002): 403–21.

M. Marchington and A. Wilkinson, 'Direct Participation and Involvement', in S. Bach (ed.), *Managing Human Resources: Personnel Management in Transition* (4th edition) (Oxford: Blackwell, 2005, pp. 398–423).

M. Marks and P. Mirvis, 'Merging Human Resources: A Review of Current Research', *Merger and Acquisitions*, 2 (1982): 38–44.

A. McWilliams and D. Siegel, 'Corporate Social Responsibility: A Theory of the Firm Perspective', *Academy of Management Review*, 26, 1 (2001): 117–27.

T. Melewar, M. Meadows, W. Zheng and R. Richards, 'The Influence of Culture on Branding in the Chinese Market: A Brief Insight', *Journal of Brand Management*, 11, 6 (2004): 449–61.

P. Meschi and J. Hubler, 'Franco-Chinese Joint Venture Formation and Shareholder Wealth', *Asia Pacific Journal of Management*, 20 (2003): 91–111.

R. Miles and C. Snow, *Organizational Strategy, Structure and Process* (New York: McGraw-Hill, 1978).

P. Miller, 'IKEA with Chinese Characteristics', *The China Business Review*, 31, 4 (2004): 36–8.

H. Mintzberg, B. Ahlstrand and J. Lampel, *Strategy Safari: A Guided Tour through the Wilds of Strategic Management* (New York: The Free Press, 1998).

J. Morris, J. Sheehan and J. Hassard, 'From Dependency to Defiance? Work-unit Relationships in China's State Enterprise Reform', *Journal of Management Studies*, 38 (2001): 697–718.

E. Morrison and S. Robinson, 'When Employees Feel Betrayed: A Model of How Psychological Contract Violation Develops', *Academy of Management Review*, 1 (1997): 226–56.

Motorola Inc., 'Motorola Opens R&D Centre in Hangzhou, China' (2006), Internet source: http://www.webwire.com/ViewPressRel.asp?SESSIONID=&aId=11583, accessed on 6 April 2006.

S. H. Ng and M. Warner, *China's Trade Unions and Management* (London: Macmillan, 1998).

P. Ngai, *Made in China* (Durham: Duke University Press, 2005).

I. Nikandrou, N. Papalaxandris and D. Bourantas, 'Gaining Employee Trust after Acquisition: Implications for Managerial Action', *Employee Relations*, 4 (2000): 334–45.

P. Nolan, *China and the Global Economy* (London: Palgrave, 2001).

P. Nolan, 'China and the Global Business Revolution', *Cambridge Journal of Economics*, 26 (2002): 119–37.

P. Nolan, *Transforming China: Globalisation, Transition and Development* (London: Anthem Press, 2004).

I. Nonaka and H. Takeuchi, *The Knowledge-Creating Company* (New York: Oxford University Press, 1995).

I. Nonaka and D. Teece (eds), *Managing Industrial Knowledge: Creation, Transfer and Utilisation* (London: Sage Publications, 2001).

D. Normile, 'Chinese Telecom Companies Come Calling' (2005), Internet source: http://www.reed-electronics.com/eb-mag, accessed on 15 March 2005.

OECD, *Technology and the Economy: The Key Relationships* (Parris: Organization for Economic Co-Operation and Development, 1992).

OECD Observer, 'Chinese innovation' (2003), Internet source: http://www.oecdobserver.org/news/printpage.php/aid/967/Chinese_innovation.html, accessed on 6 April 2006.

C. Oliver, 'Sustainable Competitive Advantage, Combining Institutional and Resource-based Views', *Strategic Management Journal*, 18 (1997): 697–713.

Organization Internationale des Constructeurs d'Automobiles (OICA), *OICA Statistics 2004* (2005), Internet source: http://www.oica.net/htdocs/statistics/tableaux2004/statistics_2004.htm, accessed on 25 March 2006.

J. Paauwe and P. Dewe, 'Human Resource Management in Multinational Corporations: Theories and Models', in A. Harzing and J. Ruysseveldt (eds), *International Human Resource Management: An Integrated Approach* (London: Sage Publications, 1995, pp. 75–98).

K. Parris, 'The Rise of Private Business Interests', in M. Goldman and R. MacFarquhar (eds), *The Paradox of China's Post-Mao Reforms* (Cambridge, MA: Harvard University Press, 1999).

M. Peng, 'How Entrepreneurs Create Wealth in Transition Economies', *Academy of Management Executive*, 15, 1 (2001): 95–108.

M. Peng, Y. Luo and L. Sun, 'Firm Growth via Mergers and Acquisitions in China', in L. Kelley and Y. Luo (eds), *China 2000: Emerging Business Issues* (London: Sage Publications, 1999, pp. 73–100).

M. Peng, J. Tan and T. Tong, 'Ownership Types and Strategic Groups in an Emerging Economy', *Journal of Management Studies*, 41, 7 (2004): 1105–29.

People's Daily Online, 22 July 2002, Internet source: http://english.people.com.cn/200207/22/eng20020722_100150.shtml, accessed on 31 March 2006.

People's Daily Online, 26 July 2004, 'Efficiency, Quality and Innovation: Before China Becomes World's Plant', Internet source: http://english.people.com.cn/200407/26/eng20040726_150799.html, accessed on 6 April 2006.

People's Daily Online, 26 October 2005, Internet source: http://english.people.com.cn/200510/26/eng20051026_216818.html, accessed on 18 November 2006.

People's Daily Online, 13 August 2006, Internet source: http://english.people.com.cn/200608/19/eng20060819_294782.html, accessed on 1 February 2007.

D. Perkins, 'Industrial and Financial Policy in China and Vietnam: A New Model or a Replay of the East Asian experience?' in J. Stiglitz and S. Yusuf (eds), *Rethinking the East Asia Miracle* (The World Bank, 2001).

T. Peters, *Thriving on Chaos* (London: Pan, 1989).

J. Pfeffer, *The Human Equation: Building Profits by Putting People First* (Boston, MA: Harvard Business School Press, 1998).

R. Pomfret, *Investing in China: Ten years of the Open Door Policy* (Ames: Iowa State University Press, 1991).

M. Porter, *Competitive Strategy* (US: Free Press, 1980).

M. Porter, *The Competitive Advantage of Nations* (Basingstoke: Palgrave Macmillan, 1990).

W. Powell, K. Koput and L. Smith-Doerr, 'Interorganizational Collaboration and the Locus of Innovation: Networks of Learning in Biotechnology', *Administrative Science Quarterly* 41, 1 (1996): 116–45.

C. K. Prahalad and G. Hamel, 'The Core Competence of the Corporation', *Harvard Business Review*, May–June (1990): 79–91.

PricewaterhouseCoopers, 'Mainland China Leads in Asia as Country with Most Growth Potential for Retail and Consumer' (2003), Internet source: http://www.pwc.com/extweb/ncpressrelease.nsf/docid/7F540C363EC766DC85256CC2004C71B5, accessed on 15 April 2005.

V. Pucik, 'Strategic Alliances with Japanese: Implications for Human Resource Management', in F. J. Contractor and P. Lorange (eds), *Co-operative Strategies in International Business* (New York: Lexington Books, 1988, pp. 487–98).

J. Purcell, 'The Meaning of Strategy in Human Resource Management', in J. Storey (ed.), *Human Resource Management: A Critical Text* (London: Thomson Learning, 2001, pp. 59–77).

M. Rajan, 'Chinese Pharmaceutical Industry Estimated at US$19.4 billion in 2002' (1998), Internet source: http://www.bccresearch.com/editors/RB-123.html, accessed on 18 March 2005.

D. Ralston, D. Holt, R. Terpstra and Y. K. Cheng, 'The Impact of National Culture and Economic Ideology on Managerial Work Values: A Study of the United States, Russia, Japan and China', *Journal of International Business Studies*, 28, 1 (1997): 177–207.

R. Reich, 'Who Is Us?' *Harvard Business Review*, January–February (1991): 53–64.

S. Robinson and D. Rousseau, 'Violating the Psychological Contract: Not the Exception but the Norm', *Journal of Organizational Behaviour*, 2 (1994): 245–59.

P. Rodriguez, D. Siegel, A. Hillman and L. Eden, 'Three Lenses on the Multinational Enterprise: Politics, Corruption, and Corporate Social Responsibility', *Journal of International Business Studies*, 37, 6 (2006): 733–46.

Roland Berger Strategy Consultants, 'From Middle Kingdom to Global Market: Expansion Strategies and Success Factors for China's Emerging Multinationals' (2003), Internet source: http://www.rolandberger.com/pdf/rb_press/public/RB_from_middle_kingdom_2_global_market_20030818.pdf, accessed on 15 April 2005.

P. Romer, 'Human Capital and Growth: Theory and Evidence', *Carnegie-Rochester Conference Series on Public Policy*, 32 (1990): 251–86.

D. Roseman, 'The WTO and Telecommunications Services in China: Three Years on', *Info: the Journal of Policy, Regulation and Strategy for Telecommunications*, 7, 2 (2005): 25–48.

P. Rosenzweig and N. Nohria, 'Influences on Human Resource Management Practices in Multinational Corporations', *Journal of International Business Studies*, 25, 2 (1994): 229–51.

J. Rubery and D. Grimshaw, *The Organization of Employment: An International Perspective* (Basingstoke: Palgrave Macmillan, 2003).

T. Saich, *Governance and Politics of China* (Basingstoke: Palgrave Macmillan, 2001).

A. Salama, H. Holland and G. Vinten, 'Challenges and Opportunities in Mergers and Acquisitions: Three International Case Studies – Deutsche Bank-Bankers Trust; British Petroleum-Amoco; Ford-Volvo', *Journal of European Industrial Training*, 6 (2003): 313–21.

M. Schraeder and D. Self, 'Enhancing the Success of Mergers and Acquisitions: An Organizational Culture Perspective', *Management Decision*, 5 (2003): 511–22.

R. Schuler, 'Human Resource Issues and Activities in International Joint Ventures', *International Journal of Human Resource Management*, 1 (2001): 1–52.

R. Schuler, R. Jackson and J. Storey, 'HRM and Its Links with Strategic Management', in J. Storey (ed.), *Human Resource Management: A Critical Text* (London: Thomson Learning, 2001, pp. 114–30).

R. Schuler and S. Jackson, 'HR Issues and Activities in Mergers and Acquisitions', *European Management Journal*, 3 (2001): 239–53.

R. Schuler, S. Jackson and Y. Luo, *Managing Human Resources in Cross-Border Alliances* (London: Routledge, 2003).

T. Schultz, 'Investment in Human Capital', *American Economic Review*, March (1961): 1–17.

Science and Engineering Indicators (2006), Internet source: www.nsf.gov/statistics/seind06/figures.htm, accessed on 2 December 2006.

Scrip Magazine, 'The China Syndrome', April (2004), Internet source: www.scripmag.com, accessed on 20 May 2005.

S. Sesser, 'Local Legend Takes Over PC Rivals in China', *Asian Wall Street Journal*, 31 May (1999): 13.

J. Sheehan, *Chinese Workers: A New History* (London: Routledge, 1999).

I. Shen, 'MG Car Line Reborn with a Made-in-China Label' 10 June 2007, Internet source: http://www.boston.com/cars/news/articles/2006/06/10, accessed on 23 June 2007.

J. Shen, 'International Performance Appraisals: Policies, Practices and Determinants in the Case of Chinese Multinational Companies', *International Journal of Manpower*, 25, 6 (2005): 547–63.

O. Shenkar, 'International Joint Ventures' Problems in China: Risk and Remedies', *Long Range Planning*, 23 (1990): 82–90.

O. Shenkar and M. Von Glinow, 'Paradoxes of Organizational Theory and Research: Using the Case of China to Illustrate National Contingency', *Management Science*, 40 (1994): 56–71.

S. Shi and D. Weisert, 'Corporate Governance with Chinese Characteristics', *The China Business Review*, 29, 5 (2002): 1–5.

M. Shipman, *The Limitations of Social Research* (3rd edition) (New York: Longmans, 1988).

V. Shue and C. Wong, *Paying for Progress in China: Public Finance, Human Welfare and Changing Patterns of Inequality* (London: Routledge, 2007).

SinoCast China Business Daily News, 'Shanghai Held 276 Conventions, Exhibitions in 2005' (2006), Internet source: http://proquest.umi.com/pqdweb?did=986786951&sid=6&Fmt=3&clientId=44986&RQT=309&VName=PQD, accessed on 17 April 2006.

P. Smith and Z. M. Wang, 'Leadership, Decision-making and Cultural Context: Event Management within Chinese Joint Ventures', *Leadership Quarterly*, 8, 4 (1997): 413–31.

J. Song, 'Brief report on the Chinese exhibition industry', *Shanghai Flash*, No. 1 (2005), Internet source: http://www.sinoptic.ch/shanghaiflash/texts/pdf/200501_shanghai.flash.pdf, accessed on 1 April 2006.

P. Sparrow, C. Brewster and H. Harris, *Globalising Human Resource Management* (London: Routledge, 2004).

G. Stahl, V. Pucik, P. Evans and M. Mendenhall, 'Human Resource Management in Cross-Border Mergers and Acquisitions', in A. Harzing and J. Ruysseveldt (eds), *International Human Resource Management* (2nd edition) (London: Sage, 2004, pp. 89–113).

E. Steinfeld, 'China's Shallow Integration: Networked Production and the New Challenges for Late Industrialization', *World Development*, 32, 11 (2004): 1971–87.

Strategic Direction, 'Inside China, They're Looking out: International Trade Is No One-way Route', 21, 3 (2005): 1–3, Internet source: http://docserver.emeraldinsight.com, accessed on 25 April 2005.

J. Sun, 'China: The Next Global Auto Power', *Far Eastern Economic Review*, 169, 2 (2006): 37–41.

J. Tan, 'Innovation and Risk-taking in a Transitional Economy: A Comparative Study of Chinese Managers and Entrepreneurs', *Journal of Business Venturing*, 16 (2001): 359–76.

J. Tan, 'Impact of Ownership Type on Environment-Strategy Linkage and Performance: Evidence from a Transitional Economy', *Journal of Management Studies*, 39, 3 (2002): 333–54.

B. Taylor, K. Chang and Q. Li, *Industrial Relations in China* (Cheltenham: Edward Elgar, 2003).

D. Teece, G. Pisano and A. Shuen, 'Dynamic Capabilities and Strategic Management', *Strategic Management Journal*, 18 (1997): 509–33.

S. Tenev, C. Zhang and L. Brefort, *Corporate Governance and Enterprise Reform in China: Building the Institutions of Modern Markets* (Washington DC: World Bank and the International Finance Corporation, 2002).

The Economist, 'Chinese Firms Abroad Spreading their Wings', Shanghai, 4 September 2003.

The Economist Intelligence Unit, *CEO Briefing: Corporate Priorities for 2005* (London: The Economist, 2005).

The Epoch Times, 8 June 2006.

The Ministry of Information Industry, *The Tenth Five Year Plan (2001–5)* (China: Beijing, 2001), Internet source: http://www.trp.hku.hk/infofile/2002/10-5-yr-plan.pdf, accessed on 13 May 2005.

The Ministry of Science and Technology of People's Republic of China (2001), 'Overview of 863 Programme in the Tenth Five-Year Plan period', Internet source: http://www.863.org.cn/english/annual_report/annual_repor_2001/200210090007. html, accessed on 1 April 2006.

The Ministry of Science and Technology of the People's Republic of China (2005), Internet source: http://www.most.gov.cn/eng/statistics/2005/t20060317_29724. htm, accessed on 1 April 2006.

The Ministry of Science and Technology (MOST) of the People's Republic of China (2005), 'Outline of S&T Activities', Internet source: http://www.most.gov.cn/eng/statistics/2005/ t20060317_29725.htm, accessed on 1 April 2006.

The Ministry of Science and Technology of the People's Republic of China (2005), 'Output Indicators', Internet source: http://www.most.gov.cn/eng/statistics/2005/t20060317_ 29722.htm, accessed on 1 April 2006.

The Ministry of Science and Technology of the People's Republic of China (2005), 'R&D Activities', Internet source: http://www.most.gov.cn/eng/statistics/2005/t20060317 _29724.htm, accessed on 1 April 2006.

The Ministry of Science and Technology of People's Republic of China (2006), 'National High-Tech R&D Programme (863 Programme)', Internet source: http://www.most.gov.cn/eng/programmes/programmes1.htm, accessed on 1 April 2006.

The Ministry of Trade and Industry (2005), 'Finland-China Innovation Centre', Internet source: http://www.ktm.fi/index.phtml?l=en&s=1317, accessed on 6th April 2006.

The Standard, Sing Tao Newspaper 2004, Internet source: http://www/thestandard.com.HK, accessed on 15 March 2005.

The World Agenda, the BBC's International Journal, April/May 2005.

The World Bank, 'China at a Glance' (2005a), Internet source: http://devdata.worldbank.org/ AAG/chn_aag.pdf, accessed on 19 April 2006.

The World Bank, 'Investment Climate Surveys Draft Country Profile: China 2003 Survey' (2005b), Internet source: http://rru.worldbank.org/InvestmentClimate, accessed on 19 April 2006.

The World Bank, 'China Quick Facts' (2006), Internet source: http://web.worldbank.org/ WBSITE/EXTERNAL/COUNTRIES/EASTASIAPACIFICEXT/CHINAEXTN, accessed on 11 May 2006.

I. Thireau and L. S. Hua, 'The Moral Universe of Aggrieved Chinese Workers: Workers' Appeals to Arbitration Committees and Letters and Visits Offices', The China Journal, 50 (2003): 83–103.

Thomson, 'Thomson partnership set to accelerate Chinese innovation' (2005), Internet source: http://scientific.thomson.com/press/2005/8301748, accessed on 6 April 2006.

E. Thun, Changing Lanes in China: Foreign Direct Investment, Local Governments, and Auto Sector Development (Cambridge: Cambridge University Press, 2006).

E. Tsang, 'Threats and Opportunities Faced by Private Businesses in China', Journal of Business Venturing, 9 (1994): 451–8.

E. Tsang, 'Managerial Learning in Foreign-invested Enterprises of China', Management International Review, 41, 1 (2001): 29–51.

T. Turpin and X. Liu, 'Balanced Development: The Challenge for Science, Technology and Innovation Policy', in C. Havie (ed.), Contemporary Developments and Issues in China's Economic Tansition (Houndmills: Macmillan Press, 2000, pp. 191–211).

D. Ulrich, 'Intellectual Capital=Competence × Commitment', Sloan Management Review, 39, 2 (1998): 15–26.

UNCTAD, World Investment Report 2002, United Nations Conference on Trade and Development, United Nations.

UNCTAD, China: An Emerging FDI Outward Investor (2003), UNCTAD, United Nations.

UNCTAD, World Investment Report 2004, Internet source: http://www.unctad.org/fdistatis tics, United Nations Conference on Trade and Development, United Nations, accessed on 12 May 2006.

UNCTAD, *World Investment Report 2006*, Internet source: http://www.unctad.org/fdistatistics, United Nations Conference on Trade and Development, United Nations, accessed on 12 June 2007.

J. M. Utterback, *Mastering the Dynamics of Innovation: How Companies Can Seize Opportunities in the Face of Technological Change* (Boston, MA: Harvard Business School Press, 1994).

M. Vatikiotis, 'Investment in China: Outward Bound', *online edition of Daily News* (2004), Internet source: http://www.dailynews.lk/2004/02/06/fea01.html, accessed on 8 April 2005.

G. Walter, 'Culture Collisions in Mergers and Acquisitions', in P. Frost, L. Moore, M. Louis, and C. Lundberg, (eds), *Organizational Culture* (London: Sage, 1985, pp. 301–14).

M. Wang, D. Chen and K. Chen, 'China Evolves from Imitation to Innovation', *Drug Discovery & Development*, 8, 6 (2005): 53–6.

M. Warner, *How Chinese Managers Learn: Management and Industrial Training in the PRC* (London: Macmillan, 1992).

M. Warner, 'Chinese Enterprise Reform, Human Resources and the 1994 Labour Law', *International Journal of Human Resource Management*, 4 (1996): 779–96.

M. Warner, *China's Managerial Revolution* (London: Frank Cass, 1999).

M. Warner (ed.), *Human Resource Management in China Revisited* (London: Routledge, 2005).

Y. Weber, 'Corporate Cultural Fit and Performance in Mergers and Acquisitions', *Human Relations*, 9 (1996): 1181–95.

S. Weiss and D. Forrester, 'China's Pharmaceutical Industry', *The China Business Review*, Nov/Dec, 31, 6 (2004): 16–17.

S. White and X. Liu, 'Transition Trajectories for Market Structure and Firm Strategy in China', *Journal of Management Studies*, 38, 1 (2001): 103–24.

R. Whittington, *What Is Strategy and Does It Matter?* (London: Routledge, 1993).

B. Wilkinson, J. Gamble, J. Humphrey, J. Morris and D. Anthony, 'The New International Division of Labour in Asian Electronics: Work Organization and Human Resources in Japan and Malaysia', *Journal of Management Studies*, 5 (2001): 675–95.

P. Williamson and M. Zeng, 'Strategies for Competing in a changed China', *MIT Sloan Management Review*, 45, 4 (2004): 85–91.

World Investment Report 2005: Transnational Corporations and the Internationalisation of R&D (New York and Geneva: United Nations, 2005).

H. Wu and C. Chen, 'An Assessment of Outward Foreign Direct Investment from China's Transational Economy', *European-Asia Studies*, 53, 8 (2001): 1235–54.

W. J. Xing, 'Automakers in the Fast Lane', *The China Business Review*, 29, 4 (2002): 8–16.

Xinhua News Agency, 'Major High-tech Projects Planned for 2006–2010' 6 March (2006), Internet source: http://www.china.org.cn/english/2006lh/160294.htm, accessed on 18 November 2006.

D. X. Yang, *Foreign Direct Investment from Developing Countries: A Case Study of China's Outward Investment*, Unpublished PhD thesis (Victoria University, Melbourne, Australia, 2003).

G. Yeung, 'The Implications of WTO Accession on the Pharmaceutical Industry in China', *Journal of Contemporary China*, 11, 32 (2002): 473–93.

P. Yoshida, 'China's R&D/Innovation Growing Fast', *Research Technology Management*, 48, 6 (2005): 2–4.

S. Young, 'Policy Practice and the Private Sector in China', *Australian Journal of Chinese Affairs*, 21 (1989): 57–80.

S. Young, N. Hood and T. Lu, 'International Development by Chinese Enterprises: Key Issues for the Future', *Long Range Planning*, 31 (1998): 886–93.

Y. Yu, *Comparative Corporate Governance in China: Political Economy and Legal Infrastructure* (London: Routledge, 2007).

M. Zeng and P. Williamson, 'The Hidden Dragons', *Harvard Business Review*, October (2003): 92–9.

A. Zhang, 'China's WTO Accession: Implications for the Auto Sector' (2001a), Internet source: http://www.pwc.com/extweb/newcolth.nsf/docid/F117826C7D792B3D85256A15 0058D014, accessed on 18 March 2005.

A. Zhang, 'The Future of China's Pharmaceutical Industry' (2001b), Internet source: http://www.pwc.com/extweb/newcolth.nsf/docid/4CE903FAD5FB1DF985256A 31007820CB, accessed on 18 March 2005.

H. Zhang and D. Van Ben Bulcke, 'China: Rapid Changes in the Investment Development Path', in J. Dunning and R. Narula (eds), *Foreign Direct Investment and Governments: Catalysts for Economic Restructuring* (London: Routledge, 1996, pp. 380–422).

M. Zhang, 'Transferring Human Resource Management Across National Boundaries: The Case of Chinese Multinational Companies in the UK', *Employee Relations*, 25, 6 (2003): 614–26.

M. Zhang, T. Edwards and C. Edwards, 'Internationalisation and Developing Countries: The Case of China', in T. Edwards and C. Rees (eds), *International Human Resource Management: Globalisation, National Systems and Multinational Companies* (London: Prentice Hall Financial Times, 2006, pp. 129–47).

Y. Zhang and R. Cheng, 'China Making a Brand New Name for Itself', *China Daily*, 18 March (2002).

H. Zhao and Y. Luo, 'Product Diversification, Ownership Structure, and Subsidiary Performance in China's Dynamic Market', *Management International Review*, 42, 1 (2002): 27–48.

X. Zhou, 'Signing in Tune', *Beijing Review*, Internet source: http://www.breview.com.cn/ 200418/world-200418(C).htm, accessed on 18 March 2005.

Y. Zhu, 'Economic Reform and Human Resource Management in Vietnamese Enterprises', *Asia Pacific Business Review*, 8, 3 (2002): 115–34.

Y. Zhu and M. Warner, 'HRM in East Asia', in A. Harzing and J. Ruysseveldt (eds), *International Human Resource Management* (London: Sage, 2004, pp. 195–220).

J. Zinkin, 'Maximising the "Licence to Operate": CSR from an Asian Perspective', *Journal of Corporate Citizenship*, 14 (2004): 67–80.

References in Chinese

Beijing Youth Newspaper, 'The Most Popular Employers in the Eyes of HR Managers', 15 November (2002).

B. Buo, 'M&As in China's Pharmaceutical Industry', *Modern Management Science*, 2 (2004): 102–3.

L. Cai and Y. H. Shen, 'An Analysis of Entrepreneurs' Behaviour in the Low Performance of SOE Mergers and Acquisitions', *Journal of Zhejiang University*, 1 (2002): 137–43.

C. M. Chen, 'A Study of the M&As of SOEs by MNCs', *Industrial Technology and Economy*, 6 (1999): 34–5.

J. G. Chen and Q. Wang, 'MNC Acquisition and Large SOE Reform', *China Industrial Economy*, 4 (2003): 30–6.

J. G. Chen, Z. Lu and Y. Z. Wang, *China Social Security System Development Report* (Beijing: Social Science Document Publishing House, 2001).

Q. T. Chen, 'Promoting the Healthy Growth of Private Economy', *Xinhua Wenzhai*, 4 (2003): 40–2.

Q. T. Chen, S. J. Liu and F. Feng, *The Coming of Auto Age in China* (Beijing: China Development Publishing House, 2004).

X. Chen and Y. Wei, 'The Electronic Industry', in S. J. Liu, F. Feng and J. L. Yang (eds), *The Blue Book of the Development of the Chinese Industries 2003* (Beijing: Huaxia Publishing House, 2003, pp. 207–24).

China Business, 7 April 2004.

China Business, 7 June 2004.

China Business, 21 June 2004.

China Business, 9 August 2004.

China Business, 16 August 2004.
China Business, 30 August 2004.
China Business, 20 September 2004.
China Business, 15 November 2004.
China Business, 22 November 2004.
China Business, 29 November 2004.
China Business, 13 December 2004.
China Business, 27 December 2004.
China Business, 17 January 2005.
China Business, 31 January 2005.
China Business, 28 February 2005.
China Business, 7 March 2005.
China Business, 14 March 2005.
China Business, 9 May 2005.
China Business, 29 May 2005.
China Business, 6 June 2005.
China Business, 8 August 2005.
China Business, 10 August 2005.
China Business, 15 August 2005.
China Business, 17 October 2005.
China Business, 24 October 2005.
China Business, 31 October 2005.
China Business, 23 November 2005.
China Business, 12 December 2005.
China Business, 26 December 2005.
China Business, 13 March 2006.
China Business, 20 February 2006.
China Business, 7 August 2006.
China Business, 18 September 2006.
China Daily, 6 January 2005.
China Labour Statistical Yearbook (Beijing: China Statistics Publishing House, 2005).
China National Conditions and Strength, 'Domestic Express', 9 (2004): 62.
China Science and Technology Statistical Yearbook (Beijing: China Statistics Publishing House, 2002).
China Statistical Yearbook (Beijing: China Statistics Publishing House, 2002).
China Statistical Yearbook (Beijing: China Statistics Publishing House, 2003).
China Statistical Yearbook (Beijing: China Statistics Publishing House, 2004).
China Statistical Yearbook (Beijing: China Statistics Publishing House, 2006).
Development and Management of Human Resources, 'Review', 11 (2005): 4–5.
M. Fan and Z. R. Cui, 'Pharmaceutical Industry Still Has Room to Grow', *China National Conditions and Strength*, 12 (2005): 47–8.
C. Fang, 'Four Stages of Development, Four Streams of Enterprises, and Four Models of Winning Profit', *China Business*, 7 June (2004).
L. Fu and J. Zhang, 'The Automobile Industry', in S. J. Liu, F. Feng and J. L. Yang (eds), *The Blue Book of the Development of the Chinese Industries* (Beijing: Huaxia Publishing House, 2003, pp. 157–173).
Y. W. Fu, 'Capacity Growth of Auto Product and Its Change of Demand and Supply', in G. G. Liu, L. L. Wang, J. W. Li, S. C. Liu and T. S. Wang (eds), *Analysis and Forecast on China's Economy 2006* (Beijing: Social Science Academic Press, 2005, pp. 186–93).
W. J. Gu, 'Constraining Factors of M&As in China and Measures of Optimisation', *Enterprise Economy*, 12 (2003): 146–8.
International Statistical Yearbook (Beijing: China Statistics Press, 2004).
Q. P. Jiang and X. D. Wang, 'The Situation of Information Talents and the Challenges Faced with China', in C. G. Pan and L. Wang (eds), *The Report of the Development of Chinese Talents*, No. 1 (Beijing: Social Sciences Academic Press, 2004, pp. 166–80).

B. S. Jin and P. X. Nie, 'Observations of International Mergers and Acquisitions in 2003', in *China Mergers and Acquisitions Yearbook*, The Global M&A Research Centre (ed.) (Beijing: Posts and Telecom Press, 2004, pp. 627–46).

C. X. Jin, P. R. Qi and W. J. Li, 'An Analysis of the Issues in MNCs' Acquisition of SOEs', *Modern Economy Research*, 1 (2003): 32–37.

P. Jin, P. Y. Li and Y. M. Feng, *Blue Book of China's Enterprises Competitiveness* (Beijing: Social Sciences Documentation Publishing House, 2003).

J. Li, 'The Pharmaceutical Industry', in S. J. Liu, F. Feng and J. L. Yang (eds), *The Blue Book of the Development of the Chinese Industries 2003* (Beijing: Huaxia Publishing House, 2003, pp. 206–24).

J. Li and L. Li, 'Prerequisite to Transnational Chinese Enterprises: Reformation of Administrative System', *Gaige*, 2 (2000): 49–50.

J. T. Li and Z. G. Yang, 'A Study in the Automobile Market of Baiyun District of Guangzhou', in J. T. Li, L. Y. Jiang, C. L. Tu and P. Peng (eds), *Guangzhou (China) Economy Development Report 2005* (Beijing: Social Sciences Academic Press, 2005, pp. 337–54).

L. Li, 'Enterprise M&As in China: Problems and Solutions', *Digest of Management Science*, 3 (2003): 54–7.

M. Li and S. H. Zhang, 'A Study in the Status Quo and Suggestions on the Development of Guangzhou's Automobile Industry', in J. T. Li, L. Y. Jiang, C. L. Tu and P. Peng (eds), *Guangzhou (China) Economy Development Report 2005* (Beijing: Social Sciences Academic Press, 2005, pp. 329–36).

Q. Li, 'The Quantitative Analysis of and Forecasting on the Development of Chinese Talents', in C. G. Pan and L. Wang (eds), *The Report of the Development of Chinese Talents*, No. 1 (Beijing: Social Sciences Academic Press, 2004, pp. 437–68).

W. H. Li and Y. Li, 'Chinese Key Enterprises Have Increased Their Technological Innovation Capacity', *China National Conditions and Strength*, 9 (2004): 14–17.

C. R. Liu, 'Opportunity and Challenge: MNCs' Acquisition of Chinese Enterprises', *Policy and Management*, 12 (2000): 4–9.

Q. S. Liu, M. Bai and C. D. Yin, 'M&As of Chinese Enterprises in the Early 21st Century', *Journal of Yunan Finance and Trade College*, 3 (2001): 30–4.

Y. Q. Liu and Z. X. Xu, *Report on the Competitiveness of Non-state-owned Enterprises No.1: Competitive Quality and Competitiveness Index* (Beijing: Social Sciences Academic Press, 2004).

R. Mo, 'Shortages of Rural Migrant Labour and Skilled Workers in the Context of Labour Market Over-supply', in X. Yu, X. Y. Lu, P. L. Li, P. Huang and J. H. Lu (eds), *Analysis and Forecast on China's Social Development (2005)* (Beijing: Social Sciences Academic Press, 2004, pp. 260–72).

P. F. Ni, Q. H. Hou, M. Q. Jiang and C. Q. Wang, *Annual Report on Urban Competitiveness No. 2: Positioning: Way to Mutual Prosperity* (Beijing: Social Sciences Documentation Publishing House, 2004).

C. G. Pan and H. Fang, 'Choices of Training Industry in China', in C. G. Pan, L. Wang and X. L. Wang (eds), *The Report of the Development of Chinese Talents*, No. 2 (Beijing: Social Sciences Academic Press, 2005, pp. 310–31).

C. G. Pan and W. Lou, 'Study on Situation and Development Environment for Chinese Talents', in C. G. Pan and L. Wang (eds), *The Report on the Development of Chinese Talents*, No.1 (Beijing: Social Sciences Academic Press, 2004, pp. 1–46).

People's Daily Overseas Edition, 13 February 2006.

People's Daily Overseas Edition, 16 March 2006.

People's Daily Overseas Edition, 30 May 2006.

People's Daily Overseas Edition, 13 November 2006.

People's Daily Overseas Edition, 13 January 2007.

Z. W. Qian, *Chinese Auto Industry in the 21st Century* (Beijing: Beijing Institute of Technology Press, 2004).

Y. Qin, 'An Analysis of Enterprise Competitiveness: The Medicine Industry', in P. Jin, P. Y. Li and Y. M. Feng (eds), *The Blue Book of China's Enterprises' Competitiveness (2004)* (Beijing: Social Sciences Academic Press, 2004, pp. 119–49).

M. J. Rui and Z. G. Tao, *Report of China's Industrial Competitiveness* (Shanghai: People's Publishing House, 2004).

L. Shi, 'China's Investment: The Problems and the Legal Countermoves', *Touzi Yanjiu* (Investment Research), 5 (1998): 33–7.

Q. Shu, 'The Situation of China's Environment Protection and Policy Options in 2005–6', in G. G. Liu, L. L. Wang, J. W. Li, S. C. Liu and T. S. Wang (eds), *Analysis and Forecast on China's Economy 2006* (Beijing: Social Science Academic Press, 2005, pp. 162–7).

Z. Song and R. Li, 'The Growth of Goods Distribution Industry in China in Its 11th Five-year Plan Period: Trends Forecast, Planning Principles and Policy Focuses', in X. J. Jiang, C. H. Fei, D. X. He and P. Y. Gao (eds), *IFTE Report Series on Service Industry in China*, No. 3 (Beijing: Social Sciences Academic Press, 2004, pp. 81–98).

J. Tian (ed.), *Research Report on the Mainstream Consumption Market in China* (Beijing: Enterprise Management Publishing House, 2003).

C. L. Wang and X. Feng, 'Problems, Trends and Counter-measures of the Chinese Exhibition Industry', in X. M. Zhang, H. L. Hu and J. L. Zhang (eds), *Report on Development of China's Cultural Industry (2005)* (Beijing: Social Sciences Academic Press, 2005, pp. 196–206).

C. S. Wang, J. P. Fan, H. Y. Xu and X. Y. Zhang, *China and the World Economy Development Report: Economic Policies and Development Forecast* (Beijing: Social Sciences Academic Press, 2004).

J. Wang and X. Liu, 'An Analysis of the Constraining Factors for MNCs' Acquisition of SOEs', *Modern Economic Research*, 8 (2002): 51–3.

R. Z. Wang, 'An Analysis of MNCs' Acquisition of Listed Companies in China', *Listed Companies*, 3 (2003): 2–6.

W. Wang, Q. S. Zhang and J. J. Zhang, *China Mergers and Acquisitions Yearbook* (Beijing: Posts and Telecom Press, 2003).

W. Wang, J. J. Zhang, B. Li, J. Dong and S. L. Lin (eds), *China Mergers and Acquisitions Yearbook* (Beijing: Posts and Telecom Press, 2004).

Workers' Daily, 26 September 2004.

Workers' Daily, 12 October 2004.

Workers' Daily, 19 October 2004.

Workers' Daily, 3 November 2004.

Workers' Daily , 9 November 2004.

Workers' Daily, 5 December 2004.

Workers' Daily, 9 August 2005.

Workers' Daily, 7 September 2005.

Workers' Daily, 14 September 2005.

Workers' Daily, 29 October 2005.

Workers' Daily, 17 November 2005.

Workers' Daily, 27 December 2005.

J. Xu, 'Capital Merger and Acquisition and Enterprise Consolidation', *Journal of Yunnan Finance and Economics University*, 6 (2003): 126–8.

Yangcheng Evening News, 23 August 2005.

H. Zhan, 'Koda's Acquisition of the Photographic Industry of China: An Investigation and Consideration', *Enterprise Vitality*, 4 (2003): 10–12.

H. L. Zhang, *Evaluation Report of China Two Years After its Accession to the WTO* (Beijing: Renmin University Press, 2004).

J. R. Zhang, W. L. Li and J. Zhou, 'An Analysis of the Performance of M&As in the Stock Market in China', *Nankai Business Review*, 6 (2002): 51–7.

Q. Z. Zhang, 'An Analysis of Enterprise Competitiveness: The Wine-Making Industry', in P. Jin, P. Y. Li and Y. M. Feng (eds), *The Blue Book of China's Enterprises' Competitiveness (2004)* (Beijing: Social Sciences Academic Press, 2004, pp. 95–118).

Z. Z. Zhang, 'A Study in the Development of Huadu Automobile City', in J. T. Li, L. Y. Jiang, C. L. Tu and P. Peng (eds), *Guangzhou (China) Economy Development Report 2005* (Beijing: Social Sciences Academic Press, 2005, pp. 355–74).

Y. Zhao, 'An Analysis of Enterprise Competitiveness: The Automobile Manufacturing Industry', in P. Jin, P. Y. Li and Y. M. Feng (eds), *The Blue Book of China's Enterprises' Competitiveness (2004)* (Beijing: Social Sciences Academic Press, 2004, pp. 69–94).

Q. Zhou, and G. Li, 'Analysis on the Supply and Demand of China Retail Talents', in C. G. Pan, L. Wang and X. L. Wang (eds), *The Report of the Development of Chinese Talents*, No. 2 (Beijing: Social Sciences Academic Press, 2005, pp. 97–112).

X. B. Zuo, 'Unpacking a Century's Secret of the "Empire of the Wine Industry": An Investigation of the Eleven Competitive Advantages of Wuliangye', *China Business*, 20 September 2004.

Useful websites

http://www.aphr.org
http://www.atimes.com/atimes/South_Asia
http://www.cashq.ac.cn
http://www.china.org.cn
http://www.chinadaily.com.cn
http://www.chinaHR.com
http://www.ChinaHRD.net
http://www.chinatoday.com
http://www.china-hr.org
http://www.China-training.com
http://www.ceic.gov.cn
http://www.cnnic.net.cn
http://www.csia.org.cn
http://www.edu.cn/20011102/3007992.shtml
http://www.mii.gov.cn
http://www.most.gov.cn/eng/statistics/2005/t20060317_29725.htm
http://www.stats.gov.cn
http://www.unctad.org/fdistatistics
http://www.51e-training.com
http://www.800hr.com

Index

Non-textual references, such as Boxes, Figures or Tables, are in *italic* print. Headings beginning with numbers (e.g. 20) are filed as if spelled out (e.g. twenty)

Academy of International Trade and Economic Cooperation (Ministry of Commerce), 74
Academy of Science, Chinese, 40
Accenture, survey by, 88, 89
ACFTU (All China Federation of Trade Unions), 276
Africa, investment in, 236
Agres, T., 149
Ahlstrom, D., 252, 253
Akiyama Publishing Machinery Company, 74
All China Federation of Trade Unions (ACFTU), 276
altruistic approach, CSR, 84
Amighini, A., 157
Ansoff, H., 70
Asia Economic Crisis (1998), 188
Association for Asian Research, 139
AstroZeneca China, *141*
Auchan (retail giant), 182
automotive industry, 117–35
  brand-name international auto firms, acquiring, 130
  building industry cluster, 131
  component parts manufacturing, 121–2
  domestic brand products, development, 128–9
  history, 118, 134
  human resources implications, 131–4
  industrial policy (1994), *118–19*
  joint ventures, 118, 119, 126–7
  maintenance business, 132
  market entry strategy, foreign firms, *129*
  MNCs, strategic alliance with, 129–30
  opportunities, 127–8
  as pillar industry, 22
  problems/competitive pressure, 123–7; dispersed geographical location, 126; domestic brand-name products, lack of, 125–6; economies of scale, lack of, 124; JVs, limited scale, 126–7; R&D/technology level, low, 124–5; removal of protection, 127
  production capacity, investment in, 123
  production outputs, 119–20, *121, 122*
  sales volumes, 120, *122*
  skill shortages, 132–3
autonomy, management, 247–8

Bai, X., 84
Bamber, G., 254
Bank of China, 232
Baoye Group, 76
Baron, D., 85
Baron, S., 84
Bartels, J., 255
Bartlett, C., 240, 241
Beamish, P., 236
Becker, G., 54
beers, foreign, *275*
Beijing
  China-Germany Hi-Tech Dialogue Forum (2001), 48
  China Promotion Committee for Top Brand Strategy, 78
  Hualian Supermarket Group, 186, 189
  Jeep Corp. Ltd, 123
  Schroeder's visit (2004), 234
  Zhingguancun Haidian Science Park in, 49
Beijing Automotive Industry Corporation, 118
Beijing City Light (retailer), 185
Beijing Four New Exhibition, 198
Beijing Tongrentang (Chinese medicine company), 150–1, 179
Beijing Wangfujing Department Store, 178–9
Bennington, L., 84
Benson, J., 70, 90
Bernthal, P., 272
Björkman, I., 212, 214, 225
Boisot, M., 12
Boxall, P., 8, 211, 221
Boyarski, J., 52
branding
  acquisition of brands, 79
  automotive industry, 125–6, 128–9, 130
  brand management, 70
  Chinese MNCs, abroad, 237–8
  concept of brand, 77

branding – *continued*
  exhibition industry, 203
  extension of brands, 79
  Fortune 500 companies, brand names, 276
  pharmaceutical industry, 149–52
  revitalization of brands, 79
  Shenzhen Huaqiaocheng, *80–1*
  as success factor, 77–80
  Wuliangye Group Co. Ltd (distillery), *80–1*
  Xinfei Refrigerator Series, *82*
Branine, M., 60
Braun, W., 225
Briscoe, D., 230
Brown, G., 1
Brunner, J., 213
Budhwar, P., 249, 250, 253, 256
Bulcke, D., 16, 140, 141, 143, 231
Buo, B., 145
business environment, 21–66
  analytical framework, 5–8, *6*
  Chinese government, role, 22–4
  fund sources, *32–6*
  industrialization and development of
      industries, 24–38
  Porter's factors, 7
  science and technology output, 51–3
  skill shortages, *see* skill shortages
  technology and innovation, *see* technology
      and innovation
  workforce, 55–60

Cai, K., 16, 231, 234, 248
Cai, L., 218
capital constraints, outflow investment, 246
Carrefour (retail giant), 180, 182, 186, 190
Cartwright, S., 221, 255
Castells, M., 70
CEOs (chief executive officers), 74, 85, 86–7,
    246, 248
Chan, A., 224, 254
Chandler, A., 70
Chang, C., 259
Changchun, First Automotive Works (FAW),
    118
Chen, B., 63
Chen, C., 16, 24, 231, 236
Chen, C. M., 211, 216
Chen, D., 63
Chen, J., 124
Chen, J. G., 216
Chen, K., 63
Chen, Q. T., 67
Chen, R., 157
Chen, X., 160, 164, 169
Cheng, R., 77, 78

Child, J., 6, 8, 12, 13, 15, 60, 67, 70, 212,
    213, 218, 225, 232, 234, 247, 248, 260
China Association of Automobile
    Manufacturers, 121
China Auto Industry Yearbook, 121
China-Germany Hi-Tech Dialogue Forum,
    Beijing (2001), 48
China Great Wall Computer, 160
China Information News, 195
China Internet Network Information Centre
    (CNNIC), 164
China National Offshore Oil Corporation
    (CNOOC), 74
China National Petroleum Corporation
    (CNPC), 74
China Promotion Committee for Top Brand
    Strategy, Beijing, 78
China Software Industry Association, 164, 167
China Technology Center (CTC), 50
China Western Region International
    Exhibition, Chengdu, 200
Chinese Academy of Science, 40
Chinese government
  exhibition industry, 197–8
  government-sponsored programmes and
      Sino-foreign collaborations, 46–50
  industrial policies, effectiveness, 262–4
  information technology (IT) industry,
      160–2
  interventions by, 23
  pharmaceutical industry, 138–40
  push strategy, 234
  retail industry, 186–7
  role, 22–4, 65, 262–4
  'techno-nationalism' of, 262
Chinese Hotel Association Professional
    Management Specialist Committee, 64
Chinese MNCs, abroad, 229–60 *see also*
    foreign direct investment (FDI); outward
    FDI
  Chinese R&D centres, 244, *245*
  cross-border acquisition experience, 244
  growth of Chinese outward investment,
      231–3
  host countries, choice, *241*
  human resource management, 249–5;
      subsidiaries, in developed countries,
      250, *251*, 252–6; subsidiaries, in
      developing countries, *251*, 256–8;
      subsidiaries, in knowledge-intensive
      businesses, 258–9
  internationalization strategy and choice of
      host countries, 239, 240–5
  international players, aspiration to be, 238
  investment strategy, *241*
  restructuring activities, 232

strategic choices, 244
Chinese National Human Genome Centre,
    Shanghai, 149
Chinese SOEs, acquisition by foreign MNCs,
    207–27
  barriers to foreign investors' acquisitions,
    220–1
  FDI acquisitions, driving forces, 213–14
  film manufacturing industry, 217
  foreign capital, utilization, 208–9
  human resources implications, 221–7, 222;
    post-acquisition integration and
    harmonization of terms/conditions,
    226–7
  local governments, intervention from,
    219–20
  managerial skills and behaviour, 217–19
  objectives alignment?, 216–17
  patterns of international acquisitions,
    215–16
Chinese Transport and Distribution
    Association, 191
Ching, P. S., 225
Chuangzheng programme, 64
Chun, R., 157
Clark, T., 6, 249
CNC (computerized numerical controlled)
    machines, 59
CNNIC (China Internet Network Information
    Centre), 164
CNOOC (China National Offshore Oil
    Corporation), 74
CNPC (China National Petroleum
    Corporation), 74
Compaq Computer, 157
competition strategy
  CEOs, 86–7
  corporate governance, reform, 87
  corporate social responsibility, 84–6
  diversification as growth, 71–3
  exhibition industry, 202–3
  factors influencing competitiveness, 69–71
  human resource management, strategic,
    82–4
  information technology (IT) industry,
    168–74
  internationalization as, 73–5
  managerial implications, for Chinese firms,
    270
  new strategic orientations, 88–9
  pharmaceutical industry, 147–52
  of private firms, leading, 67–90
  product branding, and targeting customer
    groups, 149–52
  product innovation and quality
    enhancement, 75–7

R&D, collaboration in, 148–9
retail industry, 179–88
success factors, top private enterprises,
    91–112
computerized numerical controlled (CNC)
    machines, 59
Cooke, F. L., 22, 24, 60, 61, 67, 77, 190,
    193, 212, 214, 214, 218, 220, 221, 223,
    224, 226, 250, 253, 255, 259
Cooper, C., 221, 255
corporate governance, reform, 87
corporate reputation, need for, 271–2
corporate social responsibility (CSR), 84–6
  CEOs on, 85
  and competition strategy, 69
  MNC activities, 276–7
  as new concept, in China, 85
CTC (China Technology Center), 50
Cui, Z. R., 137, 139, 140, 145
Curtin, S., 236, 243, 255
customer groups, targeting of in
    pharmaceutical industry, 149–52

Davies, G., 70, 77
Davies, H., 278
Davila, A., 250, 253, 256
Debrah, Y., 249, 250, 253, 256
Dedrick, J., 23, 157, 160, 161, 169
Delixi Group, 87
Dell, 79, 170
Deloitte, survey by, 88
demand conditions, 7
De Meyer, A., 65, 77, 78, 139
developed countries
  Chinese MNCs in, 250, 252–6
  developing countries contrasted, HRM,
    250, 251, 254–5
  employee participation and involvement,
    253
  exhibition industry, 195
  knowledge management, 253
  labour/employment law, 250, 252
  organizational image/identity, 255–6
  performance management and reward
    system, 252–3
  recruitment, 252
  retail industry, 177
  trade unions, relationship with, 254–5
  training and development, 253
developing countries
  Chinese MNC subsidiaries in, 256–8
  developed countries contrasted, HRM, 250,
    251, 254–5

developing countries – *continued*
  employee participation and involvement, 253–4
  employee welfare/well-being schemes, 254
  knowledge management, 253–4
  labour/employment law, 250
  recruitment, 252
  trade unions, relationship with, 254–5
  training and development, 253
Development Dimensions International, 272
Dewe, P., 249
Dicks, A., 221
Ding, D., 84, 212, 254
diversification, 70–3, 150, 203
domestic firms, vs. foreign firms, 272–7, *273–4*
Dong, J. L., 213, 214
Dongfeng-Citroën Automobile Co Ltd, 123, 127
Dongguan IT industrial cluster, 159–60
Drucker, P., 70, 258
'Drug Management Law', 139
Dunning, J., 7, 70, 233, 234, 240

economies of scale, automotive industry, 124
Economist Intelligence Unit (EIU), 272
economy of China, structure, *3*
education and skill levels, 55–60, *56–8 see also* skill shortages
Edwards, T., 13, 258
863 High-tech R&D Programme, 46, *47–8*
8th China International Fair for Investment and Trade (2004), 234
EIU (Economist Intelligence Unit), 272
Ellis, P., 278
Elvira, M., 250
employee participation, human resource management, 253
employee welfare/well-being schemes, 254
employment statistics, *27–8, 30–1*
  automotive industry, *133*
entrepreneurs, 60, 218
Ernst & Young European Investment Monitor (EYEIM), 240
Eun, J., 22, 119, 124
Evans, P., 211, 225, 226
exhibition industry, 194–204 *see also* retail industry
  background, 194–6
  Beijing Four New Exhibition, 198
  branding, 203
  competition strategy, 202–3
  compositional structure, *199*
  development problems, 196–202;
    government intervention, 197–8;
    insurance difficulties, 199; lack of
    economies of scale, quality and
    branding of exhibitions, 197; lack of
    human resources, 200–1; lack of
    industrial clusters, 198–200; lack of
    industrial planning, regulation and
    integration, 196; opportunistic
    behaviour, 198; overcapacity of
    exhibition space, 196–7
  diversification, 203
  environmental and ecological orientation, 203
  innovation and informalization, 203
  internationalization, 202–3
  jewellery exhibitions, 198–9
  large corporate groups, formation, 202
  specialization and professionalization, 203
EYEIM (Ernst & Young European Investment Monitor), 240

factor conditions, 7
Fan, M., 137, 139, 140, 145
Fan, P., 158, 170, 212
Fan, X. C., 225
Fan, Y., 77
Fang, C., 71, 75
Fang, H., 59, 63
Faulkner, D., 13, 70, 212, 213, 260
FAW (First Automotive Works), 118, 123
FDI (foreign direct investment), *see* foreign direct investment (FDI)
Feng, X., 194, 195, 196, 197, 201, 202, 203
Ferner, A., 258
film manufacturing industry, price wars, 217
Finland-China Innovation Centre (FinChi), Shanghai, *49*
First Automotive Works (FAW), 118, 123
'500,000 Senior Technicians in Three years' training plan, 64
fixed assets, newly increased, *32–6*
Fletcher, A., 241, 242
foreign direct investment (FDI) *see also* Chinese MNCs, abroad
  acquisitions, driving forces, 213–14
  by sector, *37*
  in Germany, 240–2
  increasing levels, 29
  inflow, 238, 246
  in Japan, 242–5
  manufacturing sector, 211
  outward, *see* outward FDI
  overview, selected years, *230*
  recipient country, China as, 207, 232, 261
  in Southeast Asian countries, 243
foreign firms, vs. domestic firms, 272–7, *273–4*
Foreign Trade Commission, 231
Foreign Trade Corporations, 231–2
Forney, M., 248

Forrester, D., 139, 140, 143
Fortune, 500 companies, brand names, 276
Francis, J., 276
Francois, J., 117
Freeman, R., 84, 85
French, P., 79, 275
Frenkel, S., 217
Friedman, M., 84
Frost, T., 233
Fu, L., 125, 126
Fu, Y. W., 119, 120, 121, 123, 124
Fuchs, H., 77

Galanz (microwave oven manufacturer), 233, 237
Gallagher, M., 224
Gan, L., 123
Garg, S., 65, 77, 78, 139
Garnaut, R., 15, 67, 214
GDP (Gross Domestic Product), 2, 25–6
General Electric (GE), 50
Germany, 140
    China-Germany Hi-Tech Dialogue Forum, Beijing (2001), 48
    Chinese FDI in, 240–2
    science and engineering research, 42
Ghoshal, S., 240, 241, 279
GlaxoSmithKline, 149
globalization, 269 see also internationalization
    competition strategy, 74
    global economy, and China, 2
'Go Global' strategy, 234, 262
Goldstein, A., 262
Good Manufacturing Practices (GMP), 22, 140
good sales practices (GSP), 22
Grace, C., 145
Grange, A., 225
Grimshaw, D., 225
Gross Domestic Product (GDP), 2, 25–6
GSP (good sales practices), 22
Gu, E., 213
Gu, W. J., 213
Guangdong Midea-Holding Co, 242
Guangdong Province, 59, 196
Guangzhou Automobile Group, 127
Guangzhou Pharmaceutical Co Ltd, 143, 150, 192

Haier (white goods manufacturer), 73, 78, 233, 237, 244
Hailiang Group, 76, 79
Haining City, Yangzi River Delta Area, 60
Hamel, G., 54, 70
Harzing, A., 230
Hayiao Group Stock Ltd, 150

Heavens, S., 225
Hempel, P., 259
Hermawan, A., 253, 256
'Hero' brand gold pens, 78
higher education sector, 61–2
high tech zones, 49
Hill & Knowlton, Annual Global Survey of Senior Executive Opinions, 85, 246
Hillman, A., 84, 85, 86
Hitt, M., 70
Ho, D., 79
Hoffe, J., 128, 134
Hofman, B., 1, 271
Honda Motors, Japan, 127
Hong Kong, Sino-foreign JVs, 76
Hoskisson, R., 5, 70
Howell, J., 254
HRM, see human resource management (HRM)
Hu, J., 213, 214
Huahong Pharmaceutical Ltd, 149
Hualian Supermarket Group, Beijing, 186, 189
Huang, C., 38, 39, 40, 65
Huang, Y. P., 15, 67, 214
Huawei Technologies Co Ltd
    case study, 172–3
    ICT market, expansion in, 73
    joint ventures, 238
    R&D centres, establishing, 237, 245
Huayi Group, 236
Hubbard, N., 211, 221
Hubei Province, Second Automotive Works built in, 118
Hubler, J., 248, 249
human capital, see workforce
human resource management (HRM) see also workforce
    automotive industry, 131–4
    Chinese MNCs, abroad, 249–55; subsidiaries, in developed countries, 250, 252–6; subsidiaries, in developing countries, 256–8; subsidiaries, knowledge-intensive, 258–9; transfer of practices between home and host countries, 257
    Chinese SOEs, acquisition by foreign MNCs, 221–7, 222; post-acquisition integration and harmonization of terms/conditions, 226–7
    Chinese subsidiaries in developing countries, 256–8
    competition strategy, 82–4

human resource management – *continued*
  employee participation and involvement, 253–4
  employee welfare/well-being schemes, 254
  employment regulations and labour disputes, 224–5
  industry comparison, 9
  information technology (IT) industry, 165–8
  job security, 223
  knowledge-intensive businesses, subsidiaries in, 258–9
  knowledge management, 253–4
  labour/employment law, 250, 252
  organizational image/identity, 255–6
  performance management, 84, 224, 252–3
  pharmaceutical industry, 152
  recruitment, 252
  trade unions, relationship with, 254–5
  training and development, 223–4, 253
  Western management techniques, adoption, 225–6

IBM PC business, acquisition by Lenovo, 73, 248
ICT (information communication technology) products, 157 *see also* information technology (IT) industry
IFPMA (International Pharmaceutical Industry Association), 137
IKEA group, *183–4, 276*
Ilari, S., 225
image problems, outflow investment, 246–7
'Implementation Procedures for the Drug Management Law of China', 139
industrialization
  and development of industries, 24–38
  employment statistics, *27–8, 30–1*
  fixed assets, newly increased, *32–6*
  foreign direct investment, by sector, *37*
  gross domestic product, composition, *25–6*
  investment sources, *32–6*
  light manufacturing, 29
  service industries, 29, 38
inflow FDI, 238, 246
information technology (IT) industry, 154–75
  affordability, 157
  challenges facing, *165*
  comparison of market, *156*
  competition strategy, 168–74
  development of computer industry, 155–8
  electronics, 157
  government, role of, 23, 160–2
  human resources implications, 165–8
  industrial clusters, 158–60
  MNCs, foreign, 167, 169

objectives, 167
opportunities and challenges, 163–4
outward investment, 232
research and development (R&D), 166, 167
as strategic industry, 22, 160
structure of computer industry, *156*
Infosys (Indian software export company), 168
Inkpen, A., 236
innovation
  challenges facing Chinese businesses, 271
  competition strategy, 75–7
  exhibition industry, 203
  new concept of innovation, in China, 65
  pharmaceutical industry, 146
  policy framework and institutions, 38, *39, 40*
  scope, 70
  and technology, *see* technology and innovation
intellectual property rights (IPR), 52, 145–7, 246
International Intellectual Property Alliance, 145–6
internationalization *see also* globalization
  Chinese MNCs, abroad, 239, 240–5
  as competition strategy, 73–5
  exhibition industry, 202–3
  motivation for, 74
International Pharmaceutical Industry Association (IFPMA), 137
IPR (intellectual property rights), 52, 145–7, 246
IT industry, *see* information technology (IT) industry

Jackson, R., 221
Japan
  automotive industry, 127
  Chinese FDI in, 242–5
  industrial policy (1950s-1960s), 22
  JETRO (Japanese External Trade Organization), 234, 236
  science and engineering research, 42
Jarvis, L., 140
JETRO (Japanese External Trade Organization), 234, 236
Jia, H. P., 148, 149
Jiang, M. Q., 166
Jiang, W., 166, 196
Jiangsu Yonggang Group, 86, 87
Jiashijie Commercial Chain Shops Group, 74
Jin, B. S., 211
Jin, C. X., 180, 181, 186, 214, 215, 216, 218, 220, 223
Jin, P., 80, 81, 136, 140, 146, 147, 150, 151
Jinzhou Group, 85, 86

job security, 223
Johnson, G., 6, 8, 11, 70
joint ventures (JVs)
    acquisitions of Chinese SOEs, by foreign
        MNCs, 223
    automotive industry, 118, 119, 126–7
    Huawei Technologies Co Ltd, *238*
    outward FDI, 232
    Sino-foreign, 76, 225

Kambil, A., 157, 158
Kangna Group, 79
Kanter, R., 70
Keim, G., 84, 85, 86
Key Technologies R&D Programme, 46
Khanna, T., 71
knowledge-intensive businesses, subsidiaries,
    258–9
knowledge management, 253, 254
Korea, industrial policy (1960s-1970s), 22
Kotler, P., 77
Kracht, J., 220
Kraemer, K., 23, 157, 160, 161, 169
Kunshan IT industrial cluster, 159

labour/employment law, developed countries,
    250, 252
Labour Law of China, 224
Lai, H., 159, 160
Lasserre, P., 70, 77, 225, 275
Lau, C., 14, 72
Lazonick, W., 5
Lee, K., 22, 119, 124
Lee, P., 157, 158
Legend, *see* Lenovo
Legewie, J., 225, 255
Lenovo
    case study, *170–2*
    IBM's PC business, acquisition, 73, 248
    location, 50
    targeting of markets, 244
Leonard-Barton, D., 38, 70
Leung, K., 226
Levine, M., 254
Li, D., 24
Li, G., 7
Li, J., 141, 143, 145, 148, 149, 247
Li, J. T., 131, 134
Li, K., 238, 244, 256
Li, L., 229, 232, 246, 247, 248
Li, M., 70, 71, 72, 125, 128, 261
Li, R., 177, 178, 179, 189
Li, W. H., 76
Li, Y., 76
Lin, S. F., 258
Lin, S. L., 258

Linden, G., 22
Lindholm, N., 84
Liu, C. R., 214, 217, 220
Liu, H., 238, 244, 248, 256
Liu, J., 196
Liu, Q. S., 215
Liu, X., 5, 40
Liu, Y. Q., 15, 65, 68, 85, 112
local governments, intervention from, 219–20
Lou, W., 59, 62
Lou, X. G., 59, 62
Lu, Q., 158, 160, 161, 170, 174, 175
Lu, Y., 212, 214, 225
Lubman, S., 221
Lucas, R., 54
Luo, Y., 13, 70, 72, 212, 213, 260, 276
Lyengar, J., 245

M&As, *see* mergers and acquisitions (M&As)
Macao, Sino-foreign JVs, 76
Makino, S., 233
Mallory, G., 6, 249
management and managers
    'Qualification Requirements for Practising
        Professional management and managers
        in the Hotel Industry', 64
    autonomy and competence, 247–8
    managerial implications, for Chinese firms,
        270–2
    skills and behaviour, 217–19
    in SOEs, appointment of managers, 134
    strategic management, 8, 70
Maotai Corporation, 80
Marchington, M., 253
market entry strategy, auto firms, *129*
Marks, M., 221
McWilliams, A., 85
Melewar, T., 78, 275
mergers and acquisitions (M&As)
    automotive industry, 126
    cross-border, overview, *231*
    diversification, 73
    failure rates, 226
    internationalization, as competition strategy,
        73–5
    outward FDI, 237, 248
    pharmaceutical industry, 148, 211
    skill shortages, 247
    state-owned enterprises, acquisitions by
        foreign MNCs, *see* Chinese SOEs,
        acquisition by foreign MNCs
Meschi, P., 248, 249
Metro (retail giant), 180
Microsoft Research Asia (MSRA), 50
MII-Thomson innovation initiative, IT
    industry, *162–3*

Miller, P., 183, 184
Ministry of Information Industry (MII), 161–2, 164, *165*
Ministry of Labour and Insurance, 59, 60, 64
Ministry of Science and Technology (MOST), 38
Mirvis, P., 221
MNCs, *see* multinational corporations (MNCs)
Mo, R., 59, 60
Moltech Power Systems, 236
Morris, J., 22
Morrison, E., 221
MOST (Ministry of Science and Technology), 38
Motorola, R&D centre, *168*
MSRA (Microsoft Research Asia), 50
multinational corporations (MNCs)
  and automotive industry, 129–30
  branding, 78
  Chinese, abroad, *see* developed countries, Chinese MNCs in
  competitive advantages, 1
  foreign, acquisition of Chinese SOEs by, *see* Chinese SOEs, acquisition by foreign MNCs
  information technology (IT) industry, 167, 169
  pharmaceutical industry, 141, 211
  repatriation of talent, 63
  retail industry, 180

Nanshan Group, 73, 75–6
naobaijin (health product), 150
Narula, R., 70, 233
National Development and Reform Commission, 127
National High-Tech R&D Programme (863 Programme), 46, *47–8*
'National Training Programme for Advanced Technical Talents', 65
New High Technology Zones, 47
Ng, S. H., 254
Ngai, P., 224
NGOs (non-governmental organizations), 49, 85
973 Programme, 47
Ni, P. F., 196, 197, 199, 200, 201, 202, 203, 204
Nie, P. X., 211
Nikandrou, I., 221
Nohria, N., 258
Nolan, P., 23, 68, 71, 72, 151, 152, 214, 263, 264, 269
Nonaka, I., 38, 70
Normile, D., 238

Oliver, C., 87
open door policy, 29, 67, 214, 231
organizational image/identity, HR practices, 255–6
original equipment manufacturers (OEMs), 125
OTC (over-the-counter) products, 137, 146
Otsuka (Japanese MNC), 141
outflow investment, challenges to
  capital constraints, 246
  image problems (technical and social), 246–7
  management autonomy and competence, 247–8
  stock market confidence, 248–9
  system inefficiency, 245–6
  technical, 246
outward FDI *see also* foreign direct investment (FDI)
  brand-name product building and market access, 237–8
  challenges to outflow investment, *see* outflow investment, challenges to
  driving forces, 233–40
  expansion and support of exports, 239–40
  financial factors, 236
  growth, 231–3, 243
  increased competition, 238–9
  increase in, 229
  and inward FDI, 232
  knowledge and know-how seeking, 236–7
  mergers and acquisitions, 237, 248
  push and pull strategies, 234
  reasons/patterns, *235*
  and system inefficiency, 245–6

Paauwe, J., 249
Palepu, K., 71
Pan, C. G., 59, 62, 63
Pan Asia Technical Automotive Centre (PATAC), 50
Parris, K., 15, 67, 214
PATAC (Pan Asia Technical Automotive Centre), 50
patents, *52, 53*
pay systems, 252–3
Peetz, D., 217
Peng, M., 12
performance management, 84, 224
  and reward system, 252–3
Perkins, D., 22, 263
Peters, T., 70
Pfeffer, J., 85
Pfizer, research centre (Shanghai), 149
Pharmaceutical Administration Law, 139

pharmaceutical industry
  background, 136–8
  barriers to growth, Chinese firms; deficiency
    in marketing, pricing and distribution,
    147; IPR protection, low, 145–7; low
    technology level/lack of new products,
    145; R&D, low level, 145–7; small firm
    size/low level of specialization, 143–5
  chain stores operation, 144–5
  competition strategy, 147–52
  drug prices, 139
  five-year plan, 140
  foreign pharmaceutical firms, in China,
    140–3
  government, role of, 138–40
  human resources implications, 152
  innovations, low level, 146
  manufacturing enterprises, 137
  mergers and acquisitions, 148, 211
  multinational corporations, 141, 211
  retail drug stores, 144
  scope, 136
  as strategic industry, 136
  WTO implications, 142
pillar industries, establishing, 22–3
Pomfret, R., 214
Porter, M., 7, 9, 38, 54, 70, 158, 220, 277
Porter, M., on business environment, 7
poverty, in China, 2
Powell, W., 70
Prahalad, C., 54
Prahalad, C. K., 70
PRC (People's Republic of China), State
    Intellectual Property Office, 52
PricewaterhouseCoopers, 177
private enterprises
  above designated size, 68
  Chinese business environment, 59–60
  competition strategy, 67–90
  network, need to create, 72
  Top 50, see Top 50 Chinese private
    enterprises
problems/barriers
  acquisitions, foreign investors', 220–1
  automotive industry, 123–7
  challenges facing Chinese
    businesses/strategic response, 264–9,
    265–7
  deficiency in marketing, pricing and
    distribution, 147
  dispersed geographical location, 126
  economies of scale, lack of, 124
  exhibition industry, 196–202; overcapacity
    of exhibition space, 196–7
  industrial planning, lack of, 196
  integration, lack of, 196

international acquisition practices, 212
joint ventures, limited scale, 126–7
pharmaceutical industry, 143–7
regulation, lack of, 196
removal of protection, 127
research and development, low level, 124–5,
    145–7
retail industry, 177–8, 183
small firm size (pharmaceutical industry),
    143–5
specialization, low level of, 143–5
technology, low level, 124–5, 145
product branding, see branding
products, output, 4
professionalization of occupations, 64
Prouska, R., 259
Pucik, V., 70
Purcell, J., 8, 9, 211, 221
push and pull strategies, outward investment,
    234

Qian, Z. W., 118, 119, 124, 125, 126, 129
Qin, Y., 143, 145, 146
Qingdao Jiante Biology Stock Ltd, 150
Quintanilla, J., 258

R&D (research and development), see research
    and development (R&D)
Rajan, M., 137, 143
Ralston, D., 60, 218
'Recommendations on the Nation-Wide
    Implementation of the Initiative "To
    build a Learning Organization, To Be a
    Knowledge Worker"', 64
recruitment, developed countries, 252
Rees, C., 13
Reich, R., 13
research and development (R&D)
  and automotive industry, 124–5
  Chinese centres, abroad, 244, 245
  863 High-tech R&D Programme, 46, 47–8
  expenditures by activity type, 45
  experimental development, investment in,
    42
  funding sources, 43
  gaps in funding/activities, 76
  General Electric, workforce, 50
  gross expenditure, 44
  institutions, 40
  investment in, 41–6
  Key Technologies R&D Programme, 46
  low levels, 124–5, 145–7
  Motorola, R&D centre, 168
  national science and technology financing
    indicators, 43
  973 Programme, 47
  personnel, 45, 46

research and development – *continued*
  and pharmaceutical industry, 145–7, 148–9
  software, 166, 167
  Spark Programme, 46
  Torch Programme, 46–7
research implications, 277–80
retail industry, 176–94 *see also* exhibition
    industry
  background, 176–9
  Chinese enterprises, strategies, 185–8
  Chinese government, 186–7
  competition strategy, 179–88
  growth, 177, 179
  human resources implications, 188–93
  pharmaceutical stores, 144
  problems, 177–8, 183
  status of ownership, *181–2*
  Western retail giants, strategy of, 180–5,
    181–2
Robinson, S., 221
Rodriguez, P., 84, 86
Roland Berger Strategy Consultants, survey
    by, 74, 88, 89
Romer, P., 54
Roseman, D., 154
Rosenzweig, P., 258
Rousseau, D., 221
Rubery, J., 225, 260
Rui, M. J., 14, 124, 128, 132, 137, 155, 156,
    164, 166, 167, 169, 170
Ruysseveldt, J., 230

SAIC (Shanghai Auto Industry Corporation),
    124, 238
Saich, T., 15, 67, 214
Salama, A., 211, 212
Sanjiu (pharmaceutical company), 151–2
Sanyo Electric Co, 242
SARS epidemic, 137, 139
SAW (Second Automotive Works), 118
Schiess (lathes and boring machines
    manufacturer), 241–2
Schneider Electronics, 236
Scholes, K., 6, 8, 11, 70
Schraeder, M., 221
Schroeder, Gerhard, 234
Schütte, H., 70
Schuler, R., 9, 212, 221, 230, 259, 270
Schultz, T., 54
science and technology (S&T) *see also*
    technology and innovation
  Chinese Academy of Science, 40
  high-technology products, national
      imports/exports, *52*
  high tech products, exports, 52
  patents, *52, 53*

science parks, 48
SEC (Shanghai Electric Group Corp), 74, *243*,
    255
secondary data, drawbacks, 69
Second Automotive Works (SAW), 118
Self, D., 221
service industries, 29, 38
Sesser, S., 157
SFDA (State Food and Drug Administration),
    140
Shanghai, 49, 149, 159
Shanghai Auto Industry Corporation (SAIC),
    124, 238
Shanghai Electric Group Corp (SEC), 74, *243*,
    255
Shanghai Fuxing High-tech Group, 83, 86
Shanghai Huayuan Group Corporation, 236
Shanghai Institute of Materia Medica, 149
Shanghai Volkswagen, 123
Shanghai World Exposition 2010, *201–2*
Sheehan, J., 254
Shen, I., 131
Shen, Y. H., 218
Shenkar, O., 12, 260
Shenyang Machine Tool Group, 241–2
Shenzhen Broadcast and TV Group, 198
Shenzhen Huaqiaocheng, *80–1*
Shenzhen International Exhibition for the Art
    and Culture Industry, 197–8
Shenzhen International Trust & Investment
    Corpn, 183
Shenzhen IT industrial cluster, 159
Shi, L., 238
Shi, S., 236
Shipman, M., 69
Shu, Q., 38
Sichuan Province, 149
Siegel, D., 85
skill shortages *see also* human resource
    management (HRM); workforce
  auto industry, 132–3
  Chinese business environment, 55, 60, 66
  information technology (IT) industry, 167
  initiatives to combat, 63–5
  mergers and acquisitions,
      negotiation/integration in China, 247
  reasons for, 60–3
  technicians/senior technicians, 59
SMEs (small and medium-sized enterprises),
    268
Smith, P., 60
social approach, CSR, 84
SOEs, *see* state-owned enterprises (SOEs)
Song, J., 196, 197, 203
Song, Z., 177, 178, 179, 189
Spark Programme, 46

Sparrow, P., 230, 259
specialization, 143–5, 203
Spinanger, D., 117
Stahl, G., 212
stakeholder approach, CSR, 84
State Council, 22, 117, 139
  State Steering Committee of S&T and
    Education, 38, *39*
State Food and Drug Administration (SFDA),
  140
State Intellectual Property Office (PRC), *51*
state-owned enterprises (SOEs)
  Chinese, acquisition by foreign MNCs, *see*
    Chinese SOEs, acquisition by foreign
    MNCs
  in coal mining industry, 84
  electronics industry, 160–1
  international acquisition practices, 212
  management autonomy and competence,
    247–8
  poor-performing, and M&As, 73
  private enterprises contrasted, 67
  reform, 213–14
  retail industry, 188, 192
  senior managers, appointment, 134
State Restructuring Regulations, 220, 224
Steinfeld, E., 22
stock market confidence, outflow investment,
  248–9
strategic choices, 8, 244
strategic industries, establishing, 22–3
strategic orientations, new, 88–9
subsidiaries of Chinese MNCs (HRM
  practices)
  in developed countries, 250, 252–6
  in developing countries, 256–8
  employee participation and involvement,
    253–4
  employee welfare/well-being schemes, 254
  knowledge-intensive businesses, 258–9
  knowledge management, 253–4
  labour/employment law, 250, 252
  organizational image/identity, HR
    practices, 255
  performance management and reward
    system, 252–3
  recruitment, 252
  trade unions, relationship with, 254–5
  training and development, 253
Sun, J., 121, 122, 125, 126
system inefficiency, outflow investment, 245–6

Taiwan, high-tech firms in, 258–9
Takeuchi, H., 38
Tan, J., 12

Tao, Z. G., 124, 128, 132, 137, 155, 156,
  164, 166, 167, 169, 170
targeting of customer groups, pharmaceutical
  industry, 149–52
Taylor, B., 221
TCL Group, 233, 236
  acquisition of Thomson's DVD business,
    73, 237, 244
technology and innovation, 38–53 *see also*
  innovation
  and automotive industry, 124–5
  government-sponsored programmes and
    Sino-foreign collaborations, 46–50
  innovation policy framework and
    institutions, 38, *39*
  R&D, investment in, 41–6
'techno-nationalism', 262
Teece, D., 38, 70
tertiary sector, and retail industry, 177, *178*
Tesco, 276
'The Outline of State Industrial Policy in the
  1990s' (State Council), 22
Thomson DVD manufacturing business,
  acquisition by TCL Group, 73, 237,
  244
Thun, E., 134
Tian, J., 119, 129, 144, 152, 180, 182
Tongwei Group, 72–3, 83–4
Top 50 Chinese private enterprises
  corporate social responsibility (CSR), 85
  diversification strategy, 71
  innovation and technological upgrading, 76
  Roland Berger Strategy Consultants study
    (2003), 74
  self-reports, 68, 69, 87
  success factors, *91–112*
Top 500 Private Enterprises, 60
Torch Programme, 46–7
Trade Union Law, 224
trade unions, 254–5
  All China Federation of Trade Unions
    (ACFTU), 276
training and development, human resource
  management, 223–4, 253
Tsang, E., 12, 72, 218, 226, 227
Tse, D., 67
Tsingtao Brewery, 78–9
Turpin, T., 40
TVEs (township and village enterprises), 24,
  86, 87
'Twelve Year Plan for Science and Technology
  Development' (1956), 155

Ulrich, D., 258
UNCTAD, 50, 229
United Kingdom, 44, 252, 255–6

United States, 42
Utterback, J. M., 38

Van Ben Bulcke, D., 16
Vatikiotis, M., 244
Vietnam, 233, 257
vocational training, in China, 60–1, 64
Von Glinow, M., 12

Wal-Mart, 180, 182–3, 186, 276
    research centre donation, 184–5
Wang, C. L., 194, 195, 196, 197, 201, 202, 203
Wang, C. S., 60, 123, 125
Wang, J., 217, 220
Wang, Q., 216
Wang, R. Z., 138, 143, 145, 148, 178
Wang, W., 140, 179, 180, 186, 187
Wang, X. D., 166
Wang, Z. M., 60
Wanxiang Group, 75
Warner, M., 60, 221, 250, 254
Warner, W., 225
Weber, Y., 221
Wei, Y., 160, 164, 169
Weiss, S., 139, 140, 143
Welsh Development Agency, 74
White, S., 5, 65
Wilkinson, A., 253
Wilkinson, B., 217
Williamson, P., 269, 275
wine-making industry, 80
Wong, Y., 70, 71, 72, 261
workforce see also human resource
    management (HRM)
    education and skill levels, 55–60, 56–8
    most needed skills, 59
    professionalization of occupations, 64
    skill shortages, see skill shortages
    vocational training, in China, 60–1, 64
World Bank, Investment Climate
    Surveys, 54
World Trade Organization (WTO), Chinese
    accession, 127
    competitive pressures caused by, 6
    globalization, challenge of, 269

pharmaceutical industry, 142–3, 144
    retail industry, 179
Wu, H., 16, 231, 236
Wuliangye Group Co. Ltd (distillery), 80–1
Wuxi City, skill shortages in, 59

Xinfei Refrigerator Series, 82
Xing, W. J., 123, 134
Xinxiwang Group, 85
Xu, J., 180, 216
Xu, Z. X., 15, 68, 85, 112

Yang, D. X., 40, 46, 54, 243
Yang, Z. G., 131, 134
Yeung, G., 136, 138, 141, 142
Yoshida, P., 46, 47
Young, S., 16, 72, 232, 235, 248
Youngor (garment manufacturer), 73
Yuejin Motor Group corporations, 130–1

Zeng, M., 269, 275
Zhan, H., 217, 223
Zhang, A., 120
Zhang, H., 16, 231
Zhang, H. L., 124, 125, 131, 146, 148, 177
Zhang, J., 125, 126
Zhang, J. R., 77, 78
Zhang, M., 70, 90, 247
Zhang, Q. Z., 80
Zhang, Ruimin, 237, 238
Zhang, S. H., 120, 125, 128
Zhang, Y., 77, 78
Zhang, Z. Z., 120
Zhangjiang High Tech Industrial Park, 50
Zhao, H., 70, 72
Zhao, Y., 124, 125, 128, 129
Zhejiang Province, 60
Zhingguancun Haidian Science Park, 49
Zhongguancun Electronics Avenue, 159
Zhongtian Construction Group, 72, 79
Zhou, H., 7, 188, 189, 190, 191, 192, 193
Zhou, Q., 7, 188, 189, 190, 191, 192, 193, 234, 242
Zhou, X., 234, 242
Zhu, Y., 70, 90, 250, 257
Zinkin, J., 86
ZTE Corporation, 237, 239